THE
Best Care
IN THE AIR

**The Complete History of the
109TH AEROMEDICAL
EVACUATION SQUADRON
(Minnesota Air National Guard)**

TSGT RICHARD H. CHILDS, USAF, RET.
COL MICHAEL A. GERMAIN, USAF, RET.

The Best Care In The Air
The Complete History of the 109th Aeromedical Evacuation Squadron (Minnesota Air National Guard)
All Rights Reserved.
Copyright © 2021 TSgt Richard H. Childs, USAF, Ret. / Col Michael A. Germain, USAF, Ret.
v7.0

The opinions expressed in this manuscript are solely the opinions of the authors and do not represent the opinions or thoughts of the publisher. The authors have represented and warranted full ownership and/or legal right to publish all the materials in this book.

This book may not be reproduced, transmitted, or stored in whole or in part by any means, including graphic, electronic, or mechanical without the express written consent of the publisher except in the case of brief quotations embodied in critical articles and reviews.

Outskirts Press, Inc.
http://www.outskirtspress.com

Paperback ISBN: 978-1-9772-3688-3
Hardback ISBN: 978-1-9772-3689-0

Library of Congress Control Number: 2020923496

Cover Photos © 2021 TSgt Richard H. Childs, USAF, Ret. / Col Michael A. Germain, USAF, Ret. All rights reserved - used with permission.

Outskirts Press and the "OP" logo are trademarks belonging to Outskirts Press, Inc.

PRINTED IN THE UNITED STATES OF AMERICA

Dedication

This book is dedicated to all

past and current

109th Aeromedical Evacuation Squadron members

whose sacrifice and service

while caring for the sick, injured and wounded

warriors of our nation

has been greatly appreciated by our

Soldiers, Sailors, Airmen and Marines.

This publication was made possible in part by the people of Minnesota through a grant funded by an appropriation to the Minnesota Historical Society from the Minnesota Arts and Cultural Heritage Fund. Any views, findings, opinions, conclusions, or recommendations expressed in this publication are those of the authors and do not necessarily represent those of the State of Minnesota, the Minnesota Historical Society, or the Minnesota Historic Resources Advisory Committee.

The appearance of U.S. Department of Defense (DOD) visual information does not imply or constitute DOD endorsement.

Front and back cover photo courtesy of U.S. Air Force Tech. Sgt Amy Lovgren, 133rd Airlift Wing's Public Affairs.

Flag image on front cover courtesy of XTOCK/Shutterstock.com.

Table of Contents

Preface i
Acknowledgements ii
Introduction v
Prologue vii
Chapter 1—The Command of Maj Edward Doyle 1
Chapter 2—The Command of Col Harry "Jerry" Nelson 20
Chapter 3—The Command of Lt Col Henry Capiz 45
Chapter 4—The Command of Col Harry "Jerry" Nelson 61
Chapter 5—Command Vacancy 64
Chapter 6—The Command of Lt Col David Molin 65
Chapter 7—The Command of Col Julia (Julie) Eszlinger Jensen 72
Chapter 8—The Command of Lt Col Darlene (Darcy) Anderson 112
Chapter 9—The Command of Col Sandra (Sandy) Carlson 173
Chapter 10—The Command of Col Karen Wolf 228
Chapter 11—The Command of Lt Col Sharon Rosburg 243
Chapter 12—The Command of Lt Col Georgeanne Johnson 257
Chapter 13—The Command of Col Penny Hodges-Goetz 301
Chapter 14—The Command of Col Matt Peterson 326
Chapter 15—The Command of Lt Col Sue Behrens 338
Chapter 16—The Command of Lt Col Curtis Mathsen 359
Squadron Patch History 363
Squadron Coin, Flight Scarf, Hat History 370
Credits 375
Past and Present Flight and Squadron Commanders 381
Aeromedical Evacuation Training Flights (A Historical Perspective) 382
Dates of Conflicts 395
Mission Aircraft of the 109th AES 396
From "Breakfast with Zak" to 109th Get-Togethers, No Stronger Bond! 401
Abbreviations 407
Validating Our Early Research 416
Index 419
The Authors 438

Preface

In August of 2013, a Founders Day/Reunion was held to recognize the 109th Aeromedical Evacuation Squadron (AES) founders, and to dedicate the red cross on the C-131 aircraft parked at the Minnesota ANG (Air National Guard) Museum in honor of Col (Colonel) Maureen A. Hunt - one of the founders of the 109th Aeromedical Evacuation Flight.

In preparation for the dedication, the authors were asked to write a history of the 109th AES for the event. Given the limited time constraints before the celebration, we decided to concentrate on the first seven years of unit history, with an emphasis on the efforts and accomplishments of our founders. A fifteen page "early" unit history was drafted and distributed at the event.

Our ultimate goal was to build on this document and write a complete and comprehensive history of the 109th AES, culminating in this book. (Several "partial histories" were written in the past, but none encompassed the incredible 60-year history of this military unit.) We accepted this monumental challenge and took the plunge. We genuinely hope that our efforts to honor the extraordinary accomplishments of all past and present unit members are realized by this project.

Acknowledgements

Even small endeavors require great help. This undertaking was no exception. The authors are greatly indebted to those individuals, both known and unknown, whose contributions have made this project possible.

A good portion of our history came from previously written articles in the Northstar Guardian (133rd base monthly news publication), the Vital Signs (109th AES monthly unit newsletter), and various other histories that were written over the years. Our goal of crediting all sources resulted in exhaustive research, listing nearly 200 footnotes/credits at the end of this book. Photo and article credits are noted where known. Some of this data (especially early histories, articles, and photos) contained little information as to who wrote the article or took the picture. To that end we would like to both apologize for any unintentional "plagiarism" and at the same time give credit to those unnamed individuals who indirectly helped contribute to this book - you know who you are. You have our gratitude and heartfelt thanks for your efforts.

At the top of the list is Col Julie Eszlinger Jensen. She was in on the genesis of this project and remained the driving force that kept us at our computer keyboards throughout the writing of this book. She organized several very important meetings bringing together early medical technicians (med techs) and flight nurses (FN) that the authors would have been unable to accomplish on their own. If she didn't have the answers to our far-reaching questions, she knew where to find them. Without her help, this book would not exist. Thanks, Julie.

We owe much of the early part of this written history to two groups of aeromeds. Dorothea Tenney, Betty Cook, and Jean Cool were able to give us an early account of unit activities from the nursing point of view at a meeting on a cold December day in Alexandria, MN. Likewise, Richard Vosika, Terry Ripley, Dick Oehlenschlager, and David Lund helped fill in the blanks and provided critical information from the early med techs' standpoint in a separate meeting held in the Twin Cities. It was truly an honor to meet these early aeromeds who had such an incredibly positive and lasting impact on the 109th AES.

Lt Col (Lieutenant Colonel) Henry Capiz met with us twice and provided a huge amount of lost information, pictures, and insight into his tenure as commander.

Lt Col Georgeanne Johnson had written several short histories on the 109th AEF (Aeromedical Evacuation Flight) and AES for the unit newsletter, the Vital Signs. Portions of her research are used throughout the book and we are indebted to her work and use of her writings in numerous chapters.

We could not have written this book without help from the staff at the Minnesota Air National Guard (MNANG) Museum. Stan Christiansen provided us with historical issues of the Northstar Guardian which put some of the "meat on the bones" of our book outline. Kirk Ransom and his computer files of archived materials and expertise provided us with many pertinent photos and information on our early commanders and unit activities.

A special thanks to MSgt (Master Sergeant) Rachel Maloney (109th AES) who was instrumental in assisting us with more specific unit level historical documents, newsletters, pictures, etc. Our phone calls were always answered, e-mails promptly replied to, and requests always honored.

Another stalwart unit member who answered every e-mail and went above and beyond to assist us in any way possible was MSgt Robert Buresh. Thanks, Rob!

Although the "Howard Era" of 90 cumulative years is over, their contributions continue to be present within the 109th AES today. Lt Col Ed Howard could always be counted on to provide us with the correct names that went with unidentified faces on a photo, as well as assist us in solving any number of puzzling questions we encountered during the writing of this book. Lt Col Pat Howard graciously contributed the narrative of himself and his siblings who were a fixture in the unit for 47 of the 60 years that the 109th has been in existence. A respectful thanks and salute to both of you.

One should always appreciate those who make them look better. To that end, we owe a debt to SSgt (Staff Sergeant) Taylor Juvland Nielsen, a past med tech in the squadron, who edited our book for proper military terminology and made it appear that the authors (with our combined 50 years of military service) knew what we were talking about. She also helped us with a number of other activities ranging from access to historical resources within and outside the wing and publication assistance. Thank you for your help during these critical phases of the book.

We couldn't think of two more qualified, seasoned aeromeds from the past to help us out with the aeromedical in-flight equipment section of the unit's history than Maj (Major) Dayton Carlson and TSgt (Technical Sergeant) Robert Ball, both former aeromeds in the 109th AES. We were able to incorporate their contributions into the Aeromedical Evacuation Training Flights section found later in the book. This historical perspective added tremendously to our story. They may want to use the word *strong-armed* while the authors like to think that they volunteered for this task. Thanks, guys!

A heartfelt thanks to Tom Stangl for the chapter in the book entitled "From 'Breakfast with Zak' to 109th Get-Togethers, No Stronger Bond!" Finer words were never spoken. This tribute to Zak, an iconic aeromed, continues to this day with mini-reunions due to Tom's monumental efforts.

We are forever indebted to the Public Affairs (PA) office for their cooperation and assistance in obtaining the front and back cover photos for our book.

Our deepest gratitude goes out to each of the commanders who contributed their thoughts and pictures to our project.

To all of the aeromeds who contributed a picture, story, or answered our e-mail questions throughout this endeavor - thank you for your time and involvement.

Any undertaking of this magnitude will incur substantial costs, and this project was no exception. The total cost of publishing this book (manuscript evaluation, interior formatting, editing, indexing and publishing in hardcover, paperback, and three different e-book versions) ran just north of $8,200. We would like to thank Col Karen Wolf (Vice Chairperson, MNANG Historical Foundation) for encouraging us to apply for and assisting us with our application for a grant from the Minnesota Historical Society. Her help and guidance through the grant submission process resulted in a subsequent grant approval which removed this daunting financial burden from the authors' shoulders. Thanks, Karen!

We should also emphasize that the book price was set as low as possible, just enough to cover the costs of printing and to make the book available for world-wide distribution. We were able to accomplish this by setting the royalty at a very low value. Having a royalty per copy is a requirement of the publisher. It is one step in their process of determining the cost of publishing any book. That being the case, the authors have established that all royalties will go to the Minnesota Air National Guard Historical Foundation to cover the costs of a digital storage fee which is charged annually by the publisher to maintain the book in a "print on demand" status in perpetuity. The authors will make no money on any book sales.

And finally, to our spouses, Margaret Childs and Cindy Germain - we couldn't have accomplished this 8-year project without your patience and understanding of the tremendous time commitment that this book entailed. Thank you for the thousands of hours that you gave up for us to pursue this venture.

Again, we are most appreciative for those who assisted and contributed to this massive undertaking and apologize to those whose names were inadvertently omitted.

Introduction

This book is organized by chapters which correspond to the tenure of the squadron commanders of the 109th AES. Each living commander was contacted and was asked to give us his or her thoughts, recollections, memories, etc. during their tenure. You will find their comments highlighted in both **bold** and *italics* at the beginning and sometimes throughout each chapter, while our research will appear in normal type.

The commanders were given carte blanche as to what they wanted to share with the readers in the introduction of their chapter. To that end, you will notice a difference in style, content and length of their comments. The authors felt that the readers would want to hear directly from those who led this incredible unit throughout the years without any preconditions as to what we wanted them to document as part of their legacy.

Within each chapter, you will find the timeline divided into specific years, and further subdivided into months (when known). Nonrelated activities within each month are separated by decorative embellishment dividers (☆☆☆☆☆). These conventions serve two purposes. First, it will be easy to locate a specific event if one has the precise date. Second, when reading the book, it will be easy to see where an event falls in the overall time frame of the unit's history.

Although some may find this way of organizing a history to be somewhat unconventional as opposed to free-flowing text with which we are all familiar, we believe that the above two purposes will serve the reader well.

Some readers may find that an event in the book might be "lacking" more detailed information. For example, "Forty aeromeds participated in the annual hospital tour which was held at the Tripler Army Medical Center in Honolulu, Hawaii." One would expect more information from this one-liner detailing who was involved and what was accomplished. However, in this case as in many others, this was all the information we were able to obtain from a source document (Vital Signs, Northstar Guardian, etc.). No aeromeds came forward with any additional material either. Even though this information was lacking, we felt that it was warranted to at least enter what we had into the book to give the reader as complete a history as possible.

Additionally, the reader might find information lacking as to the specific location of a deployed aeromed when they penned a "Letter from the Field" as found throughout the book. Not knowing if they wanted their location known and having a sincere desire to honor their "letter" as written, we sought no further input.

Throughout the book, readers will notice that picture quality varies tremendously. The photos displayed in this publication were obtained through newspapers, newsletters, scrapbooks, public websites, squadron/wing archives and personal collections - some well over a half century old. Those images that were taken before today's digital photography format had to either be photographed or scanned to convert them in order to be digitally inserted into this book.

Obviously, some of these "pictures of a picture" did not always turn out as well as we hoped. Extraordinary efforts were then utilized using several photo enhancing programs to bring out the best in each picture. We hope that the actual "visual content" of each photo will negate any imperfections that may exist in the actual picture itself, and ultimately strengthen the textual history of the unit.

Readers will also find a list of abbreviations at the end of the book with the definition of numerous military terms, abbreviations and acronyms. Even seasoned veterans may want to use this source of information as the authors have found that some of these terminologies have been dropped, added to or changed, altering the lexicon over the many years that the unit has been in existence.

In the Index, one will find many instances of just a rank and last name in the entry, with no first name listed. Many passages in the book were taken from articles written or letters penned by others who did not include this information. For the authors to research over 60 years of writings to document a first name would be an impossible undertaking. Despite this limitation, we are confident the reader will find this comprehensive Index very useful in their search for information.

One of the most perplexing problems in writing this book was deciding on the proper use of capitalization and punctuation throughout the manuscript. Our references, The Air University Style and Author Guide (Second Edition) and the Air Force Tongue and Quill (May 2015) often had conflicting guidance on how to handle these two subjects. We incorporated both of these resources and adopted a format which was used throughout the book.

Although we have painstakingly made every effort to be as accurate as possible in writing the history of the 109th AES, it is inevitable that some of the data may be incomplete or in error. Each commander was provided a copy of his or her chapter just prior to publication as a final check in this process. If you notice any erroneous information, we would ask that you contact us directly so corrections can be made to help produce a more complete and accurate product for subsequent editions.

Prologue

"We'll take one!" - Brig Gen (then Col) Leo Goodrich

It took forty years from the founding of the Minnesota Air National Guard to the establishment of the 133rd Aeromedical Evacuation Squadron (AMES) and the 109th Aeromedical Evacuation Flight (AMEF). The history of these two units would not be complete without a brief history of the origin of the Minnesota ANG and events leading up to the creation of the 133rd AMES and 109th AMEF.

The Minnesota ANG received federal recognition on January 17, 1921. Capt (Captain) Ray Miller flew a rented open-cockpit Curtiss Oriole biplane to Washington, D.C. to propose the formation of the Minnesota ANG; and thus it became the first Air National Guard unit in the United States to receive federal recognition. It was designated as the 109th Minnesota Observation Squadron.

The 109th flew a series of aircraft in its long history over the years. In 1930 they flew the Douglas O-38, in 1938 they acquired a new observation plane the O-47A, in 1941 the O-47B, in 1943 the unit received the P-51B (Mustang), in 1953 the P-51D (Mustang), in 1954 the T-33A (Shooting Star), then the F-94C (Starfire), and in 1957 the F-89H (Scorpion).

From its inception, the Minnesota ANG was called upon to support U.S. (United States) efforts in WWII (World War II), the Cold War, Korean Conflict, Berlin Crisis, Bay of Pigs, Vietnam, Desert Shield/Desert Storm, and many subsequent operations in Afghanistan and Iraq. The unit also assisted in humanitarian efforts, e.g. Operation Guinea Pigs, Operation Hospital Equipment, Operation Warmth, etc.

The Minnesota ANG received numerous awards for safety and operational readiness such as the Winston P. Wilson Trophy and the Spaatz Trophy. The Winston P. Wilson Trophy, named after Winston P. Wilson, former Chief of the NGB (National Guard Bureau), is presented to the most outstanding ANG flying unit equipped with fighter or reconnaissance aircraft. The Spaatz Trophy is named in honor of General Carl S. Spaatz, first Chief of Staff of the U.S. Air Force. This award is based on overall combat readiness during the reporting year and the unit's performance with respect to all other Air Guard flying units.

During the first week of January 1960, the Minnesota ANG was notified that the 109th AW (Airlift Wing) received a new mission - air transport using the Boeing C-97A Stratofreighter aircraft. The 133rd Air Defense Wing became the 133rd Air Transport Wing (Heavy) and was assigned nine C-97As. (Heavy airlift referred to large aircraft vs. small aircraft, i.e. cargo aircraft vs. fighter aircraft.)

By the end of the year, the 133rd was well along in its transition to the large four-engined aircraft, meeting its goal of upgrading its pilots, flight engineers and loadmasters. The 133rd transition to a transport mission ushered in the aeromedical evacuation (AE) mission.

The history of how the 133rd Air Transport Wing (ATW) acquired an aeromedical evacuation unit is quite an interesting story. The revelation of this remarkable narrative happened at the Founders Day/Reunion in August of 2013, where the 109th AES was privileged to have both Maj Gen (Major General) John Dolny (former 133rd ATW Wing Commander) and Brig Gen (Brigadier General) Leo Goodrich (former Air Officer in the Adjutant General's Staff) in attendance.

Photo courtesy of the Minnesota ANG Museum
Maj Gen John Dolny

Photo courtesy of the Minnesota ANG Museum
Brig Gen Leo Goodrich

Brig Gen Leo Goodrich tells the story in speaking to the group assembled at the reunion and in subsequent interviews:

"The Air Force was very, very short of aeromed units, so they asked the National Guard Bureau if they could talk to their state's Adjutants General and see if they would agree to organize the aeromed units. A meeting was held in Washington, D.C. with the new units converting to transports from fighters and Maj Gen Dolny and I were at this meeting. The director of the ANG told us that they wanted these aeromed units to be organized in the Guard and asked the Adjutants General to agree to it. I looked over at John Dolny and nodded and he nodded back in the affirmative so I just said, 'We want one in Minnesota!'

General Nelson, my boss said, 'Now wait a minute. We have to think this over.' We finally convinced him that afternoon that an aerovac unit would be good for Minnesota. I always kidded him that the Army was not used to making snap decisions like we did in the Air Force. We finally convinced him that it would be a good thing. I also told him that since we were the first fighter unit in the ANG, we wanted to have the first aeromed unit - and we were! They got us federal recognition. The founders took over and did a magnificent job developing the unit over the years." [1]

Maj Gen Dolny confirmed this information in a phone interview with the authors a few years after the Founders Day/Reunion. He added that, later in the game, Guard Bureau was thinking about pulling aerovac units in some states because they were complaining that it was costing them money "flying around to do their training." At one point, there was even opposition to keeping aerovac in the Guard at all, but with everything going on upon the world stage, the Guard Bureau decided that keeping aerovac would be beneficial. [2]

So it started with a simple "We'll take one!" - and the rest as they say is history - the history of the 109th Aeromedical Evacuation Squadron...

THE *Best Care* IN THE AIR

CHAPTER 1
The Command of Maj Edward Doyle

(Jun 1961 - Apr 1963)

Photo courtesy of the family of Maj Edward Doyle

Maj Edward Doyle attended St. Rose of Lima and Nativity grade schools, and graduated from Cretin High School in 1948. In 1953 he was awarded a Bachelor of Science Degree in Business from the University of Minnesota. Doyle served in the Minnesota ANG as the first Squadron Commander of the 109th AMEF. He also spent time in the Air Force Reserve (AFR) and then on active duty in the Air Force. He served twenty-three years and retired at the rank of major.

Maj Doyle began his career in the medical equipment field, eventually starting his own company. He was later a consultant to entrepreneurs in business development in Orange County, California.

1961

June. The proud legacy of the 109th AES began on Thursday evening, 1 June 1961, when two new Minnesota ANG units were born. After official inspection from Col Haun, 133rd ATW Wing Advisor, along with four medical staff members from the Eastern Tactical Air Force (EASTAF), general orders were published and federal recognition was granted to the 133rd Aeromedical Evacuation Squadron and the 109th Aeromedical Evacuation Flight.

The organic units of the 133rd AES were announced as:

Headquarters 133rd Aeromedical Evacuation Squadron, MSP IAP, MN (MNANG)

(and the three geographically separated aerovac flights)

109th Aeromedical Evacuation Flight, MSP IAP, MN (MNANG)

133rd Aeromedical Evacuation Flight, Grenier, New Hampshire (NHANG)

139th Aeromedical Evacuation Flight, Schenectady, New York (NYANG)

(authors' note: Both the 133rd Squadron Headquarters (HQ) and the 109th Aeromedical Evacuation Flight were co-located in Minneapolis.)

(authors' note: Readers should be aware that the acronyms AMES and AES were used interchangeably for Aeromedical Evacuation Squadron and are used in this book as found in source documents. Similarly, AMEF and AEF were both used for Aeromedical Evacuation Flight and are again used in this book as found in their respective source documents.)

Charter Members of the Twin Cities Units

AF Form 634 Attendance Roll dated 1 July 1961 reveals the following personnel who reported for duty:

133rd Aeromedical Evacuation Squadron

Lt Col John Drayna
Capt Thomas Forsythe, Jr.
2d Lt Harry Nelson
MSgt Leslie Krinke
SSgt Barron Brewer
SSgt William Stucky

A1C Bruce Smith
A2C George Ash
AB Daniel Koontz

Officers present - 3
Airmen present - 6

<u>109th Aeromedical Evacuation Flight</u>

1st Lt Edward Doyle
2d Lt Helen Grundberg
2d Lt Carolyn Weinzetl
A1C Robert Hecht
A2C James Farrell
A2C Robert Pitha
A3C Robert Boisclair
AB Raphael Belanger
AB David Lund
AB Leslie Olson
AB Terrance Ripley
AB Thomas Thunnel
AB James Mulroy

Officers present - 3
Airmen present - 10

The roll was certified as correct by: James H. Haun
Colonel, USAF
AF Advisor

The new squadron was assigned directly under the 133rd Air Transport Wing.

Their mission aircraft, the C-97A Stratofreighter, was a military transport cargo aircraft with a cargo capacity of 96 troops or 69 stretchers. The new 109th AMEF mission would be both strategic and domestic, encompassing the in-flight care of patients from overseas bases to stateside hospitals. Another addition to the 133rd ATW was the influx of women into the military due to the flight nurse positions that were created for the 109th AMEF.

4 ☆ THE BEST CARE IN THE AIR

Photo courtesy of USAF
Boeing C97A Stratofreighter of the Minnesota ANG in 1960.

History was being made on two fronts. Locally, the Minnesota Air National Guard received a new tasking. In addition, this was the inauguration of aeromedical evacuation for Reserve and Air Guard units. It no longer was exclusively an active duty United States Air Force (USAF) mission, which resulted in anxieties with the AF active duty aeromeds. According to some of the early flight nurses within the 109th AEF, the active duty component was not happy with the Guard being involved in aerovac.

It was widely known that there had not been enough aircraft with trained on board medical personnel to care for the sick and injured during and after the Korean War. Therefore, it was only a matter of time before additional medical air evacuation units would be formed. This expansion within the Reserve and Guard components gave the Air Force greater airlift capability by utilizing in-flight care for patients on a global basis.

The mission of these newly mandated units was to provide a highly trained, professional force of AE flight crews to provide transportation and care of the sick and wounded in the safest manner to medical facilities in the shortest possible time to meet state and national emergencies. The capability would soon be in place to haul cargo into an area and provide evacuation and in-flight care for patients on the return trip.

Lt Col John Drayna was assigned as the initial Squadron Commander.

Photo courtesy of the Minnesota ANG Museum
Lt Col John Drayna

1st Lt (First Lieutenant) Edward Doyle was selected as the first Flight Commander of the 109th AMEF. Newly commissioned 2d Lt (Second Lieutenant) Harry "Jerry" Nelson was assigned as the 133rd AMES Medical Administrative Officer.

Photo courtesy of the Minnesota ANG Museum

On 1 June 1961 (the same day the new 133rd AES was federally recognized), Lt Col John S. Drayna, the new Commander of the 133rd AMES pinned the gold bars on newly commissioned 2d Lt Harry "Jerry" Nelson.

In the original Unit Manning Document for the 133rd AES, twelve Airmen and six officers were assigned to provide command and control through the Aeromedical Evacuation Control Center (AECC) and the Unit Type Code (UTC). (authors' note: Airmen is used in early unit history to denote enlisted and med tech personnel. In later years it was used to encompass both enlisted and officers within the Air Force.) Each flight was composed of 16 medical in-flight care teams consisting of one flight nurse and two med techs, and an air evacuation control team with an officer and four Airmen who supervised patient onloads/offloads and coordinated with medical facilities and airlifters. This complement of one flight nurse and two med techs worked well for domestic and intratheater, that is, within U.S. Air Forces in Europe (USAFE) and Pacific Air Forces (PACAF) flights. Prior to 1971, intertheater flights that flew "across the pond" - from Germany to Continental United States - could have an augmented crew complement of two nurses and three med techs. (In 1980, the crew complement would be increased to two flight nurses and three med techs.)

Lt Col Drayna immediately began interviewing personnel for both units. The officers and Airmen of this initial cadre were drawn largely from the 133rd Dispensary in the Minnesota ANG. This was also the case of the flights at their respective East Coast bases.

These new members faced a daunting task in meeting the specified manning and qualification requirements set forth by the USAF, but didn't waste any time getting started. Utilizing the summer field training period, they organized facilities, procured supplies, and continued to recruit additional nurses and Airmen to fill the existing vacancies. Squadron Headquarters made several staff visits to our East Coast sister units to assist them wherever possible. Unit personnel were completely unaware that orders calling them to active duty (the Berlin Crisis) were only one hundred and twenty days away.

As was to be expected, the primary emphasis was on recruiting. AF requirements for nurses at that time stated that they be a graduate of a National League of Nursing accredited diploma or baccalaureate educational program. Nurses also had to be between the ages of 21 and 39, without minor dependents. The rank at appointment (second lieutenant, first lieutenant or captain) would depend upon the nurse's age and professional experience. The supervisor of nurses had the potential of being promoted to the rank of major. Supplemental training would also be required for certification status as a flight nurse, which carried added financial benefits. This additional rating was mandatory to fly any aerovac mission. [3]

Some of our early nurses though, remember that basic training was not mandatory for nurse officers. The nurses, all women, were expected to learn by reading, observing and being mentored by other officers (which during those times were all male). Mentoring was not what it is today; in fact, you could say it was rather primitive. One of the "Golden Rules" was to "salute anyone in uniform." This made for some awkward and memorable experiences. 1st Lt Dorothea Tenney remembers attending an AF Convention in Las Vegas: "We wore our 'whites' as that was all we had." Concurrently in the same hotel there was a Firemen's Convention being held with its attendees also dressed in their uniformed finery. She recalled, "Moving about the lobby and convention areas, we got a lot of puzzled looks as well as received a lot of smiles as we rendered the proper military courtesy to anyone in uniform." [4]

On the other side of the coin, 1st Lt Jean Cool, one of the early flight nurses said that she ran across an Airman who told her in no uncertain terms that he would never salute a woman in uniform. [5]

1st Lt Tenney also remembers, "We didn't know that much about military uniforms either. As a 1st Lt, we had silver bars on our shoulders. I really liked the looks of the gold (2d Lt bars) so much that I asked someone what we had to do to get those. That's how naive we were." [6]

These initial nurses came from backgrounds with various specialties, e.g. anesthetists, Red Cross nurses, operating room nurses, supervisors in large medical facilities, and general duty nurses. The ideal nurse recruits (like many that joined the 109th AEF) were in their mid- to late-20s. It was felt that by that point in their careers they had many of the basic nursing skills mastered. The nurses would train with their organization one full weekend each month and a 15-day annual training period. All Airmen and nurses were required to be on flight status.

For enlisted personnel, med tech requirements were rather basic – a high school diploma and a passing score on the enlistment test and flight physical. Like the nurse applicants, the enlistees who came forward brought with them experiences in various backgrounds, e.g. postal service, college students, businessmen, contractors, building engineers, etc. There was no requirement necessary for work experience or training in the medical field.

Members of all four units continued the difficult task of recruiting new personnel to fill their existing vacancies. The Minnesota unit wasted no time and soon their efforts began to bear fruit as their ranks began to fill.

2d Lt Carolyn Weinzetl transferred from the 133rd USAF Dispensary and joined the fledgling unit. SSgt Barron Brewer and SSgt William Stucky (both qualified med techs) soon followed.

Volunteers from the civilian world began to come forward as well. In June, 2d Lt Helen Grundberg, 1st Lt Betty Cook, and 1st Lt Jean Cool were among the first of the non-prior service members to join the unit.

With few exceptions, the original nine nurses did not all know each other prior to joining the 109th AEF. A few were working acquaintances in their civilian jobs and talked about it. Others heard about the formation of this new unit through the grapevine or saw advertisements and decided to sign up.

Photo courtesy of the 50th Anniversary Book, 133rd Military Airlift Wing (1971)
Original nine flight nurses.

**Back Row (L - R): Lt Carol Eckelberg, Lt Maureen Hunt, Lt Dorothea Tenney, Lt Dorothy Ludwig
Front Row (L - R): Lt Jean Cool, Lt Geraldine Hendrickson, Lt Helen Langemo, Lt Helen Grundberg, Lt Betty Cook**

Over this same four-month period, the 109th AMEF was able to recruit twenty new members into its enlisted ranks. The senior enlistee, SSgt Raymond Marabella was soon joined by Robert Hecht, John Fredericks, Lloyd Gilbert, Robert Pitha, Raphael Belanger, Robert Boisclair, David Lund, James Mulroy, Terrance Ripley, Thomas Thunnel, Richard Vosika, Robert Anderson, Larry Daudt, Dennis Fitzsimmons, Thomas Hedin, Robert Miller, and Robert Moss – all designated as Aeromedical Evacuation Specialists.

Nearly six decades later A1C (Airman First Class) David Lund recalls, "After graduating from college, I was about to start a new job, but the draft board advised me that I was going to be drafted. There were two things I didn't want – full-time military and joining the Army. I searched for part-time alternatives and focused on the AFR and ANG. One difference between the two involved the possibility of active duty. The AFR had the option of activating individuals and sending them out of state, whereas, if the ANG needed personnel, they had to activate the entire unit. I joined the Minnesota ANG and went to Lackland AFB (Air Force Base), TX for basic training. When we returned to Minnesota, I remember walking down the ramp and being told our unit had been called to active duty. They must have really wanted me." [7]

Also recruited were James Farrell, Organizational Supply Specialist and Leslie Olson, Medical Material Specialist.

July. Three additional civilians signed up for duty with the 109th AEF. 1st Lt Helen L. Langemo, 1st Lt Dorothea Tenney and 1st Lt Geraldine Hendrickson became the newest members of the unit. All three nurses were employed at Fairview Hospital.

August. This month brought two more nurses into the unit - 1st Lt Carol Eckelberg and 1st Lt Dorothy Ludwig.

September. Maj Wayne Janzig replaced Lt Col Drayna as Squadron Commander, and 1st Lt Maureen Hunt received her commission as the newest nurse in the unit.

Photo courtesy of the Minnesota ANG Museum
Maj Wayne Janzig

October. On 1 October 1961, the Berlin Crisis brought the unit to Active Federal Service. The squadron found itself with only 20 officers assigned out of 57 authorized and 48 Airmen out of 120 that were authorized. Only one nurse was qualified as a flight nurse and none of the newly recruited Airmen were qualified as med techs. Thus, the recruitment, training and qualification of flight nurses and med techs became the paramount concern.

The active duty AF, realizing the need for an expanded AE specialty, recalled previously discharged med techs (on an eight-year obligation) back to active duty. Many of the personnel recalled either had no aeromedical background or were unfamiliar with the changes since their discharge. Members came to Minnesota from all across the country. For example, several early med techs remembered that SSgt Donald Carr came from South Carolina to fill in for the Berlin Crisis. Many of those recalled to active service, especially those from the southern states, were not happy to be sent to Minnesota with its cold weather just around the corner.

The training in those early days consisted of three phases: (1) basic medical ground training with transition to in-flight medical care at the local level coupled with basic procedures in static aircraft on the ramp or on local flights; (2) flight nurse training at the School of Aerospace Medicine at Brooks AFB in San Antonio, Texas and formal school training for the Airmen at Gunter AFB, AL (beginning in 1962); and (3) participation in actual strategic and domestic AE missions.

Med techs would first complete their basic training at Lackland AFB, TX. All other medical and aeronautical schooling was conducted back at their unit as mentioned above. It wasn't until a year later that new med techs would go straight from basic training to Gunter AFB, in Montgomery, AL where they received 10 weeks of hospital instruction. In the future, med techs would also begin to go to Brooks AFB, TX for their aeromedical training which lasted for five more weeks.

Systemwide, there was a severe shortage of AF school slots to train flight nurses and med techs. It became very evident that if the squadron was to meet the fully operational projection date of January 1962 (set by the Wing Commander), an intensive in-house training program had to be developed.

To complicate matters even more, the 109th AMEF, treated somewhat as a "homeless orphan," had yet to be given a designated location for their operations. Therefore, their training was conducted wherever they could find a space that met their needs.

Lacking the necessary training and a formal school to quickly train the med techs, the challenge was getting them qualified. 2d Lt Harry Nelson was put in charge of training the initial med techs locally, which consisted of a two-phase process. First, they underwent med tech training, since the med techs were either new to their jobs or unfamiliar with the changes since they were previously discharged. The second phase was the aeromedical training.

The initial nine nurses were appointed to accomplish this training. "We had to develop our own medical agenda and classroom lectures and were given very little guidance," recalled 1st Lt Dorthea

Tenney. "We had yet to be issued AF uniforms, so when instructing in the classroom we wore our white civilian hospital uniforms." [8] These innovative and forward-thinking nurses single-handedly wrote all of the training plans and the curriculum that became the cornerstone of flight nursing as we know it today. The lessons they were assigned to prepare were chosen based on each nurse's clinical areas of expertise.

"The training program was developed by assigning each nurse a system of the body," recalled Lt Dorothea Tenney. "The assigned nurse would develop a teaching tool for that subject area. These lesson plans were then reviewed by all the other nurses. We also assigned the teaching schedule in the same manner. By working together in this way, close friendships and a high degree of trust was developed." [9]

1st Lt Jean Cool recalls, "In our first hectic months we literally flew by the seat of our pants with very little direction. Independently, we set up classes from our own books and papers. Though we were not teachers, we taught medical classes to our med techs. Sometimes we were a team of two simply for support. The med techs were attentive and cooperative and were able to do their duties quite completely." [10]

Years later, Lt Col (Ret) (Retired) Robert Hecht remembers, "It was really a crash course. We put in eight hours a day in classroom training and various tests. It was quite intensive, especially for those not already in the medical field." [11]

Fortunately, the caliber of nurses recruited by the unit was excellent and it was their willingness and ability to instruct that finally made the programs a success. Capt Anita M. Routhier of the 133rd AMEF, New Hampshire ANG, held a Master's Degree in Nursing Education and was quite logically made training officer for that unit and in this endeavor she was ably assisted by 2d Lt Harry Nelson.

A1C David Lund recalls, "When we joined the Minnesota ANG, we became students in classes taught by officers - the flight nurses. We all assumed they had military training and had taught the classes before. Years later, we were told that not only did they not have military training, but this was their first medical teaching assignment. We didn't know it. All we knew was that they were very good at their job." [12]

It is interesting to note that by all measures (both locally and AF-wide) these med techs performed at a level on par with their active duty counterparts – a testament to the local training programs developed by the 109th AMEF and the talented, hardworking med techs that were recruited into the unit.

It was tough going at first as there were limited nursing personnel to conduct this training. Six of the nine newly recruited nurses were sent to Brooks AFB, TX for flight nurse training in early October. The six-week course was intense with some students (from other units) even washing out in the last week. When these nurses returned to Minneapolis, the remaining three were sent to Brooks and the six qualified nurses took over the training.

PROGRAM

FLIGHT NURSE COURSE, CLASS 61-E

1st Week

Mon, 23 Oct 61

0815-0905	CT	In-Processing
0915-1005	CT	Welcome
1020-1110	FN	History of Air Evacuation
1115-1205	AS	Flying Safety
1305-1450	AI	Atmosphere
1500-1550	ENT	Effects of Flying on Ear, Nose & Throat
1555-1645	NP	Introduction to Psychiatry & Development of the Normal Personality

Tue, 24 Oct 61

0815-1205	FN	Orientation Flight (Sec I)
1305-1355	FN	Aeromedical Supplies (Sec I)
1400-1450	FN	Litter Preparation (Sec I)
1500-1645	FN	Litter Securing Devices (Sec I)
0815-0905	FN	Aeromedical Supplies (Sec II)
0915-1005	FN	Litter Preparation (Sec II)
1020-1205	FN	Litter Securing Devices (Sec II)
1305-1645	FN	Orientation Flight (Sec II)

Wed, 25 Oct 61

0815-1005	IM	Cardiovascular Diseases
1020-1110	NP	Mental Defense Mechanisms & Symptoms of Mental Disease
1115-1205	FN	Aircraft Used in Air Evacuation
1305-1355	FM	In-Flight Medical Considerations
1400-1450	FN	MATS Air Evacuation Systems
1500-1645	AI	Hypoxia

Thur, 26 Oct 61

0815-1005	NP	Clinical Psychiatry
1020-1110	AI	Pressure Cabins & Rapid Decompression
1115-1205	AI	Acceleration
1305-1355	IM	Cardiovascular Diseases
1400-1450	FN	Operational Procedures
1500-1645	FN	Aircraft Loading

Fri, 27 Oct 61

0815-0905	NP	Principles of Psychiatric Treatment
0915-1005	NP	Psychological Considerations in Disaster Situation
1000	CT	Reception
1115-1205	FN	Aeromedical Nursing I
1305-1645	FN	Watermanship

1961 Flight Nurse Course Syllabus for week one of six weeks.

The training continued with classroom lectures, practical demonstrations, and then basic procedures in static aircraft on the ramp or on local flights. Periodically, one Minnesota C-97 departed for San Antonio to be used by School of Aerospace Medicine students. These flights were utilized for on-the-job training (OJT) of in-flight medical care procedures. Two crews a week would depart for Scott AFB, IL to train with the 11th AMES to work on actual domestic air evacuation flights.

When the aeromeds began flying, the mission was considered strategic airlift – that is, overseas missions only. Typically, these were flown from Rhein Main AB, Germany to the United States. When the unit was activated in October of 1961, they also picked up the domestic aerovac missions – those within the United States.

1st Lt Dorothea Tenney recalled one such domestic air evac deployment. "1st Lt Maureen Hunt and I were sent to Scott AFB, IL on 10-day orders. We were either to fly aerovac missions stateside or work in the office with the scheduling system. After our 10-day orders were up, we sat on our B4 bags (military issue garment suitcase) out on the tarmac waiting for an aircraft from Minneapolis to come and pick us up. They forgot all about us! Finally, the crew from the office came out to tell us there was a mix-up and there was no plane scheduled for our return flight. They told us to take some time off and go into St. Louis for the day - which we did. A few days later, our aircraft arrived to bring us back to Minneapolis." [13]

Lt Col Robert Hecht recalls another flight: "We were dropping off a patient in North Dakota and they didn't have a ramp or anything to deplane our patients. We had to wait for someone to get a forklift so we could offload the litter patients. That was quite an experience." [14]

Every third week one crew would depart for Rhein Main Air Base (AB), Germany to participate in and supplement crewmembers on AE flights utilizing the C-135 Stratolifter (Boeing 707), - a jet propelled airplane - which could carry 126 troops and 44 liters. After qualification, the crews flew with their active duty counterparts on either the CONUS (Continental United States) or European missions for one- to two-week periods throughout the Berlin Crisis. These flights were continued well after the end of the Berlin Crisis, providing valuable "hands-on" experience to unit members.

"On my first flight from Rhein Main, I was seated next to a psych patient who was classified as '1C', a psychiatric patient who is cooperative and stable traveling in the ambulatory status," recalled 1st Lt Dorothea Tenney. "After taking off in the C-135, he told me that he was going to open the door 'for just a few minutes to get a breath of fresh air.' After alerting the charge nurse, this patient's classification was quickly changed to '1A' where he was quickly sedated and restrained on a litter for the rest of the flight." [15]

During this hectic period, the 109th AMEF was faring better than its two sister flights, in part due to the fact that it was co-located with Squadron Headquarters. The 109th AMEF was able to obtain assistance and support more readily than the other two units. In fact, at one time it looked doubtful that the 139th AMEF in New York would succeed as a unit.

December. With the arrival of Maj Katherine Simpson from Eglin AFB, FL, the Squadron Headquarters became fully manned. She assumed the duties of Squadron Chief Nurse.

By the end of the month, two units were flying either local or round-robin training missions. Our sister flight, the 139th AMEF in New York, was still plagued with many problems; scant flying support, no uniforms, late pay, no telephones, and no publications. Six of their Airmen had to be transferred out because of refusal to fly, thus severely reducing their already thin Unit Manning Document. The 109th AMEF sent two nurses, 1st Lt Carol Eckelberg and 1st Lt Dorothy Ludwig, to assist the 139th with their training as time was running out.

1962

April. Due to time constraints and the immensity of the task, the 133rd AMES target date of January 1962 for fully operational readiness was not met. However, by mid-April of the new year not only was the fledgling aeromedical squadron well organized, but 25 out of 25 nurses assigned were fully qualified as were 80 out of 109 Airmen. The squadron's three flights had logged a total of 5,633 flying hours, had participated in 66 simulated missions and 10 crews had flown actual missions in the overseas strategic program. Despite the many problems that had to be overcome and the countless moments of hopeless frustration, the success of the recruiting and training programs were paying huge dividends, largely due to the hard work and high standards set forth by the men and women assigned to the squadron's three flights.

May. Word was received that the activated National Guardsmen would be released in August. In June, the exact date of 31 August 1962 was announced and planning began for out-processing. The release date would be one month short of a full year of active duty for the newly established AE units.

The training continued, however, throughout the summer with local classroom work and in-flight training on local flights as well as the overseas missions. The 133rd AMEF in New Hampshire was performing temporary duty (TDY) training with the 12th Military Air Transport Service (MATS) at McGuire AFB, NJ, but had to discontinue the program due to the summer training of reservists by the McGuire unit. Under the direction of Capt Helena Moran, a movie depicting the 133rd AMEF activities was produced and finished in July.

June. The following article appeared in the St. Paul Pioneer Press on 24 June, 1962.

"Ambulances" that fly - at a speed of 650 miles an hour - were being used by the Military Air Transport Service to bring wounded and ill U.S. armed forces personnel home from overseas.

The first ANG medical crew to make such a flight came from Minnesota's aeromedical squadron of the 133rd Air Transport Wing with headquarters at Wold-Chamberlain field.

The flying ambulances were military versions of the Boeing 707 jetliner and made up MATS' jet ambulance service. The Air Guard's first mercy mission crew included Lt Helen Langemo (flight nurse), and A2C (Airman Second Class) Lloyd Gilbert, along with A1C Emmett Panzella (med techs).

The 109th AMEF medical crews were soon flying regularly scheduled aeromedical missions transporting injured and ill servicemen and dependents from Europe and the Far East. These aeromedical crews worked closely with the front-end crews during the speedy high-flying mercy missions.

A typical flight from Germany to McGuire AFB, NJ took six to seven hours with the C-135 Stratolifter flying 650 miles an hour at 35,000 feet. Thanks to these aircraft and their medical crews, sick or wounded armed forces personnel could be transported quickly, safely and comfortably to hospitals and treatment facilities in the U.S. [16]

Photo courtesy of St. Paul Pioneer Press (June 24, 1962)
Lt Helen Langemo (center) points out a loading ramp entrance at Rhein Main AB, Frankfurt, Germany, to A2C Lloyd Gilbert (left) and A1C Emmett Panzella (right). In the background is the MATS C-135 Stratolifter preparing for take off with a load of 57 patients for the U.S. as soon as it is loaded.

August. Many of the reserve fillers began clearing the base and the flights began to wind down their training programs in anticipation of demobilization. After 11 months of active duty, the squadron was deactivated on August 31, 1962 and returned to state control.

There is nothing more disruptive to a well-trained organization than demobilization. Thus, it was with a bleak outlook that the squadron looked forward to 1963. Dismantling the well-oiled machine it had built during the previous year left many with a heavy heart. 2d Lt Helen Grundberg, one of the charter members, resigned her ANG commission to remain on active duty. She was accepted for career reserve status and was assigned to Clark AB, in the Philippines. Capt Maureen Hunt would soon follow and accept an active duty position in the AF as well. 1st Lt Helen Langemo also resigned and moved to Duluth.

During the federal activation for the Berlin Airlift, the 133rd AMES and 109th AMEF were assigned active duty medical advisors from the Nurse Corps (NC). Capt Pandicio (Chief Nurse) and Maj Katherine Simpson (USAF Advisor) initially filled these positions. An active duty med tech advisor position was also authorized and was filled by TSgt John Peterson. A Medical Service Corps officer, Maj Clyde Hanson, filled another active duty advisor billet. The advisor program continued into the early 1970s. After that time no active duty advisor positions were utilized, despite the fact that the need for these positions became more apparent when the aerovac mission went to TAC (Tactical Air Command).

Several aeromeds were selected as First Sergeants (affectionately known as First Shirts) throughout the early unit's history. Although the authors were unable to determine the specific order of these First Shirts, SSgt William Stucky, SSgt Barron Brewer, SSgt Raymond Marabella, and SSgt Don McCormack all served in this position.

The focus remained on training throughout the year with an emphasis on the overseas strategic missions. The recruiting of both nurses and Airmen remained a priority and to aid in this effort the "Try One" program was established base-wide. (authors' note: Despite extensive research, the authors were unable to uncover any additional information detailing this program.) Flying training periods were scheduled twice a week on Wednesday and Saturdays. Recruits were scheduled for Medical Service School at Gunter AFB, AL.

Since its release from Active Federal Service in August of 1962, 109th AMEF unit members frequently participated in live aerovac missions with the United States Air Force. They assisted the USAF with airlifting patients on domestic flights as well as supporting AE needs in Europe.

1st Lt Betty Cook recalled one such flight. "I was participating in a two-week USAFE aeromedical evacuation rotation flying from Germany to Turkey," she said. "On one flight I was given the assignment of checking patients' records and discovered that one patient had the wrong record! I reported this to the nurse in charge who was then obligated to tell the pilot who was in turn obligated to return to base for the current records. This resulted in much frustration as such errors were not usually corrected, but I was simply doing my job. I ended up with an 'Excellent' rating on my evaluation, but ended up with ulcers due to the food we ate in Turkey!" [17]

October. The fall of the year would bring change not only in the weather. The Technician Program was created on 1 October. Within the month, TSgt Richard Fox filled this first full-time squadron position. These full-time technicians were and remain vital to the organization's readiness and ability to deploy at a moment's notice.

November. Because the 133rd Aeromedical Evacuation Squadron and 109th Aeromedical Evacuation Flight were organized only a few months before the wing was activated in October 1961, the unit required 17 fillers to reach active duty strength. With the departure of all of these fillers after deactivation, extensive recruiting began. Six med techs left for basic training at Lackland AFB, TX and then completed their training at Medical Technician School located in Gunter AFB, AL.

The flight nurse situation was also moving forward rapidly. Several nurses expressed interest in the AME (Aeromedical Evacuation) program and began their application process.

Overseas flights resumed this month. The squadron had been assigned to the strategic air evacuation system, and was assigned overwater flights to and from Europe. To prepare for these missions, twice-weekly training flights were conducted. In addition, all of the flight nurses made a Rhein Main flight, which consisted of missions flown from Rhein Main AB, Germany to McGuire AFB, NJ on a MATS sleek swept-wing jet, the C-135 Stratolifter. [18]

"We also flew training flights to Alaska," recalled 1st Lt Dorothea Tenney. "We carried Army units one way and ran a training flight for the nurses and med techs on the deadhead return routes." [19]

December. Maj Katherine Simpson, the unit's Aeromedical Advisor, left the squadron after she accepted a new assignment at USAF Hospital, Andrews AFB, MD.

Acceptance of the women flight nurses was difficult for some of the traditional male flight crew positions. "The first flight in which women were included with the men was a training flight to RAF (Royal Air Force) Mildenhall, England," stated 1st Lt Dorothea Tenney. "They were not very happy to now have women flying with them. We tried to stay out of their way in the billeting and dining areas. 1st Lt Jean Cool and I left Mildenhall to go into London where we enjoyed a lot of sightseeing. Again, we were on our own, just trying to stay out of their way. One evening we went to the theatre to see the play 'Oliver.' After the play, we attempted to return to our hotel and found ourselves enveloped in a major fog. In fact, we had walked a block beyond our hotel before we realized it! Enroute we met some of the aircrew who in the past were not happy with us on flight status, but now seemed to accept us as equals." [20]

Photo courtesy of the Northstar Guardian (Feb '63)
1st Lt Jean Cool (left) and 1st Lt Dorothea Tenney (right) were feeding the pigeons in Trafalgar Square when snapped by a London photographer. They were on a flight orientation to RAF Mildenhall England while waiting for England's worst fog in years to lift so they could return to the States.

1963

March. The Squadron Commander, Maj Wayne Janzig, was promoted to Lt Col.

CHAPTER 2
The Command of Col Harry "Jerry" Nelson

(Apr 1963 - Jul 1967)

Photo courtesy of the Minnesota ANG Museum

Commander's Comments: *We were a very young unit at the time we went on active duty. We were just in the process of getting people to join and get organized. We had a wonderful time.* [21]

Col Harry Nelson

April. 1st Lt Harry "Jerry" Nelson became the new Commander.

☆☆☆☆☆

Later that spring, the unit held a disaster drill in conjunction with the hospital in Rochester, Minnesota. The exercise was designed to test the ability of the 109th AMEF to airlift, provide medical care and unload patients while working with civilian medical services. 1st Lt Dorothea Tenney, having just returned from an overseas deployment, was selected to be one of the simulated patients. In fact, she was chosen to be the dependent wife in the later stages of pregnancy. Once the simulated patients were ready and loaded, the flight departed the ANG Base in Minneapolis and landed at the civilian airport in Rochester.

"They did a very good job of making me look like I was about ready to deliver," Lt Tenney remembers. When the plane landed in Rochester, the local news station had a film crew on hand to cover the exercise. As she was being offloaded from the aircraft, Lt Tenney realized she was being filmed by the news media. "I remember thinking to myself, 'If my mother sees this on the news this evening, I'm going to have a lot of explaining to do.'" [22]

June. A staff writer for the St. Paul Pioneer Press wrote the following article for the paper entitled "Writer Works as Novice 'Flight Nurse'":

Flying about 9,000 feet somewhere over Michigan, the schizophrenic patient thrashed wildly and clawed at the safety belt that held him to a litter in the ANG aerial ambulance. Three med techs grabbed restraints. By the time they reached him, the flight nurse had started unlacing his boots so he wouldn't injure the patient on the bottom litter.

The scene had all the characteristics of a military medical air evacuation flight. But this time it was only for practice. The flight was a training mission staged by the 109th Aeromedical Evacuation Flight based at the Minneapolis-St. Paul International Airport. And to get a first-hand look at the procedure aboard a military flying ambulance, this reporter was a "flight nurse" for an evening. Armed with a carefully marked map to lead me to the ANG operations building, I arrived at the briefing room about 6:30 p.m.

First order of airborne business was to make a hasty change into appropriate attire. The flight nurses' costume is AF blue slacks, jackets, blouses and hats. But since I was a flight nurse for only an evening, I was given a less chic flight suit and jacket. With some assistance from Capt Carol Eckelberg, Chief Flight Nurse, in rolling up the sleeves and trouser legs, I was ready for the patients, although my formal medical training consists of only one public health course.

We moved into the briefing room where a control center representative was waiting for us. Our mission was assigned. We were to fly six litter and four ambulatory patients from Rhein Main, Germany, to McGuire AFB, NJ. Since we would have no actual patients on board, 10 med techs were assigned diagnoses ranging from asthma to a broken femur. A few minutes before 7:00 p.m. we walked onto the airstrip and headed for a C-97A Boeing Stratofreighter assigned to the 133rd Air Transport Wing.

With some noble pushing and pulling from Lt Col Wayne Janzig, Squadron Commander, the ground-accustomed reporter ascended the steps and sat down in one of the canvas seats that line both sides of the plane.

Our pilot, Col Edmund Antonini, Deputy Commander of the 133rd, and copilot, Brig Gen John Dolny, Commander of the 133rd, announced our flight plan. Since this was a simulated flight, we would fly to Duluth, along the shore of Lake Superior, over the upper peninsula of Michigan to Houghton, Michigan, up the lake shore to Lakeland, Canada, and then back to our starting point by way of Two Harbors.

As soon as the ship was airborne, the litters were prepared. First, a sheet and blanket were placed on the litter. Then it was attached to a stanchion pole and litter straps which were released from the ceiling of the plane. Altogether, the C-97A can carry about 70 patients. The litters can be placed three wide and five deep down the length of the plane.

Now it was time for the 10 med techs to react to the symptoms of their diagnoses. And act and react they did. Suddenly the asthmatic patient clutched his chest and collapsed to the floor. Lt Dorothea Tenney, Senior Flight Nurse, grabbed a resuscitator and ran to his aid. Soon the patient was breathing normally, and we carried him to an empty litter. As the flight progressed, so did the acting. The patients had everything from air sickness to throbbing headaches to internal bleeding.

All of the aeromedical equipment is portable, and much is improvised. Blankets and sheets were draped around the poles to provide "modesty screens." Intravenous solutions were tied to the poles with gauze.

On our flight, the nurse's duties had started just before flight time. If it had been a live mission, our job would have started the day before. The flight nurse visits the patients in the hospital, reads their charts and briefs them on the flight. Then she plans the patient loading and holds a briefing session with the crew. At the meeting, the crew adjusts altitude and air routes for the patients' comfort. For example, a cardiac patient would require a lower altitude.

Once the plane is in flight, the patients are the two flight nurses' complete responsibility. Seldom is there a doctor aboard. When the plane reaches its destination, a representative from the control tower meets the nurse and she turns the patients over to him.

Our flight was one of the 36 flying training periods the nine flight nurses attached to the 109th AMEF are entitled to a year. Their yearly training also includes 48 unit training assemblies - classroom training - and 15 days of active duty field training spent on live missions. If I had been an actual registered nurse recruit, I would have been given three weeks of training at officer candidate school and six weeks of flight school.

As we neared the airport, the patients became med techs again and disassembled the litters. As the lights of the Twin Cities came into view, we fastened our seat belts and approached the runway.

Lt Tenney who was sitting next to me as we landed said, "I wanted something extra to do, but I didn't want to leave Fairview Hospital. Flight nursing is a lot different from floor nursing - mainly because the patients are the nurses' responsibility. It's a wonderful experience for girls who like to meet people and want to travel. But it takes a person who can adapt to many situations."

As we left the plane, the med techs and nurses headed for home and their civilian ways of life. This had been only a practice mission. But they were training for the day when it might be necessary to fly a live mission from the Twin Cities. [23]

September. Maj Margaret Lynch, an active duty flight nurse, was assigned to the squadron as Administrative Aeromedical Advisor. She replaced Maj Katherine Simpson who had been with the squadron through her active duty assignment in Dec 1962.

Photo courtesy of the Northstar Guardian (Dec '63)
Maj Margaret Lynch

According to Lt Col Russell Jensen, former pilot in the MNANG who flew both the C-97A and G models, the unit gradually transitioned from the A to G model during this time period. He also mentioned that some of the G models that Minnesota received were actually converted KC-97G tankers that had cargo doors installed! [24]

Photo courtesy of Lt Col Henry Capiz
Boeing C-97G Stratofreighter of the Minnesota ANG.

1964

January. The New Year would begin with a noteworthy change for the aeromeds of the 109th. Effective 1 January, the 133rd ATW was reorganized. This resulted in a significant transformation for the 109th AMEF. Previously, the aeromedical unit was independent, only attached to the base for local support. The new organizational structure placed the unit under command of Brig Gen John Dolny, Wing Commander. This made the 109th AMEF a permanent fixture of the 133rd Air Transport Wing (ATW).

The National Guard Bureau also announced the realignment of air transport units. In the consequent reshuffle, the 133rd ATW lost the 109th Air Transport Group in Schenectady, NY and so the squadron lost its 139th AMEF. The wing then gained the 170th Air Transport Group of Newark, NJ and gained for the squadron the 150th AMEF. Staff visits were planned and made to Newark to acquaint the new flight with its Squadron Headquarters personnel.

February. Obviously, planners were in tune with morale when the 18-22 February field training was set for Hickam AFB, HI. With new directives and policies being initiated by the AF and MATS, the unit took advantage of an opportunity to combine that education with field training. Both the 133rd AMES and the 109th AMEF participated along with other wing members to accomplish various exercises, including survival training, weapons instruction on the firing range, and an introduction to the new policies and procedures that MATS had established. The host units, the 1502nd ATW, MATS and the 1453rd AES not only welcomed Minnesota's winter weary Air Guardsmen with the AF Band of the Pacific playing on the tarmac as they deplaned, but provided well organized and prepared training as well. [25]

Photo courtesy of the 50th Anniversary Book, 133rd Military Airlift Wing (1971)
**The AF Band of the Pacific was on hand to welcome Minnesota's Air Guardsmen as they deplaned at Hickam AFB, HI. Capt Gibbons, 1453rd AES (center) greeted Capt Jean Cool (left) and Maj Margaret Lynch (right) with Hawaiian leis.
Note the heavy, winter uniforms sported by the Minnesota flight nurses.**

The highlight of the week was the wet ditching drill. The group first attended a morning of classes on the use of the 20-man life raft, ditching procedures, survival equipment aboard the raft and the Mae West life preserver.

In the afternoon, 20 officers and 40 Airmen of the 133rd Wing Headquarters, 133rd AMES and the 109th AMEF lined the dock to practice what they had learned that morning. The exercise consisted of jumping off the dock and swimming approximately 200 yards to the assembly of orange-colored life rafts dotting the harbor. The sea was choppy but the air was a pleasant 80 degrees. Once the swimmers reached the raft, they pulled themselves aboard and followed the directions of the raft commander. It was his task to see that the dye markers were released, that the various signaling devices and water purification kits were assigned and operated properly and that the raft was secure.

Dorothea Tenney recalled that "The raft was very crowded! I remember my foot getting sat on, but I couldn't say anything - he was a general!" [26]

Photo courtesy of the 50th Anniversary Book, 133rd Military Airlift Wing (1971)
Maj Lynch makes the leap while other flight nurses and med techs wait their turn during a wet ditching drill in Hickam Harbor.

The exercise was considered a huge success. As one would expect, organization members "managed" to find time for some fun on the beach and enjoyed their evenings off-duty. [27]

Photo courtesy of the 50th Anniversary Book, 133rd Military Airlift Wing (1971)
Aeromeds swim to 20-man life rafts.

With spring around the corner, it was once again Military Ball time which was held at the Prom Ballroom in St Paul. A1C Larry Daudt of the 109th AMEF was named one of the co-winners for the Honor Airman Award. It was the first tie of the award since its inauguration in 1958. A1C Daudt was also named one of the four McElvain Scholarship winners for the year along with TSgt Robert Hecht, another squadron member.

May. With an emphasis on recruiting, members of the 109th AMEF participated in an event at the annual Upper Midwest Hospital Conference. Held at the Minneapolis Convention Hall 4-6 May, an AE display was set up to gain the attention of civilian nurses. Labeled "U.S. AIR FORCE, The Age of Space through Education for Men and Women," the display attracted considerable interest from those attending. Lt Dorothea Tenney with other squadron officers, dressed in the various uniforms worn by AF officers, spent the weekend extolling the benefits of becoming an AF flight nurse. The unit was working towards its goal of 17 authorized flight nurse positions, but sadly found that this event did not produce any new nurses for the unit.

☆ ☆ ☆ ☆ ☆

Richard Vosika, who served as a med tech from 1961-1964, recounted his time with the early aeromeds:

> I transferred from the Minnesota Army Reserve H/H Co (Headquarters and Headquarters Company), 3rd BG (Brigade), 3rd Infantry, 103rd Division at Ft. Snelling as a fully qualified medic to the 109th AMEF effective 19 July 1961. I made this transfer for several reasons: 1) the ANG unit was looking for qualified medics, 2) I was not happy sitting at the Army Reserve every Monday night doing nothing when I had so much studying to do for college, and 3) I was fascinated that the medical career field would put me on flying status. Shortly thereafter, the 109th was notified that they would be activated 1 Oct 1961 for the Berlin Crisis, and stationed in our home town of Minneapolis. This was not what I expected, since my goal at that time was to finish college at the U of M and become a Physical Science teacher at the high school level.

During our period of activation (1 Oct 1961-31 Aug 1962), the 109th grew as other medically qualified personnel from around the USA were activated and assigned to our unit. Even though most of us lived in the Twin Cities area, those of us in the lower ranks were provided on-base quarters, which meant we could not draw a housing allowance, even though we were allowed to continue living at home.

A typical day on active duty consisted of training in the classroom. The nurses became our instructors. Normal duty day was 0800-1700 Monday through Friday. Occasionally we were required to be there on a Saturday for room inspection. Since many of us lived in the same neighborhoods, it was not unusual for several of us to carpool from a neighborhood location to the base for training each day.

Being on flying status, we were required to complete a minimum of four hours of flying each month. This training was normally completed on the C-97 while the pilots were fulfilling their training requirements. During these training missions, we would install litters in the aircraft and practice our medical procedures on our fellow Airmen. On one occasion, we accomplished our monthly training in a Navy C-54 when we all flew out to California on one day and returned the next day. Some of us also recorded flying time in the C-119G. On one such occasion, we all had to wear parachutes because our mission was to drop a lot of - I don't remember how many - but a lot of balloons over an activity taking place in Minneapolis. To drop the balloons, we had to open the rear jump doors and throw them all out. Even though we all had parachutes on, none of us had ever been trained on how to use them. Luck was with us - no one fell out.

In addition to the mock training missions, we were all rotated through the normal air evacuation system. On these occasions we supplemented the domestic and strategic system by flying stateside missions out of Scott AFB, IL on the C-131A, or flying overwater missions from Rhein Main AB, Germany to McGuire AFB, NJ on the C-135A.

Since we were flying at high altitudes - normally 30-35,000 feet - we were all required to complete physiological training periodically - I believe every three years. This training was completed at an active duty base. In addition to the classroom training, we all were exposed to the effects of hypoxia and rapid decompression in a barometric chamber.

One surprising fact I still remember to this day, was that up to 40% of our patients were classified as "psychiatric." This meant that these individuals were unable to adjust to military life while living overseas, for whatever reason. It could have been home sickness, inability to speak the native language, social problems, drinking problems, loneliness, or a host of other problems brought on by their experience working in the military overseas.

In January 1962, ten med techs from the 109th AMEF, including myself, received TDY orders to Brooks AFB, TX to attend the School of Aerospace Medicine Evacuation Technician Course AZR 90270. Brooks AFB was located seven miles southeast of downtown San Antonio, Texas. We joined 39 other med techs from across the USA to form the class of 62-A. The course began on 17 Jan 62 and commencement was held on 20 Feb 1962. Five of us drove from Minneapolis to San Antonio in one car. I don't remember how the other five travelled to San Antonio.

En route to San Antonio, we stopped at the Kansas City Steak House to enjoy one of their world-famous steaks. The steaks were so good, we asked the manager how much a second steak would cost, without the bread and salad. He gave us a great price and we all ordered a second steak.

The C-97 engines were known for their oil leaks, especially in the winter in Minnesota. It was not uncommon to be scheduled for a training flight, arrive at base and find out the mission had to be cancelled due to an engine oil leak. Worse yet, even when we did take off on a training mission, we had to return early due to engine problems.

On one occasion, we were headed to the West Coast for training, but turned around at the Minnesota-North Dakota border due to engine problems. I do not remember exactly which engine had what problem, but it was something like this: Engine 1 was running fine, engine 2 was shut down for some reason, engine 3 was feathered, and engine 4 had an oil leak. The pilots felt our chances of getting to the West Coast were very limited with the problems which had already developed only a few hundred miles out of Minneapolis-St Paul Airport.

One training trip took us all to Hawaii for about a week in the middle of a Minnesota winter. I do not remember all the details, but I do remember there was a lot of training, and a lot of free time. We all enjoyed this trip immensely. A few of the things I do remember:

   a. We all bought Hawaiian shirts and enjoyed many nights in Waikiki watching the luau shows.
   b. Some of us rented a car and drove across many of the remote parts of the island.
   c. We loaded enough pineapples onto the aircraft when we left for each of us to have two when we returned to Minnesota with snow on the ground.
   d. The live raft training in the Pacific Ocean was probably one of the highlights of our training that week.

During my entire time with the 109th, I remember we all worked together, never had any serious disagreements, and always enjoyed ourselves, whether working or having fun.

Supplementing the strategic air evac system was one of the greatest rewards of training with the 109th. These trips usually consisted of one flight nurse and two med techs, flying from the USA to Germany and back over a seven-day period. I always flew these trips during quarter break from the University of Minnesota. My classmates thought it was great to do winter or spring break in Florida. I think I had the better deal - a trip to Germany, not to mention that my trip was paid for and their trip was on their own nickel.

My first training trip overseas was from 26 April 1962 to 2 May 1962 while on active duty for the Berlin Crisis. 1st Lt Jean Cool, A1C Rolland Breth and myself A3C (Airman Third Class) Richard Vosika deadheaded to Rhein Main AB, Germany. Once there, we were provided a tour of the aeromedical facilities, then assigned to a specific flight which was to leave a few days later. In the meantime, we were free to do whatever we wanted to do. So we rented a car and became tourists. I do not remember where we went - I think Heidelberg, but I do remember being at a restaurant at a castle, sitting outside and looking over the river below. Having taken German in high school for one year, and having been somewhat proficient in my use of it in ordering our meals, I asked the waiter - in German - for a glass of cherry brandy. When the waiter brought me a piece of "cherry pie," we all had a good laugh at my proficiency in German, and I enjoyed the pie.

On another trip to Germany, we again had a few days free to visit this wonderful country. This time, with two nurses and another med tech. We travelled to a small town and enjoyed a fine meal and some drinks in the local gasthof. Shortly after 2200, we returned to the small hotel we were staying in and found the doors locked and the entire hotel dark. Unbeknownst to us, the hotel locked the doors and all occupants were assumed to be in bed. After a lot of "banging" on individual room windows, we were able to get in and go to our rooms that night.

I remember the C-97 was such a huge airplane when I flew with the 109th. Then at the 50th reunion, I was able to walk through a C-97 again - the first time in about 40 years. I was so disappointed in its size after having flown in much larger aircraft, both in the military and in civilian life over the last 40 years. Time moves on!

Richard Vosika

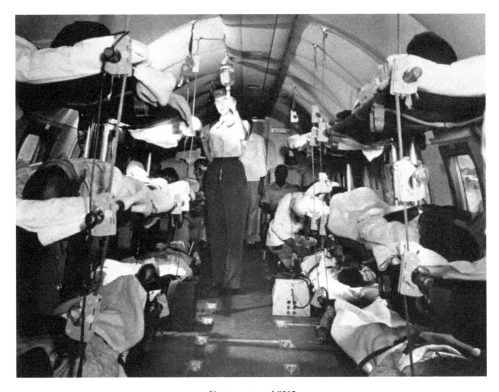

A flight nurse makes her rounds on litter and ambulatory patients in a C-131A Samaritan aircraft.

June. Members of the Squadron Headquarters traveled to Manchester, New Hampshire to observe the Operational Readiness Inspection (ORI) which was conducted that month by Headquarters EASTAF and MATS personnel. An ORI is a tool for the AF to evaluate a wing's readiness and the capability of the wing and its assigned units to perform their wartime mission. The inspection measures the effectiveness and efficiency of mobilization and mobility processing, assessment of the training for the ability to survive and operate during war and the ability of the units to perform their specific functions.

September. A full squadron AE exercise was held involving all three of its flights. Two C-97 Stratofreighter aircraft and one C-121 Constellation aircraft were utilized to transport patients with simulated injuries and ailments. The sick and injured were treated to test the responses of the flight nurses and med techs. After the flight, the crews met and discussed various problems involved in such an operation and what changes would be necessary to improve their effectiveness in the event of an actual emergency.

November. The 133rd Squadron Headquarters personnel made a follow-up staff visit to the 133rd AMEF in New Hampshire to coordinate training, regulations and procedures during the Unit Training Assembly (UTA) weekend.

☆☆☆☆☆

The recurring theme of training and more training continued through the end of the year. The focus was on the new members as well as attempting to maintain all of the qualifications set forth by the AF.

☆☆☆☆☆

MSgt Bob Kolbo joined the ANG in 1964 and was assigned to the aeromeds primarily due to his past experience serving with a U.S. Army evacuation hospital. A quiet but personable individual, he brought a wealth of medical evacuation experience and leadership to the organization as a result of his prior military service. He proved to be a very positive and strong mentor to all of the enlisted personnel. These qualities served the aeromeds well when he was assigned as their First Sergeant later in the unit's history.

Col Julie Eszlinger Jensen remembers, "He worked tirelessly for the benefit of the unit and never looked for praise. MSgt Kolbo was also a great role model for all members as he understood our people, had a gentle approach but was stern when necessary, always listened intently and never passed judgment.

"Then there was the playful and humorous side. One example was when then-enlisted med tech Norman Hendrickson was about to marry his fiancee Barb, two of his fellow med techs, who were invited to the wedding, approached MSgt Kolbo asking him a favor. 'Would you have someone type up a set of orders stating that Norm is being called to active duty and is ordered to report to the base first thing Monday morning?' MSgt Kolbo was more than happy to comply with this request. To make it look official, Capt Harry Nelson signed the orders and fellow med tech Dan Hilliker brought them to the ceremony. When the orders were presented to Norm at the wedding, he looked absolutely shocked and Barb looked like a deer caught in the headlights!"

Photo courtesy of Col Julie Eszlinger Jensen
MSgt Bob Kolbo

December. Fifteen members of the 109th AMEF traveled to Torrejon AB, Spain, on an eight-day TDY. Capt Henry Capiz coordinated the members in numerous AE training exercises while the aircraft completed its cargo mission.

☆☆☆☆☆

The year ended with official approval of the new squadron patch, which was worn by both squadron and flight members. This patch was designed during the 1961 Berlin Crisis active duty period and it bears many similarities to the patch that is worn today. Please see the "Squadron Patch History" section at the back of the book for further details.

1965

Records and achievements for the year 1965 are not available. This is in all likelihood due to the fact that MSgt Richard Fox, the unit air technician, resigned his position early in the year, but remained in the unit as a traditional guardsman. His post was filled in the latter part of the year by TSgt Walter Foster Jr., formerly of the 47th AMES, Air Force Reserve. TSgt Foster served until the late 1980s with the exception of a one-year period where TSgt Jim Hughes filled in for this position.

Col Julie Eszlinger Jensen remembers, "SMSgt (Senior Master Sergeant) Foster was the first and only one full-time technician for the unit. His weekday supervisor was a pilot officer having no knowledge of AE and provided little to no guidance. With that, Foster had many freedoms to manage the unit.

"With the arrival of computers, he was one of the first to obtain one on base, purchasing it with his own funds. Since there were no other computer users on base and no computer classes, he taught himself how to use it.

"He had a quiet demeanor, never raised his voice and handled everything in a very calm and professional manner. All of his work was very neat and professional. A true role model, his uniform and dress was always impeccable."

Another 109th AES member remembers, "SMSgt Foster was the man in charge. He always attempted to be on the cutting edge with computers, possessed vast aeromedical experience and had networked in the aerovac community. He discouraged having enlisted members making up drills by having them wash windows or some other tasks, motivating them to never miss drills in the future."

Photo courtesy of Col Julie Eszlinger Jensen
SMSgt Walt Foster

Photo courtesy of the Northstar Guardian (Sep '65)
Capt Dorothea Tenney and Sherm Booen during his televised "World of Aviation" TV program from the Minnesota State Fair Grounds. Capt Tenney described the flight nurse kit and other equipment used by the 109th AMEF nurses on their aeromed flights.

<u>November.</u> 1st Lt Julie Eszlinger became the newest flight nurse to join the 109th AMEF. She was recruited by her friend and coworker at Fairview Hospital, Capt Dorothea Tenney. Dorothea remembers hearing Julie talking about her interest in joining the AFR and convinced her that she would "like it better in the Guard."

1966

<u>January.</u> MATS became the Military Airlift Command (MAC).

<u>March.</u> Headquarters MAC sent Maj Margaret Lynch to conduct a field visit to assist the unit's training program. Ironically some of the findings show challenges similar to those found today. Some of the recommendations:

1. UTAs could be more productively utilized in record maintenance as some documentation was inaccurate or not up-to-date.
2. Home Study Guides for ground training requirements should be more promptly and properly complied with.
3. Better attendance needed to be enforced at appropriate classes.
4. Aircrew member currency requirements should be complied with as specified in applicable directives. [28]

☆☆☆☆☆

A separate Air Force Specialty Code (AFSC) for flight nurses was approved. The new Code, 9675, was reflected in AF Manual 36-1, Officer Classification Manual, September 1966. [29]

May. Maj Franklin Snapp became the third 133rd AMES Commander on May 26. He formerly commanded the 47th AES of the AFR and replaced Lt Col Wayne Janzig.

Maj Snapp was a 23-year veteran of the military having served on active duty from 1942-1955 and remained in the reserves since then. He received a direct commission in 1949 and served at Travis AFB, CA in Air Evacuation Control and later was a hospital adjutant in the Surgeon General's (SG) office.

Maj Snapp remained in the reserves because "I like the diversion." He said he was impressed with the "tremendous people you meet" in the Guard. Members of the Minnesota Air Guard, he said, "make a genuine and sincere effort to make you feel at home." [30]

Capt Henry Capiz became the new administrative officer in the 133rd AMES. He was formerly a medical supply officer in the dispensary.

Capt Dorothea Tenney, part of the original cadre, left the 109th after accepting a Director of Nursing position in Hartford, Connecticut. Her contributions and her hard work, along with that of the other founders were immeasurable. The numerous later successes that the flight/squadron garnered would be a direct result of their hard work getting the fledgling aerovac unit off the ground.

June. On 4 June, an open house was held to recruit local nurses for flight nurse openings within the unit.

☆☆☆☆☆

Col Eszlinger Jensen remembers that this was the month she went to Flight Nurse School. She recalls, "Guard and Reserve units were given the first choice of slots in flight school over the active duty. This made it very uncomfortable because the active duty was not happy with the priority given to the Guard and Reserve." [31]

July. Capt Dorothy Ludwig, a flight nurse, received the State of Minnesota Commendation Ribbon with pendant during July UTA activities.

Capt Ludwig was to have received her award during the June UTA, but was not present as she and four Airmen from the 109th AMEF were attending 15 days of aeromedical evacuation training at Kelly AFB, TX for their summer camp.

"I worked in the control center scheduling patients and setting them up on the appropriate flight," Capt Ludwig said. She also flew on two or three aerovac flights to Denver with multiple stops to pick up and drop off patients. "They were a very cooperative group of people," she said. "They let us participate rather than just observe."

Capt Ludwig's award was for "having distinguished herself by unusually meritorious achievement in assuming joint responsibility of the assembly and writing of aeromedical personnel training programs." [32]

Photo courtesy of the Northstar Guardian (Aug/Sep '66)
Col Robert Peterson presents Capt Dorothy Ludwig with the Minnesota Commendation Medal.

Water survival training at a local lake or in a nearby body of water during a field training exercise (FTX) would take place on a recurring basis in the years ahead for the 109th. Most aeromeds looked at this as one of the more enjoyable training events on their schedules. It usually consisted of lectures by the life support staff, followed by water activities consisting of the use of the life preserver and life raft.

On one such occasion, however, things took a different turn. As SSgt Larry Daudt, one of the early med techs writes:

> Now for the incident in Lake Nokomis. Be advised, the incident is real and factual from my viewpoint. Fifty years may have numbed the incidentals however.
>
> On a beautiful weekend morning in July or August we reported for duty which, today, was a rescue exercise to be done in Lake Nokomis with the assistance of a Navy Reserve helicopter doing the recovery.
>
> We rode an ANG bus to the lake where the helicopter was waiting. The day prior, we had been advised to dress in street clothes or flight suits, for they would be getting wet.
>
> Once at the lake, we were directed to get in the water and wait for the helicopter to fly overhead and for the crewman to lower a line which had a horse collar rescue device attached. I waited in the lake with an attached life preserver as did the other med techs and nurses.
>
> Once the rescue training operation started, one by one we were picked out of the water with the use of the horse collar and deposited on the shore. When my turn came, the helicopter hovered overhead as I swam closer to the horse collar. The crewman was lowering the collar from his position in the cargo compartment as the helicopter hovered. As I neared the collar, I sensed that the chopper was descending and that was verified because the crewman had abandoned his duty station on the floor of the chopper and was standing on the web seat in the cargo compartment.
>
> The collar was floating in the water and as I reached for it, I also realized that my first instinct was correct. With the engines roaring in my ears, the helicopter was in fact descending and was semi-floating in the water in an attempt to remain upright. I believe the term used was "descending through ground effect." My concern now was with those big rotor blades spinning over my head.
>
> I tried to disconnect from the Mae West and swim deep into the water and then away, to get outside the arc of the rotor but for some reason the release buckle was jammed and the Mae West held me afloat. I then frantically swam on the surface until I was outside the arc of the rotor and turned to look as the pilot made a last pull on the cyclic as the lake released it. Somehow that maneuver worked and he managed to rather forcefully land on the shoreline.

I believe the engine had been over stressed and the helicopter was hauled back to the Navy base on a truck. Needless to say, the training for the day was canceled and we were bussed back to the ANG base to be dismissed.

In researching this incident, the authors uncovered an article written by the actual pilot who was flying the helicopter mentioned above. His view from the cockpit!

"Sink or Swim... or What?"

The annual request from the Minnesota ANG to provide helo water hoists for their aircrew was welcomed. It would provide an opportunity for the pilots and aircrew to complete their requirements. Time selected was a Sunday in July, 1966 at Lake Nokomis in the south part of Minneapolis. It was also Aquatennial time, an annual summertime festival and celebration. There were about 3,500 people at the lake that Sunday. The helo exercise was an added attraction to the other scheduled events. The weather was typical Minnesota July... hot and humid.

The SH-34J helicopter was being used by the Navy and Marines at the NAS (Naval Air Station) at that time. I was assigned to HS-813 which was the unit assigned to do the hoists. Lake Nokomis is about five miles from the NAS. A portion of the shore line was cordoned off as a landing area to permit the ANG crew to debark after the hoist.

The drill called for two helos to fly at the same time: one hoisting and the other landing and debarking. A large raft, up to 40-man size, was anchored in the lake. The people to be hoisted left the raft and would swim out about 100 yards and await their turn. The helo would enter a hover at 35 feet and lower the sling for recovery.

As I started an approach, everything was normal. As power was applied to establish the hover (took a lot of power on "hot and humid") there was a tremendous BANG and the rotor RPM (revolutions per minute) started to drop rapidly. A frantic "milking" of the collective had no effect as the helo headed down to the water. I was told later that the guy waiting to be picked up almost "walked on water" as he tried to get out of the way.

As the helo contacted the water, full up collective pitch was applied and we made a really soft landing. It did not start to sink as I had feared. Of course it couldn't fly but it had neutral buoyancy. This was not expected. I nudged the cyclic stick and the helo started to move slowly through the water...just like a boat. My crewman was frantically trying to get the hoist cable back into the helo before it tangled with the rotor. My co-pilot turned on the windshield wipers...they were needed.

I applied slight pressure on pedals and turned the plane toward shore where the ground crew moved the "rubberneck" spectators off to a safe distance. As we got into shallow water, I could feel the wheels contact the lake bottom. The rotor RPM started to increase as the helo weight was starting to be supported by the wheels. With the RPM again at normal, I was able to "gingerly" lift off and ease into the landing area.

The helo was shut down and inspected. The lower cylinder head of the R-1820 engine had cracked all the way across. The blades were folded and the helo was towed back to NAS Minneapolis...to fly another day. We had accomplished a successful water landing in a SH-34...is not 'sposed to be an amphibian! [33]

Photo courtesy of the Minnesota ANG Museum
Rescue exercise with 109th aeromeds at Lake Nokomis.

September. Unit members began to volunteer for overseas AE missions in support of the Vietnam War effort. The 109th AMEF was not officially placed on Active Federal Service during the conflict. However, members continued to volunteer and support the war until February 1971 (when the unit transitioned to a tactical mission), culminating in thirteen live overseas missions.

The United States had been clandestinely involved in the political process of bringing democracy to this small country since the end of World War II. Concerned about the spread of communism, especially with the fall of mainland China to Mao's Communist forces in 1949, President Truman adopted a policy of containment. This policy was designed to slow or stop the expansion of communism throughout the world. Believing that Ho Chi Minh, president of the North Vietnamese political party, was working with the Soviet Union, Truman authorized the sending of military aid in the form of weapons and other military equipment to the French forces then reoccupying Vietnam. In 1950, he sent in a small group of military advisors to train South Vietnamese troops to fight the growing threat of the Viet Minh, the future Viet Cong. For the first time, U.S. military personnel were committed to the fight in Vietnam. President Eisenhower continued this commitment, and even increased the number of U.S. military personnel in that country. When President Kennedy took office in January 1961, he continued U.S. support of the South Vietnamese government. By the middle of 1962, close to 9,000 U.S. troops were in Vietnam fighting South Vietnamese insurgents who now called themselves the Viet Cong.

President John Kennedy was dissatisfied with the way South Vietnamese President Ngo Diem was governing the country. In November 1963, he secretly approved a coup to remove Diem from power and form a committee of South Vietnamese military officials to establish a temporary government. The result was an increase in the number of Viet Cong attacks on South Vietnam's military forces. Just two weeks after the coup, President Kennedy was assassinated and Vice President Johnson became the new Commander in Chief. In June of 1964, he placed General Westmoreland in command of U.S. forces in Vietnam. Westmoreland favored expanding the war and received another five thousand troops which brought the total number of U.S. forces in that tiny country to 21,000. With the expanding role of U.S. military personnel in field operations, U.S. casualties steadily increased. The demands placed upon the small aerovac community in the active duty USAF to transport the wounded began to tax its capabilities.

In July of 1964, it was reported that two U.S. Navy destroyers had been attacked by North Vietnamese torpedo boats just off the coast of North Vietnam. President Johnson responded by ordering air strikes against North Vietnamese military bases. In August, Congress granted President Johnson the power to use whatever force he deemed necessary to assist South Vietnam. Although no official declaration of war was passed by Congress, the U.S. was now committed to a war in Southeast Asia.

In 1965, President Johnson steadily widened the U.S. commitment to the war. He initiated Operation Rolling Thunder, the strategic bombing of numerous targets in North Vietnam. He also sent an additional 100,000 troops to support the war effort. U.S. ground forces were now actively seeking out Viet Cong/North Vietnamese forces and engaging them in battle. With this increased commitment, U.S. casualty rates rapidly reached the point where active duty aerovac capabilities were being overwhelmed. Additional trained personnel were clearly needed. AFR and ANG medical personnel could now volunteer to assist in AE missions in support of U.S. efforts in Vietnam.

The war would continue for another decade with U.S. casualties continuing to increase proportionally and with it the need for qualified AE personnel as well. Many members of the 109th AEF gained valuable hands-on experience answering this call.

This divisive war, unpopular at home, ended with the withdrawal of U.S. forces in 1973 and the unification of Vietnam under communist control two years later. More than 3 million people, including 58,000 Americans, were killed in the conflict.

As for the aerovac mission, evacuated patients were staged at Clark AB in the Philippines and at Yokota AB/Tachikawa AB in Japan. "Mother MAC," the successor to MATS, handled all patient movement to the United States, utilizing standard transport planes including the C-7 Caribou, the C-130 Hercules, and the C-141 Starlifter outfitted with litters. Only one of those aircraft still performs the AE mission as part of its many duties – the venerable C-130 – and is still in use for this mission today. The first mobile casualty staging facility of the war was stood up and was manned by the 903rd AES in PACAF.

C-141 aircraft carried the sick and wounded back to stateside military hospitals - Travis AFB, CA, Scott AFB, IL, Dover AFB, DE, and Andrews AFB, MD. AE crews flew on commercial airlines to San Francisco IAP (International Airport) in civilian clothes. From there they took a bus to Travis AFB. USAF orders stated that military personnel were NOT to be seen in uniform in public. Directives dictated that civilian clothes were changed to uniforms and vice versa in restrooms both when departing for an overseas flight and upon returning to the States.

On the return trip home on the C-141 the troops cheered upon wheels up in Japan. The mood got considerably more somber as they approached their destination base hospital. When the aircraft landed at the destination hospital bases, some of the wounded stated their family had no longer communicated with them, would not be meeting them and didn't know they were injured and returning. It was then that Lt Eszlinger mentioned to the flight crew, that she had a feeling "someday our country will have to reckon with this."

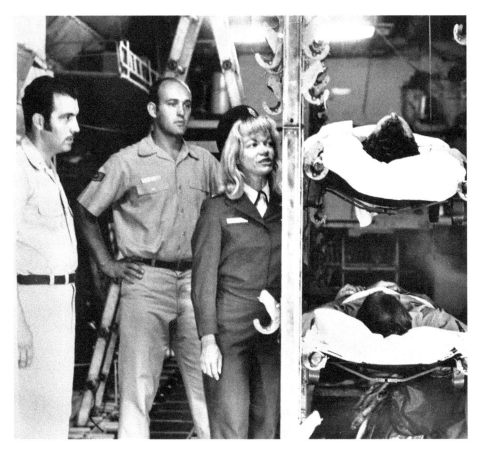

Photo courtesy of Col Julie Eszlinger Jensen

Capt Julia Eszlinger aboard a C-141 aircraft enroute from Yokota AB, Japan to Andrews Air Force Base, MD.

December. The 133rd AMES hosted a conference on 3-4 December for several aeromedical organizations throughout the country. Representatives were in town from the 133rd AEF, New Hampshire ANG, Pease AFB, NH and New Jersey's 150th AEF from McGuire AFB. Our own 109th AEF officers and non-commissioned officers (NCOs) were responsible for operations, administration and training. The purpose of the conference was to discuss problems common to each of the units and to aid in standardizing activities within the air evac organizations. [34]

It was an excellent opportunity for direct sharing of ideas and experiences related to their mission. Col Eszlinger Jensen recalls that "during this and subsequent conferences, many other units (Personnel, Maintenance, etc.) from the attending aerovac squadrons participated in these conferences. Friendships developed and some families even vacationed together." [35]

1967

The year 1967 began with two new nurses joining the 109th - Lt Judith Alsip and Lt Christina Thompson. Both brought to the unit an abundance of training and experience making them very well qualified to meet the challenges required of AF flight nurses.

CHAPTER 3
The Command of Lt Col Henry Capiz

(Jul 1967 - Aug 1973)

Photo courtesy of Lt Col Capiz

Like so many of his generation, Lt Col Capiz began his military career at the age of 18. He received his draft notice in March of 1944 while attending Humboldt High School. During his infantry training at Camp Hood, Texas, he volunteered for airborne training. Capiz earned his jump wings in October of 1944 at Fort Benning, Georgia. After this advanced training, he was assigned to the 503rd Regimental Combat Team and sent to New Guinea as a paratrooper. His next stop was the Philippines where he fought to liberate the Islands from the Japanese. With Japan's surrender, he was reassigned to the 11th Airborne Division and sent to Japan for occupation duty. In May of 1946, he returned to the United States and was discharged at Camp McCoy.

In August 1947, Capiz joined the 4th Marine Battalion at Wold-Chamberlain NAS in Minneapolis and was sent to Camp Lejeune, North Carolina for training. Due to a lack of transportation, his enlistment lasted until April 1948.

In May 1948, "Hank" Capiz joined the Minnesota ANG. The following year he enrolled at the University of Minnesota to pursue a degree in pharmacy. His studies were interrupted in March 1951 when he was recalled to active duty for the Korean War. TSgt Capiz served as a Basic Training Instructor at Holmen Field in St. Paul.

Returning to the University in September 1954, he graduated in 1957. He was then commissioned as a 1st Lt, became a Medical Service Officer, and was assigned to the Minnesota Air Guard's 133rd Dispensary. He was once again called to active duty in 1961 in response to the Berlin Crisis.

In 1964 he was transferred to the 133rd AES.

In 1969 Maj Capiz did a short tour of duty at Clark AB, Republic of the Philippines as the Medical Operations Officer staging and handling the casualties arriving from Da Nang, Vietnam.

In 1972 he was promoted to Lt Col, and retired in 1974.

Capiz continued his pharmacy practice and was appointed Chief of Pharmacy for St. Luke's Hospital, known today as United Hospital in St. Paul, MN. He received an acknowledgement from the Minnesota State Pharmaceutical Association, which recognized one pharmacist annually for outstanding service to the profession of pharmacy. His contributions to pharmacy education and practice extended close to 40 years when he retired in 1991.

His military decorations include the Bronze Star, Combat Infantry Badge, Philippine Distinguished Unit Citation, Asiatic Pacific Campaign Medal, American Campaign Medal, Philippine Liberation Medal, National Defense Service Medal and State Commendation Medal.

July. 1st Lt Harry Nelson relinquished command of the 109th AMEF to Maj Henry Capiz.

August. Our parent command, the 133rd AMES was deactivated and the flights formerly under its command were made autonomous units. With this change, the 109th AMEF became an independent flight and was expanded to 22 officers and 32 Airmen. Additionally, the two Medical Service Corps (MSC) officers were also required to maintain flying currency. The only "ground" positions were two medical administrative personnel. Even at that time, recruiting the nurses was a challenge, and recruiting remained a priority item for the unit.

October. The 109th AMEF and St. Paul Ramsey Hospital (now Regions Hospital) entered a joint community service and ANG training program agreement which became the first military-civilian community service project in the state, and only one of two in the nation.

Maj Henry Capiz (109th AMEF Commander), Capt Dorothy Ludwig, Capt A. Marlene Ausen (a nurse civilian employee at St. Paul Ramsey Hospital), Otto Janke (St. Paul Ramsey Hospital Administrator) and Minna Moehring (Director of Nursing at St. Paul Ramsey) initiated this effort to train aeromedical flight nurses and med techs in the hospital over UTA weekends. Hospital personnel supervised this on-the-job training in the specialty areas of psychiatry, medical, surgery, coronary, orthopedic, neurology, pediatric, burn and emergency departments within the hospital. This program filled a gap in aeromedical training - the lack of patient contact within the reserve AE units.

Although this type of training program was emulated by other Reserve and Guard units, it wasn't until a decade later that the AF realized the benefits of this type of training for its medical personnel and introduced the "Annual Hospital Tour." (Future 2-week hospital tours in 1971 and 1972 were conducted at the St. Paul Ramsey Hospital.)

In the fall of 2016, the authors met twice with Lt Col Capiz. When we mentioned that "his" hospital program not only still existed, but has grown over the past 49 years, Capiz seemed pleasantly surprised and beamed with pride. He told us that, "I thought it was a good program when we came up with the idea and I am glad that the med techs have found the training helpful."

☆ ☆ ☆ ☆ ☆

Looking back and just seven years after its authorization, the hard work accomplished by the original 29 members of the 109th had firmly established itself as an AE flight of the highest caliber in the AF inventory. Though always undermanned and often using creative and novel methods to accomplish its training goals, unit members always met or exceeded every mission and requirement given to them by the active duty AF. The dedication to each other, to the squadron/flight and the country has continued to this day. The example they set years ago and which has been maintained to the present has firmly established the 109th AES as "the best of the best." Its level of achievement is the barometer by which all other AE units are measured today.

☆ ☆ ☆ ☆ ☆

Fast forward 56 years later when SSgt Larry Daudt, one of the early med techs writes:

> As I ponder the events of fifty plus years ago, a new name emerges, and then another, and another, names I haven't thought of for all those many years.
>
> I came to the realization, as did so many of my friends in the early '60s that it was decision time. We were about to be drafted into the U.S. Army, given a shovel and a weapon and sent

off to foreign lands to fight someone else's fight.

So what did we do? We started to search for an alternate plan for our lives. Some joined the Navy, others the Marine Corps, and still others the Air Force, while a few just toughed it out in the Army. They spent their time marching, digging holes and ditches, washing dishes on KP duty, and sleeping on a canvas cot in a tent or out in the open.

My first choice was always to fly in one capacity or another so the USAF was my choice. And then one day a friend introduced me to the ANG. He said that it would be six years of weekend duty and summer camps each year plus training for a useful job classification. Since I had thought of medical school (once I could afford to go), the 109th Aeromedical unit was being organized at the MNANG, and so I became an Airman Basic (AB) on my way to somewhere. As the years progressed and I matured, I was promoted through the ranks to Staff Sergeant.

My life was a whirlwind of activity in the years 1961 through 1967. I started college at the University of Minnesota. I was married. I took flying lessons and became a commercial pilot with an instrument rating which qualified me to apply with the airlines, namely Northwest and North Central. I met pilots from both local airlines while flying FTPs (Flying Training Periods) as an aeromed in the C-97 in the Minnesota ANG. In September of 1965, I was accepted by NWA (Northwest Airlines) for a pilot position and continued flying there for 36 years until my mandatory age 60 retirement date of 12/21/2001.

But what about those six years as a med tech? Who were the people of the 109th? Be advised that the names are slowly emerging one by one from the crevasses of my 75-year-old mind, so if spelling isn't correct or places are changed please forgive. I'm sure that your research will make the corrections.

First, I recall the flight nurses who so patiently schooled me in the care of the patient - Lt Helen Grundberg, Lt Julie Eszlinger, Lt Cool, Lt Cook, Lt Tenney, Lt Hunt, Lt Osteboe, and there may have been more.

Next, my class of six, all sworn in on the same day in the fall of 1961:
Robert Moss...optometrist...now deceased
Dennis Fitzsimmons...lost contact
Robert Anderson...lost contact
Robert Miller...lost contact
Tom Hedin...college professor and drug addiction counselor...deceased
Larry Daudt...living in Fair Oaks Ranch, Texas

We six were trained to the 30 level at Gunter AFB, AL and also trained to the 50 level at Brooks AFB, TX.

In the class immediately ahead of the six of us were:
Terry Ripley...Minneapolis area
Tom Thunnel...lost contact
David Lund...lost contact
James Mulroy...pharmacist...lost contact
Robert Vosika...AF officer - retired
Robert Hecht...lost contact
Ray Ballenger...lost contact

The sergeants and upper-class Airmen:
Ken Morrow...farmer and postal worker...lost contact
William Stucky...deceased
Baron Brewer...lost contact
Ray Marabella...lost contact (Ray swore us in and actually taught our initial training locally instead of sending us to Lackland AFB, TX)
Don McCormack...lost contact

We traveled in the C-97 and the C-135 on aeromedical duties to and from Europe and Asia. Our summer camps were sometimes two weeks or so on duty with the regular AF in Europe. We practiced ditching and recovery in Lake Nokomis with the Navy Reserve and in Hawaii. We were activated for one year during the Berlin Crisis during which time we actually learned the AME skills in Alabama and Texas. I was awarded the McElvain scholarship for one year at the U of M. And believe it, the $500.00 actually paid for all my books and tuition for one year. I was also named Airman of the Year.

All in all, of the six years I spent studying and learning, the thing that stands out are the people that I met. These were some of the happiest years of my life.

If you can use this information in some way in your book, please do so with my regards.

Larry K. Daudt

1968

January. Three nurses joined the ranks of the 109th AEF. 1st Lts Elizabeth Kane, Brenda Olson and Diane Erdman. The three left for Flight Nurse School at Brooks AFB, TX later that month.

Since a number of qualified nurses left the unit over the past few months, these three new nurses helped the unit maintain its manning roster as well as allowing the unit to continue to meet its training requirements. Accepting attractive job offers in other states was the primary reason for the loss of qualified flight nurses.

February. The 109th AEF began an intensive nurse recruiting program. In Southeast Asia, things were heating up and the demand for qualified aerovac crews was increasing. Members of the 109th were already involved.

Three members of the unit returned to Minnesota after completing two weeks of duty in the Pacific. Capt Dorothy Ludwig, SSgt Paul Rempfer and SSgt Denny Fitzsimmons were flying aerovac missions in support of the U.S. efforts in Vietnam. They logged 150 hours on flights to and from Alaska, Japan, the Philippines, Guam, Hawaii and California.

SSgt Fitzsimmons, reflecting on his two weeks said, "Home is the biggest word in their vocabulary, and just because you are doing your job helping them to get home, they think of you as some kind of hero."

☆☆☆☆☆

Capt Maureen Hunt, a former 109th AEF flight nurse, was recognized by MAC for her work while assigned to the 2nd AE Group in Rhein Main, Germany. At that time, she was assigned to the Aeromedical Research Center at Brooks AFB, TX.

June. Lt Elizabeth Kane was one of two honor graduates in her class of 60 students from the School of Aerospace Medicine at Brooks AFB, TX. 2d Lt R. J. Hecht was also in that graduating class.

This month also saw the graduation of Amn (Airman) J.D. Fabio and Amn D. L. Hoim from Aeromedical Evacuation School at Sheppard AFB, TX.

August. Capt Olivia Theriot joined the unit later in the month. Capt Theriot was assigned to the wing and assumed the newly created post of advisor to all the medical units under wing jurisdiction as well as assisting the Chief Nurse. Capt Theriot joined the AF in 1959 and since graduating from Flight Nurse School in 1966, had acquired extensive AE experience. This was accomplished by flying numerous aerovac missions from Clark AB, Republic of the Philippines to Japan and Korea in support of U.S. efforts in Vietnam.

☆☆☆☆☆

In the summer of 1968, the C-9A Nightingale rolled out at Scott AFB, IL. Between 1967 and 1971 there were 21 C-9As purchased by the U.S. Air Force.

Photo courtesy of Col Michael Germain

Medical crew preparing C-9A Nightingale to receive patients at Scott AFB, IL.

The Nightingale was mainly utilized for inter-CONUS patient movement and eventually served in other theaters. The aircraft was fitted with hydraulic folding ramps to easily move litter patients on and off the aircraft. The C-9 also boasted separate areas for patients requiring isolation or intensive care.

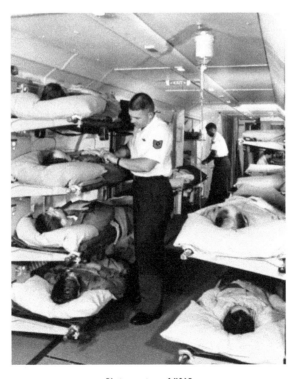

Photo courtesy of USAF

C-9A aeromedical crewmembers prepare for a mission at Scott AFB, IL.

With more medical amenities and comfort features than other aerovac airframes, the C-9s were sometimes referred to as the "Cadillac of Medevac." In the years ahead, many 109th AES members had the opportunity to participate in missions flown on the C-9 as part of a week-long indoctrination program.

1969

August. Air Guard Amn Bruce Olson ranked as the Honor Graduate upon completing his studies at Sheppard AFB, TX.

☆☆☆☆☆

Capt Eszlinger was appointed Chief Nurse.

☆☆☆☆☆

In the fall of this year Capt Alice Graner transferred to the 109th AEF from the 187th AEF, Wyoming Air National Guard. A native Minnesotan, Capt Graner moved back to her home state as a result of a job opportunity. While serving with the 187th, she initially qualified on C-121 aircraft, flying domestic and offshore aerovac missions with Wyoming aeromed crews and aircraft. She frequently volunteered for Southeast Asia missions where she flew with the regular AF, flying AE missions in C-135 and C-141 aircraft from Japan and the Philippines. While with the 187th she served as a Flight Instructor (FI) and Flight Examiner (FE). With her qualifications and experience, Capt Graner was a valuable addition to the growing 109th AEF.

Photo courtesy of TSgt Richard Childs and Col Michael Germain
109th AMEF Flying Schedule circa 1969.

1970

June. American women were allowed to enter the Reserve Officers Training Corps (ROTC) programs in colleges and universities. [36]

☆☆☆☆☆

MSgt Billy Boswell received the Air Medal as well as his First Oak Leaf Cluster to his Air Force Commendation Medal. MSgt Boswell was awarded the Air Medal for "meritorious achievement while participating in aerial flight with Detachment (DET) 1 of the 57th AES. During the period of July 27, 1969 to May 23, 1970, Sgt Boswell's outstanding airmanship and courage were exhibited in the successful accomplishment of important missions under extremely hazardous conditions."

The First Oak Leaf Cluster to the AF Commendation Medal was awarded for "meritorious service while assigned as Non-Commissioned Officer in Charge (NCOIC), Aeromedical Evacuation Operations, DET 1, 57th AES from July 27 1969 to July 26, 1970. During this period Sgt Boswell supervised the planning and coordination of 400 AE missions and directed the ground support for over 15,000 patients. The professional manner in which he served those patients who were mostly battle casualties, the support he gave this detachment on and off duty and the efforts he displayed in aiding the Vietnamese people went far beyond normal duty requirements. The distinctive accomplishments of Sergeant Boswell reflect credit upon himself and the United States Air Force."

December. The 50th Anniversary Yearbook of the 133rd Military Airlift Wing (MAW) was published and made available for wing members.

Photo courtesy of the 50th Anniversary Book, 133rd Military Airlift Wing (1971)
Flight nurses.

Back Row (L - R): 2d Lt Eileen Mohr, Capt Robert Hill, 1st Lt Robert Hecht, 1st Lt Lorraine Kunze
Front Row (L - R): Capt Darcy Simmons, Capt Alice Graner, Maj Henry Capiz (Commander), Capt Julie Eszlinger, Capt Janet Johannsen, 1st Lt Mary Huber

Photo courtesy of the 50th Anniversary Book, 133rd Military Airlift Wing (1971)

Med techs.

Back Row (L - R): A1C George Tourville, Amn Robert Dehen, A1C John de Rosier, A1C John Colomy, AB Edward Howard, A1C George Carlberg
Middle Row (L - R): Sgt James Schweigert, Sgt Thomas Skaro, Sgt Gregory Shields, Sgt Jerry Floden, A1C David Leonard, A1C Robert Hill
Front Row (L - R): SSgt James Hughes, SSgt Wayne Matula, TSgt William Stucky, Maj Henry Capiz (Commander), MSgt Walter Foster, SSgt Dennis Webster, SSgt Henry Rotell

1971

February. A major change was in the wind for the 133rd MAW as they began to prepare for the transition from the Boeing C-97G to the Lockheed C-130A aircraft. After the wing had received its total allotment of six C-130As, the 133rd flew its first C-130A cargo mission Sunday morning, 21 Feb, to Wilmington, Delaware and picked up C-130A maintenance dock equipment for the wing's hangar.

Those first six Minnesota ANG C-130As came from the 374th TAW at Naha AB, Okinawa, Japan, which was being phased down for deactivation. These aircraft, painted in green and tan camouflage with black undersides, contrasted sharply with the shiny bare-metal C-97s the wing was accustomed to. But the somber paint scheme had a purpose. In service with the 374th TAW, the C-130As had been used on "Blind Bat" flare drop missions over Vietnam, in conjunction with night-time gunship missions.

With the arrival of the new aircraft, the mission changed from a strategic global airlift responsibility to one of close tactical geographical support. [37]

The C-130A had a range of 3,100 miles, cruising speed of 334 mph and a ceiling of 30,000 feet. Normal complement was a crew of five. The Hercules was capable of carrying 25,000 pounds of payload or 90 troops. [38]

Photo courtesy of Troy Prince, MidwaySailor.com
Minnesota ANG Lockheed C-130A.

March. Most of the C-97Gs were retired to Davis Monthan AFB, in Tucson, AZ, more commonly known as "the Boneyard."

☆☆☆☆☆

The unit was reorganized when the 133rd Military Airlift Wing became the 133rd Tactical Airlift Wing.

☆☆☆☆☆

Bruce Olson, one of the early med techs writes:

The Pineapple Express Flight. This month the unit participated in an aeromed overwater training mission to Hickam AFB, HI. There were 28 members assigned to this mission, including the flight crew and a 21st AF Advisor. After all, it was March and we needed some tropical training.

The flights were broken down into several missions - one to Travis and two to Hickam, since at the speed we flew in the C-97G was not blistering with the same pattern on our return. When we landed in Hawaii, we found that there was no BAQ (Bachelors Airmen's Quarters) or VAQ (Visiting Airmen's Quarters) available on base - after all, there was a very active war going on. We were forced off base and had to stay in a hotel on Waikiki Beach in downtown Honolulu. We had 23 hours of crew rest coming so we put the location to good use. At this time the subject of pineapples came up. Several members thought they had a connection either through the Base Exchange (BX), Commissary, or other means to get freshly picked pineapples for our return flight. They were $3.00 a case of 12, with a maximum of three cases per person. The time went quickly and I managed to rent a surfboard and get so harshly sunburned I could have been considered an active patient. When we got back to the base and headed to our plane there was a good-sized truck with DOLE written on the door. It pulled up and we unloaded the 100 cases of fruit into the belly cargo compartment of the plane. I don't know if the flight crew was prepared for that much weight. We flew back, running our missions amidst the delectable odor of pineapples. We were able to get by the California ban on all fruit and vegetable products by not saying anything.

I had all but forgotten about this episode until I went to the memorial services for SSgt Greg Shields in 2019. He was my Flight Instructor on those training missions. His children were introduced and I said I served with their dad. They asked me if I knew about the Pineapple Express Flight and I said I was there. I had never heard that expression before. Obviously, it was a story Greg lived with and told often. They took me to a photo wall and there was the DOLE truck in several shots.

July. Members of the 109th AMEF attended the Tactical AE Conference at Pope AFB, NC to become familiar with the upcoming changes going from MAC to TAC. There was confusion with some of the new requirements, including appropriate uniforms, training procedures, as well as the mission that the 109th was going to support. For the 109th, the new tasking was to provide trained crew cells and liaison teams to support the 1st AE Group's deployment mission. The Commander of the 109th, Maj Henry Capiz, documented the importance of sending unit members to the training. He remarked how the unit was fortunate to participate, since the 109th was one of the first units to be assigned to the Tactical Airlift Command. His speculation was that other AE units, which remained under MAC, would soon be deactivated. Never happened!

☆☆☆☆☆

The 109th AMEF initiated and implemented the requirement that all med techs become EMT (Emergency Medical Technician) qualified. This was a first within the ANG and many other aeromed units were displeased with adding another requirement which they felt would also be adopted by the National Guard Bureau. This was a very forward-looking view that the 109th AMEF took as it wasn't until Oct of 2002 (31 years later) when the ANG mandated that all aeromedical evacuation technicians (AETs) be nationally registered EMTs. (authors' note: med tech is used in early unit history and was replaced with AET in later years.)

In addition, throughout the next several decades, the unit would either conduct the following courses at the unit level or send its members for training in Basic Life Support/Cardiopulmonary Resuscitation (BLS/CPR), Advanced Cardiac Life Support (ACLS), Trauma Nursing Core Course (TNCC), Advanced Burn Life Support (ABLS), Prehospital Trauma Life Support (PHTLS), Combat Casualty Care Course (C4), Battlefield Nursing, and Sustainment Training to Advance Readiness (TOPSTAR). (authors' note: These courses will be mentioned only once at this point in the book and not as they occurred in the specific year/month to reduce the sheer number of redundant entries.) Needless to say, this enhanced coursework provided exceptional and advanced training for the unit's flight nurses and med techs enabling them to provide the very best care for their patients.

August. The 109th AEF was featured in a Northstar Guardian article describing their work assisting the staff and members at the St. Paul Ramsey Hospital on the UTA weekends. The unit was commended by the directors and staff of the hospital for their "medical professionalism and devotion to duty."

September. The unit began to cross-train and qualify in the C-130A aircraft that replaced the C-97G. The squadron had twenty-four qualified AE crews on board. SSgt Jim Hughes, after completing the initial cadre training, took the first C-130A checkride in September. He, in turn, qualified the rest of the enlisted med techs in the unit.

October. The last C-97G left for its final resting place at Davis Monthan AFB, AZ. Aboard to record the last journey of tail number "365" was WCCO-TV's Sherm Booen, who filmed the trip for his "World of Aviation" show. [39] In addition, aircraft tail number "332" went to the Confederate AF in Harlingen, TX to be maintained as a part of this civilian association's fine collection of vintage aircraft. [40]

☆☆☆☆☆

An Operational Readiness Inspection took place over the UTA weekend. The Operations Group received a grade of "Satisfactory" due to the lack of a formal mobilization plan, which could have adversely affected the unit in its state of readiness if needed in wartime. The 109th AEF was also awarded "Satisfactory" for its medical training mission. However, manning remained limited in the squadron with only 11 of 21 flight nurse and 24 out of 31 med tech positions filled.

1972

March. Effective 30 March 1972, there was a Change of Command from MAC to TAC. This increased the 109th AEF's strength to 39 officers and 36 Airmen.

April. The 133rd TAW experienced a first. Judith Gunelius became the first female enlistee in the 109th AMEF as well as the 133rd TAW and in any TAW aeromedical evacuation unit, serving as the first female med tech. Previously, women serving in the MNANG had all been commissioned officers serving mainly in the base hospital or in the 109th AMEF as flight nurses. It would take the active duty AF another year before it accepted their first female med techs into its ranks. [41] The local TV stations and newspapers covered and publicized the event. Women, with the exception of nurses, were not recruited in the ANG ranks until 1 July 1968, when the authority of Public Law 90-180 that was enacted by Congress in November 1967 went into effect.

May. The 133rd TAW was one of the first Air Guard C-130A equipped units to be given an ORI. It passed the inspection with high marks, but it was noted that "there were some areas in which the unit can use some improvement."

☆☆☆☆☆

Judy Van Sambeck and Linda Kelly, both registered nurses in the Surgical Intensive Care Unit (SICU) at St. Paul Ramsey Hospital decided to become Airmen in the unit while waiting for their papers to be processed and for their two months at Brooks AFB, TX. In this way, they got a chance to meet the people they would be working with, got used to military ways, took care of all the forms that had to be completed and became involved in the program. Previously, new flight nurses coming in signed up, waited four to six months for their commission papers to come through and then after only one UTA went off to Flight Nurse School, not completely aware of everything that would be happening to them. [42]

Photo courtesy of Lt Col Capiz
Lt Col Capiz, Commander 109th AEF, on a training flight with one of the unit's "new" C-130A aircraft. Note part of the aeromed crew and patients in the background.

July. Unit members participated in a wet ditching exercise. 109th AEF members on flight status donned flight suits, orange air wings and entered the windy, turgid waters of Lake Nokomis for the TAC mandatory wet ditching drill. Based on the photos taken, Darcy Anderson seemed to enjoy the exercise. After the training was completed, a number of unit members took advantage of the sunny weather by "catching some rays" while waiting for the bus to return them to the base.

1973

February. The 109th AMEF received orders assigning the flight to the 1st Aeromedical Evacuation Group (AMEG) during federal activation. Also, the 12th AF would be responsible for conducting inspections and safety for the 109th.

☆☆☆☆☆

The unit was commended for its flight training program and the St. Paul Ramsey Hospital Training Program. The St. Paul Ramsey Hospital and the 109th AMEF coordinated on-the-job training for nurses and med techs to work under hospital personnel during UTA weekends. This program, now six years old, was demonstrating its worth as a valued asset allowing unit members to gain beneficial hands-on training.

April. From 4-6 April, the 1st AMEG conducted a Staff Assistance Visit. The only discrepancy for the 109th AMEF was in recruiting nurses.

June. From 16-23 June, the 109th AMEF deployed to Volk Field, Wisconsin for its annual field training requirements and a wing-wide pre-ORI exercise. The primary focus was to develop a comprehensive training program for both the ground and flying positions for the aeromedical crews. Aeromeds flew daily missions with simulated patients to the Twin Cities and Duluth. The remaining unit members became proficient under the new TAC standards.

On 24 June, a Management Effectiveness Inspection (MEI) was performed at the 109th AMEF. The results indicated that moustaches and haircuts were "a problem." As the Commander, Lt Col Capiz ordered monthly open ranks inspections until the discrepancy was resolved. If members did not comply with the uniform standard, the Commander was authorized to withhold their pay. Another setback was issuing proper hospital attire to members. By requesting an updated Unit Individual Equipment Authorization and thereby receiving an increase in uniform funds, the unit was able to work out this issue.

CHAPTER 4
The Command of Col Harry "Jerry" Nelson

(Aug 1973 - Feb 1977)

Photo courtesy of the Minnesota ANG Museum

Commander's Comments: We were a very young unit at the time we went on active duty. We were just in the process of getting people to join and get organized. We had a wonderful time. [21]

Col Harry Nelson

August. Maj Henry Capiz turned over the command of the 109th AMEF on the first of the month to Maj Harry "Jerry" Nelson. This was Maj Nelson's second time as Commander of the 109th AMEF. (His first appointment as Commander was from 2 April 1963 to 1 July 1967.)

1974

February. The Unit Manning Document was changed due to realignment and the unit was therefore authorized 24 officers and 36 Airmen. In May, another realignment and reorganization reduced the strength of the 109th AEF from 60 to 42 members. By December, the 109th AMEF was reassigned to the Military Airlift Command for all federal mobilizations.

☆☆☆☆☆

MSgt Walter R. Foster, the NCOIC of In-Flight Medical Care for the 109th AEF, was named Distinguished Graduate of the ANG Non-Commissioned Officer Academy, graduating fourth in his class of seventy-four students.

☆☆☆☆☆

Due to the national energy shortage, primarily in gasoline and aviation fuel, flying hours for the 133rd TAW were cut by 50%. In February that flying time was cut by another 25%. These cutbacks resulted in fewer cross-country training missions for aeromeds and more local training sorties.

April. There were two UTA weekends this month. The first UTA, held the first weekend of the month, was strictly a mobility training weekend. In addition, there was no scheduled UTA in June because of the eight-day field training scheduled held at Volk Field that month.

October. Maj Julie Eszlinger was appointed by the Surgeon General, ANG to unify all ANG nurses into a professional association known as the Association of ANG Nurses. This was accomplished only after overcoming major obstacles and many hindrances from other AE units. Having the support of the NGB to ease tension, she was appointed to the National Guard Medical Advisory Council (the <u>first nurse</u> and <u>first female appointment</u>). Maj Eszlinger was then elected as the first president of the newly formed professional association of nurses, the Association of ANG Nurses.

1975

November. SSgt John Balow and 1st Lt Marianne Lahman joined the unit.

1976

June. Twenty-nine unit members attended annual training exercises at Volk Field, Wisconsin along with other members of the 133rd TAW, from 7-12 June.

July. From July 17-21, Capt Judy Van Sambeck and MSgt Walter Foster were in Gulfport, Mississippi to observe the handling of simulated war casualties in an exercise staged by the AFR. The two Minnesota Guard members were invited to observe and meet with NGB personnel to study the feasibility of ANG AE flights in their ability to participate in similar training.

Two staging tents were located 100 yards from the runway. C-130 aircraft would land after making a cargo drop and pull into the staging area, where a flight nurse and med techs boarded the aircraft and reconfigured the inside for medical evacuation. Ambulatory personnel were escorted single file to the aircraft, after which litter patients were then carried to the C-130. All of this took place with engines running which meant the aeromeds were dealing with heat, humidity, engine turbulence, flying dust and a demanding time frame. This was the 109th's introduction to working in real field conditions. A hint of things to come.

MSgt Foster remarked in a unit briefing that the exercise "was as close to the real thing as you could get."

☆☆☆☆☆

Maj Alice Graner returned to the 109th AMEF after spending her annual training with the 57th AES at Scott AFB, IL. The squadron was responsible for moving patients inside the continental United States. This unique experience gave Maj Graner the opportunity to train with her active duty counterparts. Of the sixteen days she spent with the 57th, from July 24 through August 8th, Maj Graner spent the first five days in ground school orienting to the C-9A aircraft and the up-to-date medical equipment it carried for patient care. The last eleven days were spent flying regular air evacuation missions, often in the role of Medical Crew Director (MCD).

CHAPTER 5

Command Vacancy

(Feb 1977 - Oct 1977)

1977

February. Maj Harry Nelson relinquished command of the 109th AMEF which left the position vacant for over seven months. There is no information as to who was the acting commander during this period. Col Eszlinger Jensen recalls that despite the vacancy in the commanding officer's post, during that time period unit members reported for duty on the designated weekends and performed their assigned duties.

March. Thirty-nine members participated in the Samaritan training exercise held at Pope AFB, NC. This exercise marked the introduction of the 109th AMEF to working in staged positions under field conditions. It was here that members of the 109th received their initial training in the Mobile Aeromedical Staging Facility (MASF). Members returned to Minnesota with a host of new challenges to be mastered as the role of AE not only changed but expanded as well. Armed with the knowledge gained from this and subsequent exercises plus additional assistance given by the 1st AES at Pope, the 109th implemented a training program designed to prepare and equip its members to be able to function effectively in any of the new roles demanded of aerovac, whether as a member of an AE crew or a health care provider in the field. [43]

CHAPTER 6
The Command of Lt Col David Molin

(Oct 1977 - Nov 1980)

Photo courtesy of Lt Col David Molin

Commander's Comments: I had a very good time during my tenure as the Commander of the 109th. The equipment we had to train with was resurrected from the Korean War and even some from WWII. Successfully working with this outdated equipment was quite a tribute to and demonstrated the dedication of our crews.

Lt Col David Molin

October. Maj David Molin took over command of the 109th AEF.

New members joining the unit this month were: Capt Jarl Bergland, SSgt Dennis Smith, SSgt Alan Johnson, SSgt Dayton Carlson, SrA (Senior Airman) Michael Cunniff, Jr., AB Nancy Glaeser and AB Robert Redmond, Jr.

☆☆☆☆☆

Training flights for the 109th AMEF were long and strenuous. Launching in the gathering darkness of a fall evening, these training flights often took the crews to such destinations as the Black Hills of South Dakota or over northern Michigan.

SSgt Judy Gunelius remembers, "We never were sure just where we would be going, only that it would be where the weather was best. The flights were often long and exhausting. Often it would be close to 11:00 p.m. local time when we landed back at the Minneapolis airport. We would then have to unload and haul our equipment from the plane to the building. After putting it away we would usually debrief at the Contact Club." (authors' note: The Contact Club was the on-base bar and grill located 25 steps from the doorway of the Aeromed building.)

A medical crew at this time consisted of three crewmembers; one MCD and two med techs. One such flight was made up of Capt Glen Ramsborg as MCD with A1C Doug Dahlquist and TSgt Diane Schmidt as crew. Eighteen-year old A1C Dahlquist was making his initial flight. His performance would be closely monitored and evaluated by SSgt Larry Bild, his instructor. They had a patient load of five personnel, all members of the 109th AMEF with simulated conditions. The patients' symptoms and reactions to the flight were all played out with as much realism as possible.

1978

April. Members of the 109th AMEF participated in the week-long Samaritan II tactical exercise held at Pope AFB, NC. It was strictly field conditions for the participants. Tents that served as sleeping barracks at night were used as a hospital during the day by unit members. C-rations and field sanitation combined with a constant flood of simulated patients were daily fare. After being triaged, the patients were treated, stabilized and made ready for airlift. They were then "hot loaded" aboard a waiting C-130. From a tactical perspective, officials pronounced the exercise a great success. [44]

May. A Health Services Management Inspection was performed from the 18th to the 21st. The purpose of the inspection was to evaluate readiness, training, and internal management of the unit. The 109th AMEF was authorized to have twelve aeromedical crews, which consisted of one nurse and two AETs. However, only nine crews existed and all but one were current with training requirements, qualified in their respective positions, and operationally ready. The nurse shortage remained a problem for the unit, while the med techs were staffed at 120 percent. Despite the noted shortages, the result of the inspection was "Outstanding."

1979

Photo Courtesy of Maj Joe Jensen
Local Flying Training Period.

Standing (L - R): Alice Graner, Dan Bougoeis, Ed Howard
Sitting: Jim Hughes
Litter Patients (L - R): 1st three are unidentified, Mike Cunniff, Dayton Carlson

February. The unit participated in the hospital care of patients at Wilford Hall Hospital, Lackland AFB, TX. Taking a look back in history, it should be noted that General Wilford F. Hall, a distinguished and decorated medical officer, was recognized as the man who spearheaded the DOD policy for air evacuation, replacing surface transportation as the primary means of patient movement in both war and peacetime. As a patient advocate, he was influential in the improved design of aircraft used in aerovac, resulting in comfort and maximum care improvements without affecting cargo and patient capabilities. The concept of AE as a primary AF mission was General Hall's inspiration. Wilford Hall Medical Center at Lackland AFB, honors both his contributions and his name.

Photo courtesy of Lt Col Darcy Anderson
Squadron photo.

Back Row Standing (L - R): Bob Kolbo, Gerry Blilie, Shawn Brede, Jarl Bergland, Dan Bramsford
Middle Row Standing (L - R): Tony Carroll, Patricia Benson, Val Yantz, Darcy Anderson, Judy Gunelius, Alice Graner, James Small
Front Row Standing (L - R): David Molin (Commander), Diane Schmidt, Paula Funk, Nancy Glaeser, Pam Shelly, Catherine DeVaan, Donna Alt
Back Row Kneeling (L - R): Doug Dahlquist, Larry Bild, Terrance Bergren, Walt Foster, Jim Hughes, Dan Bougoeis
Front Row Kneeling (L - R): Richard Lee, Dennis Ferretti, Norm Hendrickson, Mike Cunniff, Terry Wellner

April. Based on initial experiences gained with the MASF in the previous two Samaritan exercises, Maj Graner saw the need for additional training in this area. The 1st AES at Pope AFB,

NC was contacted and asked if they would let the 109th use their training manual as a guide and foundation for the unit to develop their own program. They informed Maj Graner that it was new to them as well and they had no formal training program at that time. The 1st AES requested that the 109th AEF develop the curriculum and bring it to Pope to conduct the exercise. Maj Graner, Maj Darcy Anderson, MSgt Ed Howard, MSgt Walt Foster and personnel in the training section began to do the research into Army and AF regulations. From that, a week-long curriculum was developed.

The 109th AEF accomplished all of the typing of the curriculum via IBM Selectric typewriter, and Xerox copies were sent via U.S. Postal Service to West Virginia, Delaware and Pope AFB. The 1st AES was included in the training exercise.

109th AEF personnel then deployed to North Carolina to participate in Samaritan III, which was held in a wooded area at Mackall Army Airfield, Fort Bragg, NC. "The exercise was designed to train and test AE personnel in field conditions that come as close to actual wartime circumstances as possible," emphasized Maj Julie Eszlinger, 109th Chief Flight Nurse and project officer for this exercise. In the trenches with the 109th AEF were AE personnel from the 142nd AEF out of Delaware, the 167th AEF from West Virginia and the 156th AEF from North Carolina.

Maj Darcy Anderson, 109th AEF Coordinator of Education for this exercise, stated the schedule was made extremely tight to emphasize training. As soon as the troops deplaned the work began. Four twenty-man tents were erected and personal gear was unloaded and stowed. Equipment was set up and made functional. Radio communications were established between the various points and made operative. Maj Alice Graner, the mission evaluation coordinator said, "Personnel were trained to coordinate and administer patient care in the Mobile Aeromedical Staging Facility, use the medical equipment needed to treat the patients with their simulated injuries and to communicate with patients rapidly in this tactical setting."

Seven missions were planned. Two had been completed when heavy rains arrived in the area. The third mission was accomplished in a downpour. The exercise continued despite the adverse weather. Classes were held in place of four missions that were cancelled. [45]

Photo courtesy of Col Glen Ramsborg
Samaritan III Participants.

Back Row (L - R): (unidentified), Shawn Brede, Gerry Blilie, Judy Gunelius, Tony Carroll, (unidentified)
Front Row Standing (L - R): Mike Cunniff, Kate DeVaan, Larry Bild, Nancy Glaeser, Jim Hughes, Bruce Olson
Front Row Kneeling: Doug Dahlquist

1980

AE crew complements were increased from one flight nurse and two med techs to two flight nurses and three med techs. This resulted in an increase in authorized personnel and new faces in the ranks. [46]

☆☆☆☆☆

Unit med techs and flight nurses continued to spend one-fourth of each month's weekend drill period at St. Paul Ramsey Hospital, helping hospital staff under an agreement that allowed 109th AEF flight nurses to supervise their own technicians. The teamwork built here paid off on the unit's training flights as the crews converted their newly acquired knowledge into better and more efficient care for their simulated patients.

Clinical areas that provided experience related to Strategic, Tactical and Domestic missions continued to be utilized: the emergency room (ER), intensive care, orthopedic and medical/surgical wards. Although flight nurses remained in one clinical area, technicians rotated every four months to a new area. While providing a variety of experience for the technicians, this system encouraged continuity as the flight nurse leader became increasingly familiar with a specific area and staff.

Each nurse supervised no more than two or three technicians at one time. Unit OJT supervisors coordinated with the flight nurses as to what specific training experiences were needed by each of the technicians. The flight nurse then selected patients and patient care activities that best meet the needs of the med techs. This program is still a critical part of the 109th's continuing training. [47]

August. Two unit members were awarded the Minnesota State Medal for Merit: Maj Julie Eszlinger and Maj Darcy Anderson.

☆☆☆☆☆

A 30-member delegation of United States Nursing Service Administrative Leaders, including Maj Julie Eszlinger, spent two weeks on a People-to-People Goodwill Tour to Sweden, Poland, Hungary and England this past summer.

The purpose of the mission was to give delegation members an opportunity to carry messages of friendship to their counterparts in Western Europe. It also allowed members to visit typical nursing operations to compare methods and procedures. The mission was an official program of People-to-People International, a nonprofit, private sector organization founded in 1956 by President Dwight D. Eisenhower to promote World Peace through international understanding. The trip included visits to hospitals, health care agencies, community health care agencies and meetings with nursing organization leaders in Stockholm, Warsaw, Budapest and London with an excursion to Zelazowa Wola, near Warsaw, Poland.

CHAPTER 7
The Command of Col Julia (Julie) Eszlinger Jensen

(Nov 1980 - Mar 1989)

Photo courtesy of Col Julie Eszlinger Jensen

Commander's Comments: My 24 years in the MN ANG...

I did not make the most ideal/positive impression when I was interviewed by Col John R. Dolny, Commander of the 133rd Air Wing, during my initial recruitment interview back in 1965. During the interview he asked both why and how long I planned to stay. I told him I was interested in traveling and after having been to all 48 states, I would leave. "Not to worry. I only plan to stay for 2-3 years." He said, "Well, that's not exactly what I was hoping to hear. We are investing a lot of time and money to get you trained. I think you ought to reconsider that." I said I would and with that I was sworn in as a 1st Lt in the Nurse Corps on 18 November 1965 and served in the unit for another 24 years.

In 1965, the National Guard Bureau saw the need to increase aerovac strength as a result of the increasing U.S. involvement in the Vietnam War since they felt that the active duty Air Force would not be able to meet the demands. Therefore, our recruiting effort was intensified to meet the required number of flight nurse and med tech slots specified on our Unit Manning Document. And thus, I began my 24 years in the 109th AEF.

For nurse commissioned officers, Officers Training School was optional. We could choose to attend, but attendance was not required and it would have delayed flight school for a year. Instead, Lt Cool and Lt Cook gave us an orientation of protocols – how and who to salute, rank and uniform wear.

There was a push to get us flight nurse qualified. Command emphasized the importance of making ourselves available for flight school. So, until a flight school date became available, we studied the ground school curriculum that the 109th nurses had created along with assistance from Lt Harry Nelson. The Air Force was not able to provide printed education materials. We learned in later years that the 109th curriculum and training materials were adopted and used in other newly established aerovac reserve forces. This was at the very initial acceptance from the USAF of AE reserve components - the Air National Guard and Air Force Reserve.

The active duty Air Force aeromedical staff were not happy about our being tasked to support them. That feeling seemed to carry on through all the years I was in the ANG. There was always a "negative-rub" toward us – the ANG aeromedical personnel.

The School of Aerospace Medicine was at Brooks AFB, TX. It was the location for all schools that related to medical flying and was the school to qualify flight nurses, flight surgeons, biomedical technicians, etc.

Some of the instructors had just returned from their one-year rotation in Vietnam. This was planned so they could teach us the reality of what they had just experienced. The course syllabus consisted of a thorough review of anatomy and physiology, the effects that altitude has on the body at various altitudes, in-flight care of different wartime injuries, patient emergencies, emergency aircraft procedures, loading and offloading patients, wet ditching, etc. Our flights were conducted in the C-131 aircraft.

There was a disconnect with some of the active duty nurses and/or reserve nurses. The active duty nurses could only attend flight school if they were recommended by their charge nurse and commander. They were not guaranteed a flight nurse position upon completion of the course. Whereas, for the reserve nurses, it was our only mission.

Graduation was 8 July 1966. We had the flight nurse wings pinned on our uniforms at which time we were granted the aeronautical designation of flight nurse.

Following graduation, we returned to the 109th and immediately began our orientation to the C-97 aircraft. Training for qualification consisted of five missions. We had four orientation training flights and our fifth flight was the examination, which was the initial qualifying checkride. Usually, this was accomplished on a 3-5 day overwater training mission known as a Nav-Overwater. I became a qualified flight nurse in the C-97 on 27 August 1966.

Our summer Class A uniform was a striped seersucker skirt and short sleeve jacket which was loved by everyone. Our summer flight uniform was navy blue cotton trousers and a light blue chambray blouse that had to be tucked into the trousers. If needed for warmth, a navy-blue woolen, button sweater was authorized. It was known as the "Perry Como" sweater - the type of sweater worn by singer and actor Perry Como.

In September 1966, I was assigned the position of Flying Training Officer. From 1966 to early 1968 the unit lost a number of valuable members as several flight nurses resigned for various reasons. Capt Tenney resigned for a Director of Nursing Position in Hartford, CT. Capt Cook and Capt Cool resigned to continue their work with the American Red Cross. Capt Lou Campbell, Flying Training Officer, resigned her commission to return to the civilian sector to continue her work in anesthesia. As a result, additional duty assignments came in rapid succession - Flight Nurse Instructor (1967), Flight Nurse Examiner (1968), Assistant Chief Nurse (1968), and Chief Nurse (1969).

From the beginning, when I applied for a flight nurse position, I was especially motivated to experience live aerovac. We were required to participate in one live aerovac mission a year. Prior to overseas aerovac, there was a requirement that we had to participate in a two-week domestic aerovac mission.

I volunteered and in July 1967 was assigned to McGuire AFB, NJ. The Medical Crew Director I was assigned to was Maj Maureen Hunt. Maj Hunt was one of the original flight nurses that started the 109th AEF. She went on and joined the active duty Air Force.

Our route was Army, Navy and Air Force bases along the South and East Coast states. The days were very long. Wakeup call at 0430, briefing 0600, patients loaded 0700 and wheels up by 0730. Enroute, even though we notified the arriving base of our arrival, often the buses with patients had not arrived at the airplane. This resulted in long delays in an already long day. However, I was learning and impressed with the good crew coordination and camaraderie among everyone.

For overseas aerovac, we were given a round trip commercial airfare to get us to a domestic departure base in the U.S. For USAFE missions, we were flown to Philadelphia, PA and took a bus to McGuire AFB, NJ. For PACAF missions, we were flown to San Francisco, CA and took a bus to Travis AFB, CA, a two-hour drive north of the city. We did not receive overseas commercial airfare orders to our destination base, so our transportation for overseas bases was to fly as an additional crewmember on a USAF aircraft to that destination. I flew missions in Morocco, Turkey, Africa, Greece, Spain, Italy and Libya on the C-131 aircraft.

Because of the Vietnam War, the 133rd recognized the dire need to recruit nurses. One interesting recruiting story was told by Col Robert Eriksen, 133rd Personnel Flight. They decided to contact hospitals in Rochester, MN as there likely were an abundance of nurses with two large hospitals - Methodist and St. Mary's. Arrangements were made to fly the C-97 there and give them a flight on the aircraft. What they weren't prepared for was a group of nuns (sisters) from St. Mary's Catholic Hospital waiting in their black habits (which was the required attire for nuns during those years) ready to board the C-97. Upon completion of their ride, the nuns went back to St. Mary's and the 109th aircrew returned home empty handed, with no nurse recruits.

In September 1968, the Vietnam War was in full swing. I was employed in a supervisory position at St. Paul Ramsey Hospital and knew the Vietnam experience would be a once-in-a-lifetime event.

I resigned my position and volunteered for Southeast Asia. SMSgt Alan McCormick, SSgt Richard Oehlenschlager and I participated in PACAF AE missions. We were assigned to the 56th AES at Yokota and Tachikawa AB, Japan. Our mission back to the U.S. was augmenting the active duty aeromed crew in our respective roles. The active duty crew was 1 MCD and 2-3 med techs aboard the C-141 aircraft. Our patient load could be 30 liters - many with traumatic limb amputations, traumatic body injuries, burn patients, 2-3 psychiatric patients and 1-2 Stryker frames.

The routes to the U.S. bases were via Clark AB, Philippines to Travis AFB, CA or Elmendorf AFB, AK, with the final destination of Scott AFB, IL, Dover AFB, DE and/or Andrews AFB, MD.

In summary, there was the "good" and the "not so good" with these missions. Through higher headquarters' directives, the 109th assigned one nurse and two med techs to these missions. The aeromed crew was given the opportunity to schedule their own flight times for departure from the Twin Cities. This was done to help the individuals with their work schedule and employer. Once we arrived at our domestic departure base, we made our own additional crewmember request. Sometimes we were on different flights.

Upon checking in at the assigned AES, we were given our aerovac assignments and were never on the same mission. As a result, we never really saw each other until the flight back to the U.S. That was both the "good" and "not so good." As the nurse, I was in officer quarters which was usually quite separated from the enlisted quarters. Also, at the time, Officers Clubs and Enlisted Clubs were separate, and being on active duty bases, protocol was strictly enforced.

Starting in the late 1960s and early 1970s, the Lincoln Del (Delicatessen) in Bloomington conducted the Lincoln Del Races in July. The race was held in Bloomington, along designated streets. Because the Emergency Medical System was not established as it is today, they requested our assistance in providing first aid services at intervals along the route. Dressed in white uniforms, the 109th did just that for as long as they were held.

"The Sky is Falling, The Sky is Falling" was the feeling most of us had when we heard we would be losing the C-97 MAC mission and transitioning to the C-130 tactical mission. We women would no longer be wearing our Eisenhower wool blue flight suits nor our summer flight uniform. We would be required to wear the Nomex flight suit - sloppy, too large for most of the women and unable or at best very difficult to use the latrine on the aircraft. Wait - what latrine? What could be worse? The C-130 was a noise hazard and resulted in all of us wearing heavy, clumsy earmuffs.

Do we now resign and decide we have had enough and this isn't for us?

And so, life went on in the 1970s as we began to see major changes for the 109th AEF. It began with clothing supply to obtain our Nomex flight suits, followed by all the other required C-130 gear. It also meant for the 109th that live aerovac missions in USAFE and PACAF were no longer a part of their assigned tasking.

The unit training office began to plan our new tactical training requirements. It was a night and day difference from C-97 AE. From slowly and methodically carrying liters aboard the C-97 for safety with no consideration for time, to loading up the back ramp of the C-130A as rapidly as possible with the engines running – "hot loading."

The change to the tactical mission came at the right time, although we didn't realize it when it was happening. We were getting stale operating in the MAC mission concept and we needed a change and a challenge.

All of the aeromeds took an interest in learning and working together. We had to change the Standards and Evaluation (Stan/Eval) regulations, documents and the ever-present paperwork requiring documentation. Training had a huge responsibility in developing a curriculum. The loyalty to each other and their dedication prevailed and never stopped. Many of the aeromeds were in their qualified positions in the C-130A by the end of 1971.

Samaritan III in 1979 was a ten-day FTX (Field Training Exercise) conducted at Pope AFB, NC. I was the Project Officer. The work was enormous and lengthy. Plans had to be developed and communicated with other ANG units. This was a significant exercise in that the 1st AES relied on this exercise as a model for future tactical FTXs, etc. It could not have been done without the dedication of aeromeds - TSgt Jim Hughes, TSgt Ed Howard, Sgt Mark Latourelle, TSgt Paul Walker, TSgt Larry Bild, TSgt Gerry Blilie, Lt Norm Hendrickson, Capt Karen Wolf, Lt Joe Jensen, Capt Valerie Yantz, MSgt Walter Foster, Maj Alice Graner, and MSgt Robert Kolbo. I likely unintentionally missed some of the dedicated and committed hard working aeromeds.

The 109th was always about training. In addition to the FTXs, we also participated in hospital training. We requested and were accepted for annual training at the hospital at Langley AFB, VA. It was probably a given as the Chief Nurse, Col Maureen Hunt, was one of the original nurses in the 109th AEF before she went on active duty. Wilford Hall Hospital, San Antonio, TX was another hospital training site frequently utilized by the 109th AEF.

While we in Minnesota were working to get a top-notch tactical curriculum, it occurred to me that most of the training decisions which became regulation were being made by a few nonmedical personnel at the National Guard Bureau Air Division. Col James Weaver was the Surgeon General, and if needed they would consult with him. However, the reality was that the officer and enlisted staff in the division would contact the superintendents of the tactical ANG squadrons in different states. Usually, because of proximity to Washington, DC, it would be those located in the Eastern U.S. The ANG Superintendents and ANG Headquarters staff were not nurses, yet they were promulgating our curriculum and rules.

Annually, the Association of Military Surgeons of the United States (AMSUS) held numerous conferences. The flight surgeons had their own organization and designated meeting time, as did the enlisted superintendents. Through the years, there was no scheduled meeting time for nurses. For several years I had trouble with that. It was at the 1972 convention that I began having conversations with nurses from other AE squadrons about my concern that nonmedical people were making decisions that I felt nurses should be making and that there was no meeting time designated for nurses.

At that time, nurses could attend any of the medical sessions as well as the Nurse Luncheon hosted by the Chief Nurse of the USAF. It didn't take long for them to hear me and understand my concerns. My past connections with nurses in flight school - Lt Kathleen Murray (FN), Capt Patricia Dwyer (FN) and Maj George Pate (MSC), the Commander of the Pease aeromedical unit, were some of the supporters. With that we decided we needed our own organization.

Lt Col Grace Hart, Chief Nurse from McGuire AFB, NJ and I met with Col Weaver to discuss our goals. He gave us his full support and agreed with us that we needed to do a survey of all nurses within the ANG.

With that we started our survey. As we suspected, some of the superintendents opened the mailing that was intended for the nurses in their unit. They sent a letter to the Department of Defense informing them that Lt Col Hart and Maj Eszlinger were intending to form an organization within the USAF. The Department of Defense then sent a letter to our commanders - Gen Dolny for me. I was called in and questioned. It took some explaining for him to understand. He then contacted Col Weaver at the NGB to receive the verification.

The recommendation was that we not use the word "organize" which was not acceptable in the military as it implied sedition of some sort. We instead used the word "association" and got our survey underway.

In 1973, Col Weaver assigned me the responsibility of unifying all ANG nurses into a professional organization. During the next year we had meetings with the Chief Nurse of the USAF, Col Claire Garracht, who without hesitation endorsed the plan and gave us her full support.

It was hard to believe, but the most challenging part was what to call us. We didn't want to be like the physicians – "Association of Flight Surgeons." We searched the Roget's Thesaurus for identifying words. Since fraternity was not a male identification but a unifying of similar beliefs, we finally settled on Fraternity of ANG Nurses. That was different and would be remembered.

In October 1974 at the AMSUS conference in San Diego, CA, The Fraternity of Air National Guard Nurses became an official association. I was elected the first president and we were off and running with our own identity. Officers included Maj Julie Eszlinger, MN ANG (President), Maj Elinor Reed, TN ANG (Vice President/President Elect), and Maj Mary Wallace, AZ ANG (Secretary/Treasurer).

In later years the name was changed to the Association of Air National Guard Nurses. A good decision.

In 1974, I was appointed to the ANG Medical Advisory Council made up of senior medical personnel from all health disciplines within the ANG. The purpose was to discuss unit issues, concerns, upcoming USAF directives, etc. We heard, and were heard. Our opinions mattered.

From 1976 to 1985, at the request of the Surgeon General, I was asked to facilitate and chair the aeromedical evacuation meetings. At the AMSUS conferences there were scheduled meetings for AE. We presented the Samaritan FTX at several of the conferences. These meetings were attended by commanders, flight nurses, medical technicians, superintendents, MAC and TAC Headquarters and staff from various ANG AE squadrons which usually consisted of 70-100 participants. They were usually quite heated and controversial, often taking aim at the staff of the Surgeon General's office. I suspect that is why I was asked to facilitate. We usually got some helpful responses and the attendees left with positive impressions. I didn't know how I was doing until Col Schuknecht, Deputy Commander for Aeromedical Evacuation, 375th Aeromedical Airlift Wing –Reserve Affairs Branch complimented me on the success of the meetings which was followed by a telegram stating as such.

The ANG Medical Advisory Council was established in 1972 and was composed of senior medical personnel from all disciplines in the ANG. In May 1974, Col Weaver in a request to Brig Gen Dolny stated, "We are requesting Maj Eszlinger to serve on this council because of her demonstrated expertise in her medical specialty and ask for your favorable consideration."

Permission was granted. Meetings were held twice a year. The one in the spring was usually over a long weekend at the Hyannis Resort located near Otis AFB, MA. The fall meeting was held a day before the AMSUS conference where we would discuss unit issues, concerns, upcoming USAF directives, etc. Our opinions were voiced, considered and voted on. All of us felt satisfied with the outcome.

November 1980 brought a new responsibility. Brig Gen Robert Schaumann, 133rd TAW Commander, asked me to consider becoming the 109th AEF Commander. We had a long discussion about the history of aerovac commanders. Commanders had always been men. As I recall, the requirements were to be a Medical Service Corps officer with a business background. Pharmacists were acceptable. Nursing was not included. This was a concept that Brig Gen Schaumann could not understand and asked, "Pilots are in charge of pilots, why aren't nurses in charge of nurses?" I suspect it was not difficult for him to convince the "powers that be" of the nurse in command philosophy. In ANG units, the interpretation for commanders in aerovac also included pilots, teachers, etc. - but not nursing. I also mentioned the uncertainty of higher headquarters, Office of the Surgeon General, Air National Guard Bureau - Col Weaver, and Chief Nurse of the USAF, Col Sarah Wells accepting a woman and nurse. He assured me he had made a trip to Washington to meet with the NGB and the Chief Nurse. The NGB told him he likely would receive approval from the CN, and if he chooses to do so, they too, would also support me. The Chief Nurse, Col Wells said, "Go for it! I highly endorse." A breakthrough for nursing.

I was humbled and honored. I welcomed the opportunity to finally have nursing in a leadership position of all things nursing and medical. The realization of the responsibility for the entire 109th AEF - The Buck Stops Here - was awesome. At Brig Gen Schaumann's Commander Staff Meetings I was always respected and well received by other base commanders.

I knew when I was selected to be Commander that I would be facing some negative glances and behaviors. Not so much from the 133rd members, but from the MSC officers within the reserve forces military-wide. The MSCs were men with backgrounds ranging from pharmacists, teachers, pilots, auto supply store managers, and except for pharmacists, all with no medical background. My appointment could likely appear to be predicting and threatening a change in qualifications. Nurses and women had never been in command positions, neither in the USAF nor the ANG. It was a first and likely would instill future change.

This became evident when I was the only female at commander conferences sponsored by either or both the National Guard Bureau and USAF. They were all polite during meeting sessions. However, when the day ended and the conferees gathered for the usual "happy hour", I was not invited nor included. On one occasion, I decided I would go to the cocktail lounge and perhaps when seen, I would be invited to join. No such luck. Perhaps I should have invited myself. Then again, maybe their moral values did not allow socializing with a woman. At any rate, the barriers were there.

At this time women weren't fully integrated into the MNANG and NGB. I requested to attend the seminar course for Air War College, which was held locally on base along with neighboring members of the 934th Air Force Reserve unit, also housed on our airfield. I was questioned by Base Personnel, "Why would you, a woman and a nurse, want to take that course - it is really a military man's course." Well, I took the course and passed! It was a definite asset for my promotion to colonel.

When Brig Gen Schaumann retired, Col Boab was named the 133rd Commander. As is expected, I offered my resignation to Col Boab. He asked me to remain in the position.

After all we felt we had accomplished, we worked up our bravery to submit the 109th AEF for an award – an award that was presented by the Director of the National Guard Bureau annually to the outstanding medical unit at the AMSUS Convention. In discussions with the 109th leadership, we decided to go ahead. Lt Col Graner, Maj Anderson, Maj Wolf, Capt Hendrickson along with advice and suggestions from unit members, submitted our application. To our surprise, we received a call a few days before the conference that we not only received the Theodore C. Marrs Award but also the George Schafer Award. It was unusual for one unit to receive both awards. The judges were so impressed with the application and how well it was written that it left no doubt of our accomplishments.

It was the lift that the 109th needed and certainly deserved. We had a large contingent attending the conference and award ceremony in Las Vegas, NV. The awards were presented to the 109th by Maj Gen John Conaway, Director of the Air National Guard Bureau. USAF Chief Nurse, Col Carmalleta Schmenti was in attendance and congratulated us. This was the first time that the unit had won either award. In the evening we hosted another gathering and invited other ANG AE units, NGB staff and Col Robert Self, who was an assistant to Col Weaver, the ANG Surgeon General.

Col Julie Eszlinger Jensen

November. Lt Col Julie Eszlinger assumed command of the 109th AEF. At an AMSUS conference, it was announced that she was the first nurse commander of an aerovac unit for both the Guard and Reserve. [48]

Lt Col Eszlinger stepped into the job highly qualified. She received her nursing degree in 1959 and a Master's Degree in Education Administration in 1978. In her civilian role she was a supervisor of nursing and worked in health occupation education for the State Department of Education.

Upon assuming command, Lt Col Eszlinger said of the unit, "I believe the members of the flight are persons who are talented, eager, imaginative and creative. They have the ability to meet the challenge of high standards and have an appreciation for their recreational time." [49]

Lt Col Alice Graner was selected as the unit's Chief Nurse.

December. MSgt Walter R. Foster was awarded a 30-Year Federal Service Award. MSgt Foster became the Aeromed Evacuation Superintendent in December 1965 as a technician.

1981

February. Four members of the unit spent their annual field training in Panama. These aeromeds were assigned to the USAF Hospital at Howard AB, where they worked alongside their active duty counterparts.

September. Karen Wolf was sworn into the MNANG by her husband, Capt Lewis Wolf. Commissioned as a captain on the 11th of the month, Karen was assigned to the 109th AEF. She came to the unit with eight years of nursing experience and was currently attending classes at the University of Minnesota, working towards a Master's Degree as a Nurse Practitioner. [50]

☆☆☆☆☆

The 133rd TAW took delivery of its first C-130E model on 15 Sep. On hand were approximately 100 Guard members and friends. Maj Gen James Sieben, Adjutant General, was present to officially accept the aircraft on behalf of the state of Minnesota. Eight more E-model Hercules aircraft would be delivered during the next four months. When the final E-model arrived, the last C-130A was transferred to other units who flew the "A" Herks.

From the outside, the E-model didn't look much different than the A-model, which the 133rd had flown since 1971. Both models were the same size and shape, had four turboprop engines, lots of cockpit windows, sat low to the ground and sported a combination of colors.

However, the E-model Hercules was newer, heavier, had a longer range and sported more modern avionics (flight instruments) than its predecessor. It could haul the same cargo farther or fly the same distance carrying heavier cargo than the A-model. The A-model could carry about 8.5 hours of fuel, but the E could carry 14 hours of fuel, enough to fly nonstop from the East Coast to Central Europe.

The easiest way to tell the difference between the two models is to look for three external features on the E-model. The first two are large fuel tanks hanging under the wings, between the inboard and outboard engines. These fuel tanks are the largest on the airplane, each holding 9,100 pounds or 1,400 gallons of jet fuel. The standard A-model has smaller external tanks. The E-model also has a small radome on top of the fuselage behind the cockpit. It houses a device called station-keeping radar that enables a flight of C-130Es to remain in formation, regardless of visibility and weather conditions.

The E-model Hercules when empty weighed about 73,000 pounds - 4,000 more than the A-model. Stronger wings and landing gear enable it to haul more weight. It can take off at 155,000 pounds, compared to the A's normal gross weight of 123,000 pounds. Actual volume capacity is the same for both aircraft, about 4,150 cubic feet. Each model can carry 92 passengers, 74 litter patients or 64 paratroopers.

The E and A use similar turboprop engines, although the E is quieter on the ground because its engines have a "ground idle" setting that reduces engine speed to 69-75 percent rpm.

Inside, the E-models are more comfortable for the crews. By rearranging equipment and some hardware, designers created room for two bunks and a galley. The avionics are more modern on the E, giving the crew more information with a fewer number of instruments. On the E, both pilot and copilot have identical instruments, making position transition easier.

The 133rd flies the Hercules under the authority of the governor of Minnesota or the United States Air Force. State missions could include hauling firefighting personnel and equipment to fire zones in the state. AF missions include carrying defense cargo or passengers anywhere in the world.

The readiness of the unit was improved by the acquisition of the E-models. Built in 1956, the A models were becoming progressively harder to maintain. Replacement parts were becoming increasingly scarce and qualified technicians to repair them were all but gone. The E-model was common to the AF inventory, so parts and qualified technicians were readily available.

Built in 1962, the C-130E models saw some tough service, much of it in Southeast Asia. However, they were maintained and operated with a high degree of care by the Georgia ANG. [51]

Photo courtesy of USAF
C-130E.

Past trips that were routinely limited to Germany, Puerto Rico and Panama were now history for the 109th AEF. With the new C-130Es future travel destinations were virtually unlimited. [52]

☆☆☆☆☆

Nine members of the 109th AEF underwent "wet ditching training" as part of their ongoing training program.

"It was a chilling experience - using the life preservers was cold and very strenuous," SSgt Violet Ruff remarked. Amn Tim Evavold replied, "That's what made it realistic, something that could happen in a real situation."

Detailed training in using the life raft, handheld radio and other survival equipment were part of the wet ditching class. [53]

Photo courtesy of the Northstar Guardian (Nov '81)
"Survivors" signal rescue aircraft.

October. A portion of the unit participated in a four-day training session on tactical AE with the 1st AES at Pope AFB, NC.

1982

March. Lt Col Julie E. Eszlinger graduated from the Health Services Executive Management Course.

April. Aeromeds deployed to Langley AFB, VA. Despite the poor, unfavorable weather, which set three separate records for bad weather during the period the aeromeds were there, a great deal of training was accomplished.

The trip to Langley was the annually scheduled two-week active duty period required to maintain their medical proficiency. The Langley Hospital has the only 24-hour emergency room facility that services Army, Navy and AF personnel in the immediate area. The busy emergency room provided training in areas the Minnesotans would most likely meet in a tactical aeromedical setting. On one day, the hospital logged over 180 patients during a two-shift period. One of the patients delivered her baby in the front seat of her car outside the emergency room doors. 109th personnel also worked in intensive care, the recovery room and in the medical/surgical ward.

Maj Darcy Anderson and MSgt Bob Kolbo stated that the Langley staff made them feel most welcome and were very cooperative and supportive in meeting the aeromeds' training requirements.

Col Maureen Hunt, a former flight nurse in the 109th AEF, was the Chief Nurse at the Langley Hospital and was on hand to see that unit personnel received the training that benefited them the most.

Unit members attending were: SSgt Gary Fee, MSgt Bob Kolbo, SSgt Judy Gunelius, SrA Joe Cordova, 1st Lt Joe Jensen, Maj Carol Schulz, Maj Darcy Anderson, Maj Valerie Yantz, Maj Marie Taylor and SSgt Tony Carroll.

Maj Carol Schulz addressed a group of civilian and military nurses on risk management, a subject about which she was well experienced. [54]

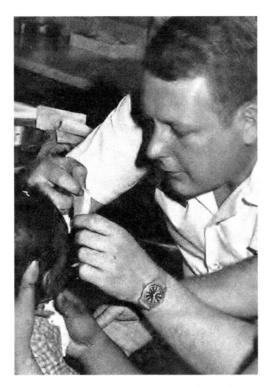

Photo courtesy of the Northstar Guardian (May '82)
SSgt Gary Fee treats a patient in the emergency room at Langley AFB, VA Hospital.

May. Brig Gen Sarah P. Wells, the Chief Nurse of the Air Force, arrived in Minneapolis to speak to the American Nurses Association Convention. She was greeted by Col Howard E. Mangin, 934th TAG (Tactical Airlift Group) Commander and Lt Col Julie E. Eszlinger, 109th AEF Commander.

Col Eszlinger Jensen recalls, "The 109th AEF was designated as the host unit. This honor would have normally gone to the Air Force Reserve but because of our connection on the national level for many years, we were selected. Lt Col Ausen, a former Minnesotan who had served with the 109th as a flight nurse from 1966 to 1973 and now working in the office as ANG/Reserve Assistant made this happen." Lt Col Eszlinger, Lt Larry Perkins and Lt Joe Jensen were required to be available 24/7 for her five-day stay in the Twin Cities.

Photo courtesy of Col Julie Eszlinger Jensen
**Brig Gen Sarah Wells and Lt Col Julie Eszlinger
at the American Nurses Association Convention in Minneapolis.**

<u>**July.**</u> The second Saturday of the month and the first running boom was in full swing. "It was a time," said former race director Scott Schneider, "when you could put a chalk mark on the street and draw 1,000 runners."

Aeromeds and other 133rd TAW members volunteered to support this first Annual Kaiser Roll. More than five dozen Air National Guard members volunteered to assist in this charitable event. It was a sunny, but steamy, hot Saturday with temps well into the upper 80s and the humidity level not much lower.

The Kaiser Roll sponsored two races for runners and wheelchair competitors whose proceeds go to the three centers for rehabilitation - the Courage Center, Sister Kenny Institute and Vinland National Center. The aeromeds staffed a first aid tent and manned two ambulances. The heat and humidity resulted in the aeromeds treating about a dozen runners for heat-related problems alone. Brig Gen Robert Schaumann remarked, "I think the Air Guard should participate in community events, especially charitable ones. This not only gives us visibility, but because the Guard is part of the community, we should participate." [55]

Photo courtesy of Capt Jean Cool
Flight nurses.

Back Row (L - R): Joe Jensen, Dayton Carlson, Alice Graner, Val Yantz, Norm Hendrickson, Cortland Arlien
Front Row (L - R): Darcy Anderson, Marie Taylor, Julie Eszlinger, Joan Dawson, Carol Schulz, Terry Wellner

November. The School of Aerospace Medicine established a course in Battlefield Nursing as part of the AF Medical Service's readiness training initiative. In the first year, 258 nurses attended. [56]

Maj Darcy Anderson and Capt Norman Hendrickson completed this 5-day Battlefield Nursing course at the School of Aerospace Medicine, Brooks AFB, TX.

The course was divided into five parts. First, there were classroom lectures delivered by authorities with field combat experience in Vietnam. Then the nurses moved to the laboratory where they practiced their skills on mannequins. The third day was spent with veterinarians in the dog lab. On the fourth day, the nurses donned complete chemical warfare ensembles and worked in tear gas chambers. Finally, the training culminated by going into the field and working in lifelike situations. Teams of nurses worked on simulated patients in chemical warfare garb and had to decontaminate and treat whatever injuries needed attention.

Maj Darcy Anderson stated, "The training was very intense and terribly realistic, almost frightening. It really made me feel more confident and better prepared." [57]

December. The Nurse Corps began to require a minimum of a Bachelor of Science in Nursing for all new AF nurses. The only exception was for career fields deemed critical, such as anesthesia. [58]

1983

The 133rd Tactical (TAC) Hospital was one of several units on base that provided medical support to the Annual Kaiser Roll. This charitable race generated funds in support of the Sister Kenny Institute, Vinland National Center and Camp Superkids (American Lung Association).

1984

April. A medical milestone was reached for the 109th AEF. It was tasked with the first actual airlift of a cardiac patient. A member of the 133rd TAW had suffered a heart attack while on a deployment in Panama. In early April, the patient had stabilized so his doctors were willing to discharge him. MAC indicated it would be several weeks before a C-9 Nightingale could be dispatched to fly the patient home. A 133rd TAW C-130E was leaving Minneapolis to support the A-7 operation at Howard AB, Panama. It was decided to equip and dispatch an aeromedical team on the flight. The crew was made up of Capt Terry Wellner, TSgt Lawrence Bild, and SrA Timothy Evavold, who successfully transported the patient back to Minnesota.

Capt Wellner went to work. He gathered an evac team and collected the needed drugs and medical equipment from the TAC Hospital. A portable defibrillator and cardiac medication required special handling. The C-130E departed Minneapolis for Arizona, spent the night and left the next morning, landing at Howard AB eight and a half hours later. Checking with the hospital the next day, April 8th, Capt Wellner was provided with an update and other vital information concerning the patient. The evac team then prepared for the return flight to Minnesota the next day.

Arriving at the hospital the next morning, Wellner was shocked to learn that there might be an indefinite delay in releasing the patient. Analyzing the situation, Capt Wellner made a few well-placed calls and corrected the problem and the patient was discharged. Even with the delay at the hospital, the flight departed Howard AB only a half hour late.

Upon landing back in Minneapolis, the C-130E had to clear customs. "The agent, after seeing the 'special cargo' released us in five minutes," Wellner remembers.

"TSgt Bild and SrA Evavold were outstanding in their performance as was the entire flight crew," Capt Wellner stated. "They each initiated and applied the extra effort needed to create a smooth, safe and controlled flight all the way." [59]

July. The 109th AEF deployed to Fort McCoy, Wisconsin for the purpose of conducting a field training exercise with the 204th Medical Battalion, ARNG (Army National Guard). This was the first ever joint exercise between these two Minnesota medical units and was believed to be the first of its kind in the nation.

Joining land and air advance parties, which included 11 personnel from the 1st AES, Pope AFB NC, the 109th AEF established and operated one entire Tactical Aeromedical Evacuation System (TAES) for a period of three days.

The setting for this training was a three-day combined arms exercise involving nearly 12,000 members of the ARNG's 47th Division. While F-4s, A-7s, A-10s, Chinooks, Huey's and C-130s competed for air space, the infantry, tanks and heavy artillery units fought the land battle. The 109th AEF was to provide the final tactical medical evacuation link.

As casualties occurred in battle, they were treated and then processed through the Army and TAES. First by the Army field medic, then the battalion aid station and finally the clearing stations for more definitive treatment. In order to move casualties from the combat zone by air, a MASF was established by the nearest runway capable of "handling" a C-130. Through a series of radio communications initiated by the user service (the 204th Medical Battalion), patient movement and aircraft deployment was coordinated by the TAES of the 109th AEF. Manned by four flight nurses, seventeen med techs and two radio operators, the MASF prepared the casualties for flight and continued the prescribed medical treatment.

And the casualties did come! All the while the temperatures soared, the rain never stopped, and the humidity hugged them in a dense wet blanket - and still the casualties kept coming, by ground ambulances (called "cracker boxes" by the troops), by Huey and Chinook helicopters and on foot.

Although most casualties were simulated, their injuries appeared real: blood stained dressings, IVs and fractures splinted with tree branches, with the leaves still attached, was the norm.

The 109th medical crews were kept busy. Working at times on hands and knees near litter patients and caring for overflow ambulatory patients outside the tents, the 109th personnel treated, manifested and prepared for flights with up to 56 patients per mission. Flying three missions per day and utilizing only one MASF, the 109th moved 296 patients through the system in 2½ days.

The exercise was incredibly successful, not only in enhancing the 109th AEF's readiness posture, but also in demonstrating the coordinating capabilities of the 204th Medical Battalion and the 109th AEF. Gen Walden, Commander of the 47th Division, ARNG, while observing the joint operation termed it "damned impressive" and indeed it was. [60]

Photo courtesy of 2d Lt Ann Dryer (Steinmetz)
Transporting patients to the MASF in preparation for airlift from a CH-47 Chinook helicopter.

<u>**November.**</u> Representatives of the 133rd TAC Hospital and the 109th AEF attended and actively participated in the 91st meeting of the Association of Military Surgeons of the United States, held in San Diego, California.

"Planning Effective Inservice Education" was this year's theme. More than 100 nurses - active USAF, ANG, and AFR - who attended not only gained in knowledge, but received continuing education credits authorized by the state of California.

Key members of the 109th responded to a request from Capt Tim Adams at National Guard Bureau and took charge of the aeromed workshop. Lt Col Alice Graner, Chief Nurse of the 109th, chaired a group discussion, part of the MAC Command Nurse Breakout Session. Its topic was to emphasize the importance of nurses within AE units and to evaluate specific problems and successes with nurse recruitment into aeromed units.

Lt Col Julie Eszlinger, Commander of the 109th AEF, was in charge of a one-day workshop covering a number of topics in the areas of operations, training, executive management and standardization/evaluation. Nearly 200 nurses, med techs, flight surgeons and MSC officers participated in the workshop. Within Lt Col Eszlinger's topic area of Stan/Eval were specific discussions on office management practices and AFORMS (AF Operations Resource Management System) interfacing. [61]

1985

January. Temps over the UTA weekend: -30s F. Engines would not start and tires went flat.

☆☆☆☆☆

Unit Members participated in Operation Brim Frost '85. This exercise was designed to determine the ability of Joint Task Force Alaska to conduct winter operations. The exercise ran from December 10th, 1984 through January 24th, 1985 and involved more than 18,000 military personnel.

The 109th AES provided two crews for aeromedical evacuation support from Elmendorf AFB, Anchorage, AK during this exercise. Then 1st Lt Dayton Carlson recalls, "One of the most memorable experiences was a live aeromedical evacuation mission 109th AES unit members performed. We were alerted for an URGENT mission to transport a critically ill Army dependent from Ft. Wainwright, Fairbanks, AK to the medical center at the University of Alaska, Anchorage. The aircraft used was a U.S. Coast Guard HC-130E, which did not carry litter stanchions. We borrowed two litter stanchions from the Alaska Air Guard's 210th Rescue Squadron which flew HC-130Hs.

"My crew included Maj Terrence Wellner, myself, TSgt Lawrence Bild, SSgt Paul Walker, and A1C Eugene Conrad. On landing at Fort Wainwright, we found the patient had an Army physician and an ICU (Intensive Care Unit) qualified Army nurse accompanying her. The patient was a very heavy individual, requiring six crewmembers to carry the litter and her various IV bags and monitors up into the HC-130E. In preparation for takeoff, TSgt Bild and his med techs quickly rigged a duct tape "clothesline" between the two litter stanchions and had all of her IV bags neatly hung along this "clothesline" so they could be easily monitored throughout the flight.

"Our aerovac crew took primary responsibility for continually monitoring her vital signs, meeting her personal needs, and attempting to make her as comfortable as possible throughout the flight. The Army nurse commented to me that, 'We were the hardest working aerovac crew she had ever seen.'

"On arrival at Elmendorf AFB, Maj Wellner and I accompanied the patient to the medical center at the University of Alaska, Anchorage to provide a report on her condition and transfer her medical records to their staff. The ICU staff told us that she was in much better shape than she had been prior to being transferred from Fort Wainwright."

July. The 109th AEF held their second annual Joint Army/ANG Tactical Aeromedical Evacuation Field Training Exercise at Camp Ripley, MN (Samaritan V) which took place over a period of six days. Capt Joe Jensen and TSgt Mark Latourelle were the 109th AEF leads in this exercise.

Photo courtesy of Col Michael Germain
Patient care and onloading procedures at Samaritan V exercise, Camp Ripley, MN.

A second full-time technician position was authorized and filled by SSgt Joseph Cordova.

December. MSgt Lawrence Bild, First Sergeant for the 109th AEF, was selected as the Outstanding Senior NCO for the 133rd Tactical Airlift Wing.

1986

March. A spouse flight was held this UTA weekend on a local aeromedical training flight to Duluth. During the flight, the ramp and door were opened after a retaining fence was strung across the opening. Spouses were able to stand at the ramp and door and take in a spectacular view as the C-130E flew along the north shore of Lake Superior. They were also able to watch a simulated aeromed mission and sit in the co-pilot's seat while "flying" the C-130E.

Photo courtesy of Col Michael Germain

Cindy Germain, wife of then 1st Lt Michael Germain, takes her turn at "piloting" the mighty Hercules along the North Shore during a recent spouse flight.

May. History was made recently when A. Marlene Ausen became the first woman to be promoted to full colonel in the ANG. Col Ausen, ANG Nurse Advisor to the Chief of the AF Nurse Corps, received her eagles from Lt Gen (Lieutenant General) Murphey Chesney, AF Surgeon General and Maj Gen John B. Conaway, Director of the ANG at a ceremony held at the Pentagon.

Col Ausen received her diploma in nursing from Hamline University and her Bachelor's Degree in Nursing from the University of Wisconsin, graduating with honors. In 1965, Col Ausen began her military career by joining the AFR in Minneapolis. A year later, she served with the 109th AEF as a flight nurse from 1966 to 1973. Col Ausen then transferred to the Wisconsin ANG and in 1978 became a member of the Virginia ANG where she received her Master's Degree in Nursing from the University of Virginia. [62]

June. The crew of Channels Five's "Good Company" flew with the aeromeds of the 109th AEF. Gary Lumpkin, Good Company's field host, was one of the mission's patients. The training flight was filmed from mission briefing, to hot onload, through the flight and back to base. The filming effort was to inform the public of the work of the 133rd TAW, and more specifically, the mission of the 109th AEF. [63]

☆☆☆☆☆

During the summer, an intensified effort was made to recruit flight nurses for the unit. Maj Karen Wolf had been filling a 60-day temporary position, with the sole responsibility of "getting the word out" to the nursing schools, hospitals, nursing associations, radio and TV audiences and the public in general, that the 109th AEF had openings for flight nurses. She had been involved in live radio interviews and assistance in the development and execution of public service announcements with Channel 9 and 11.

1st Lt Michael Germain and SSgt Cheryl McLean were selected to film individual 30 second commercials to recruit new flight nurses and med techs (respectively) into the unit. Germain recalled, "After 20-30 'takes' to get the timing exactly down to 30 seconds, I looked forward to seeing the commercial on broadcast TV. Unfortunately, I had to record the commercial as it aired in the 0100 to 0200 time frame. So much for my star on the Hollywood Walk of Fame."

☆☆☆☆☆

The 109th AEF participated in Sentry Independence at Volk Field, WI. The exercise was run annually by the Wisconsin ANG, simulating warfare conditions the unit would experience in northern Europe.

All of the flight nurses and med techs lived in tents - without running water or light bulbs - at Young airstrip, a 3,500-foot dirt runway bulldozed from the woods at the end of a gravel road. Six radio operators (co-located with the aeromeds) from the Tennessee ANG provided essential communications for the exercise.

Photo courtesy of Col Michael Germain

Aeromeds unloading a "cracker box" field ambulance and transporting patients to the MASF in the background at Volk Field, Fort McCoy, WI.

"It's like the wartime situation in which we would work," said Maj Karen Wolf, Deployment Project Officer. "The mission is to take care of the casualties...or whoever needs the services of air evacuation out of the combat zone."

Since the unit had no physicians, patients would arrive with instructions from Army doctors in the field, but at the airstrip, the nurses and med techs had to make decisions that could mean the difference between life and death.

"I'm allowed to do a lot more around here than I am as a licensed practical nurse," said SSgt Debra Hodnett. In civilian life, she worked in a treatment center for chemically dependent adolescents, but in the Air Guard, she had responsibilities not allowed as a civilian - for example, giving intravenous fluids. At Fort McCoy, she was learning principles of triage.

"There's a lot of training in emergency medicine," said Lt Sue Redalen.

During Sentry Independence, the 109th AEF treated 180 simulated patients. "They had blast injuries, broken bones, amputations and chemical injuries," Maj Wolf said. "Plus, there were some psych patients." The wounded were brought in by ambulance or helicopter, given intravenous fluids if needed, rebandaged and tended to for up to four hours before being loaded aboard one of the five C-130 Hercules aircraft supplied during the exercise. The aeromeds flew with the patients for about an hour, simulating a trip to a rear area, before returning.

The experience "trains us to be operationally ready for a time when the governor or the president might call us to go somewhere and take care of casualties," Maj Wolf said.

"This is when they shine; they really get down and work together," she said. "Everybody works especially well in a hard situation like this." [64]

Photo courtesy of Col Michael Germain
"The Hilton" crew at Volk Field, Fort McCoy, WI.

Back Row (L - R): Mike Cunniff, Larry Perkins, Joe Jensen, Gerry Blilie, Jim Bouthilet, Tim Evavold
Front Row (L - R): Mike Germain, Joe Cordova, Tim Schenk, Mark Latourelle, Jim Hughes, Larry Bild

Sept. SrA Mark Freund, a recent graduate from the six-week Aeromedical Evacuation Technician Course, was honored by Lt Col Julie Eszlinger Jensen, the 109th Commander for being the only student to graduate with a course average over 90%.

November. Lt Col Darcy Anderson became the Chief Nurse and was elected President of the ANG Nurses Association at the annual AMSUS meeting.

1987

January. SMSgt Walter Foster was named the Outstanding Senior Non-commissioned Officer of the Year by the 133rd Tactical Airlift Wing.

April. Minnesota Air Guard members participated in a 3-day NDMS (National Disaster Medical System) exercise that ranged from California to Ohio. Named April Fault '87, this exercise tested the nation's ability to provide medical care for victims of a disaster. In this case, it was a simulated catastrophic earthquake in California. The victims were scheduled to be flown to the Twin Cities, St. Louis, MO and Dayton, Ohio for treatment.

Members of the 109th AEF participated, along with Reservists from the 934th's 47th AEF, as well as personnel from twelve Twin Cities area hospitals. The 109th was the only Air Guard AE unit in the exercise.

The local portion of the exercise centered on a hangar at the 934th TAG, which simulated the earthquake area and was the victim collection point. 109th personal performed triage - classifying patients by severity of injury - and briefed the flight crews about the mission requirements. An augmented 109th AEF flight crew consisting of three flight nurses and five med techs flew a 90-minute mission.

"On each mission there were 50 seriously injured patients," Lt Col Darcy Anderson, 109th Chief Nurse, explained. "There were 25 moulaged Army personnel and 25 sets of records representing additional patients. It was a realistic test of our abilities because we didn't know any of the casualties, and they were instructed to simulate emergencies during the flight. We were involved in doing what we do best, transporting or evacuating critically ill patients from the disaster area to whatever part of the country they are designated to go to." The exercise was the first nationally coordinated test of the NDMS, which was devised in 1984.

The system has only been tested once before, in a regional exercise at Andrews AFB, MD, that was coordinated with local agencies like the American Red Cross and the Maryland area Veteran's Administration hospitals. The flight crews dealt with numerous trauma conditions and patients who were suffering from various degrees of psychological shock as the exercise scenario called for the evacuation to occur 48 to 72 hours after the earthquake.

The 934th TAG Command Post controlled the Twin Cities portion of the exercise and coordinated with units from Rickenbacker ANG base in Ohio and Richards-Gebaur AFB, MO.

"We're just a small part of a huge exercise," said Lt Col Anderson. "It's really been a positive atmosphere. All the agencies have pulled together and the planning has been going very smoothly."

The nationwide system is designed to respond in the event of floods, earthquakes or toxic spills as well as an overseas conventional war. It is intended to be capable of handling approximately 100,000 victims in 71 locations nationwide with 150 alert teams fully staffed and trained. The network is set up to augment the facilities of individual states and regions. It is not designed to be a response force in the event of a nuclear war.

"This was a real test of our communications skills and training," Lt Col Anderson added. "This scenario was excellent because we had to be flexible, we never knew what we would get into. In the military, you always have to deal with uncertainties."

"It showed us what we need to plan for," Lt Col Anderson said. "For example, we learned that we may be picking up patients where the local medics do not have the medications and dressings to send along with the patients. We may have to take those with us. Our original assumption was that we'd carry a specified amount of drugs, dressings and supplies such as IVs and that they'd be enough as long as we could be supplied by people at our destination. Now we realize that might not be enough. So, we're asking ourselves, 'What do we want to go in with?' We've got to reassess what we'll be carrying. The medical crew director and the triage physician were talking the same language because all our nurses are well-versed and well-experienced in triage so we had the kind of information the physicians were looking for."

"If there was a disaster, the system would work," Lt Col Anderson said. "We'd have to augment the crews and re-evaluate our supplies, but it would work. We would make it work." [65]

June. Sentry Independence '87 was held at Volk Field, Wisconsin. The 109th AEF was the only Guard AE unit participating in this exercise. The unit's teams consisted of flight nurses, med techs, supply, radio operators and administrative personnel. With sites at three locations, forty of the members were at Camp Ripley, Minnesota while the remaining forty-four members were split between Volk field and Young Field, Wisconsin. The 109th AEF was supplemented with members from the 1st AES based at Pope AFB, NC.

The exercise provided realistic training in scenarios similar to wartime battlefield conditions. The actual field conditions included eating, sleeping and showering in tents. Personnel were exposed to heat, insects, rain and the dust from the nearby dirt airstrip.

Radio operators and administration personnel practiced the art of communication by Pacer Bounce radio. All communication, movement of aircrews, aircraft and patient conditions could only be done by radio transmission between the three sites. The medics had the opportunity to train in and simulate patient care and procedures while dressed in chemical warfare gear.

Army personnel from the 32nd Brigade and various other units served as patients to be airlifted by helicopter from the battlefield to the makeshift tent hospitals. At these Mobile Aeromedical Staging Facilities, the medics provided care to stabilize the patients while waiting for additional airlift to military hospitals where they would receive more definitive care.

Photo courtesy of Lt Col Darcy Anderson

Lt Col Darcy Anderson (left), in the field discussing resupply problems with AECC representative TSgt Dennis Ferretti (right).

Four med techs from the unit driving home from this exercise suddenly put their training to use in aiding a real accident victim.

TSgt Dale Roiger, A1C Tad Hengemuehle, A1C Lisa Plombon and SSgt Micki King were driving from Camp Ripley, MN after participating in the Samaritan VIII exercise (a portion of Sentry Independence '87), when on 18 June they came upon a car that had smashed into a concrete pillar under a bridge on I-94 near Rogers, MN. The car, driven by a 17-year-old, had gone off the road, hit a guardrail and then the pillar. It had been heading north, so it was on the opposite side of the highway from the med techs.

"Being medics, we stopped on the spur of the moment," SSgt King said, "got out and grabbed all our mobility gear from the back of our car and headed to the smashed car. None of the bystanders were medically trained, so they were just standing around although a trucker had called for medical and police assistance."

A1C Hengemuehle ran to the driver's side of the car and TSgt Roiger moved to the passenger side. They discovered that the driver was pinned inside with unknown injuries. "I climbed into the car and immediately put him in a surgical collar so he wouldn't move his head in case of a neck injury," said TSgt Roiger. "Tad kept asking the boy if he had any pain or injuries. That was to keep the boy talking and keep his mind off what had happened while we did an assessment to see if he'd sustained an injury to the head."

They improvised the collar out of bandages rolled together from their personal first aid kits. The medics also checked the youth's vital signs and tried to keep him calm so he wouldn't go into severe shock. They said that the brake pedal apparently had dug into the boy's leg, and every time he moved, it hurt worse. They continued to monitor him until the paramedics arrived about ten minutes later.

After the paramedics had given the youth an IV and stabilized his condition, they told TSgt Roiger they appreciated all the information and help they had rendered and they had done "a hell of a good job."

Flight nurse supervisors familiar with the incident said later that from what they were able to learn, the youth could be expected to recover.

"We didn't want recognition or anything for our actions; our concern was for the safety of the boy," said TSgt Roiger. "We just gathered as much information as we could. We were glad we could help." [66]

☆☆☆☆☆

Maj Karen Wolf and her husband, Maj Lew Wolf, were the first married couple in the Air Guard to attend Air Command and Staff College (ACSC) together in residence. While attending ACSC, the Wolfs made the most of their "academic sabbatical" by also completing a Master's Degree in Personnel Management through an evening school program at Troy State University.

The Wolfs were two of only twelve Air Guard officers chosen to attend the ten-month course at Maxwell AFB, AL. Maj Wolf was most impressed by what she learned about worldwide political, military, and economic environments and how they shape national policy and by the way the course gave them an understanding of the USAF and total force structures.

July. Col A. Marlene Ausen, former 109th AEF flight nurse, was the first ANG nurse and women selected to attend Air War College in residence at Maxwell AFB, AL.

September. In an effort to improve aircrew retention, the AF issued leather jackets to flyers. The jackets, which closely resembled the flying jackets worn in World War II, were intended to help address aircrew perceptions that they were not adequately recognized and to increase esprit of combat-ready aircrew members.

The jackets cost about $100 each, with initial expense to be less than $5 million. Lt Gen Thomas Hickey, Deputy Chief of Staff of Personnel, said that training an F-15 or F-16 pilot to operational status costs more than $1 million. "If this initiative alone enables the AF to retain several operational pilots who would otherwise have left the service," he said, "it would have paid for itself in the first year." [67]

November. The 109th AEF won the top two awards for medical units - the George Schafer Award for being the best medical unit in the air reserve forces and the Theodore C. Marrs Award for the best medical unit in the ANG. This is the only AE unit to win these two prestigious awards simultaneously - making the 109th AEF the number one AE unit in the AF system.

Lt Col Julie Eszlinger Jensen and flight members accepted both awards in November at the annual Association of Military Surgeons of the United States conference in Las Vegas, Nevada. The awards annually recognize outstanding medical units. The Air Guard has 110 medical units and the 109th AEF is believed to be the first AE unit to win both awards.

Winners were chosen for medical readiness demonstrated through training and inspection results, recruiting, individual and unit awards, community work and other professional activities. The awards were for the period of July 1986 through June 1987.

"I've felt for a long time that our people perform in an outstanding manner," Lt Col Eszlinger Jensen said. "They are very dedicated, they put in a lot of their own time and they are always willing to attend field training exercises even though some of this extends them beyond their 15 days. It's nice that someone recognizes that we've got dedicated people."

"This unit has been exceptional for many years," she said. "This year I felt that we could compete and win." The awards are the first of any kind that the 109th AEF has won since it began in 1961.

When the awards package was submitted, Lt Col Eszlinger Jensen hoped the unit would win the Marrs award, but when the Air Guard Surgeon called, he told her that the 109th AEF had won both awards. "I was shocked," remarked Lt Col Eszlinger Jensen. As she called unit members to tell them about the award, she began to feel elated.

Her feelings were echoed by unit members, most of whom hadn't known that an application for the Schafer Award had been submitted. "I was a little bit surprised, but it's nice, for once, to get recognized," said SSgt Tracy Soderholm, quality-assurance NCOIC. "I was delighted for the unit," said Lt Col Darcy Anderson, Chief Nurse. "I think the unit has long deserved some recognition and not gotten it. Now, I keep touching the trophy and asking people 'Do you know what you've done?'"

"It was a real high because when I was at field training at McDill AFB, FL last year they had the George Schafer Award on a pedestal," said Lt Col Anderson. "I teased a full-time nurse down there that, 'this award is going north next year.'" They laughed and said, "'Sure, Darcy, sure.' When I saw her at the conference I said, 'guess where the George Schafer's going?' She said it was wonderful that we'd won. It's really like a dream come true."

The Schafer Award is named for a former Surgeon General of the AF who believed strongly in the idea of active and reserve components as a total force. The Marrs award is named for a former physician with the Alabama Air Guard who also was an Assistant Secretary of Defense for Reserve Affairs and an assistant to President Gerald Ford for national organizations.

The Marrs award is a modest plaque, but the Schafer Award is a traveling trophy almost three feet high, and it spent most of the next year at the 109th AEF, a busy place where members worked long hours on a strong program of training and readiness.

Photo courtesy of TSgt Richard Childs and Col Michael Germain
Theodore C. Marrs Award

"IT IS WITH PLEASURE THAT I CONGRATULATE THE 109TH AEROMEDICAL EVACUATION FLIGHT, MN ANG ON BEING SELECTED AS WINNERS OF THIS AWARD. THE PROFESSIONALISM AND DEDICATION DISPLAYED WAS EXEMPLARY AND REFLECTS GREAT CREDIT ON YOURSELVES, YOUR STATE AND THE ANG."

Maj Gen John B. Conaway
Director, ANG

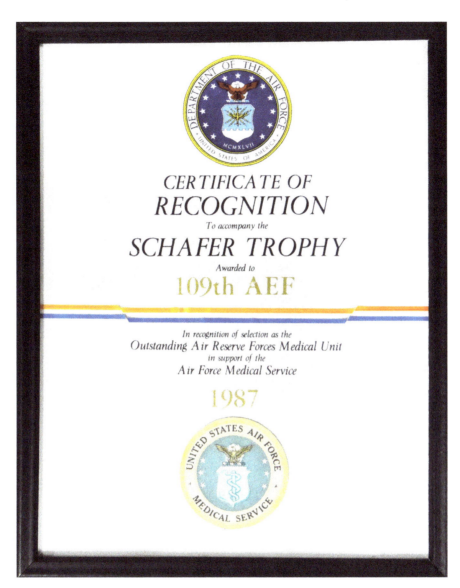

Photo courtesy of TSgt Richard Childs and Col Michael Germain

"CERTIFICATE OF RECOGNITION TO ACCOMPANY THE SCHAFER TROPHY AWARDED TO 109TH AEROMEDICAL EVACUATION FLIGHT IN RECOGNITION OF SELECTION AS THE OUTSTANDING AIR RESERVE FORCES MEDICAL UNIT IN SUPPORT OF THE AIR FORCE MEDICAL SERVICE."

Medical readiness field training was accomplished by participating in Samaritan VIII - a portion of Sentry Independence - where members lived in tents by a dirt landing strip at Fort McCoy, WI. They also did field training at Camp Ripley, MN, and other major AF exercises such as Winter-Cimex 1987, Brim Frost and Solid Shield.

The flight also was the only Air Guard unit to participate in the first exercise of the National Disaster Medical System, which involved units from across the country and a dozen Twin Cities-area hospitals in April.

Another training program linked the military and civilian medical communities by sending flight members to work at St. Paul Ramsey Medical Center. Members of the unit spent a portion of each UTA at the medical center.

The flight also participated in the annual Kaiser Roll race held annually to benefit the disabled as well as supported activities of the Civil Air Patrol and Boy Scouts. [68]

"The members of the 109th AEF have worked long and hard to achieve this performance," said Maj Gen James Sieben, Minnesota's Adjutant General. "It's great to see them finally get the recognition they so richly deserve." [69]

Photo courtesy of TSgt Jerry Brown, Minnesota ANG, Northstar Guardian (Jan '88)

Proudly displaying awards for the best medical unit in the ANG and air reserve forces are (left to right) Lt Col Julie Eszlinger Jensen, 109th AEF Commander, Brig Gen Patrick Boab, Wing Commander, and SMSgt Walt Foster, 109th AEF AE Superintendent. The plaque is the Theodore C. Marrs award for the top Air Guard medical unit, and the trophy is the George Schafer Award for the top air reserve forces medical unit.

Lt Col Anderson was a featured speaker at the fourth annual AMSUS AE workshop. Her topic: "Aeromedical Evacuation Role in the National Defense System."

1988

January. From January 29th to February 11th, a number of unit members were in Germany testing an underground system for treating battlefield casualties. They were part of a team testing the Air Force's Survivable Collective Protection System-Medical (SCPS-M). The good work they did during this test gave them claim to the free world's fastest time for satisfactorily processing 66 chemically contaminated casualties in a particular series of underground buildings. There were only two such systems in existence. One was located at Wright-Patterson AFB, OH and the other at Ramstein AB, Germany. The teams worked in the SCPS-M for 96 hours, about the time expected to survive a chemical attack, during which they processed a total of 264 patients. The goal was to process 66 patients in four hours. On the second day, our Air Guard team set a record of three hours and thirty-seven minutes - better than the regular AF had done.

March. The 133rd TAW was awarded the AF Outstanding Unit Award. The award was given for the wing's accomplishments from February 1, 1985 to January 31, 1987.

☆☆☆☆☆

Also this month, the unit moved to the newly renovated Building 644 from their overcrowded quarters above the TAC Hospital. The 109th AEF's authorized strength had grown from 60 to 150 people.

☆☆☆☆☆

Seventeen members worked with their active duty counterparts at Wilford Hall in Texas for a week to increase their abilities and confidence. "We buddied up with an active duty person and got all kinds of hands-on experience," said TSgt Sue Clark, OJT supervisor. "We had a lot of flexibility. If the med (medical) floor wasn't busy, then we'd go down to the emergency room or the intensive care unit and do our eight-hour shift."

April. Wing members practiced to improve their ability to aid their fellow countrymen when they participated in the second annual test of the NDMS.

The premise of the exercise, titled April Touchdown '88, was that a tornado had ripped through the Dallas - Fort Worth Metropolitan area. The path of this massive storm included a sports stadium holding a capacity crowd. The resulting carnage and injured overwhelmed the area's medical systems.

The exercise was intended to test the ability of aeromedical specialists and civilian hospitals outside of the disaster's immediate area to respond to such a large-scale emergency. The NDMS provides training so civilian medical facilities, Veterans Administration (VA) hospitals, and military medical units can practice and fine tune swift and coordinated responses to national disasters anywhere in the country. This exercise featured heightened realism with patients dressed up with wounds that looked very real. Not only that, as TSgt Joe Cordova recalled, "We got to work on patients who were medics in other military units, so they really knew how to fake injuries and make it realistic."

The realism was to feature an exchange of patients between Denver and Minneapolis, thus challenging 109th AEF members to care for seriously injured patients during cross-country flights. This flight was canceled at the last minute due to bad weather around the Denver area so the exercise was limited to local flying.

Despite the last-minute cancellation, Capt Michael Germain, 109th AEF Project Officer, was very satisfied with the entire experience. He remembers, "The last-minute cancellation certainly caused a lot of extra work, but it also made us realize that we have to be flexible in order to deal with real disasters - they won't occur according to any plan." [70]

Photo courtesy of SSgt Allan Stahlberg, 133rd TAW PA (Public Affairs), Northstar Guardian (Fall '98)
MSgt Larry Bild secures a litter aboard the C-130 Hercules during exercise April Touchdown '88.

On June 20th, Lt Col Gene Andreotti was appointed Minnesota's Adjutant General by Governor Rudy Perpich.

November. The VA Medical Center's Women's Advisory Committee selected Lt Col Darcy Anderson to give their keynote address - "The Role of Women in the Military" - at the Women's Wellness Day.

1989

January. Bone-chilling cold hampered training for members of the 109th AEF during their participation in the annual Brim Frost exercise in Alaska. Brim Frost '89, the Army Forces Command's biennial Arctic field training exercise in January, also presented unique challenges to the Minnesotans, compelling them to deal with weather and a real-life tragedy.

The aeromeds joined 21,000 Army, Air Force, ANG, Coast Guard and Canadian Forces to gain experience working in an arctic environment. The 109th AEF was deployed at both Elmendorf AFB, Anchorage, AK and Eielson AFB, Fairbanks, AK. The weather was a constant factor with everyday sub-zero temperatures putting both people and equipment to the test. Temperatures often dipped into the minus 50-degree range in parts of the state. The Alaskan Weather Service stated it was the coldest and longest stretch in the past one hundred years. Living conditions were rustic to say the least. With the tents never really getting warm and walking the quarter-mile to the mess tent or to one's workplace in field gear became a major challenge. Exposed flesh freezes in 30 seconds at 50 below.

Lt Judy Hill stated, "Our mission was twofold. We practiced the Mobile Aeromedical Staging Facility scenarios and provided help if there was a real-life emergency like the C-130 crash."

The 109th set up the MASF, a MASH (Mobile Army Surgical Hospital) type unit, using large tents. According to TSgt Mark Grieme, "The tents were used to store medical supplies and serve as a holding area for the injured until they could be airlifted to a 'real' hospital."

Photo courtesy of Col Michael Germain
Aeromeds in the field at Eielson AFB, AK.

The aeromeds would be tested for real during this Brim Frost exercise. On 29 Jan, eight people were killed and 10 injured when a Canadian C-130 crashed in ice and fog at Fort Wainwright near Fairbanks, and the 109th AEF responded. Lt Judy Hill, a flight nurse and TSgt Tom Stangl, a med tech, were on the medical team that airlifted crash victims to an Anchorage hospital.

Lt Hill recalled, "We tail swapped from a C-130 to a C-141 three times in 50 below zero weather and finally transported on a C-141 that was originally loaded with cargo bound for the Philippines. We flew out of Anchorage, Alaska. I remember the spectacular view of Mount McKinley during sunset, arriving moments later in ice fog so thick you couldn't see the ambulance back to the aircraft until it was a few feet from the ramp. I recall that all of the aircrew were greatly humbled by the transport of the critical crash victims. This mission was extremely challenging and rewarding." [71]

"The C-130 crash showed how suddenly you can be thrown into a real-life emergency," TSgt Stangl said. "Deployments like Brim Frost help guarantee that you know what to do when it happens in brutal weather conditions."

Commander's Comments (continued):

Significant Contributions:

MSgt James Hughes for his dedication and commitment to serve the 109th in whatever way he was able. One way MSgt Hughes, aka "Jim," did this was by providing support to the 109th during SMSgt Foster's one-year National Guard Bureau assistance tour. He was a Flight Instructor and Flight Examiner. He knew his job and mentored his students. When there were challenging questions and uncertainties, he was always the go-to "Common Sense Guy" - "What did Jim say?" MSgt Hughes was recognized for his humble down-to-earth and stable manner. He was a dedicated, committed leader, hard worker and equally enjoyed fun playing guitar in his band. Jim was respected by all!

Lt Col Edward Howard, aka "Ed," for 41 years of committed and dedicated service to the 109th AEF/AES. He served in many capacities - medical technician, NCOIC of Staff Development, Superintendent of Nursing Services, Flight Instructor, Flight Examiner, Medical Service OIC (Officer in Charge) Logistics and Senior Medical Service Officer. With his many years of honorable service, he was often sought to provide historical information and referred to as "Ask Ed, he has corporate knowledge." During those years, Ed, who managed his business, also dedicated countless hours of his own personal time in whatever needed to be done to accomplish the mission. Ed says he had a great run, and the opportunity to serve with some outstanding people. Lt Col Howard retired when he reached the mandatory age requirement.

Greatest Impact for Who the 109th has Become:

MSgt Kolbo, First Sergeant, was the "gatekeeper" for the 109th AEF. In this role he had many and varied duties and responsibilities assisting predominantly the enlisted, but extended his assistance to officers as well - uniform issues, meeting USAF and 109th AES requirements, interpretation of orders, transitioning of MAC C-97 to TAC C-130 aircraft missions and UTA/active duty training. He had an innate sense of care and compassion for the troops. His impact was his exemplary understanding and concern of personnel. Because of his counseling and mentoring, many enlisted were retained and had a successful aeromedical and civilian career.

SMSgt Walter Foster for over 30 years was the only person and medical technician daily managing the 109th aerovac office. He represented the commander, OICs and NCOICs at base-wide meetings, handled the mail, answered the phones, relayed information and researched methods for improvement. Known as "Walt," he was always low-key, calm and gracious to everyone. SMSgt Foster was the role model for AFR 35-10 uniform dress requirements. He was ahead of his time in computer use. SMSgt Foster's expertise resulted in a request by the National Guard Bureau to provide a year of in-residence assistance to establish their computer format. "Walt" laid the foundation for the current 109th daily office management.

Col Alice Mae Graner's career began with the Wyoming ANG where she had gained live aerovac experience. Upon moving to Minneapolis, she became a member of the 109th AEF. She, aka "Alice," was a "stickler" for accuracy. MSgt Blilie said, "She was the best supervisor I ever had. We passed all inspections with no write-ups." It was Captain, Major and Lt Col Graner's countless hours of work researching all the areas of aeromedical evacuation, with support from all aeromed personnel, that initiated the training that resulted in the 109th becoming the role model for training which became the standard. It was adopted by higher headquarters who required it for all ANG and AFRES (Air Force Reserve) aeromedical evacuation going forward. It again was Lt Col Graner's dedication with support from 109th personnel who submitted the application that won us the Theodore C. Marrs and George Schafer Awards. Thankfully, the format has been followed since with success. Alice was always behind the scenes, never comfortable with recognition.

Who the 109th has become is in large part due to the commitment and dedication of these three 109th individuals.

My final thoughts on the 109th AES and its members:

Honored to be the first nurse appointed to the ANG Medical Advisory Council and to be the nurse selected by ANG Surgeon General, Col James Weaver, to unify all ANG nurses into their own association - Fraternity of ANG Nurses/Association of ANG Nurses.

Recognized for being the first to establish a hospital training program in the 1960s for medical technicians. This program was initiated by Capt Ardyce Marlene Ausen who transferred to the 109th from the Air Force Reserve in Minneapolis.

Recognized for being at the forefront of requiring all medical technicians to be EMT qualified. It was initially fraught with controversy from the ANG aerovac superintendents, but eventually became the NGB standard.

Appointed first nurse to command the 109th AEF.

Col Ardyce Marlene Ausen, aka "Marlene," for becoming the first flight nurse to represent ANG nurses in the Office of the Chief Nurse, USAF.

Recipient of first 109th awards - a beginning with others to follow.

Most Memorable Comment: Col Paul Carlton, SG, 375 MAC upon return from Desert Storm at a staff meeting at the 375th MAC Headquarters, Scott AFB, IL stated, "If I ever have to go to war again, it will only be with the 109th, the unit out of Minneapolis. They are outstanding. There isn't anything they can't do." (Heard and so proudly appreciated by Col Eszlinger Jensen, Individual Mobilization Augmentee (IMA) at a staff meeting at the 375th MAC Headquarters, Scott AFB, IL.)

That is who the 109th is known to be. Aim for keeping up those standards!!!

I am forever grateful for the opportunity to be part of and serve with all of the 109th aeromedical crews. Each and every one of them has exhibited outstanding care, dedication, and commitment to not only help our patients but each other. I am proud to say I was a member of the greatest AE squadron in the USAF. An unbreakable bond. Thank you.

Upon my retirement from the 109th in 1989, I was an Admissions Liaison Officer for the USAF Academy, Colorado Springs, CO. After this, I joined the AFR to be an IMA. I was assigned to Scott AFB, IL, McDill AFB, FL, and Andrews AFB, MD as Chief Nurse/Commander. I retired from Andrews in 1997.

Col Julie Eszlinger Jensen

CHAPTER 8
The Command of Lt Col Darlene (Darcy) Anderson

(Mar 1989 - Jul 1993)

Photo courtesy of Lt Col Darcy Anderson

Education - Bachelor of Science Degree in Nursing, University of Minnesota

Master of Science Degree in Nursing with an Administration and Personnel Supervision Focus, Boston University

Honor Graduate - Flight Nurse Course, Brooks AFB, TX (1970)

<u>President</u> - Association of ANG Nurses (1988-1989)

<u>Chief Nurse</u> - During which time the 109th AEF was awarded the George Schafer Trophy for being the best medical unit in the reserve forces and the Theodore C. Marrs Award for being the best medical unit in the ANG (July 1986-June 1987)

<u>Commander</u> - 109th AES would again, during her last year of command, receive these two significant awards (July 1992-June 1993)

March. Lt Col Julie Eszlinger Jensen turned over command of the 109th AEF to Lt Col Darcy Anderson. (Lt Col Eszlinger Jensen would continue to serve in the Air Force Reserve from 1989 to 1997). Anderson was a nursing instructor at Inver Hills Community College and an on-call disaster nurse for the American Red Cross. She was married to an Executive Officer in a Navy Reserve unit, with two sons ages 8 and 13, at the time of her command.

Lt Col Anderson joined the 109th AEF as an airman basic in 1969 while in a program initiated by the National Guard Bureau to retain nurses while awaiting commission. She served in the 109th AEF/AES for her entire military career.

☆☆☆☆☆

From Lt Col Anderson's command notes:

Being selected as the Commander of the 109th AEF was one of the happiest days of my life. I felt its mission was the best in the Air Force, and I was surrounded by officers and enlisted that I respected and felt were exceptional.

Yet, I knew I faced many challenges:

Our Unit Manning Document was increasing and we continued to have difficulty recruiting nurses and finding training slots for them.

Support from the base, National Guard Bureau and State Staff was lukewarm at best. We were often viewed as the "base stepchild."

We were a large unit with limited full-time help (one full-time enlisted technician for approximately 132 members, with the possibility of adding a temporary officer position).

Extensive and diverse training was required by the aerovac mission. Thirty-six AFTPs (Additional Flying Training Periods), cross-countries, FTXs, and multiple other training activities (MASF, hospital, survival, weapons, air and chemical warfare) and the list goes on. My husband, who was a Lt Commander in the Navy Reserve, frequently expressed amazement regarding the amount of time and commitment that being in the 109th required. He often said, "What happened to the just one weekend a month and fourteen days of annual training? How do you retain anyone?"

I faced a major inspection (Health Services Readiness Inspection) scheduled in five months.

I would be starting my command with a new Chief Nurse, Mobility Officer, OIC of Stan/Eval, OIC of Medical Readiness, First Sergeant and OJT Manager.

I had a new boss, 133rd Director of Operations (DO). How well would we work together? What kind of resource would he be? Basically, he told me that he was "hands-off." He would let me run the unit and I should contact him only if I had real problems that I couldn't solve. I was flattered that he trusted me. Unfortunately, as we rarely met to discuss the unit, he would not get to know me or the strength of the unit. There would come a time during Operation Desert Shield/Storm that I would need his support and respect. It would not be there.

Why then was I still so excited to be starting my command of the 109th? Again, it was the strong positive feelings I had about the members of my unit. With a unit like this and a different style of leadership, I couldn't wait to get started.

I formulated my approach to command:

1. Each member of the unit must understand and <u>value the significance of the AE mission.</u>
2. From the Commander all the way down to the airman basic - it <u>must be reinforced that each member of the unit is making a difference to the success of this mission.</u> "What each member of the unit did – mattered."
3. <u>Improve communication</u> up and down the chain of command.

   - Expand Executive Staff (OICs and NCOICs) to represent more sections within the unit. Staff would meet before each UTA to discuss issues and prepare for the upcoming UTA.
   - Establish and expand unit newsletter (Vital Signs) to be mailed to members' home before UTA. Include section messages, training schedule and social items such as birthdays, team sporting events, etc.
   - Establish Commander's Newcomers Reception. Once a quarter, hold an hour-long reception for all those in the unit less than a year. All Executive Staff will attend and discuss what is working well or poorly with the new unit members. All unit members are invited the last half hour, but the focus is on those new to the unit.

4. *Focus on the strength of the Flight Examiner /Flight Instructors.* What's working, what's not, from equipment to airframes. Special interest items go directly to the Commander.
5. *Recognize and support senior NCOs.* Open door directly to the Commander. As Commander, ask to occasionally attend one of their meetings to hear directly about their concerns, issues and sometimes be on the "hot seat."
6. *Continue strong emphasis on realistic training* in the field (FTX) with the user services and medical training at local hospitals. I have always thought the "check could be cashed" - that at some point this unit would be tasked to do what it was training for. The 109th will be well trained, the best in the field, and feel good about it. That was at the heart of my job as Commander.
7. Continue to promote *involvement with the community* - NDMS, Kaiser Roll, Youth Camp at Fort Ripley, Minnesota Stand Down for Veterans. This is the other side of the National Guard that I think is most valuable. I like the feel - I can serve my state as well as my country.
8. Effective/results-oriented *family and employer support programs.*
   - Appoint Family Assistance Officer and NCOIC.
   - Design Family Unit Deployment Assistance Handbook.
   - Arrange for Family and Employer Flights.

So, I've served nearly two decades with the 109th in various positions, have identified some of the challenges and had a plan for command to meet those challenges that fit my style of leadership.

But my first six months of command would profoundly affect me and require more of myself than I ever thought possible.

Shortly after I accepted the command of the 109th, I was visited by the State Air Surgeon. I thought he was coming to congratulate me and offer his help if needed. I was half right. After congratulating me, he said, "I'm sorry to have to tell you this Col Anderson, but there are many on this base and on State Staff who feel your unit will not exist by this time next year." Sounding urgent, he went on to say, "Your unit is like a revolving door - you can't retain your members and your C-rating is absolutely dismal. Few have hope that this unit will survive."

I was stunned. No, he's wrong, I thought. I remember mumbling something to him about disbelief and the strength of the members of the unit. I said that we were turning this situation around.

I asked myself, what do I do with this information? Do I share it with the unit or Executive Staff? It was so disheartening.

At times it was a very lonely decision, but I decided not to tell the unit about this conversation. I felt that ninety five percent of the people in the 109th were "busting their asses" already - doing much with little support from outside the unit. The current situation was not their fault. What would telling them accomplish?

But there was more "discouragement" to come. The following was a typical UTA during my first six months:

- *A senior officer comments to me about the overall feeling about the aeromeds on base. "Every unit on base does something for our flying mission. The aeromeds do nothing. They expect everyone to support them." I replied that what greater gift is there for a commander on this base to give to his troops than to help ensure that if one of his troops gets injured, we will be there for them. He rolled his eyes and said "Nice try, Col Anderson - but most commanders on this base feel their troops will never get injured."*
- *Another flight nurse commander of an aerovac unit calls me and says, "You're going to have a hell of a time. Many MSC officers think flight nurses should never be commanders. They will sabotage you every chance they get." Possibly, I thought, but I prefer to spend my energy moving this unit forward, rather than defending my back.*
- *Another ranking officer wanting to give advice: "You're the first Commander of your unit to be married, have kids and a full-time job, right? And you have just one full-time technician for over 100 people, right? Yeah - like that's going to work!"*
- *And my monthly calls from other units, which I learned to identify as "you damn aeromeds" calls. "Col Anderson, your damn aeromeds busted my mobility exercise. You guys have some real problems." I explained to him that my mobility officer was brand new, but had much strength - we are learning. And we were learning very fast.*

Growing from negative experiences is much more in tune with this unit's spirit than blaming, overreacting or self-doubt. What an adventure these next few years will be!

The unit members would prove me right. Several years later, on 7 Aug, 1992, that same Air Surgeon (who predicted the unit's demise in one year) would write:

Dear Darcy,

Now that the initial excitement of the ORI's "Excellent" rating is over, I wanted you to know personally how proud I am of your accomplishments and those of your unit. I hear the same comments from everyone around the base - "Those aeromeds sure did a great job!!" - and I agree.

We both know the struggles that you faced just a few years ago. No one could anticipate what has happened since. You have persevered and put up with all kinds of grief and disappointments and your efforts were not in vain. Your leadership makes us all glad that we are in the Minnesota ANG because you are setting an example we would all like to follow.

My congratulations on jobs well done. It is truly an honor to be recognized by your peers as well as those sitting in judgment as having that "something" that pulls a unit together against all odds. You deserve a big "attaboy" and "you done good."

My warm personal regards,

(signed)

State Air Surgeon

☆☆☆☆☆

A closer look at the 109th AEF during Lt Col Anderson's command years:

April. On the 22nd of the month, the 133rd TAW, along with other military units and 21 local hospitals, participated in Response '89, the annual test of the National Disaster Medical System.

In Response '89, the scenario was a massive earthquake that struck northern California, leaving thousands dead or injured and overwhelming the local medical system. California authorities contacted the regional FEMA (Federal Emergency Management Agency), which in turn contacted its National Headquarters in Washington, D.C. HQ FEMA then activated the NDMS. The 72 NDMS sites nationwide, including Minneapolis - St. Paul, reported how many beds they had available. That information was sent to Scott AFB, IL, where the military began coordinating the airlift to get these "injured" people to the beds.

Military aircraft that were supposed to be from California, but were in reality from Chicago and Indianapolis, brought in "patients" who were moulaged to look injured. The patients were triaged and sent to area hospitals.

This year's exercise had several firsts: being the first test of three cities simultaneously (Chicago, Indianapolis and the Twin Cities), and having "relatives" of the victims flown in to simulate the problems of dealing with bereaved and psychologically stressed people.

The 133rd TAW provided two C-130Es and upward of 50 people, 40 of whom were from the 109th AEF. The 133rd aircraft flew to Indianapolis with "patients," who after they arrived, were triaged and then whisked to area hospitals.

Then SSgt "Chip" Childs remembers, "This was my first flight as an aeromed so I was a bit nervous. I was still in student status needing to complete six flights under instruction successfully to earn my wings and qualify as an 'aeromed.' I had completed my medical training late fall of 1988 and had just finished my ground school. Walking out to the aircraft, a fellow aeromed asked me who my instructor was. I replied it was TSgt Liz Howard. He looked at me, shook his head and said, 'You poor SOB, she is one tough instructor.' That didn't help my confidence, but his words were right on the money. TSgt Liz Howard was tough and demanding, but she was also a great mentor and made sure I was more than qualified when I was finally presented my wings."

And, to top it all off, nearly every major Twin Cities media outlet covered the event and Armed Forces Radio/Television sent a film crew aboard one of our Guard planes. SSgt Childs continues: "We had the camera crew on our plane and they filmed our every move. I can't recall all of the medical emergencies we had, but our instructors kept us busy. We had at least one heart attack per flight and on the flight down to Indianapolis, right in the middle of that cardiac arrest we had one of the female 'pregnant patients' go into labor. So, while one nurse and one med tech worked on the heart attack patient, the other nurse, I and the third med tech dealt with the 'unexpected birth.' In all the excitement and desire to impress my instructor, running up and down the aircraft getting the necessary supplies, I practically ran over the cameraman. The flights to Indianapolis and back were a real workout."

According to Edward Lord, NDMS Area Manager, "The exercise was a big success. Planning and executing an exercise of this magnitude was a challenge. It worked and worked well, because everyone, from the Air Guard to the hospitals to the Civil Air Patrol, worked together. We truly demonstrated a community in action."

Capt Dayton Carlson, the Project Officer for the 109th AEF's role in the exercise, agreed. He said, "This was truly a team effort. Our people did a superb job and were able to demonstrate what a first-class unit the 133rd TAW is, in great measure because the other groups involved put the mission first."

"Everyone worked like clockwork," said Lt Col Julie Eszlinger Jensen, former 109th AEF Commander who accompanied one of the Air Guard planes to Indianapolis. "Our people responded with professionalism and enthusiasm. There is no doubt that if the need arose, we would be ready." [72]

☆☆☆☆☆

On 29 April, thirty-eight members deployed to Hahn AB, Germany for a 15-day tour. The members were tasked with not only assisting the medical staff at the base hospital, but with making an inventory, inspection, and operational testing of one-third of the pre-deployed War Readiness Materials (WRM)/MASF supplies/field equipment and assessing its wartime mobility capability.

The 109th AEF was supposed to inventory three MASFs in two weeks. Each MASF kit contained 88 four foot by three foot boxes and six tents. Each tent had to be set up to make certain it was usable. The group accomplished this task in three days and went on to inventory seven more - ALL of the equipment marked for the WRM/MASF - ultimately going through 880 boxes and dozens of tents.

Photo courtesy of Col Michael Germain
Aeromeds checking inventory of War Readiness Materials.

Sgt Dan Johnson, the unit's Safety NCO, tasked with filming the tent inspection portion of the inventory, used as much film capturing the F-16s as they flew overhead as he did documenting the inspection. The deployment also offered unit members plenty of time to enjoy the local scenery with trips on the Rhine, and down the Mosel with its many castles. TSgt Chip Childs remembered, "One evening a number of us took a bus tour to a family owned vinyard situated on a slope above the Mosel River. This family went out of their way to be hospitable and wine samples of their product were frequently offered and just as frequently accepted. To show our appreciation for their kindness we all purchased a number of bottles of their fine wine, some of which was consumed on the return trip. ….. All who went agreed it was a 'very pleasant evening'!"

Maj Norman Hendrickson, Deployment Commander said, "Everybody on that deployment worked like two people. Our people made the most out of every minute of every day, often volunteering to stay late. And, we received outstanding support from the people at Hahn." [73]

Photo courtesy of Col Michael Germain
Tent inventory and checkout (set up and teardown).

August. The AF had such a shortage of nurses that this past February the AF surgeon general said the need for nurses had reached the "wartime critical" stage. Civilian nurses over the age of 35 were now allowed to enter the AF, including the ANG.

As a result, the AF started recruiting older nurses. "This means we can now recruit nurses up to 48 years of age," said Lt Col Susan Barbi, Chief of the Nurse Recruiting Division at Recruiting Service headquarters.

"Anyone over 40, however, must sign a statement of understanding that they are ineligible to retire. They cannot complete 20 years of active duty before the mandatory retirement age of 60," Col Barbi said. She expects an increase in the number of nurses in the 36-40 age group entering the Air Force. In the past, most nurses were 35 or younger when they initially entered the military. "Conceivably we could now see a 46-year-old second lieutenant," said Col Barbi. [74]

November. Thirteen unit members traveled to San Diego, CA for the 96th Annual Conference of the Association of Military Surgeons of the United States. This association included the medical departments of the Army, Navy, AF, United States Public Health Service and the Veterans Administration.

The theme for this year's conference was "Total Quality Management: Strategies for the Federal Health Care System," where several exhibits and programs were offered which were intended to enhance all phases of the federal health services.

Two 109th AEF officers, Lt Col Donna Alt and Maj Norman Hendrickson, gave a presentation for the ANG section entitled "Mobile Aeromedical Staging Facility Continuing Operation Exercises: Lessons Learned." The presentation was well received by the dozens of medical personnel in the audience. All participants felt that the conference offered an excellent training experience. [75]

December. Operation Just Cause was executed in December with the goal of capturing and removing President Manuel Noriega, as well as preserving U.S. interests in Panama. The 109th AEF was notified by the NGB to alert one or more medical evacuation crews for possible deployment in support of Operation Just Cause. The 1st AES MASF was deployed to Howard AB in Panama to stage patients during the short-lived conflict. It was part of the Joint Casualty Collection Point (JCCP) which treated casualties and evacuated 257 military members to Wilford Hall Medical Center and Brooke Army Medical Center in San Antonio, TX. A total of 192 patients were evacuated during the first 24 hours of the operation under the care of AE crews utilizing eight C-141s and one C-130. Tammy Hayes, Mark Latourelle and Todd Highstrom were deployed to Panama for 16 days with seven other aeromeds from different units. They were billeted in housing which was vacated by military families in preparation of the invasion.

The experience gained in the deployment and use of AE crews during this operation would have a major impact on their deployment and roles in Operation Desert Shield/ Desert Storm. Unbeknownst to unit members at this time, this call to active duty would come in less than a year.

☆ ☆ ☆ ☆ ☆

Lt Col Alice Graner retired from the unit this past year. Looking back, Col Julie Eszlinger Jensen remembers, "Because of her live domestic aerovac experience before joining our unit, she was most knowledgeable in all things aerovac and did an outstanding job in teaching our aerovac crews. Everything she was responsible for was ALWAYS done according to regulation—there were no ifs, ands or buts. She served with the Air National Guard Chief Nurses, planned sessions at AMSUS, assisted with the development of a Tri-Service (Army, Navy and Air Force) Annual Conference, worked on special projects with the NGB, planned a very successful Tactical Field Training Exercise and contributed countless hours to formulate and submit the application which successfully earned the George Shaffer and Theodore C. Marrs Awards. Lt Col Graner was promoted to colonel and continued to serve in the AFR as an IMA at Strategic Air Command in Omaha, NE and Scott AFB, IL during Operation Desert Storm."

1990

February. H. T. Johnson, Commander in Chief of the U.S. Transportation Command and MAC, announced that the AF would now permit female front-end crew (pilot, etc.) aircrew members on MAC C-130H aircraft, including ANG aircraft, as well as C-141 airdrop missions and future C-17 aircraft programs.

April. From Lt Col Anderson's command notes:

Many challenging issues continued with manning, FN training slots, and full-time technician support. After all unit commanders met in Washington, D.C., I wrote a letter to the Base Commander and the Director of Operations. Their support and assistance was ever more critical. I needed to draw a line in the sand. Did they want this unit or not? There was an exceptional aerovac unit in their backyard!

12 April 1990

109th AEF/SG Lt Col Darlene A. Anderson

*After Action Report: Aeromedical Evacuation Commander's Meeting
                         (NGB Andrews AFB) 30 Mar 90*

133rd TAW/DO
133rd TAW/CC
<u>*In Turn*</u>

  1. Concept

   All 10 aerovac commanders were unexpectedly requested to attend a meeting at Andrews AFB to deal with a "serious problem": The anticipated improvement in the aerovac units' ability to meet tasking as defined by the Status of Resources and Training System (SORTS) had not been realized, even though the realignment of aerovac assets had occurred over six months ago. Working together it was hoped that the commanders could identify and implement solutions.

  2. Historical Perspective

   Since 1986 when the 109th's Unit Manning Document doubled the size of the unit, we have suffered with a lingering inability to meet our tasking as defined by SORTS. We are known throughout the system for the excellence of our training and the quality of personnel, yet we are continually embarrassed and identified with a poor "C" rating. Many other aerovac units suffer the same fate. This became a special interest item for General Killey and, I am told, the Joint Chiefs of Staff. Without consulting the aerovac commanders, the decision was made in the spring of 1989 to realign the aerovac units, specifically, to move taskings (MASF) to units who had waiting lists and backfill newly created positions in hospitals and clinics.

   I went to Andrews AFB in June of 1989 and informed Col Strate/SG that the lack of flight nurses was driving my SORTS down and the loss of only four empty flight nurse positions in our "reassigned" MASF would not alter my SORTS. I attempted to offer alternative suggestions that I thought would help our SORTS. I was told I "did not understand" and that the issue had been decided.

3. **Meeting Results**

For the first time to anyone's knowledge, all 10 aerovac commanders met and identified and prioritized what we felt were solutions. The attached talking paper summarizes the results. I have highlighted those that particularly impact the 109th.

4. **Major Factors Affecting 109th AEF SORTS**

The full-time technician manning for the 109th is intolerable and is directly responsible for many of our recruiting and retention problems. Currently, I have 132 unit members (96 percent are flyers and on mobility). We average at least three activities (GFTPs - Ground Flying Training Periods and AFTPs - Additional Flying Training Periods) per week outside the UTA. Large numbers are in upgrade training (15-20 persons). Our personnel access over 17 different schools, conferences and seminars yearly. Administrative and operations activity is enormous.

This unit faces a SAV (Staff Assistance Visit) in May, a major field training exercise with the 47th Division in June, a hospital tour to Keesler AFB in August and a major inspection (our Health Services Readiness Inspection) in September. Yet the 109th has only:

- *one full-time enlisted technician, GS (General Schedule) - 5*
- *one temporary, full-time officer who I have no idea if he will be with the unit from week to week, and*
- *one part-time enlisted technician shared with the TAC hospital*

   Note: All aerovac units are currently authorized and funded for three full-time enlisted technicians. (This can be verified with Maj McGuire at NGB, AV 858-8555). When the third authorization came to this base, it was placed elsewhere.

I cannot retain qualified personnel when I cannot support them. On any given day you can see 8-12 persons working an hour here, an hour there trying to make it work for the unit. I am currently witnessing the "burnout" of several excellent flyers. Unfortunately, I know one of them very well.

Base Recruiting is now doing a commendable job recruiting our much-needed flight nurses, but we are unable to get them to required schools in a timely manner. A 2-week Military Indoctrination for Medical Service Officers (MIMSO) followed by the 6-week flight school is a heavy commitment for these professional persons and must be scheduled early with their employers. For well over a year CBPO (Consolidated Base Personnel Office) has refused to schedule our nurses for flight school until they have completed the required MIMSO course. If both could be scheduled at the same time, slots for flight school would still be available. What might have been accomplished in one year is now taking two years! We have addressed this concern with CBPO on several occasions. Lt Col Alt, our Chief Nurse, has spoken with MSgt Linda Dvorak and Maj Moen. They stated NGB told them they could not schedule these schools at the same time. At this commander's meeting I addressed this issue. The NCOIC of Aeromedical Evacuation Training stated this was a "local problem" and the other nine aerovac units were aggressively scheduling their flight nurses for both MIMSO and flight school at the same time. In fact, they recommended it! She further stated that many CBPOs were calling her when requested slots were filled and she would often work to locate additional slots. The nine other commanders concurred with her comments.

5. Recommendations

   a. *An immediate increase in the permanent, full-time technician staff. As we are projected to be over 150 persons by August '90, give the 109th the three full-time positions we were authorized and funded.*

   b. *Fund, as the state of New York (139th AEF) has, one full-time officer position (already authorized) for the 109th AEF.*

   c. *Actively communicate your support to both General Andreotti and General Killey for:*

      - *Four full-time technicians for all aerovac units*
      - *A GS rating for each position that would retain talented, qualified individuals*

   Support in this area from the directors of operations and base commanders could make a significant impact.

   d. *Immediate change in CBPOs posture for scheduling schools for flight nurses. We cannot have nurses sitting in the unit for over a year with no flight school slots.*

   e. *Continued dialogue on and support for our flying program (weekly AFTPs and cross-countries).* <u>*No other aerovac units are*</u> *currently flying "tactical" missions. I have no problems with occasional tactical missions, but safety issues (downtime) and nausea impact negatively on our training. Cross-countries with large cargo and PAX (Passengers) loads also hurt our program. With the large number of newly recruited AECMs (Aeromedical Evacuation Crew Members), I will have a significant number of persons (about 30) to qualify in a timely manner. As the* *number of **qualified** crews drives my SORTS, I feel a real urgency to aggressively work with you to ensure additional **quality** flying time.*

A continued low SORTS rating and a poor evaluation on our upcoming HSRI (Health Services Readiness Inspection) would have significant, negative repercussions, specifically, the loss of federal recognition for the 109th. These recommendations must be aggressively addressed. As Commander of the 109th AEF, I feel what we do in the next six to eight months will determine the fate of this unit.

Darlene A. Anderson, Lt Col, MNANG, NC

Commander

☆☆☆☆☆

Thirty-one members of the unit conducted their annual training at the Wilford Hall Medical Center, Lackland AFB, TX. Capt Julie Gapstur stated, "For the technicians, the active duty rotation is an opportunity to hone their skills allowing them to maintain their skill proficiency rating or gain 'hands-on' assistance should they want to move to a higher skill level." She added, "For the flight nurses, the rotations give them a chance to learn how things are done on active duty bases."

While at Wilford Hall, unit members worked in intensive care, coronary care, trauma and general surgery, neurosurgery and the emergency room. Capt Gapstur pointed out that unit members also "practiced inserting intravenous catheters on mannequins and ultimately on each other. Starting an IV is a tricky procedure. By working with the dummies, we could make mistakes that did not hurt anyone. From there, we practiced on each other, which really helped build trust between people, that's for sure."

Not only did the aeromeds improve their medical skills while in Texas, they pitched in and proved invaluable in helping to relieve some critical staffing shortages. Gapstur stated, "For example, the trauma room was understaffed some of the time we were there. Since our people were integrated into the staffing schedule, they literally became members of the crisis team. The people who worked in the trauma room got to see a little bit of everything. You name it, from car accident victims to heart attack patients, they treated all who came through the door. More than once the presence of our people made the difference." [76]

June. The 109th AEF proved their mettle in a highly realistic combat scenario at Camp Ripley, June 22-26, during the 47th Division's Army Training and Evaluation Program (ARTEP) - the Army's version of an Operational Readiness Inspection.

1st Lt Charles Rodke designed and organized Samaritan IX, the aeromeds' part of the exercise. The focus of Samaritan IX was to deploy the unit to Camp Ripley and set up two Mobile Aeromedical

Staging Facilities on either end of a dirt runway. This was the sixth year of cooperative efforts with the Army.

"We operated the two MASF sites independently to simulate two separate locations," he said. "In conjunction with the Army Guard's 204th Medical Battalion, we ran five evacuation missions over three days, with airlift provided by one aircrew from the 109th Tactical Airlift Squadron (TAS)."

For the first time in nine exercises, the aeromeds also worked at first aid stations with the Army medical personnel of the 204th. These first aid facilities were the first stage of medical treatment provided to those injured in the battlefield.

"It gave us a chance to learn how the Army and Air Guard roles mesh together," said SSgt Marlene Johnson.

When the AE Liaison Team and Control Center planned an evacuation mission, the "wounded" (Army personnel and 109th aeromeds) were sent to an MASF by helicopter or field ambulance.

"Nurses treated the incoming wounded while escorting them throughout the MASF tents," said SSgt Johnson. "Patients were immediately arranged in the tent according to the aircraft load plan with those who could walk to the aircraft first, and then patients on litters."

The goal in MASF treatment was to carry and care for each patient only once to reduce trauma and confusion as well as conserve the medical staff's time and energy.

Aeromeds played diversified roles: marshaling aircraft, performing triage in the field and at the MASF, loading patients on the aircraft, and providing in-flight care.

Some of the injuries were not simulated.

"The Army Guard was in full chemical warfare gear for their training exercise, so we saw people with heat exhaustion, smashed fingers and other minor injuries," explained 1st Lt Rodke. "The Camp Ripley field clinic was overwhelmed with patients, so we had actual wounded coming in with intravenous fluids attached."

A great advantage of the Samaritan IX exercise was top notch training for the 109th AEF's 35-40 new members who had never participated in a field training exercise. "I was very impressed with our new members' willingness to learn and our older members' enthusiasm in a demanding scenario," stated Rodke. Army evaluators were so impressed with the aeromeds in action that they asked if the unit would deploy to exercise with their active duty units.

1st Lt Rodke credited the other 133rd Tactical Airlift Wing units with providing "outstanding support" for the Samaritan IX exercise. He gave special thanks to the people in Mobility Processing, Maintenance, Operations, and Intelligence.

"We couldn't have assisted the 47th Division in this exercise without their team effort," he said. [77]

Photo courtesy of TSgt Richard Childs

Litter bearers of the 109th AEF "hot load" simulated wounded onto a 133rd TAW C-130E for an evacuation mission.

With the deteriorating situation in the Middle East, it proved a very timely exercise.

☆☆☆☆☆

Lt Col Robert Brannon made a special trip to brief the unit on his experiences as Commander of the Field Hospital in Panama during recently completed Operation Just Cause. He stated that it was a "stark 'wake-up call' for the need to increase the coordination between the field hospital and air evacuation. There were some hard lessons to be learned. For example, time after time aircraft flew in men and supplies and were then reconfigured for aerovac, but they brought in no evacuation crews with them. As a result, they continued to siphon off needed staff personnel from my field hospitals." Lt Col Brannon would later apply the lessons learned as Commander of all AE crews in the theatre of operations during Operation Desert Shield/Desert Storm. Less than 60 days later, the Guard Bureau would call with a request for volunteers to depart within 12 hours for deployment in support of Operation Desert Shield.

July. The Health Services Readiness Inspection was scheduled during the September UTA.

☆☆☆☆☆

Lt Don Dahlquist and SSgt Micki King participated in the Internal Look Exercise in Florida.

August. On the morning of August 2nd, the world awoke to the news that the Iraqi dictator, Saddam Hussein had ordered six divisions of his elite Republican Guard to cross the Iraq-Kuwait border. Within four hours his forces were on the outskirts of Kuwait City, that nation's capital. By 10:00 a.m, Iraq had completed its occupation of that tiny emirate. Saddam then began to move his forces to the Kuwait/Saudi Arabian border.

The UN was quick to respond, condemning the action and calling for a cease-fire and an unconditional withdrawal of Iraqi troops from Kuwait. Saddam ignored these demands and continued to mass his army along the Saudi border.

On August 6th, King Fahd of Saudi Arabia invited U.S. Forces to his country to bolster its defenses. President George H.W. Bush dispatched 40,000 American troops to the kingdom.

Watching these events unfold, most members of the 109th AEF had no idea the impact this decision would have on their futures. They began to get a hint when MSgt Mark Grieme began calling unit members asking them in very official language if "they would be willing to deploy to an undisclosed location for an undetermined length of time?"

On Fri, Aug 10, a tasking message was received from Military Airlift Command for 12 AE teams, each with five people, plus a liaison team of three aeromeds. 109th AEF was to provide four of the teams, but the tasking message had not been cleared through NGB and was cancelled.

As predicted, on the 19th of August, the Guard Bureau called with a request for volunteers to depart within 12 hours for deployment in support of Operation Desert Shield. Maj Claudia Hernandez, Capt Michael Germain, Capt Tammy Hayes, 1st Lt Linnea Anderson, MSgt Gerald Blilie, and SSgt Eugene Conrad departed the base at 0430 the next day. Realizing that this was just the first call of many, Lt Col Darcy Anderson, 109th AEF Commander, made the decision to prepare the unit personnel for deployment. It proved a sound decision because by the end of September, a number of unit members had deployed in support of Operation Desert Shield. Although most were sent to the area of responsibility (AOR), other members were deployed to Germany to fill support positions.

☆☆☆☆☆

From Lt Col Anderson's command notes:

"The check is being cashed". It starts here. In all the hustle and decisions being made, I was struck by the thought that I might not see these friends again.

Had I done all that I could - to prepare them to excel at their job and survive? Possibly, right now, every aerovac commander in the country was asking themselves the same question.

☆☆☆☆☆

The 109th AEF was sometimes looked upon and often treated as the base "stepchild" in the 133rd TAW, but it transformed into Cinderella when it was the first unit within the wing to have been requested to send members overseas in support of Operation Desert Shield.

As the UTA was wrapping up for most of the 133rd Tactical Airlift Wing units, the 109th AEF was preparing an aeromed team of four nurses and two med techs to deploy on a C-130 coming from an ANG base in another state.

Capt Sharon Rosburg, Base Mobility Officer, set up a mobility processing line in the 109th AEF building. Special protection gear, including safety goggles, canteens, sunblock, face wraps, first aid kits, chemical agent detection paper, and ponchos were distributed to the six deploying aeromeds.

Col John Silliman, Jr., Deputy Commander for Operations, said, "I was amazed at how fast the aeromeds' personal equipment was squared away."

Maj Patricia May, 133rd Services Flight Commander, remarked on the emotional well-being of the aeromeds, "They were serious about going through the mobility line, but there were jokes about the MREs (Meals Ready to Eat), like 'Are these for ammunition or eating?'"

Over in the 133rd Medical Squadron (MDS), aeromeds received antimalarial medication and gamma globulin immunizations for prevention of insect and foodborne illnesses.

Capt Sandy Darula, 109th AEF Administrator, reported, "The base has just been great, you couldn't get any better support than we've had today. It's been phenomenal."

109th AEF Mobility Officer, 1st Lt Donald Dahlquist, said the recent Operational Readiness Inspection in March and field training exercise with the Army National Guard's 47th Division at Camp Ripley in June helped in the unit's readiness to respond quickly.

At 0630 on August 20, the six aeromeds departed on a C-130 for an undisclosed destination in support of Desert Shield operations, taking with them the support and good wishes of their families and fellow Guard members.

An additional tasking came from NGB on Wednesday, August 29 for five nurses, ten med techs, two radio operators and one Medical Service Corps officer to deploy for approximately 30 days. [78]

On Friday, August 31, a California ANG C-130 took off at 1642 carrying 18 members of the 109th AEF, as well as aeromeds from two other states en route to Dover AFB, DE on the first leg of their deployment overseas. [79]

Photo courtesy of Lt Col Darcy Anderson
(L - R): Capt Tammy Hayes, 1st Lt Linnea Anderson, Maj Claudia Hernandez In Dhahran, Saudi Arabia.

Initially, some aircrew members were billeted at the Riyadh Intercontinental Hotel and other hotels throughout the capital city due to the rapid influx of US military and the lack of available space to house them.

The United States coalition forces looked for a site that could be used as a temporary base for its Soldiers during the first days of Operation Desert Shield. Fortunately, the government of Saudi Arabia offered the village of Eskan as the perfect site for the coalition forces to set up camp. The housing area known only as "Eskan Village" was located some 20 kilometers south of Riyadh AB in Saudi Arabia. Built during 1983, the housing complex, composed of 44 high rise towers and 841 villas or housing units, was originally intended to house the various Bedouin tribes who lived in the desert. Unfortunately, the tribes decided never to occupy Eskan and chose to maintain their desert living lifestyle, leaving the housing complex unoccupied and free to be used by the United States Military forces as permitted by the Saudi Arabian government. [80]

Among the first to move into the new site, Col Germain recalls, "The housing units had sat vacant for a number of years. No furniture, air conditioning, or running water was the norm. Floors were thick with sand and dirt. It took a lot of effort to clean up and move into the villas. Eventually, services improved and subsequent deployers found them quite livable."

Photo courtesy of Lt Col Darcy Anderson
One of the villa housing units in Eskan Village, Saudi Arabia.

September. Initiation of the stop-loss program became necessary, in which separations, discharges, and retirements of nurses during Operation Desert Shield (and later Operation Desert Storm) were frozen. [81]

☆☆☆☆☆

On 5 Sep, the unit was notified that the HSRI had been temporarily postponed.

☆☆☆☆☆

In this month's Vital Signs, Lt Col Anderson mentioned that she was told to expect additional taskings every 30-40 days as aerovac units would be rotated in and out of the theater of operations.

She said that many unit personnel worked 18 to 20 hours a day to ensure our people were prepared and equipped. A special thanks in this effort went to Capt Dahlquist, Capt Rodke, Capt Darula, 2d Lt Ed Howard, TSgt Liz Howard, TSgt O'Keefe, and MSgt Hughes who made it work.

TSgt Childs recalls, "Just about every member in the unit was required to get the mandated immunizations for deployment overseas. We trooped over to the Medical Squadron and were told to form a line outside one of the heads, the site chosen for the inoculations. The line stretched the length of the hall. We were given two big doses, one per cheek in our derrieres. Most of us finished the drill day standing at our work stations. Sitting down didn't have much of an appeal."

Photo courtesy of the 109th AES archives
Deployment bags (in old Aeromed building) ready to be loaded for 109th AEF personnel heading overseas.

With 28 key individuals deployed, many of the staff positions in Aircrew Training, QA (Quality Assurance), Operations, and Medical Readiness were left vacant. To compound the problem, new med techs were returning from school and there were 21 new nurses to qualify.

☆☆☆☆☆

From Lt Col Anderson's command notes:

It was a strange feeling watching so many mothers, with each deployment, saying goodbye to their children. What are we doing for the families? The media (TV, papers, etc.) is so "front line" and has brought the conflict right into each deployed Airmen's family living room. I worry about the children, seeing this. So many concerns. "Is that my Mom?" and "Will she be coming home soon?"

Getting calls from unit members in Flight Nurse School in Texas. They say "rumors are that they will go straight to the Middle East. Families worried. Please advise."

Communication from NGB and the Middle East concerning unit members was unhelpful and rare. Parents are calling about hearing from their sons or daughters that they are sick with diarrhea, in tented hospitals and getting IVs. They want more information.

Radio operators deployed with special customized pallet, now separated from their pallet. NGB no help in trying to match these up again. So sad - all the work the unit members had done to go to war with the right stuff. I am getting angry and disheartened.

Calls from NGB, theater of operations threatening to send our unit members back, due to lack of aircrew chemical warfare gear. This bothers me greatly - I tried without success to find some, but the base said they had no such gear. What commander wants to send their unit to war without all of the right equipment? This equipment issue continued to be a problem for many guard units. It got to the point that when unit members returned from their rotations, their gear was taken from them at Dover to give to the next group of deploying aeromeds from other units.

☆☆☆☆☆

Several remaining home station personnel were reassigned positions in the unit in order to carry on normal day-to-day operations. When Maj Hendrickson was moved to the OIC of Aircrew Training, MSgt Latourelle commented, "Now that's desperate!" [82]

TSgt Childs, deployed in September remembers, "I had raised my hand the month previously when our Commander asked all unit members for volunteers who would be willing to deploy on short notice if called. A list was compiled. Over the course of the month and into September, as the situation in Kuwait and Saudi Arabia intensified, the Guard Bureau made a number of requests for small numbers of unit members for deployment. I was not one of those asked to deploy. The situation was tense, but not hectic. I then left town on a scheduled week long family vacation.

"I returned home to find a phone message informing me I had been 'volunteered' for active duty and was being deployed. I was actually listed to go on an earlier rotation, but as the unit was unable to contact me, they just rotated my name to the next call up. When I called the unit to report in, Major Rodke wanted to know 'where the hell I had been.' Things were getting serious.

"Amid the hustle and bustle of getting the kids ready for school, I also had to spend a couple of days on base securing my gear and completing my outgoing checklist for deployment. My group left Minneapolis on a Saturday. After an emotional family goodbye, I boarded a C-130 and we headed for Dover AFB, MD. We had no sooner landed at Dover when we were whisked out to a waiting C-5 Galaxy. This was the largest aircraft in the U.S. inventory, capable of carrying huge loads of material. This plane fit that description to a T. After climbing a short ladder into the front of the plane, we made our way down a narrow walkway to the rear of the aircraft where another ladder took us to an upper deck and our seating. The walkway was fairly narrow, barely eighteen inches wide. Some of the bigger folks had to shuffle sideways to make their way to the rear. What impressed us was the degree to which this plane was loaded. The entire cargo area was packed from floor to overhead. I found myself thinking, 'I don't believe this plane can get off the ground with this much weight on board.' Those thoughts were bolstered when the plane started to taxi. Every time it made a turn the wheels squealed so loudly I thought the tires were going to jump off the rims. During the takeoff, it felt as if we were just crawling down the runway. I was certain we were never going to get up enough speed to get off the ground, but we did and eight hours later we landed in Germany. The first leg of our trip to Saudi Arabia was behind us. After a layover to check and refuel the plane and a chance to go through the chow line, we were off again. Destination Riyadh, Saudi Arabia."

October. Fear of a chemical attack, culture shock and gratitude from Kuwaiti citizens were among experiences shared by four members of the 109th AEF as they returned from service in the Persian Gulf during a recent press conference.

"For me, gas was the biggest fear," MSgt Gerald Blilie said about the 30 days he and five other members of the 109th AEF served in Saudi Arabia. Blilie and others assisted in the evacuation of 371 American servicemen injured in Saudi Arabia. He said heat casualties and orthopedic injuries topped the list.

According to Blilie, the group had chemical warfare training with their unit, but received additional training in Germany and again in Saudi Arabia, where they were required to keep their chemical protective gear at hand.

He recalled how people who had fled from Kuwait "ran up and grabbed my hand and said they were glad we were here," an experience echoed by others at the news conference.

Maj Claudia Hernandez described how she experienced the diverse Islamic culture that required her to wear an abaya, a long black robe worn by Muslim women, when she left her quarters, and how men and women were separated in most social situations.

Capt Germain recalled listening to "Baghdad Bertha" at night on the radio, the Iraqi propaganda counterpart to Tokyo Rose of World War II and Hanoi Hannah of Vietnam. He said the propagandist "was good entertainment and very comical." [83]

Photo courtesy of the St Paul Pioneer Press, 4 Oct 1990
(L - R): MSgt Gerald Blilie, Capt Michael Germain, Maj Claudia Hernandez, SSgt Eugene Conrad answer questions during a news conference in Minneapolis, MN.

On Saturday, October 13, members from the 133rd TAW and the 109th AEF hosted a National Disaster Medical System exercise at the base. About 400 people from eleven local hospitals, the American Red Cross, Civil Air Patrol, and Army and Navy Reserve medical units cooperated in the treatment and transport of simulated casualties.

"The exercise scenario was a catastrophic earthquake which was projected to occur along the New Madrid fault line in Marktree, Arkansas later this year," said Mr. Ed Lord, NDMS Regional Director based at the VA Hospital.

About 50 patients from the Civil Air Patrol, Army Reserve and new Marine recruits were "moulaged" before the exercise began at 0800. Then at 0900, 11 aeromeds directed the loading, simulated flight, and offloading of the 50 patients from a C-130E. Triage of the wounded was conducted in the Air Guard's South Hanger where patients were organized by degree of injury. The Security Police directed civilian ambulances to the South Hangar to pick up the patients who were tagged for their specific destination. Computers were used to track where each patient was taken; 75 volunteer ham radio operators provided communication with ambulances to reroute them if necessary.

"We were testing how fast and safely the civilian and military personnel could work together to quickly treat and transport patients to medical facilities," said MSgt James Hughes who, with Capt Julie Gapstur, coordinated the exercise for the aeromeds. "Wounded patients require medical care and observation through the entire process in case of heart or respiratory failure or shock."

Minnesota NDMS teams have prepared for this type of medical response to a disaster since 1987. This exercise was planned for a year and a half and would have included flying patients from Memphis, Tennessee, but the use of C-130E aircraft was denied by the National Guard Bureau at the last minute due to Operation Desert Shield demands.

109th AEF aeromeds participating in the NDMS exercise included: Capt Julie Gapstur, MSgt James Hughes, 1st Lt Karel Stibitz, MSgt Gerald Blilie, TSgt Elizabeth Howard, TSgt Owen Seeley, SSgt Steve Sitta, SSgt Michelle Torkelson, SSgt Debra Pursley, SSgt Mark Nygaard, and A1C Darren Damiani.

Local hospitals included: St. Paul Ramsey Medical Center, Hennepin County Medical Center, University of Minnesota, Veterans Administration, Methodist, Mount Sinai, Abbott Northwestern, Divine Redeemer, Fairview Southdale, Midway, and St. Francis in Shakopee. [84]

☆☆☆☆☆

Over the past 30 days, the 109th AEF received additional tasking messages from the National Guard Bureau until a total of 51 aeromeds deployed overseas. Over the last three weeks of September, 27 aeromeds left the Twin Cities while four members returned from the Middle East on September 24. Fifteen additional aeromeds returned home the first week of this month.

According to Capt Donald Dahlquist, 32 aeromeds were still deployed overseas at this time. "On a whole, we're getting invaluable real-time experience, airlifting live patients," said Capt Dahlquist, who returned from overseas duty on October 2. "It's not a situation that anyone wants to be placed in - a potential 'hot spot' - but we wouldn't find this kind of real-world AE work anywhere else. We're dealing with aircraft and patient problems, coordinating and tracking airlift movement from Europe to the Middle East."

Capt Dahlquist worked in an AE control element for 32 days, controlling the airlift movement of Air Guard aircraft transporting aeromeds and patients.

Photo courtesy of Lt Col Darcy Anderson
Aeromeds at Al Bateen AB just outside of Abu Dhabi, United Arab Emirates in front of their sandbagged quarters.

(L - R): SSgt Richard Childs, 1st Lt Linnea Anderson, TSgt Owen Seeley

Lt Col Darcy Anderson returned from a meeting at the NGB in Washington, D.C. to report that replacements for deployed aeromeds will continue to be attempted on a voluntary basis for a couple more months.

"We expect to have more people rotating in and out as we have been the last two months," said Lt Col Anderson. [85]

☆☆☆☆☆

MSgt Thomas Stangl was named the new Outstanding Senior NCO of the Year.

November. From Lt Col Anderson's command notes:

After I returned from my own deployment to Germany and the Middle East, I planned to focus on deployed unit members' families and employers.

Deployed aerovac command structure in Operation Desert Shield for the National Guard was a series of confusion and conflicts that soon became filled with "bullying, deliberate misinformation, and favoritism."

Aerovac units competed with one another for supplies and command of different elements. Rumors and misinformation concerning commanders, units, and MSC officers were widely spread and used effectively to reposition leadership.

Photo courtesy of Lt Col Darcy Anderson

Aeromeds returning from the Middle East via Germany with a stop in Keflavik, Iceland. (L - R): Richard Childs, Sandy Darula, (unidentified), Darcy Anderson, Tom O'Keefe

December. The rotation of aeromed volunteers continued for five months involving a total of 71 individual activations. Finally, on 11 December, 1990, the voluntary deployment rotations were discontinued and partial mobilization for active duty began. [86]

☆☆☆☆☆

In a surprise move, Bob Hope traveled to the Middle East and brought laughter and Christmas cheer to troops participating in Operation Desert Shield in Saudi Arabia and Bahrain. The 87-year-old comedian has appeared at Christmas shows for American troops overseas since 1941.

Mr. Hope had to censor his materials heavily while in Saudi Arabia and was forced to leave a number of women out of the show, including the performers Ann Jillian, Marie Osmond and the Pointer Sisters. One exception was made. His wife, Dolores, was allowed to appear on Christmas Eve to sing "White Christmas" to the troops.

Mr. Hope made a European tour in May and vowed at that time it would be his last overseas tour. "I said this definitely is my final trip, this is my final tour," he stated. "But then up popped madman," he said, referring to President Saddam Hussein of Iraq. "I finally said, we have to go again." He added: "The feeling of the entire country is the same. This is our blood and guts over here and this is the day of all days, Christmas." [87]

Col Germain remembers, "We had just completed our aerovac mission in Saudi Arabia and saw Bob Hope's caricature painted on the nose of his aircraft which was parked on the ramp. We missed the show the night before as we were based in the United Arab Emirates (UAE), but wandered over and as he was leaving, I was able to take his picture, shake his hand and thank him for his support of our troops."

Photo courtesy of Col Michael Germain

Bob Hope as he was leaving the morning after one of his Christmas shows.

1991

January. From Lt Col Anderson's command notes:

Reports from the field indicated that members from the 109th were doing exceptionally well. I expected nothing different, but it gave me such joy.

As Operation Desert Shield turned to Operation Desert Storm, I decided to arrange for me to be designated as the Casualty Notification Officer for my unit. I could not tolerate the idea of a stranger walking up to the door of a family with bad news. This is one of the toughest letters I have ever written. The thought of losing a member of my unit was heartbreaking.

Below is the letter from Lt Col Anderson requesting assignment as Casualty Notification Officer:

Subject: Casualty Assistance/Notification of Death or Injury

To: 133rd DP

1. Per our conversation today, I would like to be officially designated as the Casualty Notification Officer for the 109th AEF. In the event of my deployment, I request that our Family Assistance Officer, Lt Edward Howard assume that role.

2. I have spoken with Col Lynch, the Regional Casualty Assistance Officer and in the event of a unit member's death he has agreed to accompany me and access the family to the Casualty Assistance Program.

3. I pray daily that this activity will not be necessary. However, I care deeply about members of the 109th and their families. If the news comes, I don't want them to hear it from a stranger.

Darlene A. Anderson, Lt Col, MNANG, NC
Commander

After five months of voluntary deployment rotations for Operation Desert Shield, 29 members of the 109th AEF were activated for six months duty in the Middle East.

The activation message arrived the week before Christmas. On January 2, five aeromeds departed on a commercial flight for Rhein Main AB, Germany; nine more left on a military aircraft with two pallets of equipment on January 8; and a final three aeromeds left the Twin Cities on January

17. Twelve of the activated aeromeds were already in theater, having deployed in November or December to the Persian Gulf to serve through the Christmas holidays.

"We asked for volunteers for activation, as directed by Col Broman," said Lt Col Darcy Anderson, 109th AEF Commander. "We met 85% of our initial tasking with volunteers and the remaining slots were filled by random selection. Some flight nurse and medical tech examiners were held back to qualify our people returning from schools."

Over 20 new flight nurses plus new med techs were being trained in the 109th AEF.

An MSC officer being activated said, "We're ready to go, thanks to the support of people from Supply, Resources, Mobility, Disaster Preparedness, Personnel and others all across the base. People jumped through wickets to get us ready to go and to make sure everything worked."

Besides flight nurses and med techs, MSC officers and radio operators were being activated for Aeromedical Evacuation Liaison Teams (AELT) to coordinate airlift between aircraft and Army, Navy, and Marine units requiring air evacuation of troops.

Referring to the January 15 deadline for Iraq withdrawal from Kuwait, the MSC officer said, "Hopefully, they'll come up with a long-lasting diplomatic solution, but if they can't, we're ready to do our job." [88]

And ready they were.

On January 16, Operation Desert Shield became Operation Desert Storm and the Allied forces took the offensive to liberate Kuwait. The war lasted 100 hours. Although the Iraqi army was almost totally destroyed, Allied casualties were surprisingly light. Most unit members had returned home by the end of April, some remained in Saudi Arabia until the middle of June to assist with the takedown, packing and return to the U.S. of the tons of Allied equipment sent into the AOR for the war.

Photo courtesy of TSgt Richard Childs
Desert living conditions for aerovac crews flying out of Thumrait, Oman.

On January 25th, thirty members of the 109th AEF deployed in support of Operation Desert Storm. Many of the aeromeds had previously deployed to Saudi Arabia and other adjoining countries for Operation Desert Shield. This time, they were sent to RAF Croughton, England in the Northern Aerovac Command. Lt Col Donna Alt served as Troop Commander for the deployment.

Approximately 300 aeromeds, from both ANG and AFR units across the nation, were sent to England. The mission was to evacuate patients from the Aeromedical Staging Facility in England to medical facilities in the United States. The anticipated onload was 72 litter and 8 ambulatory patients per aerovac mission with a total of six missions per day.

Fortunately, due to the abbreviated war and minimal number of U.S. casualties, these missions did not materialize.

The base at RAF Croughton was home for all 300 aeromeds deployed to England. This facility had been closed and, in reopening, it had been set up quickly. Deployed aeromeds had to augment the basic living conditions by purchasing bed linens and supplies off the local economy. This base served the billeting and messing functions while deployed in England. Crews were bussed a short distance back and forth to RAF Upper Heyford where all training and flying duties occurred.

Photo courtesy of Lt Col Donna Alt

Aeromedical Staging Facility in an aircraft hangar at RAF Upper Heyford, England.

The aeromeds did get the opportunity to train for aerovac missions in C-141s, requiring time both in the classroom and in the aircraft. Four missions were flown during the five weeks of deployment, with onloads of 45 to 80 patients. The few that were able to fly were able to get checkrides and became qualified in the C-141.

TSgt Arlene Brady summed up the experience this way, "It was reassuring to see tactical medevac C-130 crews and strategic medevac C-141 crews working effectively together to ensure the safety and well-being of our patients."

Even though the aeromeds were kept on constant alert status, they had ample time to get off base and see some of the sites in England. [89]

Photo courtesy of the Northstar Guardian (Apr '91)
109th AEF aeromeds evacuate Desert Storm patients from RAF Upper Heyford, England to medical facilities in the U.S. aboard a C-141 aircraft.

February. The Northstar Guardian noted that the 109th AEF continued to carry the heaviest load within our wing in support of Operation Desert Storm.

☆☆☆☆☆

From Lt Col Anderson's command notes:

I watched as each unit member came home. Were they the same? I was not, nor was my family.

- *My sons felt I was moody, distracted.*
- *My oldest son (age 13) was angry with me. He said I didn't care that he was so scared every day that I would die, and there was nothing he could do to save his own Mom.*

Each of us has our own stories and lives to reclaim, while we search for normal. Is it possible and how do I help them? It's not over…

Photo courtesy of Lt Col Darcy Anderson
(L - R): 1st Lt John Wyland, Maj Joe Jensen, Capt Sue Clark deployed in the AOR.

A yellow banner was flown from the 109th AEF building during the drill weekend. 2d Lt Edward Howard, the unit Family Assistance Officer, purchased the flag after several unit members asked if there was some way they could display their support for aeromeds (and all the U.S. service men and women) on active duty overseas.

The yellow flag and numerous yellow ribbons around the building were a visible reminder that unit members were thinking about those deployed.

As Commander, Lt Col Darcy Anderson said, "It's heartwarming to see the ways our members are thinking of each other, like the flag, and the yellow ribbons. Another thing we all agreed on; to wear the BDU (Battle Dress Uniform) uniform for as long as any of our members are on active duty. We are all 'deployed' until the last person who is deployed comes home." [90]

★★★★★

Lt Col Anderson was selected to be a guest speaker at the Department of Veterans Affairs Conference in Northport, New York on "Interventions in Traumatic Stress" with the focus on "Difference Between Vietnam and Persian Gulf Wars With Implications for Combat Stress, Readjustment, and PTSD (Post-Traumatic Stress Disorder)."

★★★★★

While many units took pride in having one honor graduate in their midst, the 109th AEF found that honor graduates had become the rule rather than the exception.

Of the unit's last nine recruits: seven came back after achieving 90 percent or better in their rigorous 14-week Air Force Technical Training School (Tech School) at Sheppard AFB, TX. Four of the new aeromeds were cited as outstanding or honor graduates: A1C Darren Damiani, A1C Brent Kapfer, A1C John Vandevoort, Jr. and Amn Donald Nosbisch.

What made these accomplishments all the more remarkable was the fact that these Airmen followed up Tech School by flying to bases across the country to complete an additional 8-weeks of clinical training. They were stationed at March AFB, CA, Andrews AFB, MD, Carswell AFB, TX and Wilford Hall Medical Center at Lackland AFB, TX.

Since this was a critical time when the need for qualified AE personnel was becoming acute in the Middle East theater of operations, these new members were enthusiastically welcomed by their fellow aeromeds. [91]

March. On March 10, 30 members of the 109th AEF returned home on board four Minnesota C-130Es which were returning from a two-week mission at RAF Mildenhall, England. Members and friends of the Twin Cities Chapter of the Vietnam Veterans of America were on hand with flags and signs to greet them as they deplaned from the C-130Es. Many of the Vietnam vets never had a proper welcome home, they said, and they wanted today's military to have a more joyful homecoming. [92]

Photo courtesy of Col Verne Burque and Northstar Guardian (Apr '91)

A welcoming party of family members, wing officers, media and many others streamed out to meet the first of four C-130Es returning from RAF Mildenhall, England.

Photo courtesy of TSgt Charles Mayer, Northstar Guardian (Apr '91)

Lt Col Darcy Anderson, 109th AEF Commander, is interviewed by WCCO-TV reporter Bill Hudson about her feelings as 30 members of her unit return early from what was expected to be a one-year active duty tour.

Later that month, the 109th AEF was honored as they marched in the St. Patrick's Day Parade in Minneapolis, and had a float in the annual Minneapolis Aquatennial Parade that summer.

Photo courtesy of MSgt Robert Janssen, 109th AEF, Northstar Guardian (Apr '91)
Leading the 109th AEF contingent in the St. Patrick's Day parade in downtown Minneapolis.

(L - R): SSgt Daniel Johnson, SSgt Christine Davidson, SSgt Debra Corrigan, and TSgt Eugene Doven

<u>**April.**</u> Most unit members were back at the base by the April UTA. SrA Kjellander and SSgt Edwards volunteered to extend for another 4-6 weeks in the AOR.

☆☆☆☆☆

Numerous findings were noted when looking back on both Operation Desert Shield and Operation Desert Storm. Ground UTCs were critical in the deployment and orchestration of the entire AE system. They consisted of 19 AELTs, 12 MASFs, and a number of command and control and support elements that stood up as part of the 1,950 AE personnel deployed. At that time almost 97% of the system consisted of air reserve component personnel who were essential to the plan, which spanned bases from Southwest Asia to CONUS. Ninety-nine tactical crews were assigned with AE dedicated C-130s in the Persian Gulf, and 46 strategic crews were assigned the mission of returning patients to Europe and CONUS on C-141 aircraft which were either dedicated or retrograde missions. Fortunately, the war lasted six days, not the anticipated six weeks and the projection of up to 15,000 American injuries during the initial invasion did not materialize. Most of the evacuations consisted of disease and non-battle injuries.

The NGB issued the following statistics on ANG participation in Operation Desert Shield/Operation Desert Storm:

Voluntary Deployers (Title 10 USC 672d)

    a. 87 ANG units participated
    b. Peak participation was on 23 Aug '90 when 4,036 volunteers were in active service
    c. Over 10,000 ANG members served on a cumulative voluntary basis

Involuntary Deployers (Partial Mobilization/Title 10 USC 673)

    a. 121 ANG units were partially mobilized
    b. Peak participation was on 12 Mar '91 when 11,365 were mobilized

While significant for the largest historical AE deployment and number of patients evacuated to that point (12,632 on 671 flights with no deaths in-flight), Operation Desert Storm highlighted some important AE challenges. Some of them included the fact that the Guard and Reserve had serious deficiencies in protective equipment such as Kevlar, the necessity of contingency operation training for the ground UTCs, and that the system needed a better patient regulation process.

The performance and contributions of the National Guard and Reserves in Desert Storm was one of the factors that contributed to the Allied victory, the Secretary of Defense and other military leaders said in assessing the war.

At the height of Desert Storm, reservists, including members of the National Guard, made up nearly a fifth of the forces deployed to the Middle East. More than 227,000 reservists supported the war effort in the Persian Gulf, and from bases around the world.

"Reserve Soldiers, Sailors, Airmen and Marines, as well as the Coast Guard Reserve helped create the total force our victory relied upon," Secretary of Defense Dick Cheney told the National Committee for Employer Support of the Guard and Reserve conference in St. Louis in April.

"These reservists served in battle and helped provide the combat service and support," Secretary Cheney said. "Reservists drove tanks, flew planes and helicopters, and helped plan and carry out amazing feats of logistics."

President George Bush told Congress and the nation last month that "This victory belongs to the regulars, to the reserves, to the National Guard. This victory belongs to the finest fighting force this nation has ever known in its history."

In testimony to the Congress, Army Gen Colin Powell, Chairman of the Joint Chiefs of Staff, described the contributions of guard and reserve components to Desert Storm as "magnificent."

Stephen M. Duncan, Assistant Secretary of Defense for Reserve Affairs, told Congress in April, "It is important to note that even before the armed conflict began, various combat units from the Selected Reserve were called to duty along with a wide range of support units from each of the services."

In addition, more than 11,000 reservists had volunteered for active duty by the end of August last year. "As soon as the decision was made to deploy forces to Southwest Asia, volunteers from the air reserve forces responded immediately to perform vital strategic airlift and tanker support missions with C-5, C-141, C-130 and KC-135 aircraft," Mr. Duncan said. "In August, 1990 alone, ANG and AFR volunteers flew 42 percent of the strategic airlift missions and 33 percent of the aerial refueling missions."

Moreover, by the time that Operation Desert Storm began on January 16, more than 188,000 people and 375,000 tons of equipment had been airlifted by the reserves to Saudi Arabia.

"Each and every one of them volunteered to put on the uniform, to go in harm's way if necessary on behalf of their country," Secretary Cheney said. "We've seen the sacrifice which this service required over the last six months, as our people left their homes and families to serve half a world away." [93]

As far as the participation of the 109th AEF in Operation Desert Shield/Storm went, the aeromeds were not only the first unit within the 133rd tasked with sending members overseas, they were more involved in this set of deployments than any other Minnesota ANG unit. The squadron had a total of 86 members (28 officers and 58 enlisted) serve in 145 slots via 13 levies during the crisis, with 39 members involved in one rotation, 35 members in two and 12 members serving three separate rotations. [94]

☆☆☆☆☆

On 12 April, Gen Kazek, Col Broman, Lt Col Anderson and 20 AECMs from the 109th AEF went on a cross-country to Brooks AFB, TX to celebrate with 11 new graduates from Flight

Nurse School: Capt Julie Finn, Capt Mary Sullivan, Capt Lynette Munsterman, 1st Lt Judine Lockridge, 2d Lt Colette Bornhofen, 2d Lt Susan Carmody, 2d Lt Georgeanne Johnson, 2d Lt Barbara Anderson, 2d Lt Sandra Bushey, 2d Lt Lorraine Emahiser, 2d Lt Theresa Matus.

☆ ☆ ☆ ☆ ☆

The April UTA also saw construction underway for a new entrance and gatehouse for entry into our base.

May. Lt Col Anderson asked for volunteers for a "first out crew" - individuals who could deploy for CONUS (Continental United States) or OCONUS (Outside Continental United States) contingencies on short notice. This was in response to a request by the National Guard Bureau for AE units to compile a list of volunteers for 90-day rotations to European Command (EUCOM), Turkey, and/or the AOR.

Photo courtesy of the 109th AES archives

This was a traveling tribute to those Minnesotans who served in Desert Shield/Desert Storm. The American Flag was made up of red, white and blue hearts. Each heart was adorned with the name of a veteran.

July. Cloudy skies and cool temperatures set the tone for the 10th annual Kaiser Roll held at Normandale Community College. The internationally recognized track event attracted nearly 6,000 entrants this year in a variety of categories for wheelchair, blind, and able-bodied competitors of all ages.

Sixteen members of the 109th AEF provided medical coverage at the race, as they have for the last nine of ten years, volunteering their time and expertise in medical support for the participants and spectators.

"Everyone benefits from this arrangement," said MSgt Gerald Blilie, a 109th AEF med tech. "We get good hands-on experience in treating the various injuries that are common with this type of event, and the race organizers know we come trained and equipped to handle any situation from handing out Band-Aids to administering basic life support to heart attack victims."

As in past races, the 109th set up a field first aid tent near the start/finish line, and also positioned teams at strategic points along the course. MSgt Mark Latourelle, who had worked at a number of Kaiser Rolls said, "Experience has taught us that medical emergencies can happen just about anywhere during a race, so our teams are placed so they can observe the runners from start to finish. Each team has medical supplies, and is in constant contact with the first aid tent by handheld radio."

The start/finish line is the most likely spot for trouble. At the start of the wheelchair races, a large number of competitors are bunched up and accelerating which have caused pileups in the past. The finish of most races can also be a time of potential trouble. SSgt Steven Sitta said, "We have a good view of the final stretch of each race, spot people who are showing signs of exhaustion or dehydration, and get to them very quickly without disrupting the other runners."

This year, the Kaiser Roll was a great success for both the competitors and the 109th AEF. There were some exciting finishes in the 5K and 10K races, while things were relatively quiet on the medical front. TSgt Elizabeth Howard noted that only 16 people needed treatment, and most of those were minor injuries consisting of sprains, dehydration and minor abrasions. "The two exceptions were a 39-year-old man who complained of chest pains as he crossed the finish line, and a little girl who fell out of her stroller," said TSgt Howard. "We examined the man, and sent him to the hospital by ambulance. The little girl was brought into our tent needing attention for her bloody face. She appeared to be more scared than hurt. Once we got her cleaned up and calmed down, we administered a couple of M&Ms and she was fine."

1st Lt Karel Stibitz, a flight nurse and OIC of the teams at the Kaiser Roll was pleased. "We were very lucky that the weather was just perfect for an event like this - cloudy, cool and dry. But you could see that had it been a typical Minnesota July day with high temps and high humidity, we could have been extremely busy. As it was, we mostly just handed out ice packs and lots of tender loving care." [95]

☆☆☆☆☆

The July issue of the Vital Signs carried a warning about certain items that unit members may have purchased while in Saudi Arabia. University of Pittsburgh research demonstrated that eye shadow cosmetics sold under the name of Kohl or Serma could contain a large percentage of lead. Although lead is not absorbed through the skin, the cosmetic, if used by a child, may be ingested through rubbing the eyes and then placing the fingers in the mouth which could result in lead poisoning. Another source of potential lead poisoning was lead solder used in cooking utensils, specifically copper pots and pans. In addition, arsenic and other potentially harmful heavy metals may have been used in ceramic glazes on cooking and eating utensils.

☆☆☆☆☆

Up to this point, aerovac unit inspections were known as HSRIs. It was announced that they would be replaced by the Performance Based Inspections (PBIs). The new PBI actually tasked a unit to deploy and fly. The 137th AEF in Oklahoma volunteered to be the first test unit in November.

☆☆☆☆☆

Lt Col Anderson was selected to testify before the Senate Committee on Veterans Affairs in Washington D.C. The topic was "Personal Perspectives on How Operation Desert Shield/Desert Storm Deployments Affected Families and Relationships." She was selected due to her nationally known work with deployed families.

August. After three years of planning, the first Minnesota Guard Youth Camp was held at Camp Ripley in Little Falls, MN, Aug 18-24. Going to camp took on a whole new meaning for 106 sons and daughters of Minnesota Army and Air Guard members. In fact, it was more like "you're in the Army now!" It gave boys and girls, aged 10 through 12 what camp director Richard Zilka called "a little dose of what their moms and dads do during annual training and drill weekends."

After kicking off the week-long camp with an orientation for parents and kids, the campers were divided into four groups: Bradleys, Falcons, Hercules, and Patriots. Each group had its own color T-shirts, hip packs, symbolic theme, and of course, camper counselors. The counselors were all Air Guard/Army Guard members or spouses, including the 109th AEF's own Maj Karen Wolf.

Tales of 20-mile bike hikes, tipping canoes, pillow fights and an overnight campout were the talk of campers at a family picnic on the last day. Sports games were a favorite camp activity. A little patriotism and education were slipped in, with daily flag ceremonies, first aid classes and a visit to the local fire department.

Campers and counselors alike were misty-eyed when it came time to say goodbye at the final ceremony, wearing their official Youth Camp T-shirts and singing "I'm Proud to Be an American" for their families. [96]

Photo courtesy of Col Karen Wolf
"Campers" at Youth Camp doing what they do best - having fun!

September. The 109th AEF hosted 18 crewmembers from the 68th AES from Norton AFB, CA (who flew the C-141 Starlifter) and provided C-130E familiarization training that included equipment review, configuration, walk around, egress, and on/offloading procedures.

☆☆☆☆☆

After Operation Desert Storm, the stop-loss program terminated for active duty nurses in April. However, it would take until the end of this month for the program to be terminated for reserve nurses. [97]

October. The unit expanded their one-hospital program at St. Paul Ramsey to a second health care facility, the VA Hospital in Minneapolis. Training was conducted in the trauma emergency room, intensive care unit, and burn units at the St. Paul Ramsey Hospital and the psychiatric and medical/surgical units at the VA.

☆☆☆☆☆

Also this month, all AECMs were directed to undergo C-141 Familiarization Training within the next year to become familiar with the C-141 aerovac mission and airlift operations which included a shadow flying program.

These two additional training requirements were a direct result of lessons learned from Operation Desert Shield/Desert Storm.

☆☆☆☆☆

Thirty-three employers had the opportunity to fly with the 109th AEF this month, observing simulated patient evacuation missions. Enthusiastic AECMs provided guided tours of the aircraft explaining different aspects of the equipment and how they provide medical care under flight conditions.

"I can't believe there are only two nurses!" exclaimed an RN (registered nurse) from St. Paul Ramsey Medical Center. She appeared relieved after hearing about the important role our med techs play in providing patient care. By the end of the flight, she felt at home on the aircraft as she straightened blankets and secured litter straps.

Two nursing instructors from Normandale Community College couldn't imagine taking care of large numbers of patients under these conditions. "The noise level must make it difficult to communicate with patients and there is so much to do in such a short amount of time." Both instructors were happy to have had the opportunity to participate in this experience.

Sharon Bild, a representative from the Family Support Group was equally happy to get the chance to fly. "I can't believe all the up-to-date equipment." She also felt more spouses should be allowed to fly. "They need to see what this unit is accomplishing."

Fascinating, fun, exciting, worthwhile, and impressive were just some of the adjectives used by employers to describe the experience. Many expressed the desire to fly with us again. In all, the employer appreciation flights were a success.

☆☆☆☆☆

On October 19th, MSgt Tom Stangl, representing the U.S. Air Force, threw the first pitch of the first home game of the 1991 World Series. Standing on the pitcher's mound next to Rod Carew in the Hubert H. Humphrey Metrodome along with three other service members, each representing one of the four branches of the military, Tom's was the only pitch that crossed the plate.

November. The 68th AES reciprocated by inviting sixteen 109th AEF personnel to California to participate in C-141 Familiarization Training. Egress training, systems review, and a cross-country trip to Hawaii were part of the program. Personnel shadowed the crew positions, served on set-up crews, and acted as (FCC) Flight Clinical Coordinators on the trip.

☆☆☆☆☆

Capt Tammy Hayes was recognized as the Junior Officer of The Year and MSgt Tom Stangl was selected as the Senior NCO of The Year for the 133rd TAW. Both were honored at the AF Association Banquet on 11 Nov at the Radisson Hotel in St. Paul.

☆☆☆☆☆

Several unit members attended the Association of Military Surgeons of the U.S. conference in San Antonio, TX. It was announced that MAC at Scott AFB, IL would become Air Mobility Command (AMC). All of aerovac will serve under this command. In addition, the creation of an "Aerovac Schoolhouse" at Little Rock AFB, AR was discussed. All new flight nurses and med techs would complete a standardized course and return to their units fully qualified. This proposed training was a direct result of the wide variety of flight nurse and med tech proficiency noted in Operation Desert Shield/Desert Storm.

December. Lt Col Darcy Anderson and TSgt Richard Childs presented a plaque of appreciation, signed by all of the 109th AEF, to the wing for its support of the aeromeds during Operation Desert Shield/Storm.

Photo courtesy of Lt Col Darcy Anderson
Lt Col Darcy Anderson and TSgt Richard Childs present a plaque from the 109th AEF to the 133rd Tactical Airlift Wing.

THE COMMAND OF LT COL DARLENE (DARCY) ANDERSON ★ 157

Photo courtesy of TSgt Richard Childs and Col Michael Germain

"PRESENTED TO 133RD TAW IN HEARTFELT APPRECIATION FOR YOUR STEADFAST AND DEDICATED SUPPORT OF THIS UNITS' ACTIVATION AND DEPLOYMENT FOR OPERATION DESERT SHIELD/DESERT STORM
17 AUGUST 1990 - 28 MARCH 1991
109TH AEF."

1992

January. It has already been a year since Desert Storm and the activation of the 109th AEF. The unit had learned many things through their experiences in Desert Storm affecting how they function today.

As Commander, Lt Col Darcy Anderson saw the big lesson as being ready when called. "The first group activated was told they had five hours to get ready, but they actually had eleven," Anderson commented. "We have always trained hard, but we have to be prepared for the worst and expect the unexpected."

The 109th AEF also learned from Desert Storm that intense realistic training pays off. "We have to train like we fight. This includes everything from chemical warfare training to family support and keeping employers informed," said Anderson.

Capt Charles Rodke believed that the squadron's readiness was increased. "We are mentally prepared. We know now that we can and probably will be involved in future conflicts."

Overall morale of the squadron was improved. They were more cohesive, better trained and had a clearer picture of their mission. But Anderson stressed that they are not a solo act. "This unit is filled with talent. The success of the 109th AEF is a composite of the whole base."

As a result of this, Anderson predicted that the 109th would be involved in more operations. "When other squadrons on base deploy, we will be going with them." [98]

Her prediction could not have been more accurate. In the future, the 109th AEF would find itself deployed numerous times in many varied locations.

February. The unit acquired its first fax machine.

March. During the March UTA, the entire base was involved in an extensive four-day mobility exercise as part of the countdown for the ORI in September. 100% of the unit was involved in one way or another in this event.

May. The base became a no-smoking area except for the Contact Club.

☆☆☆☆☆

TSgt Seeley began a slow transition out of the First Sergeant's office. His replacement was slated to be named in the near future.

Photo courtesy of Lt Col Darcy Anderson
TSgt Owen Seeley as First Sergeant.

1st Lt Fellman returned from the Combat Casualty Care Course. The eight-day tri-service active duty and reservist course was run by the Army at Camp Bullis, TX.

Training during the first three days focused on ATLS (Advanced Trauma Life Support), cricothyroidotomy, vein cut down, peritoneal lavage and pericardiocentesis. The course also included skills stations and a written and practical exam. Lectures covering the ABCs (airway, breathing, circulation), triage, and a system by system discussion of trauma and trauma management. In the goat lab, attendees performed chest tube insertions.

After the academic training, all course participants moved to Camp Posey, the field training site. In this setting, training topics included land navigation, escape and evasion, triage, NBC (nuclear, biological, chemical) situations, litter carry obstacle course, rope bridges, rappelling, leadership skills, and lectures on medical issues specific to the combat environment. The last five days culminated in a six-hour exercise involving setting up and moving casualties through a battalion aid station and a clearing station. [99]

☆☆☆☆☆

Seven 109th members deployed to Pope AFB, NC and then to various other sites on 5-17 May for a tactical Aeromedical Evacuation System Field Exercise. Active duty and reserve components were integrated in this FTX. TSgt Ackerman, MSgt Howard, SrA Tracy, SSgt Milsten, Maj Darula, 1st Lt Horvath and Maj Hendrickson represented the 109th in this exercise.

☆☆☆☆☆

On 28-29 May, Lt Gen Huddleston, Chief of Staff of the Canadian Forces Air Command and representative of the Secretary of the AF were on base to look at the feasibility of a National Guard AF for Canadian forces. One of their focuses was AE. With very short notice, the unit configured an aircraft with 72 litters and appropriate equipment, then provided a complete crew plus an AEOO (Aeromedical Evacuation Operations Officer). The visitors asked questions regarding aerovac resources, training, and interoperability of crewmembers between different types of aircraft.

June. The AF made a monumental move that impacted AE. Three major commands - MAC, Strategic Air Command (SAC), and TAC were all deactivated and their assets were incorporated into two new organizations - Air Combat Command (ACC) and AMC. Initially, the aerovac squadrons fell under AMC. Soon thereafter, AMC transferred the C-130 airlift squadrons, including the majority of active duty and reserve component C-130 units to ACC. The transfer involved 19 AE units and the active duty AE squadron at Pope AFB, NC. The active duty unit then at Rhein Main AB in Germany became part of the U.S. Air Forces in Europe and the one residing at Yokota AB in Japan transferred to Pacific Air Command. (Five years later the CONUS squadrons were returned to AMC.)

☆☆☆☆☆

Also this month, the aeromeds participated in the base-wide Purple Penny exercise, and were praised by exercise officials for their readiness and "can do" attitude. The unit worked 12 to 15 hours each day, sent out four crews, completed Engine Running Onloads (EROs) in Mission Oriented Protective Posture (MOPP) gear and dealt with THREATCONs (Terrorist Threat Conditions) and simulated chemical attacks.

July. The 109th AEF was officially designated a squadron - the 109th AES.

(authors' note: AEF from this point forward will refer to the new Air Expeditionary Force. The previous use of AEF referred to the Aeromedical Evacuation Flight which was replaced by Aeromedical Evacuation Squadron this month as noted above.)

☆☆☆☆☆

To prepare for the ORI at the end of the month, Round-Up '92 was held as a home station training event.

On Saturday of the July UTA, Capt Stibitz (OIC) and MSgt Liz Howard (NCOIC) did a great job of organizing the medical care for participants of the Kaiser Roll, an annual event featuring several races for the handicapped and able-bodied participants. The medic tent was staffed with 12 nurses, 12 med techs, and a physician. These volunteers were the primary source of medical care during the races. Capt Stibitz commented, "We saved them all!" and the paramedics did not need to transport anyone for further medical treatment.

Of the 57 patients needing care, 20 were treated for heat exhaustion. The remaining patients were treated for sore muscles, blisters and abrasions. Effective communication between the volunteers, stationed at varying locations throughout the course, aided in rapid identification of participants in need of care.

SMSgt Latourelle did a great job in organizing the medical crew at the finish line while 1st Lt Prickett established an efficient tent crew. Procurement was handled by Maj Hernandez, who was able to obtain donuts, bananas and yogurt for the volunteer staff. MSgt Howard obtained the ever-popular T-shirts.

As the crew left the medic tent, they knew they had left their mark. A swamp had been created in the area where they had hosed down all of those heat exhausted patients! [100]

Photo courtesy of the 109th AES archives
109th AES personnel treat a runner suffering from heat exhaustion during the annual Kaiser Roll race.

Later in the month, only one week after the conclusion of Round-Up '92 and in conjunction with the wing, the unit underwent an Operational Readiness Inspection while participating in Operation Sand Eagle. It was only the second aerovac unit to be inspected as such. The wing and the squadron both received a rating of "Excellent," the second highest score given. In addition, the 109th AES received laudatory recognition.

After spending four hot days in Georgia, spirits were high as the report spread of the 109th AES excellence shown during the inspection. Returning aeromeds told of the valuable experiences they had working with other components during the ORI. "I now have a better understanding of the AECC, AELT, AEOO, and the radio operators (RDO). It was a great opportunity to learn about the different aspects of aerovac and how it all fits together," said Capt DeSanto.

Chaplain McGuire shared similar comments after flying as a patient with the aeromeds. "It was an extremely enlightening experience. I never really knew what the aeromeds did. They worked well as a team, knew what they were doing, and worked with ease." Chaplain McGuire, experiencing the role of a patient during an ERO exclaimed, "It's hot!"

SMSgt Al Zakariasen, flying as an aircrew member, found that, "The inspectors didn't ask us anything differently than we're tasked on a typical Wednesday evening flight." Each crew flew one mission per day, usually carrying 13 patients.

The inspectors were most impressed with the command and control, specifically the modified AECC and AELT. Terms such as "extraordinary," "incredible," and "superb" were used. Our radio operators worked by flashlight throughout that first night to ensure our communications were unequaled. Although the crews had a minor glitch with equipment management, Capt Riley, one of these inspectors, stated that the crews were "something incredible to watch." The 109th AES was also the only unit specifically cited by the HQ AMC Team Chief during the closing remarks. He also remarked that "the 109th has set the standard for the rest of aerovac." [101]

Photo courtesy of Lt Col Darcy Anderson
Lt Col Anderson (left) and Maj Darula (right) at a field training exercise.

The unit received their first sets of reflective waist belts that were to be worn at night when working on or around the aircraft.

☆☆☆☆☆

Due to the popularity of the employer flights, numerous requests from unit members for spouse flights were answered when two such opportunities were scheduled and flown during September. Patty Johnson commented, "I would like to thank all of those involved with the spouse flight on Sep 26th. It was a very enjoyable experience. It was good to see what kind of training and practice our spouses go through when they fly. The high humidity added to the excitement as the plane's condensing units let off steam, making the inside of the place seem like a haunted house ride at the fair. The best scenery was from the cockpit where you could see all around. Thanks again. It will be an experience I won't soon forget." [102]

☆☆☆☆☆

No UTAs were scheduled for the months of August or September due to the time required of unit members for the recent Operational Readiness Exercise and Operational Readiness Inspection.

September. Lt Col Carolyn Sheldon, AMC, flew with the unit over four days in Sep to requalify in the C-130E. This reinforced HQ AMC's trust and reliance on the 109th AES to support their requirements and staff.

October. A celebration was held at Kelly AFB, TX commemorating the 50th anniversary of flight nursing. A poster designed by two unit members won national awards. Among 35 entries from every active duty and reserve aeromed component, the poster won "Best of Show" and "Most Patriotic." Unit members Capt Julie T. Finn and SSgt Richard H. Childs designed and created the poster for this special event. The poster was a collage depicting the history of the unit and of AE from 1961 to present. "A lot of people dug into their closets to find paraphernalia for the collage," said Childs. The poster was placed on permanent display at the Aeromedical Evacuation Museum at Brooks AFB, TX. When the museum closed, the poster was returned to the unit and is now on permanent display with the other awards won by the 109th AES. [103]

Photo courtesy of TSgt Richard Childs and Col Michael Germain

**"BECAUSE WE STAND ON THE ACHIEVEMENTS OF THOSE WHO WENT BEFORE US, WE CAN LEAD CLEARLY AND BOLDLY INTO THE FUTURE - AND PASS ON, ENRICHED BY OUR CONTRIBUTIONS; THE TORCH, BRIGHTER STILL TO THOSE WHO WILL BUILD UPON OURS.
109TH AES 1961- "**

Photo courtesy of TSgt Richard Childs and Col Michael Germain
Detailed close-up of previous picture.

Eight aeromeds participated in REFORGER (Return of Forces to Germany) '92 - Capt Jensen, Lt Bornhofen, SSgt Davidson, SSgt Berg, SSgt Childs, A1C Kisser, SrA Peterson and SSgt Conrad.

☆☆☆☆☆

The word was put out that the unit had several openings for nurses, especially those with prior service.

☆☆☆☆☆

The squadron golf team, captained by SSgt Dan Cisar (who commented that he "carried the old people on the team"), took first in the 1992 Thursday Night Men's Golf League at Fort Snelling. Other team members included Capt Charles Rodke, SMSgt Al Zakariasen, MSgt Tom Stangl, TSgt Gene Doven, and SrA Mike Tracy. [104]

November. The 1992 Senior NCO Honor Airman of the Year was MSgt Mark A. Grieme, medical service specialist with the 109th AES.

December. In keeping with the new "Total Quality Air Force," air evac units would now be evaluated during their parent Wing/Group Aircrew Stan/Eval Visit (ASEV). The ASEV was a tool for evaluating aircrew flight operations and verifying safe and effective mission accomplishment. This was achieved through aircrew testing and flight evaluations to ensure compliance with the approved operational procedures and applicable Special Interest Items (SII). In addition to ASEV testing and flight evaluations, Stan/Eval and Aircrew Training programs were evaluated to ensure compliance and standardization.

1993

February. Lt Col Donna Alt, Chief Nurse, left the unit for an IMA position at Grand Forks AFB, ND. Maj Norm Hendrickson was named the new 109th AES Chief Nurse.

March. The Guard Bureau notified the 109th AES that its medical skills were again needed overseas. Five members departed for the Middle East on a sixty-day rotation in support of Operation Provide Hope, the United Nations humanitarian effort in Somalia. Although based in Cairo, Egypt, almost all of the aeromeds spent time in Mogadishu using their medical skills to help ease the suffering of the native population. In all, 14 aeromeds would deploy to Somalia in support of this operation with the last returning home in March 1994. [105]

The first individuals deployed included SSgt Kelly Anderson-Ray, 1st Lt Georgeanne Johnson, Capt Gary Prickett, MSgt Gerald Blilie, and TSgt Dan Tracy. Initially, the aeromeds worked in feeding centers. "It was great seeing the kids," MSgt Blilie remarked, "and seeing how glad they were that we were there. Seeing the smiles on their faces - they were eating, not starving anymore."

It soon became too dangerous after killings occurred at a different center, so the aeromeds were relocated and would never see those faces again.

The crews rotated into Mogadishu, Somalia, via C-141 Starlifters, which meant the C-130E-trained crews had to cross-train onto the C-141 platform. They shuttled 20-30 patients at a time from Mogadishu to Germany. The sick and injured were primarily military members from all branches of the service.

What sticks in their minds, however, were the haunting images of Mogadishu.

"It was unbelievable - the whole city was devastated," said Johnson. "The embassy was the only complete building we saw."

While in Mogadishu, the crews stayed in a barren military compound and seldom left it. When it was necessary to leave for supplies or to convoy patients from the embassy, crews had to wear flak vests and helmets and carry weapons. It was then that the Americans saw, as Johnson did, "how little people have there and yet can still survive."

The Somalis rooted through garbage for scraps of food or building materials for their homes, which were mere huts made of sticks and rubbish teetering against walls of demolished buildings. In the "outside the compound" world, anything could happen - a Saudi physician leaving for home was shot and killed instantly moments after he left its confines. That happened the day before Prickett left for Minnesota.

"It's a very beautiful country - beautiful beaches with deep blue water," he said. "But there is no value for human life."

Johnson echoed his feelings, "I thought, 'This is terrible. This country is devastated; these people are dying - how can anyone be willing to waste this human life?'"

Tracy said that these were experiences that changed lives. "You find out what's really important in life," he said. "You have a lot of time to think and make decisions." Since his return, he has gone to his niece's school to talk to six classes of children about his time in Somalia.

Each member stressed they appreciated the total support from the 133rd they received which included unit level training, pay, supply and medical attention prior to departure.

"We were better prepared than anyone who went over there," stated Johnson. "And we'd all go back again," concluded Prickett. [106]

Photo courtesy of the 109th AES archives

Convoy crew that traveled to the university complex in Mogadishu to get supplies weekly in full gear (locked and loaded) during Operation Restore Hope.

Back Row (L - R): (unidentified), Kelly Tracy, Georgeanne Johnson, Gary Prickett
Front Row (L - R): (unidentified), (unidentified), Dan Tracy

April. Capt Horvath became the first flight nurse to become AECOT (Aeromedical Evacuation Contingency Operations Training) trained in the AELT role. As part of this training, Capt Horvath joined two MSC officers and two radio ops in isolating an advanced AELT. This was a new AF concept, linking air evac close to the troops at the front lines. They were to establish an operational site several miles from the MASF in the backyard of the "bad guys."

The first night out, they had no fuel, water, heat, or electricity, but it was the only night they didn't come under attack. As part of the scenario, the team practiced camouflage, low light, low noise, low movement discipline. Everyone at the site went on 100% alert twice daily, once before sunrise and again after dinner, until 2300. They also established firing positions in the woods to watch for infiltration.

To help ensure realism, each of the four AELT members wore sensors and carried an M16 with laser gear, also known as MILES (Multiple Integrated Laser Engagement System) gear. On the final night of the mission, the enemy forces cut the two radio ops off from the main camp site and set up two sniper teams with automatic weapons to pick off the other three team members. Capt Horvath crawled under the side of the tent, used a chem stick to illuminate the radio, sent a message for help, zeroed out the radio, destroyed the COMSEC (Communications Security) material, then went out and in two and a half hours killed three snipers and captured a fourth. [107]

May. It was announced that Operation Desert Shield/Storm participants could receive a health check as a precautionary measure for possible medical coverage for any war-attributed illnesses that were currently present or might surface in the future. The Minneapolis VA Medical Center was a participant in the health registry program. Members would undergo some lab work, chest x-ray, and history/physical data gathering.

☆☆☆☆☆

At the end of the month, the 109th AES was informed that the unit had inherited surplus Kevlar helmets and body armor vests to cover all of the mobility positions. The wing was scheduled to receive a large number of survival vests, of which 50 were allocated to the aeromeds for 10 aerovac crews.

June. The unit, led by Maj Dayton Carlson, conducted a 2-day Aircrew Training Rodeo attended by 50 AECMs. Numerous positive comments regarding content and the training pace were reported.

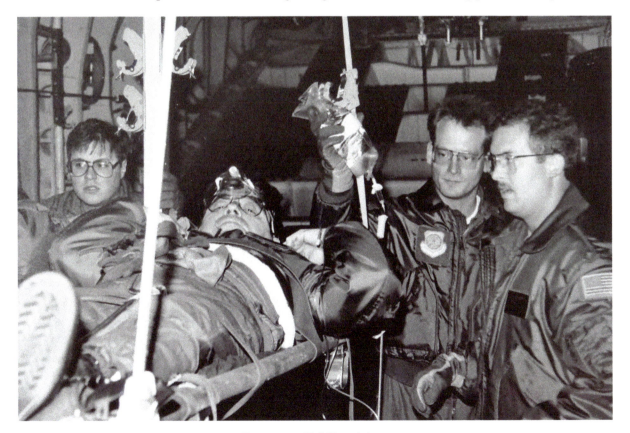

Photo courtesy of Lt Col Darcy Anderson
Local training mission (circa 1993).
(L - R): Michael Kjellander, Norman Hendrickson, John Wyland, Mark Freund

Once again, Scott AFB, IL chose the 109th AES to train and evaluate one of their staff. Maj Mortindale underwent two days of intensive training and then a checkride on his return trip to Scott AFB. This was Maj Mortindale's first exposure to the C-130 aerovac mission. He was quite impressed with the concentrated training attention given him by TSgt Dan Cisar and 1st Lt JoEllen Evavold.

☆ ☆ ☆ ☆ ☆

From Lt Col Anderson's command notes:

We are submitting the 109th for the George Schafer and Theodore C. Marrs awards for the last year of my command (July 1992-June 1993). There is no better aerovac unit in the entire medical reserve system of our country.

A special thanks to MSgt Robert Janssen, who is the creative talent in putting our nomination package together.

July. Lt Col Anderson retires.

From Lt Col Anderson's command notes:

I now recall the attitude by many on base toward the "aeromeds" at the beginning of my command and how rough that was. The base newspaper even had a name for us -- the "stepchild unit." So it is with much joy as I close my chapter as Commander - that I share a letter I received from the Commander of another squadron on base - Civil Engineering.

22 Oct 93

FROM: 133 CES/CC

SUBJ: Retirement Recognition

TO: Lt Col Darlene A. Anderson

Dear Lt Col Anderson,

On behalf of everyone in the 133rd Civil Engineering Squadron, I want to offer our congratulations and best wishes to you on this occasion of your retirement.

I know it must be difficult for you to leave a unit you have been with for over twenty years, one that you have commanded and led through wartime activation. But I'm sure you will treasure the memory of your successes with this squadron for your lifetime.

As an interested outsider, I've enviously observed the dynamics of the 109th AES as it has developed over the course of your commandership. You made it happen that the 109th AES went from among the lowest C rated units to the consistent best. You did this even while mobilizing the unit for war. You built a closeness and camaraderie among your people and their families that is unmatched in the wing. But most of all, I have envied that you have so many great cooks in your unit that enable you to have the best holiday spread, the most and the best cookies per capita on the base.

During a time when we were all chomping at the bit to get involved in our era's "Big One," the Gulf War, it was your unit that really got into it and had unit members on the ground in the theater for the duration; ready to save the lives of our soldiers. During this crazy time, you set aside your personal and professional life and worked tirelessly on behalf of your people who were off to war and their families. And thankfully everyone came back safe and sound. You and the members of the 109th AES did the Minnesota ANG proud. Then, just after your people returned, they participated in the Wing ORI, and were instrumental in that great triumph.

You know that during your command the 109th AES had nothing but success in everything it did. This can only happen when a unit has great leadership and great people. The men and women of the 133rd Civil Engineering Squadron are proud of our association with the superb unit you have built, and we offer you our heartfelt congratulations, best wishes in your future endeavors, and a fond farewell.

Sincerely,

(signed)

Commander

☆☆☆☆☆

Lt Col Anderson's last command note:

It is my hope that the members of the 109th AES that I served with during my command years know what a difference each of them made. The base "stepchild" did not disappear as foretold by the State Air Surgeon.

I am confident that this unit will soon be acknowledged as the best AE unit in the country, and will be awarded the Theodore C. Marrs and George Schafer awards. The 109th AES is the only ANG AE unit that is 100% manned and trained for the third consecutive year. Our C-rating is unequaled. After coming off thirteen different deployments for Desert Shield/Desert Storm, the unit significantly contributed to the 133rd Airlift Wing's overall "Excellent" rating in their recent Operational Readiness Inspection. Our local involvement with NDMS, National Guard Youth Camp and the Kaiser Roll continues to expand. And the list goes on-- support of REFORGER '92, Operation Restore Hope, and Samaritan (Army FTX).

Future members of the 109th AES will owe much to these exceptional officers and enlisted, who did far beyond their duty and made the critical difference, because they believed in the mission and each other.

I was privileged and fortunate to have served with them.

(authors' note: The unit would indeed be awarded both the George Schafer and Theodore C. Marrs awards in November for her last year of command.)

CHAPTER 9
The Command of Col Sandra (Sandy) Carlson

(Jul 1993 - Apr 1999)

Photo courtesy of Col Sandy Carlson

Commander's Comments: During this six-year period, the 109th AES was primarily in a training and inspection/evaluation mode. Many changes continued to be made to the AE system based on problems experienced during Desert Shield and Desert Storm. My goal was to set the 109th AES up for long-term success.

Approximately 95% of the Air Force's AE mission was done by the reserves during this time frame. Because of this heavy reliance on these reserve forces, I believed the 109th AES would get called upon again to perform the AE mission under a wartime scenario. This required that we maintain a high level of readiness and excellence. Our mission was to save lives.

We left an old two-story World War II style building behind and joined the Operations Group in the new one-story Operations building. At that time, we had approximately 160 people in the unit. Our part of the building design was intentionally flexible to accommodate new work space configurations as the unit changed in size and scope. We acquired all new modular office furniture, new meeting spaces, and state-of-the-art audio/visual equipment. The "blue" carpeting was designed to reflect our AF "blue" heritage.

Throughout this time period, our automation needs significantly increased. We continued to acquire computers which enhanced our ability to communicate, especially with our traditional guard members.

The C-130 units were moved from Air Mobility Command to Air Combat Command during this time. The Air Force's philosophy in making this move was to put all tactical aircraft into one major command. This change did not last long however and the C-130s were eventually moved back under AMC.

Our relationship with the Operations Group continued to strengthen during these years. We merged our aircrew Stan/Eval function with the airlift squadron's Stan/Eval function, forming a single Stan/Eval office for the group. Additionally, we began to have Aircrew Stan/Eval Visits every four years. These visits evaluated the effectiveness of our Aircrew Training. Aircrew members were individually evaluated. Our aircrew members consistently exceeded AF standards.

We also participated in the 133rd Airlift Wing's Operational Readiness Inspections. These inspections were a total wing effort and tested the wing's ability to deploy, conduct operations and redeploy. The 109th AES' performance always far exceeded AF standards.

Our unit was the first AE unit to participate in the Joint Readiness Training Center (JRTC). Our MASF and AELT were "in the box" during this time and faced very challenging conditions. They successfully executed the AE mission. Our aircrews flew into the box to pick-up and care for simulated patients. Our command and control elements provided operational control of the missions. Our participation in JRTC was key to receiving the grade of "Outstanding" and "best seen to date" during the following ORI.

Our Unit Type Codes went through dramatic changes. We started out with 24 AE crews and two AELTs. These UTCs were replaced with 10 AE crews, a MASF, AELT, AEOT (Aeromedical Evacuation Operations Team), Support Cell and AGE (Aerospace Ground Equipment). This significantly changed the unit with a large increase in ground support personnel offset by a reduction in AE crews. We acquired more Medical Service Corps officers, Admin Personnel, Radio Operators, Generator Maintenance Personnel and Logistics Personnel.

We also continued to maintain our War Readiness Materials. This was a huge job for our logistics personnel. The WRM was used to support our aircrew training missions and ground operations.

AE is a "hybrid" mission, involving both a medical component and an operations component. A balance needed to be struck between knowledge of the aircraft systems and medical knowledge. The medical community wanted the AE units to be evaluated under a Health Services Inspection (HSI). We were successful in holding off yet another unit inspection which would have resulted in the 109th AES being inspected every year. Instead, we did metrics reporting to the Air Force Inspection Agency (AFIA). This worked for a period of time until AFIA decided that they didn't like this process and started working toward including the AE units in the HSI process.

The unit received the George Schafer Award for the best medical unit in the air reserve forces, and the Theodore C. Marrs Award for the outstanding ANG medical unit - both for the second and third time in the 109th's history. The hard work of all unit members paid off and was acknowledged by the receipt of these prestigious awards.

Col Sandy Carlson

July. Maj Sandy Darula became the unit's new Commander, taking command from Lt Col Darcy Anderson.

Maj Sandy Darula, formerly the Medical Service Corps officer for the 109th AES since 1989, said that the secret to the unit's success was its motivated members.

"We have a special spirit in this unit," she said. "We have a lot of fun - we train hard and play hard, too. We really care for and enjoy each other and what we do. We're excited about our work - that's what allows us to do so much and be so successful."

Darula hails from Minneapolis and graduated from the Air Force Academy with a Bachelor's Degree in Behavioral Sciences in 1980. Hers was the first class of women graduating from the Academy! She earned her Master's in Engineering Management at Northeastern University in Boston. Her first assignment on active duty was in systems acquisition, followed by a position in crew station design for the AV-8B Harrier with McDonnell-Douglas through the AF Institute of Technology.

She then served in Plans and Command and Control with AF Space Command, Peterson AFB, CO. She left active duty in 1988 and became an Air Force Academy Liaison Officer for a year before joining the 109th AES.

As a civilian, Darula was a sales specialist, western region, for National Computer Systems. [108]

MSgt Jim Hughes became the unit's First Sergeant at this time as well.

☆☆☆☆☆

Family Day was held for the wing and their families on Jul 18. Speakers (Brig Gen John Broman, Maj Gen Eugene Andreotti, and U.S House Representative Martin Sabo), static displays, various unit open houses, and a variety of activities for children adorned the agenda.

☆☆☆☆☆

A mobility exercise was accomplished which consisted of mobility processing (with no discrepancies), three ERO missions, and some excellent training with the MASF and Operations Center. These activities provided some additional training that could not be duplicated on the weekly local missions. Maj Germain, Capt Dahlquist, Capt Hill, Capt Rodke, and Lt Caldwell organized the exercise and training and events.

August. Plans were being developed for the new Operations/Aeromed building scheduled to be built in FY96. In general, the design was planned with the "open concept" idea that minimized private offices and maximized the use of systems furniture. With the uncertainties involved with the upcoming aerovac restructure, it was determined that this "open concept" would best meet the long-term needs of the unit. Maj Karen Wolf was named the project officer for this undertaking.

☆☆☆☆☆

An indication of the unit's busy ops tempo (OPTEMPO, also known as operating tempo or operations tempo) during this month: 40 personnel to Tripler Army Hospital and Hickam AFB, HI, 20 AECMs on a Pacific ARM (Aeromedical Readiness Mission) training for 10 days, five airshow static displays (St. Paul Airport, Rochester, Owatonna and two at Camp Ripley), support for the Minnesota Stand Down for Veterans at the U of M West Bank over three days and finally, 11 local ARMs.

☆☆☆☆☆

Dozens of 109th AES personnel deployed to Honolulu, Hawaii for annual training. "The driving force behind the deployment was the hospital tour," explained Maj Tammy Hayes, OIC of the flying portion of the trip. "But it was great getting the flying time. The long flights are sometimes much better than the quick 'up and down' flights we normally have. We accomplished a lot of checkrides for qualification."

Hayes explained that of the 56 people deploying, 24 worked in AE and 32 at the base hospital. But the trip wasn't just doing double duty, it was doing triple duty - the C-130E was a home station aircraft, enabling the 109th Airlift Squadron (AS) crews to get some training while supporting the Army, including paratroop drops.

Maj Karen Wolf, OIC for the overall trip, explained that it was a stroke of luck getting the Hawaii assignment. "We were determined we were going to do a hospital tour this year," she said. "We called around to various medical centers to see who could accommodate us, and everything worked out perfectly with the Tripler Army Medical Center."

Wolf said that this was the first time the unit worked at an Army medical center. "Joint service training is a new venture for us, but they couldn't have been nicer," she said.

The hospital group included a variety of specialties, including radio operators, med techs, flight nurses, an administrative specialist and even an on-the-job training specialist. Capt Rose DeSanto served as OIC of the hospital portion of the deployment.

"It was a big hospital," said Wolf. "There were a lot of areas where our people could get experience - the emergency room, physical therapy, dialysis, psychiatric treatment and intensive care."

She said it was especially a good experience for med techs who don't do patient care in their civilian jobs. "And we went in there to train, to shadow a staff person - not to provide relief," Wolf said. "Our people did an excellent job."

Wolf added that though the days were long and productive, the Hickam AFB beach was handy for relaxing, snorkeling and volleyball. Pearl Harbor was also nearby for touring.

"This was nice," Wolf concluded. "Our people had been working very hard these past two years. It gave them a great opportunity for good, solid training in a wonderful place, too." [109]

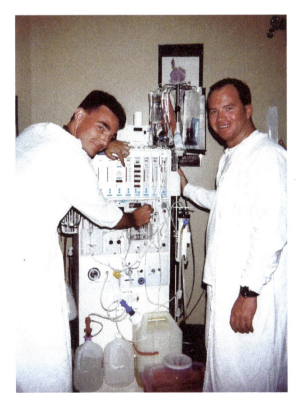

Photo courtesy of Col Karen Wolf

Darren Damiani (left) and Don Brock (right) at Tripler Army Medical Center, Honolulu, Hawaii.

Dependents of Minnesota National Guard members spent seven days at the Army Guard's Camp Ripley, MN, for the third annual Youth Camp.

The camp was intended to help youth understand their guardian's involvement in the National Guard as well as to give them an enjoyable and unique camp experience.

A total of 243 campers, ages 10-12, attended one of two one-week sessions experiencing some typical and some not so typical camp activities. There were about 130 volunteers who were active or retired members of the Minnesota Army or Air National Guard or spouses of active or retired members.

The campers tried their hands at archery, riflery and orienteering. They challenged their physical endurance at the confidence course, bicycle riding with Adjutant General Eugene Andreotti, hiking and canoeing. They practiced survival skills, camping in the woods and learning first aid. Finally, they got a taste of the military by taking rides in Army vehicles like a Bradley, an armored personnel carrier and a HUMVEE (High Mobility Multipurpose Wheeled Vehicle - HMMWV, colloquial: Humvee), watching F-16 flyovers, and touring a C-130E and a UH-1H helicopter. The youth were also taught about respect for our national flag, environmental concerns and substance abuse.

Many youth said they enjoyed the confidence course and the rides in the Army vehicles the most. They also liked making new friends and learning about the National Guard. The groups were split into four squads of about 30 campers each for both of the weeks. The squads were named Hercules, Falcons, Bradleys and Patriots. [110]

September. MSgt Larry Bild returned from Somalia after working in the MASF in Mogadishu. He recalled the day after his group arrived at the MASF that, "Things got very busy. The base was under fire every day. Luckily many of the militia members didn't know how to arm the RPGs (Rocket Propelled Grenades) so they did not detonate when they landed. U.S. service members called the rocket and machine gun mounted civilian Land Rovers 'Kling-ons,' because every vehicle we saw had at least twenty or more folks clinging onto the vehicle."

October. Lt Col Darcy Anderson retired this month. Anderson spent her entire Air National Guard career with the 109th - 23 years - starting out in 1969 as an airman basic in a special nurse commissioning program. In three months, she became a captain, since she held a master's degree and had considerable nursing experience. She then went on to hold a number of positions, including Assistant Chief Nurse, Chief Nurse and then Commander.

"This is a very emotional time for me," she said. "I believe this is the best AE unit in the Guard, and it has been the best privilege of my life to be part of it. The unit has such intense esprit de corps. I'm keeping promises to my family, but I'm leaving lifelong friendships and a mission I strongly believe in."

She fondly remembers seeing the unit pull itself up from the bottom to rise to the top, maintaining the highest readiness ratings possible - while also going to war, as the unit performed a total of 13 deployments for Operation Desert Storm.

"Some people have said, 'You're a lucky commander. You actually got to do what you train for,'" she said. She thinks that the war intensified the squadron's efforts, as members realized that training was more than just filling squares - it meant they were prepared for war.

"When I say, 'People in this unit sit on the edge,' I don't say that for dramatic effect," Anderson said. "It's reality. They accept that. They take their training seriously."

She stated that she'll always consider herself a member of the 109th AES. "It's impossible not to have intense feelings about it," she said. "I have literally lived here - seen children born and go through high school, divorces, potlucks, hospital visits - you get very, very close to unit members. I just want to say how proud I am of this unit and how significant these individuals are...we have all types of people, from bankers and bricklayers to college professors, but somehow they blend so well. Individuality is respected." [111]

Photo courtesy of the 109th AES archives
"Final Formation" for Lt Col Darcy Anderson, 109th AES Commander.

All C-130 units transferred to Air Combat Command. It should be noted that at this time, the flight scarf was to be worn with the flight suit except when flying. This was the first instance in the unit's history that a flight scarf was part of the official uniform. (authors' note: See the "Flight Scarf" section in the back of the book for details and notice the flight scarf worn by the Commander in the preceding photo.)

☆ ☆ ☆ ☆ ☆

Home station training was accomplished from 18-22 Oct. All unit AFSCs had training events scheduled. On the first day, aeromeds completed 13 hours of static aircraft training, while the second day they concentrated on medical equipment with four test out stations. The next two days consisted of multiple morning and afternoon flights.

☆ ☆ ☆ ☆ ☆

Last month, Maj Dayton Carlson, Maj Michael Germain, SMSgt Mark Latourelle and MSgt Tom Stangl attended the Worldwide AES Conference at Martinsburg, WV from 21-24 September and briefed the unit during Commanders Call during the October UTA.

☆ ☆ ☆ ☆ ☆

October was also the "kick off" month for the preparation for the ASEV which was scheduled for next September. Maj Michael Germain was selected as the OIC for this event.

☆ ☆ ☆ ☆ ☆

As this planning was getting underway, a number of aeromeds continued to fill taskings overseas. One member, SrA Nicole Fagula, recalls an interesting incident while she was a med tech serving in Mogadishu, Somalia. She and her colleagues found a live grenade inside the flak jacket of a badly wounded American Soldier sprawled on a stretcher. If they operated and the grenade exploded, it would kill scores of people. But without immediate treatment in camp, the man would die. It turned out that the awful decision never had to be made. The man died, was placed into a plastic bag and was deposited in a bunker a distance away - the grenade still on his chest. Fagula recalls that the man's hand had been chopped off by the Somalis, but the wedding ring on one finger still sparkled.

These and other instances still stand out in Fagula's mind, interrupting her sleep and prompting an occasional flashback, although she has been back from Mogadishu since mid-October.

Fagula still thinks about the medical needs of Soldiers in the war zone. So much so that she understands why some Vietnam veterans were preoccupied with going back for a second tour of duty. She made friends with service members from America and the United Nations forces, and the camaraderie helped them get through this time. Fagula said it strengthened her.

Fagula was not involved with the humanitarian part of the mission, but focused on stabilizing patients for the three-minute helicopter ride to a field hospital, then a flight to a German hospital. Even though Fagula's camp was regularly in the midst of mortar and sniper fire, on only one day were the patients arriving in waves. At that time there was no letup for the better part of the day, and at one point, Fagula stabilized about 30 patients in just 15 minutes. "We'd put an IV in them if we could and check for shrapnel, try to determine major injuries then move on to the next stretcher," she said. She once told a fellow aeromed the toughest part of one day was when "I was having a beer with an Army Ranger friend one day then assisting a doctor working to save his leg three days later."

She became acquainted with Michael Durand, the pilot who was captured and imprisoned in a much-publicized incident. The Army Rangers, who flew Black Hawk helicopters and were stationed just 35 yards from Fagula and her colleagues, blared messages over loudspeakers at night demanding his release.

The fateful day was October 3, when helicopters on routine surveillance flights were attacked, and the medics ran from their mess hall to treat the wounded. Late in the attack, an overflow caused patients to be brought back from the field hospital to the MASF, as Fagula's camp was called, for additional treatment. Broken bones and other injuries caused by jeeps hitting land mines were commonly seen.

Fagula said the camp was much like the MASH units portrayed in the popular television series, but it had no alarm to warn of incoming wounded. Unlike Hawkeye and Trapper John, Fagula volunteered for this mission but originally had been told she would work as a medic in Cairo, not Mogadishu. Much like the MASH series, the number of medics on hand was well short of what was intended.

Fagula said that upon arrival, she was amazed at the speed with which a triage unit was set up in the sand. People of other nationalities felt much safer than the Americans, and they were commonly sent into town to buy food, Fagula said. "They weren't touched. They didn't get a second look." [112]

Photo courtesy of SrA Nicole Fagula, Northstar Guardian (Jan '94), Hudson Star-Observer

109th AES aeromeds wait with other medics in Somalia for patients to arrive. The medics assess them and they are then flown via helicopter to a nearby field hospital. Pallets in the background offer protection from mortar and sniper fire.

(L - R): SrA Robert Buresh, SrA Nicole Fagula, (unidentified), MSgt Lawrence Bild, (unidentified)

<u>**November.**</u> The 109th AES was notified that it was the recipient of two awards. The unit had won for the second time the George Schafer Award for the best medical unit in the air reserve forces and the Theodore C. Marrs Award as the outstanding medical unit in the ANG. These honors were based on performance from July 1, 1992, through June 30, 1993. During that time, the unit worked numerous medical missions in Somalia in support of the UN mission there, as well as in Central America. The unit also participated in a number of community service projects, including the Kaiser Roll, a race for physically challenged and able-bodied athletes. The squadron supported the Minnesota National Guard Youth Camp and provided volunteers monthly for the VA Medical Center in Minneapolis and the St. Paul Ramsey Hospital and Medical Center in St. Paul to assist with patient care. The last time this award was won by an AE squadron was when the 109th AES earned it back in 1987, making it the only AE unit to win this award back to back. [113]

In addition to these awards, Maj Michael Germain was selected as the ANG Outstanding Nurse Corps Officer of the Year.

☆☆☆☆☆

The unit participated in a wing exercise this UTA. The ACC Vice Commander visited the base as well.

December. A newly formed Family Support Group planned and hosted the annual Christmas party. 1st Lt Pat Howard and Sharon Bild were the representatives for the 109th AES.

Photo courtesy of the 109th AES archives
Santa's helper (Tom Stangl) and Santa (Al Zakariasen) making their annual appearance at one of the squadron's Christmas parties.

1994

January. Early in the month, Capt Dahlquist, Capt Linda Jensen, MSgt Tim Evavold, TSgt Connie Erickson and SrA Kim Bruesewitz deployed for a two-week tour with the 24th Med Group in Panama. They were replaced by mid-month with Capt Chuck Rodke, Lt Gail Fellman, MSgt Liz Howard, TSgt Sharon Villagran, and SSgt Brent Kapfer.

February. Maj Germain, Capt Dahlquist and MSgt Blilie were selected by Guard Bureau to participate as members of the ORI Evaluation Team acting on behalf of the Inspector General. They attended formal training from 15-18 February at Scott AFB, IL and were placed on an "on-call" list to augment Air Force Reserve and active duty evaluators for future ORIs.

☆☆☆☆☆

The AF decided on two types of written correspondence that would be used for all future communication, thereby reducing the previous number of formats. The "Official Memorandum" (business style) and "Personal Memorandum" (personal style) examples were distributed to all sections within the unit, and members were directed to immediately begin using these formats in all future correspondence.

March. Six members of the 109th AES helped "bring up the rear" as U.S. forces wrapped up their involvement in Somalia. SSgt Darren Damiani, SSgt Patty Ehresmann, SSgt John Green, SSgt Michael Kjellander, SSgt Mark Norman, and SSgt Ken Peterson served in various locations, including Mogadishu, Somalia, and Mombasa, Kenya. Members remained on alert for urgent flights and moved from place to place as needed. Treatment ranged from delivering babies to minor surgery to treating minor coughs. A total of fourteen 109th AES members deployed in support of Operation Restore Hope. [114]

☆☆☆☆☆

Julianne Deutsch, the civilian employer of 1st Lt Georgeanne Johnson, was awarded the Pro Patria award from the National Committee for Employer Support of the Guard and Reserve (ESGR). Johnson, who nominated Deutsch, said she was selected largely because of her response to Johnson's activation for Operation Restore Hope in Somalia.

"Her first words to me were, 'Tell me what you need. I wish I were going,' and 'Come back safely,'" recalled Johnson.

The Pro Patria, a Latin expression meaning "for the nation," is the top award in the ESGR program. Only one per state is awarded annually.

Deutsch was selected from 400 nominations as the employer who most demonstrated support of the Guard or Reserve by adopting personnel policies making it easier for the employee to participate in their military duties. [115]

May. Nine 109th AES med techs supported the Combat Readiness Training Center (CRTC) at Volk Airfield, Wisconsin, 2-9 May.

☆☆☆☆☆

The AF Medical Service initiated a pilot project to develop a Critical Care Air Transport Team (CCATT). [116] A CCATT is a highly specialized and uniquely skilled three-person medical team that augments standard aeromedical evacuation crews. It is composed of a physician who specializes in an area of critical care or emergency medicine, a critical care nurse and a respiratory therapist.

June. The 109th AES hosted the ANG Aerovac Commander's Conference from 22-24 June. Attendees included aerovac commanders, senior health technicians, and aerovac representatives from the ANG Readiness Center.

✯✯✯✯✯

The unit conducted June Jamboree; a home station training event designed to prepare the unit for the upcoming Formal Stan/Eval visit (formerly known as the ASEV). The BTLS (Basic Trauma Life Support) presentations, medical hands-on training, and six contingency staged aeromedical readiness missions provided a stimulating learning opportunity for the unit. 1st Lt Evavold and MSgt Blilie were the POCs (Point Of Contact) for this activity.

✯✯✯✯✯

Both the 109th AES and the 133rd MDS continued to participate in what's known as the hospital program, arranged at both the Veterans Hospital in Minneapolis and St. Paul Ramsey Hospital and Medical Center in St. Paul, MN.

"It provides more hands-on training to med techs who may not be in medical fields in civilian life," said Maj Karen Wolf. She added that the participants are supervised by squadron nurses rather than the civilian staff of the hospitals.

The 109th AES sends 12-15 people between the hospitals each UTA. Wolf explained that a variety of working environments are available, including the emergency room, burn unit and psychiatric services.

"They come back with a baseline of skills from Tech School," said Wolf. "We build on those so our members have skills to use on the aircraft and in the Mobile Aeromedical Staging Facility. They're learning skills in peacetime to use in a contingency." [117]

July. The National Guard Bureau called the 109th AES to fill a tasking in support of medical efforts in the Rwandan refugee crisis in Zaire, Africa. After assembling the thirty-one volunteers and processing them through mobility, working overtime to collect, check and palletize needed equipment and supplies, the unit was placed on hold. Two weeks later, it was decided there were enough civilian relief agencies such as the Red Cross providing medical relief already in place and the extra personnel were not needed. The mission was scrapped. [118] Lt Col Wolf and MSgt Hughes were the POCs for this deployment.

✯✯✯✯✯

The 109th AES once again did their part by providing medical support at the community sponsored 8K Kaiser Roll. This year, because of moderate temperatures, there were very few casualties. Eight runners were treated by the aeromeds with only two individuals requiring transport to treatment facilities. The most common problem was heat exhaustion. Lt Georgeanne Johnson and TSgt Steve Sitta were POCs for this event.

Photo courtesy of the 109th AES archives
109th AES crew staffing the annual Kaiser Roll event.

Patriot Medstar was held in Westover, Massachusetts from 9-16 July. For many members of the unit, this AFR sponsored FTX was their first field experience. The purpose of this AE exercise was to test the functional capabilities of the new UTCs including the MASF, AEOT, AECC and aircrews. This was the first exposure to an AEOT, and for most, their first exposure to a MASF. "Talk to anyone and they'll tell you about the great learning experience. Even those who didn't fly weren't disappointed," said 1st Lt Pat Howard. Non-flyers were certified to drive many vehicles and received training that is not usually offered. Radio ops personnel, who were deployed on their first field exercise, performed an outstanding job.

☆☆☆☆☆

Minnesota National Guard Youth Camp was held at Camp Ripley, MN. Aeromeds volunteered both at the camp and at a static C-130E display, which always seemed to be a hit at this event.

Photo courtesy of Col Karen Wolf
Lt Col Karen Wolf and her crew of aeromeds at Youth Camp at Camp Ripley, MN.

For some time now, unit members were authorized to wear privately purchased T-shirts and hats. The T-shirts were in black with the 109th unit patch embroidered on the upper left side, while the hats were dark blue and carried a frontal C-130 silhouette over the unit's designation. These items proved very popular with unit members as they could be worn with flight suits and BDUs. In July, TSgt Sue Malecha became the new POC for purchasing these items. All profits went into the unit fund.

<u>**August.**</u> Twenty-six 109th AES members provided setup and medical support during the 1994 Minnesota Stand Down for Veterans from 5-7 August.

This event provided homeless veterans with many needed services such as medical and dental treatment and referral, voter registration, VA benefits, job services, stress counseling, and the basic requirements of food, clothing and a place to sleep. This year 317 male veterans passed through the gates at the site on the West Bank campus of the U of M. Statistics on homeless women and children attending the event were unavailable.

"I participated to show my gratitude to the veterans and to gain experience," said Capt Julie Finn. Her sentiments were echoed by several other 109th AES medical workers in the emergency/first aid tent.

The aeromeds were kept busy, treating over 60 veterans and transporting several to area hospitals. Most treatments involved ear and eye infections, foot problems, joint pain, dressing wounds, hypertension, falls and drug/alcohol abuse referrals. Many veterans required medication prescriptions. Most could no longer afford the drugs needed to control their hypertension, diabetes, or joint pain. [119]

September. More than 100 inspectors and assessors descended upon the 133rd Airlift Wing (AW) to conduct the unit's first QAFA (Quality AF Assessments). Col George "Marty" Martin, 8th AF Inspector General, ranked the 133rd among the top three units he had assessed during more than five years with "aeromedical" being one of the areas earning exceptional scores.

During the same time frame, the 8th AF conducted their Stan/Eval visit and evaluated the flying portion of our unit. Their comments: "Best C-130 AE seen to date. AE programs to emulate. The 109th AES is composed of dedicated, motivated, and professional senior leaders, aircrew members, and ground support personnel." [120]

☆☆☆☆☆

As a trainee, it instantly bothered SSgt Lawrence Cronemiller when he saw the C-130Es "sanitation kit." Recognizing this problem, SSgt Larry Cronemiller designed one and used his own money to create a prototype kit. Dubbed the "Cronemiller" by other unit members, the sanitation station received special recognition by the QAFA team and the Stan/Eval inspectors recommended it be benchmarked for worldwide aerovac. [121] What an accomplishment!

In the past, a used needle disposal canister consisted of a pop can that was secured to a litter stanchion with a bandage. Below that, a can of foam germicide was available for cleanup and wet hands were "air-dried."

Thinking of all the diseases in the world today, that didn't cut it with Cronemiller.

"This is the third-generation," he said of his compact kit. He had the lightweight case sewn at a local medical supply company. Holding everything from biological contaminant bags to cardboard urinals to face masks, it folded up to resemble a small gym bag.

"You can run into gross contamination in transporting patients," he explained. "These items could save us from becoming infected with HIV (Human Immunodeficiency Virus) or hepatitis."

Though aeromed teams carry "tactical bags" when flying, the contents are considered mobility items, according to Cronemiller. Constantly "borrowing" from those bags often leaves some items worn or unusable.

Photo courtesy of the 109th AES archives
SSgt Lawrence Cronemiller and the "Cronemiller" sanitation station.

Using his own money to avoid extensive red tape, he sank more than $200 and a year of refinements into the project, which is now under consideration in the AF Suggestion Program. The unit has given the kit several test runs on deployments.

Photo courtesy of TSgt Richard Childs and Col Michael Germain
Detailed photo of the "Cronemiller."

October. With a notice of only 48 hours, 10 members of the 109th AES deployed for 32 days to support Operation Southern Watch in Southwest Asia. This followed Iraq's troop movements near Kuwait, which started on 6 October. Approximately 64,000 military personnel were ordered to the region. Although a number of AE units volunteered, the 109th was the only unit that left Pope AFB, NC for deployment. Supporting the 4410th AES, the 109th worked with teams of active duty and reserve aeromeds on 12 medical evacuation missions. NATO (North Atlantic Treaty Organization) responded with troop build ups of its own and after a time the Iraqi troops withdrew.

☆☆☆☆☆

The 133rd Airlift Wing hosted the annual Veterans Affairs Department of Defense Exercise (VADEX). Testing civilian and military medical contingency support, the day's events included participation by more than 100 moulaged "patients," a 109th Airlift Squadron aircrew and 109th AES members. Patients were airlifted to various locations in Minnesota, Illinois and Iowa. Several crewmembers tested the computerized Pen-Pad documenting device for the Global Patient Movement Regulating Center (GPMRC), Scott AFB, IL. Highly complimentary remarks about the professionalism and care delivered were evident in the critiques. Maj Rask, Capt Hill, TSgt Campos and SSgt Brock coordinated this event.

☆☆☆☆☆

Twenty members and one aircraft from the 133rd joined seven other Guard and Reserve teams in Operation Nomad Vigil to help complete vital European missions prior to the buildup in Bosnia. The mission was to airlift Predator observation aircraft that had completed mapping missions over Bosnia from Gjader AB, Albania to Rhein Main AB, Germany. They also flew an aeromedical airlift mission for a combat control team member injured in a military motorcycle accident at Gjader.

November. While some unit members deployed for Operation Nomad Vigil, other aeromeds returned back to the desert.

"The 109th was up on all our AFORMS," said MSgt Lawrence Bild, who was in the Persian Gulf area twice during Desert Shield/Desert Storm. "And we had our equipment ready. It ended up we were the only ones activated who made it all the way."

Supporting the 4410th AEF, 109th members worked with teams of active duty and reserve aeromeds on 12 medical evacuation missions. This included three "priorities," meaning a patient was seriously sick or injured, and the first available aircraft was used for evacuation.

One of these was a highlight of the duty for SrA Adam Swierczek on his first deployment. "It was my first mission with that many patients," he said. "Everything went perfectly. It was good to do the job I've been trained to do."

Bild said the deployment was more organized and relaxed than during the Gulf War. "The fear wasn't there. We knew it wasn't a combat situation."

"There's more command structure there now," said deployment Troop Commander Capt Gary Prickett, who also was in the area during Desert Shield/Desert Storm. "Things moved much more efficiently."

In addition to the 12 missions, the 109th worked daily in the AECC coordinating missions. "There were only 10 permanent party aeromeds there," Bild said. "We had to run the operation for that part of the world."

In the AECC, they received messages from the "user force" - any agency in the area wanting to buy space on an aircraft for a patient. A nurse recorded medical information, met with a flight surgeon to prioritize the requests, and manifested them for flights. Medical Service Corps officers then appropriated aircraft or acquired aircraft space from Air Mobility Command.

Prickett and another med tech were on a mission in Germany when they were called for a priority patient in Rwanda who needed air evacuation. "It was a tight turnaround," Prickett said. "We were up 41 hours. We were also very successful over there because of the excellent training we've had here," Prickett concluded. [122]

☆☆☆☆☆

Three additional MSC officers were chosen from the enlisted ranks to fill part of the unit's new manning requirements. The in-house med techs selected were: TSgt Tracy Soderholm, TSgt Jacobson-Hanson, and MSgt Stangl.

1995

February. SMSgt Al "Zak" Zakariasen retired from the 109th AES. Since his arrival as a SSgt in the 109th in 1982, he held the positions of Flight Instructor, Flight Examiner, and finally as the Superintendent of Nursing Services. Perhaps "Zak" was best remembered for keeping the unit spirit alive and well with his unpredictable antics and humor.

Photo courtesy of the 109th AES archives
SMSgt Al "Zak" Zakariasen

March. Capt Julie Finn returned from a deployment to Guantanamo Bay, Cuba where she was deployed from 22 Dec-21 Mar in support of Operation Sea Signal. During her tour, she treated Cuban and Haitian migrants.

Finn told the story of a Cuban man who witnessed a shark eating his 15-year-old son who fell out of their overcrowded boat. Though the man could not swim well, he plunged into the ocean to save his boy, with no success.

Once back in Cuba, he attempted suicide, feeling inadequate as a father. Psychiatrists administered antidepressants. These, however, gave him more energy to be self-destructive and almost did him in, according to Finn. She was able to help him through the healing process.

"The chapel held a 'Mass of Hope' for him and a woman who had lost a son," Finn said. "This was a turning point in their recovery. It was a highlight of my tour."

Finn added that she was drawn to Cuba by the influence of her neighbor, Maria Elena, a native Cuban. "She's a marvelous person," she said. Knowing some Spanish also motivated her to volunteer.

Finn, along with 18 Army members and an AF colleague, built a psychiatric hospital from the ground up to provide care for up to 60 migrants at a time. Her co-workers were close-knit, but most were not experienced in hands-on, inpatient psychiatric care. "Psychiatric support is not a usual thing to be called up for," Finn said. "But the need was overwhelming."

She helped many people with situational depression. "These people had things happen to them four and five months before I got there, and they hadn't dealt with it yet. There was no one there to help them," she said. "We intervened, even that late, and we watched them normalize and pull through. They were able to come out as productive human beings."

Besides the situationally depressed, Finn said they dealt with those who were mentally ill in their own country and would be anywhere else. There were also groups of threatening patients.

The hospital received 50-60 Cubans in three days, many considered "very dangerous". "Our challenge was keeping track of all the new faces," she said.

During Finn's first week in Cuba, the Haitian migrants were told they would be sent home. If they returned they would face a death squad, or at least lack access to food. Though the Haitians had not rioted previously, military police thought fear might push them to that point.

"It was sad to think the military police's riot gear would be used on what seemed to be a gentle, kind and grateful people," Finn said.

The rest and unrest of the migrants changed daily as rumors circulated the camp as to who would and would not be allowed into the United States.

"The political issues follow you wherever you go," Finn said. "Issues like why the door was closed after 30 years of being open - issues like abortion."

The Cuban migrants, a westernized and educated people, wondered about these issues, she stated. They seemed to have a sense of entitlement for medical care, abortion on demand and a certain standard of living. "There were a lot of threats of lawsuits for just about anything, mainly from the Cubans," Finn said. "We were trying to make sure their rights as migrants and as people were upheld."

Added to the stress of the 90-degree, muggy, dusty days and tight living quarters was a work schedule of three 12-hour days, then two days off. "I just lived for those three days because there was little else to do except to eat and get some sleep for the next day," Finn recalled.

Support from home was one thing that kept Finn going. She said many people from the 109th AES helped, with exceptional support from Capt Don Dahlquist, Maj Sandy Darula, Lt Col Norman Hendrickson and 1st Lt Pat Howard. She also noted that base support from Intelligence, Supply, and the Airlift Squadron was critical to the success of her mission. [123]

April. The 133rd Airlift Wing conducted Coronet Gopher, an ORE (Operational Readiness Exercise), which focused on the ability to deploy, survive and operate, and redeploy. Units were operating out of Minneapolis, Camp Ripley and Duluth.

☆☆☆☆☆

Lt Col Karen Wolf was elected as the next president at the Minnesota State Guard Conference held in Rochester, on 28-29 April.

May.

Deployed - Letters from the Field: Maj Darrell Rask

In May, I was asked to go to Guantanamo Bay, Cuba, to help with Operation Sea Signal. This was the joint effort of all services to help the Cuban and Haitian migrants on their way to the United States. At one time the naval base housed over 40,000 migrants. The base was designed to house only 1,500 naval personnel. To say the least, it was crowded. When I arrived, the number had been reduced to about 20,000.

I was assigned to the TB (tuberculosis) team. When I left, over 400 migrants had been treated for this disease. Specifically, my role was working with the Haitian population. Over 80 Haitians were being treated with direct observation treatment where we made sure that the medication was administered. About half of the 80 were children down to the age of two years. Medication was given twice a week. Many of the adults had to take around 20 pills at a time. The children's medication was in suspension form. For the kids, even though the medication was in liquid preparation, it was not palatable. Juice was given to make the process somewhat easier. However, there were a few youngsters who would not voluntarily take the medication and a great deal of effort along with some creative problem solving had to be used to accomplish the task. The 95-degree heat and humidity added to the challenge. Treatment for all individuals was six months. I am glad I was only there for two.

July. The fifth annual Minnesota National Guard Youth Camp was once again held this month. According to officials, the camp provided a unique and enjoyable opportunity for dependents of the Minnesota National Guard to explore the environment in which they live and be more responsible in maintaining that environment for future generations. It also assisted campers in gaining an understanding of why their guard member served in the National Guard.

Monica Childs remembers, "I had so much fun my first year. I got to ride in the Humvees and armored personnel carriers (APC). Riding shotgun in the Humvee and standing in the open hatch on the APCs as they raced over the fields and through the woods was awesome! The night marches were fun, but kind of scary. I was really excited to go back the following year, but this was the last year I could go."

Photo courtesy of TSgt Richard Childs

Youth Camp volunteer Karen Wolf (left) checking registration for Monica Childs (right) who is accompanied by her mother, Margaret Childs.

FTX '95 was held from 25-29 July after nine months of planning. One group of personnel was deployed to Camp Ripley, MN to establish a Mobile Area Staging Facility and Aeromedical Evacuation Liaison Team. Another group deployed to MSP IAP to establish an Aeromedical Evacuation Operations Team and to maintain the AECMs.

The Army provided the casualties, which allowed them to exercise their own medical evacuation chain. The AELT worked with the Army on the procedures necessary to prepare patients for air evacuation. Patients were moved through the MASF and were flown by our AECMs on aircraft that were arranged by the AEOT. Support personnel from the 109th AES (Radio Repair, Supply, and Vehicle Operations) were also attached to AEOT. Lt Col Wolf and MSgt Rich Brcka were POCs for this very successful training event.

Photo courtesy of Col Karen Wolf
Receiving patients from the Army user service.

SMSgt Jim Hughes, First Sergeant, retired from the unit. Since the squadron did not have an official First Sergeant position, this additional duty assignment was posted as a unit vacancy.

Photo courtesy of Col Julie Eszlinger Jensen
SMSgt Jim Hughes (then MSgt)

The unit provided medical support for Kaiser Roll 1995 in Bloomington, MN, featuring five- and eight-kilometer running and walking events, including the country's largest wheeled athlete race.

<u>August.</u> Once again, the aeromeds from the 109th AES provided emergency tent coverage during the three-day Minnesota Stand Down for Veterans event this month. In some very unpredictable weather, unit members demonstrated their willingness to help in their community by performing duties ranging from emergency medical care, securing tents during a rainstorm, and entertaining children with balloon animals.

Over 400 veterans attended this event with 73 patients receiving treatment in the emergency tent. Stand Down is not only an opportunity for veterans to help veterans, but also an opportunity to work with Army and Navy counterparts. It also served as a training ground for the aeromeds. Unit members received continuing education credits after attending brief classes on certain medical procedures. After the training, the med techs put this information to good use on the veterans by starting IVs, drawing blood samples, performing blood glucose levels, and giving injections. [124]

☆☆☆☆☆

Five aeromeds returned home after 90 days at the contingency hospital in Guantanamo Bay, Cuba, where they treated Cuban and Haitian refugees.

☆ ☆ ☆ ☆ ☆

On 30 August, ground was broken for the new Ops/Aeromed building. Congressman Sabo attended the groundbreaking ceremony. The scheduled completion date was 6 December 1996. The unit was currently working on the warehouse area and systems furniture design.

September. The Aeromed Golf Team walked away with the league championship again this year, winning the playoff by one stroke.

☆ ☆ ☆ ☆ ☆

From 23-24 September, the 133rd Airlift Wing and the Minnesota Air Guard Museum commemorated the 75th anniversary of the flight of Capt Ray Miller to Washington, D.C., requesting authorization for a Minnesota air militia unit. The 109th Aero Squadron was federally recognized in January of 1921, the first unit of its kind in the country.

Numerous military and civilian aircraft were on display for this event. At 1300 on Saturday and Sunday a "built from scratch," full-size replica Curtiss Oriole was officially dedicated with a living history re-enactment of the events leading up to the preflight and flight.

Attendees were able to stroll along the flight line observing all types of aircraft. The 109th AES staffed the first aid tent as well as a C-130E AE static display. The unit also provided a booth to sell refreshments and 109th AES memorabilia.

☆ ☆ ☆ ☆ ☆

The Secretary of Defense William Perry announced the opening of a new incident reporting telephone hotline for all military and civilian members who served in the Persian Gulf region beginning in August 1990. This toll-free line offered veterans, their families, and health care professionals the opportunity to report details of first-hand experiences they believe may have led to medical problems they or others may have experienced since serving in this region. A separate toll-free number allowed military members and their eligible family members to call to register for medical examination and treatment. A self-help guide was also made available that was designed to be a working tool for those suffering from illness associated with services in the Persian Gulf. It provided strategies to obtain compensation, prove eligibility and described services available through the VA and Social Security.

In a related story, a news release from the Office of the Assistant Secretary of Defense for Health Affairs, Stephen Joseph, stated that the Comprehensive Clinical Evaluation Program (CCEP), a study involving over 10,000 clinical evaluations of active duty military personnel and their families, found no evidence of increased disease or unique illnesses in Persian Gulf veterans.

According to Dr. Joseph, the large number of participants and the thoroughness of CCEP examinations provided considerable insight for understanding the nature of illnesses and health complaints experienced by Persian Gulf veterans.

Dr. Joseph stated, "No single disease or syndrome is apparent, but rather multiple illnesses with overlapping symptoms and causes." He further stated that severe disability, based on lost work days was not a major characteristic of the CCEP participants.

This study found that the pattern of illnesses was similar to what was found in the general population, general practice, and in those patients seeking primary care. However, mental/psychological, musculoskeletal and connective tissue; and, signs, symptoms, and ill-defined conditions appeared to occur more frequently in CCEP patients.

The most common psychological conditions were tension headache, mild or stress-related anxiety or depression, post-traumatic stress disorder, and alcohol-related disorders. The musculoskeletal problems included joint pain, osteoarthritis and backache. Dr. Joseph stated that, as with similar patients in the general population, these conditions frequently did not have a clear-cut explanation.

Dr. Joseph stressed that this was not the end of efforts to help Persian Gulf veterans and their families. Ongoing research would continue to compare populations to characterize health consequences of the Gulf War. [125]

October. Training began this month for the July 1996 ORI. An exercise was conducted on Saturday of the UTA which involved all members of the unit. Chemical warfare and UTC training were also evaluated during this exercise.

November. Maj Diane Farris from the 8th AF Stan/Eval Office chose the 109th AES as the unit for her C-130E training and checkride. Maj Germain, Maj Gapstur, Capt Evavold, Capt Johnson and TSgt Cisar provided the training while Maj Hayes conducted her checkride. She had many complimentary things to say about all the AECMS who helped her successfully achieve this secondary aircraft qualification.

☆☆☆☆☆

Capt Gary Prickett was named the ANG Flight Nurse of the Year and Dolly Vinsant Nominee at the annual AMSUS convention. An annual award, the Wilma "Dolly" Vinsant Flight Nurse of the Year award is given to flight nurses who "put patient care above self" and must be involved in in-flight evacuations and healthcare missions. "I was overwhelmed when I was told about the award. The bottom line is that without all the support from my peers and subordinates, I'd never be successful in AE - if not for the in-flight med techs I work with. They're the backbone of it all."

SSgt Kenneth Petersen was named the ANG Outstanding Medical Service Specialist, and was a Brig Gen Sarah P. Wells Award Nominee which recognizes an outstanding enlisted Airman in the medical service. "I am honored to be recognized individually in a unit full of exceptional performers!"

1996

January. The Initial EMT course scheduled for this month was cancelled due to congressional budget cuts.

☆☆☆☆☆

One hundred years of aerovac experience was recognized and celebrated with the retirement party for MSgt Larry Bild, MSgt Dale Roiger, and MSgt Steve Larson this month.

Along with retirement, came the "obligatory" stories. TSgt Micki King remembers, "At roll call, MSgt Bild could never pronounce Mike Kjellander's (Chow-lander) name correctly. So one day, I asked a bunch of people to spread the word that Kjellander comes right after King and, when MSgt Bild gets to that name, we should all yell it out. It actually worked great and MSgt Bild looked up startled with a wide-eyed expression which I presumed showed his gratitude for our help."

February. From 6-20 February, twenty-nine members of the 109th AES participated in field training at the Joint Readiness Training Center at Fort Polk, Louisiana - the first ANG unit in the United States scheduled for this realistic wartime training. The 109th was the lead unit in this rotation of 80 aerovac members from 15 other Guard/Reserve units from around the country.

Unit members were transported to the "war zone" at Fort Polk to spend two weeks in wartime conditions. Helicopters and C-130s landed 24 hours a day carrying patients to a site with tents on a bare, sandy strip within sight of the flight line. Members performed medical duties while dealing with simulated artillery, low-light conditions, concertina wire, and aggressors while wearing thirty pounds of equipment including chemical gear, flak vests, night vision goggles (NVGs), and MILES gear.

In an e-mail message to the Commander, Col Deming stated, "I would like to congratulate you and the members of the 109th AES for the outstanding work that you and the organization are doing down at JRTC. Both Cols Robinson and Klosowski briefed Maj Gen Andreotti and the State Staff of your outstanding efforts. Please extend my congratulations to everyone for their outstanding contribution to making us the premier airlift unit."

☆☆☆☆☆

The "Bullpen" concept was introduced for the first time this month. It was developed for AE to provide each unit a schedule so they would know exactly what UTCs they were responsible to support in the event of any contingency operation that might arise. Individual units could then preplan for the deployment of personnel and equipment. The schedule was developed on a monthly basis. This concept outlined each UTC, and assigned a primary and alternate (or supporting) unit which was designated to provide manpower and equipment.

At the unit level, the 109th AES posted a Bullpen Sign-Up List on the Saturday morning of each UTA. The following morning, OICs and NCOICs of each of the UTCs involved met and made final selections based on AFSC and currency requirements, duration of deployment, and other unique circumstances. The monthly Bullpen Schedule was then posted by noon the same day. Individuals on this list would then be deployed for any future operations that might occur. [126]

March. The unit participated in the Operational Readiness Exercise - Phase I at Volk Field, WI from 5-10 March. Lt Col Wolf, SSgt Dave Mattson, SSgt Steven, SSgt McCann and SrA Clobes were identified by the Volk Field cadre as top performers.

☆☆☆☆☆

Capt Julie Finn was selected by the AF Association as the winner of the Juanita Redmond Award. This award was presented to an AF nurse with fewer than six years of experience who demonstrated excellence in clinical nursing. Capt Finn was selected for this award based on her deployment in support of Operation Sea Signal, a United States Military humanitarian operation in the Caribbean in response to an influx of Cuban and Haitian migrants attempting to gain asylum in the United States. The migrants became refugees at Guantanamo Bay Naval Base in Cuba. [127]

☆☆☆☆☆

The "Old Spice" policy was enacted due to the concerns of numerous unit members. The new guidance stated that "109th AES members should avoid the wearing of perfumes/colognes while performing duties in patient care settings (VA Medical Center, St. Paul Ramsey Medical Center) and on air evac missions in consideration of the sensitivities of patients and crewmembers." (authors' note: No policies were considered regarding the odors encountered on flights when JP-4 jet exhaust fumes filled the air on a hot load or the pervasive odors noted on rough and bumpy low level flights as the supply of "sick sacks" were rapidly depleted.)

April. The 1996 Tri-Service Military Reserve Nurses Educational Conference was held from 13-14 April at the Rosemount National Guard Armory. "Into the 21st Century: Reflection on Tri-Service Unity" was the theme for the conference, with Deborah Lee, Secretary of Defense, Reserves, as the guest speaker.

May. The Phase II Operational Readiness Exercise was held this UTA. It was the last opportunity to fully operate the aerovac system prior to the ORI. All six UTCs were operational throughout the weekend. The primary focus was the Ability to Survive and Operate (ATSO).

☆☆☆☆☆

SSgt Steven, SSgt Burmeister, and SrA Granlund were the first from the Minnesota ANG to arrive in Taszar, Hungary in support of Operation Joint Endeavor (Bosnia). Just before and during this deployment these three aeromeds designed the first unit coin. (authors' note: Please see the "Squadron Coin" section at the back of the book for further details.)

☆☆☆☆☆

The 109th AES hosted several medical training activities this month. Twenty-five flight nurses completed the Trauma Nurse Core Course, one flight nurse was certified in Advanced Burn Life Support, and nineteen med techs attended the Pre-Hospital Trauma Life Support training. A total of 86 students participated from the 109th AES, 911th AES (Pittsburgh), 23rd AES (Pope AFB, NC), 24th Med Group (Panama), 148th FW (Fighter Wing, Duluth), 133rd MDS (Air Guard, Minneapolis), Fleet Hospital 23 USNR (United States Navy Reserve, Minneapolis and Fargo), and several Wisconsin reservists.

June. Following the UTA, the unit held a three-day Home Station Training event designed to prepare all members for the ORI next month. Capt Schauer and TSgt Cisar were the POCs for this training.

☆☆☆☆☆

Construction on the new Ops/Aeromed building continued to proceed while unit members enthusiastically looked forward to its completion.

☆☆☆☆☆

The 1996 versions of the Lippincott Nursing Manual and Mosby's Drug Reference were placed in the in-flight trip kits as reference materials for all future flights.

☆☆☆☆☆

The AF successfully concluded its CCATT pilot project with the decision to incorporate CCATT units into the aeromedical system in fiscal year 1998. [128]

July. The 133rd AW and its active duty partner, the 189th AW, Little Rock AFB, AR participated in an Operational Readiness Inspection conducted by the Office of the Inspector General, 8th

Air Force. The inspection involved mobilizing and moving the unit to Volk Field, Wisconsin where numerous missions were performed under "combat conditions." The 109th AES achieved perfect results in overall AE operations, MASF, AE site management, and AE crews earned the grade of "Outstanding," the highest grade attainable. The squadron also received the wing's only Best Practice/Benchmark Candidate - the Patient Data Checklist for collecting medical data. The 133rd Airlift Wing as a whole received the grade of "Excellent." The following individuals were recognized by the Inspector General (IG) team as superior performers: Capt Evavold, 2d Lt Brock, TSgt Campos, SSgt McCann, and SrA Staut.

In a letter to Lt Col Carlson (109th AES Commander), Col Lloyd Dodd, Air Surgeon stated, "Congratulations for a job well done! I want to extend my personal thanks for your outstanding performance during your recent Operational Readiness Inspection. This is a very intensive inspection process that evaluates your ability to survive and operate in an exercise scenario simulating a real-world contingency operation. An 'Outstanding' score is an exceptional feat. I am extremely proud of your accomplishment.

"Your outstanding achievement is an obvious result of excellent training programs. Your overall score is a measurement of your unit's ability to exceed the standard, as well as an absolute indicator of your mission ready status. As the first ANG AE squadron to receive an ORI under Air Combat Command, you have set the stage for all other units. Please convey my accolades to all members of your unit. Their performance was superior and once again demonstrates that the 'ANG is a World Class Organization' consisting of highly trained professionals ready to go to war." [129]

While the convoy of trucks and equipment were returning to the base, a Ford Explorer blew its front tire and the driver lost control of his vehicle and crashed into a M35 (deuce) driven by 2d Lt Brock. The Explorer careened into the median and rolled to a stop. All of the convoy vehicles were maneuvered off of the highway. The aeromeds in the convoy responded immediately by going quickly to the demolished Explorer to render medical assistance. Fortunately, only one person in the vehicle suffered minor abrasions and refused medical care. Unit level training along with the quick thinking and skill of the involved 109th AES members turned a potential tragedy into a minor traffic incident. [130]

☆☆☆☆☆

The Global Patient Movement Requirements Center was developed under U.S. Transportation Command (TRANSCOM) to better coordinate and facilitate patient evacuation. In Europe and the Pacific, Theater Patient Movement Requirement Centers (TPMRCs) were established. Their responsibilities were to define and manage patient movement requirements, improve patient in-transit visibility, and collaborate with the theater or control center to coordinate plans for beds and airlift.

☆☆☆☆☆

To answer the need for standardized UTC training, the Aeromedical Evacuation Contingency Operations Training course was developed at Sheppard AFB, TX in September. Prior to this, non-standardized UTC courses were taught at places like Alpena, MI and Pope AFB, NC. The course became a required medical readiness requirement for all AE unit members.

☆☆☆☆☆

Lt Col Norm Hendrickson was named the ANG Flight Nurse of the Year. He was also a nominee for the Dolly Vinsant Award.

☆☆☆☆☆

The new Ops/Aeromed building reached 80% completion. The unit was working out final details on the systems furniture concept.

August. The 1996 Minnesota Stand Down for Veterans was held from 2-4 August. Fifteen air evac personnel participated during the three-day event where the aeromeds worked alongside the Army, Navy, and Veterans Administration Medical Center personnel. About 640 homeless veterans and their families were registered this year. One hundred-eleven of these individuals passed through the medical tent. SrA Tony Staut was chosen to represent the AF as a color guard during the opening ceremonies. [131]

September. The 133rd Airlift Wing began conversion from the older C-130E aircraft to the new C-130H3. It should be noted that the C-130 has been in continuous production longer than any other military aircraft. The unit was also working with the 934th AES and other ANG units to acquire flying time during the conversion.

Photo courtesy of TSgt Erik Gudmundson, USAF

A 133rd Airlift Wing Minnesota ANG Lockheed C-130H flies along the shore of Mille Lacs Lake in northern Minnesota during a training mission.

A tour of the new Ops/Aeromed building was conducted on Saturday of the UTA. On Sunday, an event was held to celebrate the 75th Anniversary of the 133rd Airlift Wing, acceptance of the new C-130H-models and the wing's "Excellent" ORI rating. Both retirees and family members were in attendance.

★☆☆☆☆

New federal military recognition - the Military Outstanding Volunteer Service Medal (MOVSM) was introduced this month. The prime qualifier for the MOVSM was volunteer service in the community setting over a specific period of time. Numerous unit members instantly qualified for this achievement based on their voluntary efforts in many events over the past several years.

October. The COT (Commissioned Officer Training) course officially replaced the MIMSO (Military Indoctrination for Medical Service Officers) program. COT became a 4-week, 2-day school for newly commissioned medical officers. Students were required to attend the full course instead of completing it in increments.

★☆☆☆☆

The unit had 10 personnel deployed in support of Operation Joint Endeavor. Capt Georgeanne Johnson remembers, "Camp Able Sentry was in Skopje, Macedonia and supported the Bosnia aerovac mission. We had an AEOT there made up of a crew and support personnel. Medevac helicopters brought patients to the airfield and we then transported them to Germany. An interesting memory...one night we had an urgent patient coming in and a C-9 with crew on board was coming for him. The airfield, which was run by French military personnel, operated by very unconventional rules according to our AF standards. For example, vehicles drove under the wing and were in movement while an aircraft was arriving. Most patient movement occurred during the day so this particular night there were no English-speaking French personnel on duty. My OIC and I ended up drawing in the dirt at the flight line to explain about the incoming helicopter and C-9. Very crude, but they got it! All went well with a very unusual mission."

Photo courtesy of the 109th AES archives
Operation Joint Endeavor deployed 109th AES aeromeds.

Back Row (L - R): Georgeanne Johnson, Mary Larson
Front Row (L - R): Shawn McMahon, Mike Howk, Kelly Tracy, Laura Napurski, JoEllen Evavold

The C-130H Model Conversion Training Program began in earnest this month. Aircrew Training implemented a plan for the flight instructors and crewmembers to accomplish familiarization training.

November. Several unit members attended the Association of Military Surgeons of the United States conference in San Antonio, TX. At this conference, Capt Julie Finn accepted the Juanita

Redmond Award and Lt Col Norman Hendrickson received the ANG Flight Nurse of the Year Award.

December. Lt Col Norm Hendrickson, 109th AES Chief Nurse, retired from the ANG with over 20-plus years of distinguished service with the 109th AES. MSgt Gerry Blilie also retired this month after many years with the aeromeds as well. Both of these individuals demonstrated tireless dedication to duty and commitment to the mission that contributed to making the 109th AES the best aerovac unit bar none. Col Michael Germain remembered an incident in which a med tech student on a training flight asked MSgt Blilie how long he had been involved with the aerovac mission. MSgt Blilie responded quite pointedly, "Let's put it this way. These boots (as he pointed to his well-worn flight boots) are older than you are!"

Photo courtesy of Lt Col Darcy Anderson
MSgt Blilie on a local training flight.

SSgt Steve Burmeister, SSgt Michael Granlund, and SSgt Bryan Steven earned the first NATO Medals awarded to wing members for their service in Operation Joint Endeavor.

Granlund, who spent 151 days in Hungary, also earned the singular distinction of having his medal awarded to him while still in-country, thought to be another first for the wing. He earned numerous letters of commendation and was selected as an "Airpower Superstar" in the base paper. Burmeister and Steven each spent 91 days in-country. [132]

Though daily living was rigorous - living and working in tents, serving 12-hour shifts, sleeping on cots and bathing in portable, self-contained showers - they all agreed there was never a dull moment, and all would gladly return again.

"I've been in 15 years, and this is the first time I've done what I've trained for," said Burmeister.

Granlund agreed. "It was rewarding to be able to do the job and do it well after training for so long, and our training here made the job easier," he said. "We set the standard over there, and people were really impressed with how we conducted business."

Steven explained they had understood their mission was to serve in Hungary in a MASF, which would include no flying duties. "When we got there, we took over all patient airlift from Hungary to Germany," he said. "A full complement for an MASF is 40 people. We had nine, so we really kept busy."

With no combat in that area, patients came from the sizable joint service contingent there, with mostly routine injuries, but a few urgent ones.

They enjoyed the hot meals served at Taszar but actually grew tired of having steaks, which was the usual fare along with salad, fresh vegetables and fruit. More exciting were the powerful storms with 40-50 knot winds, proving a real challenge to tent life. And though Granlund worked 138 out of 150 days, the trio were allowed a few days to visit nearby attractions, such as the capital city of Budapest on the Danube River. [133]

Photo courtesy of the Northstar Guardian (Nov '96)
(L - R): SSgt Steven, SSgt Burmeister, SSgt Granlund in Taszar, Hungary.

1997

January. Fewer training flights for the aeromeds became the new norm as the wing continued to transition to the new C-130H models.

☆☆☆☆☆

General Ronald Fogleman, AF Chief of Staff, announced a professional reading program that was designed to promote the development of AF personnel. Gen Fogleman stated, "I believe reading is one of the most important things an AF member can do for personal professional development. By reading, we can examine the thoughts and actions of important people that have faced the same kinds of challenges we face today, and we can learn from their experience. In the broad perspective, their times were different and the issue varied, but the problems were quite similar."

AF personnel were encouraged to read and broaden their understanding of air and space power, service doctrine, employment concepts and AF contributions to joint and combined operations.

Thirty-four books were chosen for the officer's reading program. Subjects included air power history, military strategy, combat experience and leadership. An enlisted reading program offered eight books as part of their professional military education.

☆☆☆☆☆

A message from Maj Gen Charles Roadman II (AF Medical Operations Agency Commander) stated, "The American public has been repeatedly informed that our Persian Gulf veterans may have been exposed to chemical weapons during Operation Desert Storm. The reports allege that this is the cause of illnesses potentially related to the Persian Gulf War.

"The Department of Defense is releasing a model of theoretical chemical agent dispersal from the munitions disposal operation at Khamisiyah, Iraq. Taken at face value, the model indicates that thousands of troops might have been exposed to sarin or cyclosarin.

"As you know, numerous military and civilian studies of Persian Gulf veterans show there is no clinical evidence of exposure or of a specific syndrome. The Office of the Assistant Secretary of Defense (Health Affairs) is planning to send letters to veterans explaining what is known about these potential chemical exposures. The letter will emphasize our commitment to provide for their welfare and to urge them to contact the Military Health Services System if they have any concerns." [134]

March. 90% of the 109th AECMs had completed the C-130H Model Conversion Training Program for the new aircraft.

April. The C-130s returned to AMC on 1 April.

☆☆☆☆☆

SSgt Mike Granlund was chosen as the ANG recipient of the Sarah P. Wells Award. He would go on to compete with the reserves and active duty for this recognition.

☆☆☆☆☆

Forty aeromeds participated in the annual hospital tour which was held at the Tripler Army Medical Center in Honolulu, Hawaii.

☆☆☆☆☆

Plans continue for the move into the new Ops/Aeromed building scheduled for next month. The actual move-in date was tied to the systems furniture installation. Some of the furniture from the existing Aeromed building was removed and refurbished for the new building as well.

May. The unit moved into the new Ops/Aeromed building this month. By all accounts the move went well.

Photo courtesy of TSgt Richard Childs and Col Michael Germain

Original number from the building the aeromeds occupied from March 1988 to April 1996.

Building 644, a wooden rectangular, two story flat-roofed "shoe box" shaped structure that dated from the World War II era served as the home for the 109th for nearly a decade. The first floor on the east half was the area for the squadron commander and full-time air technician. The west half of the first floor was the location of the 133rd Dispensary/Clinic.

The majority of 109th AEF was located on the second floor. We had one large room for a classroom and gathering location for everyone – both educationally and socially. There were other smaller rooms for Aircrew Training, Stan/Eval and USAF Nurse Advisor.

The most common description of Building 644 given by unit members who worked out of its ancient walls was, "You always knew what the temperature was outside the building, because it was exactly the same temperature inside the building!"

Photo courtesy of the 109th AES archives

__Building 644, the old Aeromed building. Note in-flight equipment storage door on the far left of the picture.__

Photo courtesy of MSgt Rachel Maloney

__Building 641, the New Operations/Aeromed building from the flight line.__

Photo courtesy of Col Michael Germain
The Aeromed side of Building 641.

Photo courtesy of Col Michael Germain
109th AES outside entrance to Building 641.

Two squadron members did well in the ANG Bowling Tournament that was held in Memphis, Tennessee. SSgt Bryan Steven ended up eighth nationally in "all events" out of approximately 3,000 Guard bowlers. Then he and his partner, CMSgt (Chief Master Sergeant) Bob Janssen, placed 19th in the "doubles" event. Both individuals were awarded cash prizes for their efforts.

Photo courtesy of MSgt Rachel Maloney
CMSgt Robert Janssen

<u>July.</u> The Total Force Aeromedical Evacuation Commander's Working Group was held from 21-25 July. A total of 116 participants came from around the world to attend this event, which was hosted by the 109th AES and the 934th AES. The unit received many kudos for the conference and the recommendation was made by several attendees to have next year's conference back in Minnesota due to the great organization and planning of the host unit.

<u>August.</u> Eighteen 109th AES aeromeds participated in the 1977 Minnesota Stand Down for Veterans which was held at the West Bank of the U of M campus during the first weekend of August. This year, 550 veterans and 124 dependents were treated at the three-day event which offered social, legal, and medical care to veterans in need.

The medical treatment tent, staffed by an Army physician's assistant and dentist, VA podiatrists and ophthalmologists, and aeromedical support staff provided an array of treatments and referrals to 100 clients. During the event, four veterans required emergency care and transportation to hospitals using the Humvee ambulance or 911 rescue vehicles. Hennepin County 911 service, apparently unaware of the Stand Down operation, was somewhat confused when they were called for assistance. Upon entering the emergency treatment tent, the paramedic asked, "What is this place?" When he found that the patient had a set of vital signs, an infusing IV, oxygen in place, blood glucose results, and EKG strip, and a diagnosis of a possible drug overdose he said, "WOW!"

Many of the aeromeds who participated in the event had the opportunity to provide hands-on medical care to a population in need, while honing their assessment and treatment skills. [135]

☆ ☆ ☆ ☆ ☆

The 109th AES also deployed to Peru and Ecuador to participate in two international Traditional Commander in Chief Activities (TCAs). These 10 day-long exchanges focused on medical and air evacuation skills.

Nine members of the 109th AES joined forces with eight members of the 109th AS, the State Air Surgeon, 20 members from the 183rd AES of Jackson, Mississippi, and two active duty translators to accomplish a military-to-military exchange of ideas with Ecuador. The training took place at an air force base in Manta, Ecuador from 8-17 August. The 83 participating students included personnel from the Ecuadorian Civil Defense, the Red Cross, Fire Department, Police, Air Force, Army, Navy, and the press.

Twenty of the students were doctors and the remaining students were nurses, medics, firefighters, and volunteers. The curriculum included trauma training, ACLS, CPR, burns, national disaster preparedness, MASF, and the USAF aerovac system. Two missions were flown on a C-130H with Ecuadorians participating as litter bearers and patients.

Many students were given tours of their city, fire departments, and experienced some of the local culture and food. Unit members stated that they gained great insights regarding this country, culture, and people.

Before this exercise, TCAs included only one unit. This was the first time the TCA was accomplished by combining the forces of two units, the 109th AES and the 183rd AES.

Photo courtesy of Col Karen Wolf
109th AES aeromeds and MN State Air Surgeon in Ecuador.

Third Row in Doorway: Jennifer Shults
Back Row (L - R): Mike Howk, Col Harry Robinson (MN State Air Surgeon), John Green, Lorraine Hennessy, Tom O'Keefe, Karen Wolf
Front Row (L - R): Dave Richter, Larry Cronemiller, Theo Williams

Also this month, twenty 109th AES members deployed to Lima, Peru to participate in subject matter exchanges in AE with both military and civilian personnel in that country and to conduct a mass casualty exercise to demonstrate the USAF Aeromedical Evacuation system. The activities were conducted at Group to Ocho, a Peruvian military compound.

Approximately 70 host nation personnel (doctors, nurses, technicians, and auxiliary personnel from both the military and civilian sectors) attended the hands-on training sessions and a mass casualty exercise using the 133rd AW's C-130H aircraft. Peruvian medical personnel were paired with 109th AES personnel as part of the flight crew and MASF team. MASF patient care, operation, and litter loading of simulated patients were exercised. Despite a shortage of equipment, translators with medical backgrounds and audio/visual equipment, the exercise was a success.

Maj Gapstur, Capt Hennessy, 1st Lt Jacobson-Hanson, MSgt Campos and TSgt Freund were the POCs for these events. [136]

Photo courtesy of Col Michael Germain

Mass casualty exercise involving a MASF and litter loading on a C-130H aircraft in Lima, Peru.

In addition to hosting an AE conference, the aeromeds found time to deliver boxes of donated supplies to some of Lima's neediest children where Peru's largest orphanage is located.

"I never expected to see so many children," said Capt Barb Anderson as she viewed rows of neatly dressed, orderly children in the orphanage courtyard. Pandemonium quickly ensued when the donated toys appeared.

The Sociedad de Beneficencia de Lima Metropolitana orphanage provides services for 550 of Lima's poorest children. Of the 100 orphanages in the city, this facility is the largest and has a unique mission. Only 50 of the children have no parents, and the remaining 500 children come from the streets or homes consisting of cardboard boxes or pieces of sheet metal.

These children are brought to the orphanage during the week. Here they are given food, clothing, medical care and an education in the public school system. The children return to their parents on the weekends.

An orphanage spokesman said 30-40 percent of these children become productive members of society. Many become skilled workers, teachers, or even doctors or lawyers. [137]

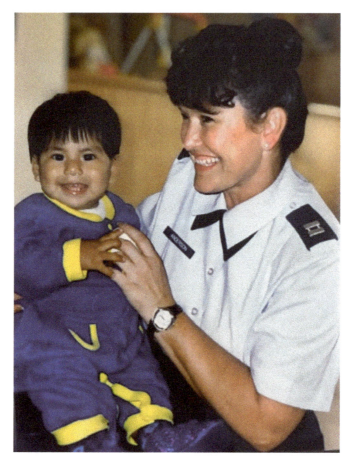

Photo courtesy of Sgt Micki King
Capt Barb Anderson at an orphanage visit in Lima, Peru.

On top of all this, an unexpected event occurred that heaped praise and recognition upon one of our aeromeds.

TSgt Mark Freund recalls, "After having observed some of the breakout sessions of our medical symposium in Peru, the Surgeon General for the Peruvian AF went to the podium to speak. His interpreter stood to follow him to the stage. He quickly turned to her and gestured with his hand to take a seat. He then announced, 'I want Mark to interpret for me.' I had no prior knowledge that this was going to happen and immediately stood and took my place in front to interpret for the General. After that event, he asked that I be his personal interpreter for the remainder of our time in Peru. The Peruvian officers could not believe that an enlisted person was allowed to dine at the same table as the officers. It was truly a unique experience that I will never forget and is one of my personal highlights."

Photo courtesy of TSgt Mark Freund

TSgt Freund interpreting for the Surgeon General of the Peruvian AF in Lima, Peru.

The 133rd AW web page was set up and running this month. The site consisted of topics concerning recruiting, history, photos, related web pages and the UTA schedule. Future plans called for an electronic copy of the Northstar Guardian which will include pages for squadrons and retiree information.

September. While on an AE training mission from Nevada to New Mexico, a 133rd AW aircraft was requested by an air traffic control facility to assist in the search of a downed aircraft in the vicinity of the Phoenix, Arizona airport. On a second flyover, the aircraft was spotted with the uninjured pilot standing on the wing. The coordinates were passed to air traffic control and a rescue helicopter arrived on the scene within 45 minutes to help the downed pilot.

☆☆☆☆☆

Unit members became eligible for a $600 Minnesota Persian Gulf Veterans bonus from the Minnesota Department of Veterans Affairs. To qualify, the Southwest Asia Service Medal must have been awarded for service outside of the U.S. between 2 August 1990 and 31 July 1991. A $300 bonus was available for those who were on active duty orders in the U.S. but out of Minnesota in support of the Gulf War.

October. A two-hour aeromed training mission was chosen for the Employer's Day Orientation Flight. Thirty employers participated in the event which was designed to both show them what their employees do in the military as well as thank them for their support.

November. When the Association of Military Surgeons of the United States convened in Nashville, the 109th AES received the Schafer Trophy - an award given to the outstanding reserve medical unit. This was the third time in 10 years that the unit received this honor. In addition, the unit was also recognized as the outstanding ANG medical unit by receiving the Theodore C. Marrs Award for the best medical unit in the ANG, again for the third time. Individual award winners included SSgt Michael Granlund - ANG Medical Service Specialist of the Year, 1st Lt Cathy Jacobson-Hanson - Young Healthcare Administrator of the Year, and Lt Col Karen Wolf - ANG Flight Nurse of the Year.

Photo courtesy of Col Karen Wolf
109th AES and wing representatives accept the Schafer Trophy, the Theodore C. Marrs Award and three individual awards.

It was announced that there were still some 109th AES coins available for purchase. The coin, designed by SSgt Granlund, SSgt Steven and SSgt Burmeister, was a limited edition coin. The mold was scheduled to be broken after 1000 coins were produced. At this time, there were less than 500 unit coins remaining, selling for $10 each. All profits went to the unit fund.

1998

January. Up to this time, the unit was not authorized an official First Sergeant position - all former occupants of the office were in an "acting" status. After careful thought and consideration, MSgt Susan Malecha was nominated for the position of First Sergeant this month after successfully graduating from the United States AF First Sergeant Academy. She held this position from 1998 until her retirement in 2003, and was also the first female to become a First Sergeant in the 133rd Airlift Wing.

Photo courtesy of MSgt Susan Malecha
MSgt Susan Malecha

In conjunction with MSgt Malecha's appointment, SSgt Mike Granlund was selected as the unit's Assistant First Sergeant.

February. Eighteen personnel from the 109th AES completed a seven-day tour at David Grant Medical Center at Travis AFB, CA. Live patient care was the focus of the training.

Personnel worked in the intensive care units, the emergency room and surgical and medical floors. In addition, the MSC officer and admin personnel gained experience in the Area Staging Facility (ASF), assisting with live patient launch and recovery.

Another highlight of the tour was an orientation to the hyperbaric medicine wing, the largest hyperbaric chamber in the country, where they treated non-healing wounds, carbon monoxide poisoning as well as the bends. (The bends, also known as decompression sickness, occurs in scuba divers or high altitude or aerospace events when dissolved gases, mainly nitrogen, come out of solution in bubbles and can affect just about any body area including joints, lung, heart, skin and brain.)

In addition, successful in-flight training was accomplished during six simulated aerovac missions on the wing's C-130H aircraft. [138]

☆☆☆☆☆

A TOPSTAR (Sustainment Training to Advance Readiness) program for AF nurses was implemented in a two-week course using actual patients, state-of-the-art mannequins, and computer-based instruction. Lackland AFB, TX, and Travis AFB, CA, hosted the training. [139]

March. 2d Lt Christine Davidson was selected as the 1997 Flight Nurse School Honor Graduate of the Year. Davidson was chosen as the honor graduate from her May 1997 class and then went on to receive national honors.

2d Lt Mary Larson was the second person in the nation to successfully complete the Flight Nurse Bypass Correspondence Course.

May. The 133rd Medical Squadron (MDS) and the 109th AES joined forces to conduct their first mass casualty exercise together. In the past, this type of training had been conducted annually by the aeromedical squadron but had only recently become a requirement for the Medical Squadron. During the exercise, the units practiced patient treatment in three basic areas. First, at the casualty collection point, patients received initial evaluation and treatment. Second, at the medical treatment facility, patients were stabilized and prepared for transport to the MASF. Third, at the MASF, the aeromeds provided medical care and prepared the patients for evacuation to medical facilities via military aircraft. [140]

June. Twenty-five members of the 109th AES and the 133rd MDS participated in a humanitarian health care deployment to Ecuador. Aeromedical evacuation technicians gained valuable experience as they treated tropical diseases, parasitic conditions, skin disorders, and other health problems erupting from poverty, lack of education, and poor sanitary living conditions. Working from the clinic area of a hospital in northern Ecuador (San Lorenzo), the medical group treated 2,297 patients in seven days. Three medical doctors, two Ecuadorian doctors, three dentists, two nurse practitioners, six nurses, and eight med techs provided physical exams and treatment to the steady stream of needy Ecuadorians. They prescribed about 6,000 medications in the process. The two unit dentists and one Ecuadorian dentist treated 300 patients and conducted 549 extractions.

Photo courtesy of Maj Darrell Rask
Hospital in San Lorenzo, Ecuador.

MSgt Steve Campos, an aeromedical technician with the 109th AES, was critical to the success of this deployment. The Ecuadorian patients were very receptive to MSgt Campos. He bridged the language barrier and through him they made their health problems known to the various health professionals and were able to receive the necessary treatment. He knew the language, medical terminology, and after eight years as an AE technician, he knew the important questions to ask to expedite numerous medical and dental examinations.

"MSgt Campos is part of the 'A' team, the advon team," said Maj Ed Howard, Officer in Charge of this Medical Readiness Training Exercise (MEDRETE) to Ecuador. MSgt Campos and two staff sergeants spent a busy week in Ecuador making sure housing, food, water and supplies were in place before the 26 team members arrived.

A 5,000-pound pallet of medical supplies arrived by military airlift in Esmeraldas a week ahead of the advance team. They hand-loaded these supplies on a barge for the seven-hour trip to San Lorenzo, where the medical mission took place.

In order to establish habitable quarters, aeromedical crewmembers had to rewire electrical circuits to power the water pump. "There was no running water in the men's barracks when we arrived," said advon team member SSgt Michael Granlund. Repairing faulty plumbing, fixing ceiling lights and cleaning foul barracks and latrines filled their spare time.

Most importantly, the advon team set the tone for relations with the Ecuadorian Navy Commandant whose base hosted the American military group.

"MSgt Campos used all of his field expertise, his vehicle expertise, and all of his cultural expertise to get this mission ready. He worked until it was done. I couldn't send someone who only works until he's tired. Steve views challenges as an opportunity to work more," Maj Howard said.

"You make your own reputation," MSgt Campos tells young people considering a military career. "Hard work will bring respect from your peers. After you earn respect, everything else falls into place. You make your own destiny."

Spanish language skills were key to this health care mission to South America. "Doc, med tech or security police, if you didn't speak Spanish, we were in trouble," said Maj Howard. "Even with 10 or 11 interpreters of varying skill levels, we still had language barriers and could have used more."

Maj Barbara Anderson agreed with the important role interpreters played in the success of the operation. "Our interpreters were worked to death. They were pushed and pulled in all directions."

MSgt Campos grew up in a home where Spanish was the primary spoken language. He admits that he lacks formal coursework, but mastered Spanish through careful listening and repetition. In his 22-year military career, MSgt Campos has traveled to Panama, Peru, Venezuela, Colombia, Ecuador, Puerto Rico, Honduras, El Salvador, and Belize. Each deployment required military personnel with Spanish language capabilities. Bilingual skills helped mesh the civilian and the military communities. [141]

Photo courtesy of Col Karen Wolf
Crowd waiting for the clinic to open in San Lorenzo, Ecuador.

Teams from the active duty Air Force, Air Force Reserve, and Air National Guard participated in Rodeo 1998, a biennial international airlift and tanker competition. Held at McChord AFB, WA, teams from 16 countries participated. Each aeromed team was judged according to response time and performance in three categories: combat configuration/loading, medical equipment preflight operation, and medical emergency scenarios. The 109th AES won a first place trophy for the best C-130 configuration enplaning team (both litter and ambulatory) whose members included Capt Cathy Cisar, Capt JoEllen Evavold, MSgt Liz Howard, TSgt Scott Gruel, and SSgt Ken Peterson. [142]

July. Fifteen unit members provided medical support for the 17th annual Kaiser Roll at Normandale Community College in Bloomington, MN. Races were again conducted for both the able-bodied runners and wheelchair participants. 109th aeromeds treated 12 racers who suffered from heat and exhaustion. Maj Espinosa and SSgt Culver headed up this event.

August. During the Minnesota Stand Down for Veterans, seven officers and eleven enlisted members from the 109th AES worked with 122 homeless veterans, contributing 472 hours of service.

☆☆☆☆☆

Ten radio operators and med techs blazed new trails at the Aeromedical Contingency Operations Course in Texas this month.

October. The 15th AF conducted an Aircrew Standardization and Evaluation Visit of the 133rd OGV (Operations Group Standardizations/Evaluations). This was a joint inspection involving the 109th AS as well as the 109th AES. The two squadrons earned a combined high "Excellent" rating based on the performance of the 109th AES, 109th AS, the Wing OGV section and the AFORMS area.

Once again, the 109th aeromeds excelled, with Lt Col Karen Wolf and MSgt Cheryl Burton earning "EQ" (Exceptionally Qualified) evaluations.

Inspectors observed that the AE technicians had an extremely high level of medical skill and knowledge. In their spot evals and general observation of our crews, the evaluators commented that it was obvious the entire unit's training efforts in this area were consistent and intense, contributing to the AETs level of expertise. Spot evals were conducted on 42% of the flight nurses and 32% of the med techs.

Another area noted by the team was the excellent CRM (Crew Resource Management) with crews and the 109th Airlift Squadron, as well as the obvious efforts of the people to take care of each other. [143]

The next inspection for the unit would not be for another three years - the longest time between inspections since 1992.

November. Six students from the Roosevelt High School Medical Magnet Program spent four hours with the 109th AES during the November drill. There, they learned the workings of patient evacuation through the tactical airlift system and some of the skills necessary to care for patients in-flight.

This mentoring program offered interested high school students the opportunity to explore medical career paths. In the 109th AES medical skills lab, students received hands-on experience inserting intravenous lines and endotracheal tubes into mannequins. "Once they were shown what to look for, with a little assistance, they were able to intubate," said SSgt Bryan Steven. This visit offered a chance for these high school juniors to see a small part of the military medical career field.

"It is so refreshing to see these young kids and witness their enthusiasm. It helps remind me of the reasons why I'm doing this job and why I'm in nursing," said Maj Georgeanne Johnson, who instructed the students on C-130H litter loading procedures.

"They really lit up when we took them on the aircraft," said Capt Pat Howard, who helped the students don chemical gear, body armor, web belts and helmets.

One of the students said her experience at the 133rd Airlift Wing has opened up some doors for the future. Future visits were scheduled for the following year. [144]

☆☆☆☆☆

Maj Georgeanne Johnson was selected as the ANG Outstanding Nurse Corps Officer of the Year, 1998.

☆☆☆☆☆

Throughout the history of the 109th AEF/AES, there has been a group of individuals who are not always recognized as much as the "flyers" or other groups within the unit, but who perform an absolutely critical function dealing with every aspect of our mission. These squadron members not only worked Monday through Friday, but many weekends and evenings as well. The "Admin" section has performed admirably in the past and will continue to provide critical support in the years ahead.

Photo courtesy of MSgt Rachel Maloney
"Admin" personnel.

(L to R): Deb Flohr, Rachel Maloney, Chuck Rodke, Betty Tomerlin, Stephanie Shegstad

1999

February. The unit ran an exercise in preparation for the upcoming rotation at the Joint Readiness Training Center, to be held this coming June at Fort Polk, LA.

☆☆☆☆☆

Maj Rodke left the 109th AES following many years of service after accepting the position as the 133rd Airlift Wing Senior Maintenance Officer. Maj Rosburg joined the unit's full-time staff as the new senior technician.

☆☆☆☆☆

A celebration was held after the Saturday UTA at the Fort Snelling Employees Club to honor and bid farewell to the following unit members who were retiring after twenty plus years of service: Capt Eric Lee, 2d Lt Tom Stangl, SMSgt Paul Walker, and SMSgt Betty Tomerlin.

CHAPTER 10
The Command of Col Karen Wolf

(Apr 1999 - Sep 2001)

Photo courtesy of Col Karen Wolf

Commander's Comments: Really, you think I'm going to remember what happened 15 years ago . . .?? Well, it certainly wasn't boring but it certainly didn't have the ops tempo that most of the Guard has these days. I remember my time as Commander as a succession of planning for exercises, maintaining crew and personnel currencies, sending people off to the AEF (Air Expeditionary Force), having exceptional unit members recognized at the national level, and providing personnel for various state needs.

I began my ANG career in September 1981. Sure, I thought I'd do my three years and then get out. However, the mission and the people I worked with in the 109th AES (Flight at the time) were so compelling that I decided to stay. I remember being awed by the expertise of the flight nurses and med techs and hoped to one day be able to emulate them. I remember the camaraderie and good times we had on cross-country training missions, and the good training we got during those missions. Each year seemed to bring more requirements from the Guard Bureau, but we were always willing and able to accomplish them. We were never short of volunteers for any tasking that came our way. When it came to field training exercises or ORIs, we all committed to show to the wing and the world that we were the best—and we wanted to see ourselves in the entertaining slide show at the end of the exercise—thanks to Lt Col Darcy Anderson's skill in putting slides, two projectors and music together.

In 1986, my husband and I were chosen to attend Air Command and Staff College in residence at Maxwell AFB, AL, for a year. Having learned to persevere from our 133rd AW experience, we finished the year-long program, met lots of interesting people, and earned our master's degrees as well. We returned to Minnesota in 1987, I got requalified and we were happy to be home for the Twins to win the World Series! 1988 took us to Washington, D.C. where my husband worked at the ANG Readiness Center. I joined the Medical Squadron of the D.C. ANG, which gave me another angle of how we, as medical providers, can impact others in the wing. Back to Minnesota in 1991, I rejoined the 109th AES, and in time to see the Twins win the World Series again!! During the '90s I concentrated on flying, becoming an instructor and then an examiner, moving on to the Wing Stan/Eval office with SMSgt Cheryl Burton. Again, another assignment that allowed me to grow with and beyond the 109th. I also completed Air War College in seminar in 1996 which eventually led to further opportunities. Lesson for all—don't neglect completing your PME (Professional Military Education)!

Throughout these years I was privileged to have wonderful commanders—starting with Col Julie Eszlinger Jensen, then Lt Col Darcy Anderson, and then Col Sandy Carlson. Each one of these women provided opportunities for me to learn and lead. It was an honor to be chosen as the next Commander, taking over from Col Carlson in April 1999.

My tenure as Commander consisted of many exercises and inspections such as JRTC, Northern Eagle x 2, mass casualty exercises, ORI, preparing and deploying unit members for AEFs x 2, hosting a wing dining-in, continuing support for the MN Stand Down for Veterans, hosting the Total Force AE Commanders Conference and continuing our excellent flying training program, including cross-country trips. I was very proud to be involved in writing nomination packages for our excellent unit members for national recognition. During my time as Commander, these national award recipients included Maj Georgeanne Johnson, Capt Jacobson-Hanson, SMSgt Cheryl Burton, Maj Sue Schuldt, and Capt Dave Richter. Of course, the 109th AES has had many recipients before and since!

In early 2001, I was chosen to go to State Headquarters to be the nurse liaison to the 133rd AW and the 148th FW. Change of Command was planned for September UTA. Of course, we all know what happened in September 2001—just a few days before the ceremony, 9/11 happened. What a blow to all of us. What devastation we felt. Where would we go from here? How should we best respond as a unit? Lt Col Rosburg had been chosen to be the next Commander and was ready to do the job. The Change of Command took place and thus began an unprecedented time of real-world deployments in support of the new reality.

The honor of being Commander of the 109th AES was a wonderful experience. I always felt the support from the unit and appreciated the hard work everyone was willing to give for the good of the unit. My philosophy of leadership was to give others the chance to contribute their ideas and know-how and to grow in their careers. There was so much knowledge and life experience from which to draw. I hope I inspired unit members as I was inspired by others throughout my career.

Col Karen Wolf

April. Lt Col Sandy Carlson turned over command of the unit to Lt Col Karen Wolf. Lt Col Carlson assumed the duties of the 133rd Medical Squadron Commander in May.

Photo courtesy of Col Karen Wolf
Change of Command Ceremony.

(L - R): Col Bill Schuessler, Col Ron Keith, Lt Col Karen Wolf, Lt Col Sandy Carlson, MSgt Sue Malecha

May. One final exercise was conducted as a final "tune up" for the upcoming JRTC.

★★★★★

On 22 May, this year's NDMS exercise was held on base at the wing's South Hangar. Twenty-eight 109th AES personnel participated in the exercise that launched three C-130H missions with moulaged "patients" consisting of members of the Civil Air Patrol and lifelike mannequins. A small AEOT and modified MASF were utilized to prepare the patients who were "exposed" to a sarin gas attack in the Twin Cities. Each aircraft carried up to 40 patients and flew to destination airfields in Milwaukee, Detroit, Cleveland and Des Moines.

June. Members from the 109th AES once again deployed to Fort Polk, LA to participate in an annual 10-day JRTC exercise that was co-located with the Army's combat support hospital. Twenty-four additional people from eight other AE units filled out the UTCs and supplied the aircrews.

Not only did the 69 unit members airlift 126 patients, they also experienced many "firsts" which included the opportunity to mark helicopter landing sites, marshal the helicopters into position, and then offload patients in the dark. There was also a first-time experience for many to complete an ERO. Those working in the MASF became proficient at adopting a defensive posture. While providing their own perimeter defense, these aeromeds learned valuable lessons while on watch. SSgt Jennifer Shults, who spent nights in a bunker with three other aeromeds said, "I learned how to sleep outside under a tree for three nights and fight the raccoons."

Co-located with the Army's C-Med and combat support hospital, two liaison teams worked with the Army, encouraging them to utilize the AE system. The AELT then assured that the patients were prepared for flight.

These Army medical units were under constant enemy attack. Subsequently, the liaison team spent much of its time coping with the barrage of missiles and the patients that followed in their wake. [145]

The exercise was a big success and numerous kudos went out for the work accomplished. Special recognition at the out-briefing was given to TSgt K. Hoffoss, Capt Jacobson-Hanson, Capt Evavold and SSgt Granlund.

☆☆☆☆☆

Once again this year, the unit participated in the Minnesota Stand Down for Veterans. Treating heat casualties and forcing fluids kept the aeromeds busy during the hottest first two days of this four-day event when temperatures reached the high 90s. Thirty-seven unit members provided around-the-clock staffing for the medical treatment tent which was located at tent city on the West Bank campus of the University of Minnesota.

Over 1,000 visited Stand Down this year. About 400 homeless veterans from all corners of the state as well as veterans from as far away as Texas and California registered. Ninety-five veterans visited the medical tent seeking treatment for ailments ranging from high blood pressure and diabetes to sprained joints and foot problems. After an assessment and minor treatment, many of these men and women veterans from the streets were referred to the VA Medical Center for follow-up care.

September. The 1930 aeromed flights were moved up half an hour to the 1900 time frame. The reason for the earlier show times was to avoid the big line-up of commercial aircraft that also had a 1930 take off time.

October. Thirty-seven members of the 109th AES deployed for Operation Northern Eagle to Camp Ripley, Little Falls, MN and to the AFR facilities at Minneapolis-St. Paul International Airport. While four 109th radio operators kept communications open between the two exercise sites, the flight crew coordinators and liaison team communicated air evacuation requirements with the Army, Navy, and the AFR. Once patients were properly prepared and airlift was arranged, the Army or Navy moved their patients to a staging facility at the flight line. The 109th marshaled C-130Hs and helicopters in position and cared for patients passing through their tents during the day. At night, members used a driving course, honing their vehicle and NVG skills on remote terrain.

Both the MASF and AELT did a wonderful job supporting this exercise despite the cold and field conditions. Lt Col Karen Wolf, Maj Ed Howard and Maj Sue Schuldt assisted in the planning and execution of the exercise for the unit.

☆☆☆☆☆

Three live C-141 air evac training missions with the Keesler AFB, MS air evac unit, were a great success for the nine 109th personnel fortunate to participate in this program. These were whirlwind trips to Germany, Puerto Rico and the Azores that airlifted patients back to the U.S.

"We flew 18.4 hours from Jackson, MS, to Andrews AFB, MD, the Azores to Keflavik, Iceland and back to Andrews AFB. The Keesler Mississippi unit and crew were great to work with. We integrated as crewmembers and the trip was a good learning experience," said Maj Barb Anderson. "This was their first rotation, so we were able to observe how they had to deal with issues concerning patients, passengers, non-medical attendants, equipment and timeline issues," she said.

SrA Shirley Janu flew as an AE technician. "I enjoyed working with real air evac patients on the C-141," she said. "All the training that we do provides the knowledge and skills necessary for us to participate as crewmembers with the Mississippi ANG." Lt John Janu found these live missions to be an opportunity to deal with "real people and real issues."

Medical Service Corps officers had the chance to think through and troubleshoot actual problems such as procuring meals, lodging and taking care of equipment. All of those who deployed on these patient missions felt it was great training. [146]

November. A combat dining-in (casual dress) was held on Saturday evening of the UTA weekend for all unit members. The joint officer-enlisted event was held at the Everett McClay VFW Post in Bloomington, MN.

☆☆☆☆☆

A scheduled overnight cross-country to Tucson, AZ turned into a five-day trip for several aeromeds this month.

Due to mechanical problems, the group was forced to extend their stay and was billeted at the posh Loews Ventana Canyon Resort. The aeromeds remained alert and ready for any medical mission that might come their way.

December. The unit held the annual family Christmas party this UTA weekend. It was a great celebration for the family with presents, food and even a visit from Santa and a couple of his elves. The unit also sponsored a holiday gift giving effort. Like last year, the 109th AES directed their generosity to the King Family Salvation Army Preschool. Unit members donated such needed items as construction paper, Big Glue Sticks, watercolor paints and other school supplies.

☆☆☆☆☆

Two unit members garnered wing-level awards again this year. MSgt Douglas Ackerman was selected as First Sergeant of the Year 1999 for the 133rd Airlift Wing and the Minnesota ANG. Maj Susan Schuldt, was chosen as the 133rd Unit Public Affairs Representative of the Year 1999 for the third year in a row!

2000

January. The Commander briefed that the upcoming year held many new and exciting challenges for the squadron. The primary responsibility of the unit was to prepare for the Air Expeditionary Force exercise which was scheduled for June through August. The squadron also had TOPSTAR, AECOT for the new troops, a deployment to Brazil, EMT refresher and TNCC to name just a few of the events on the table for the upcoming year.

February. The unit learned that Maj Sharon Rosburg served as class leader and was selected as a Distinguished Graduate of the nine-week Health Services Administration School, Sheppard AFB, TX.

As unit members continued to deploy, maintaining currency was a challenge as was keeping members' immunizations up-to-date.

✩✩✩✩✩

The squadron also conducted winter survival training for its members, with several aeromeds camping overnight in snow igloos and parachutes lined with hay bales. Class participants set up tents and AGE equipment in the challenging winter environment. Generators and Hunter heaters were also used throughout the weekend. The radio operators were able to set up and train on their equipment as well.

✩✩✩✩✩

Maj Sharon Rosburg participated in a teleconference with representatives from USAFE, AMC, AFRC, ANGRC (Air National Guard Readiness Center), deployed sites and all Guard AE units. The goal was to get answers to the many questions regarding the new Air Expeditionary Force concept.

✩✩✩✩✩

The unit experienced a lot of foggy weather and broken aircraft this month. Many AECMs had to make schedule changes to accommodate students and flight evaluations.

April. The 109th AETs began training at the 133rd Medical Squadron during this UTA. This clinic experience enhanced their skills training and provided opportunities to take vital signs, measure height and weight, perform 12-lead EKGs, as well as draw blood samples and give immunizations.

In May, technicians from the 133rd Medical Squadron joined the 109th AES at their Sunday morning hospital rotations at Regions Hospital and the VA Medical Center.

May. The first rotation for the summer's AEF left on 20 and 21 May. Eight 109th AES personnel headed for Kuwait. The unit's participation in AEF declined in August, but there were opportunities for individuals to fill shortfalls and unfilled positions. The unit was able to fill every position requested and even filled extra shortfalls. The squadron received high praise for their work during their rotation. The next commitment for the aeromeds was scheduled for September, October and November 2001.

Photo courtesy of Maj Sue Schuldt

SrA Kelly Hanzel (left) and SrA Jason Arndt (right) configuring aircraft for an aeromedical mission in Kuwait.

This year's Rodeo team, which consisted of Maj Evavold, Capt Brock, MSgt Pierson, MSgt Cisar, TSgt Petersen and SSgt Staut, headed to Pope AFB, NC to participate in the competition. Aircraft events included preflight, configuration, loading patients and proper use of medical equipment. Patients were also transported through the medical endurance course competition.

☆☆☆☆☆

Over the past year, the Medical Service Corps officers have been working to more clearly define their role as it related to flying. MSCs were required to fly at least quarterly and the unit wanted to make sure that both the flyers and MSC officers got the most out of that experience.

A two-day Aeromedical Operations Officer training seminar was scheduled for the September drill to get all MSCs "up to speed." On drill weekends, an MSC was assigned to AEOO duties whenever a flight was scheduled. An MSC would be scheduled on all cross-country training missions and serve as "Executive Support Officer," not in the chain of command of the OIC and AOIC (Assistant Officer In Charge) i.e. flight nurses. In this case, the MSC would take care of the logistical issues such as billeting, messing and transportation. When the MSCs flew on local missions, they assisted the launch and recovery, equipment movement and generally assisted the crew as requested.

August. The Guard Family Network sponsored "Get Framed," which was an opportunity for personnel to have a professional 8 X 10 family portrait taken at no cost to wing members. Several photo sessions were available at the dining facility (DFAC) throughout the month.

☆☆☆☆☆

A new Concept of Operations for AE was approved by Lt Gen P.K. Carlton, Surgeon General of the Air Force. New AE UTCs were developed based on the building block "plug-in/pull-out" principle, allowing planners to select specific UTCs capable of supporting the range of steady state, contingency or major theater war operations plans. Most of the UTCs were similar to what were already in place. Since this was now a building block concept, the number of personnel assigned to each UTC changed according to the needs of the mission. There were also several non-flying slots in the new Unit Manning Document.

☆☆☆☆☆

The 2000 Minnesota Stand Down for Veterans was held again this year and was the largest event of its kind to date. About 1,020 needy veterans and 270 family members came through the gates on the West Bank of the U of M campus during this three-day experience.

Several new elements were introduced to the medical mission for the 109th AES - Medical Service Corps officers and radio operators were incorporated into the event and additional medical testing was provided to veterans.

AOIC, Lt Julie Ritz, had some initial concerns about the logistics of this humanitarian operation, but quickly grasped the dynamics of the mission. Her practical nursing skills, as well as her MSC knowledge, helped smooth the way for appropriate medical treatment for a number of veterans seeking help.

Communicable disease screening was a priority this year. About 66 veterans had blood drawn for hepatitis C and 50 PPDs (Purified Protein Derivative - Tuberculin) were administered to test for tuberculosis.

Capt John Janu, OIC of this year's event, was pleased to see how well the AETs pulled together to make it work. When asked to draw blood for the hepatitis C testing, many of the AETs were hesitant and unsure of their abilities at first. "SSgt McMahon was the first to step up and say 'I'll do it.' That got the ball rolling," said Capt Janu.

The AETs demonstrated confidence in their blood draws and a caring attitude as they tried to understand the psychosocial needs of this population of veterans.

Twenty-one personnel from the 109th AES worked during this year's event. "SrA Ben Zappia gathered information from previous years, found out what needed to be done and did it," said Capt Janu.

Radio operators SrA Andy Reinhardt and SSgt Earnest Borrego pitched right in, driving between the Stand Down site and the VA Medical Center. When not on the road, SSgt Borrego assisted with admin tasks, learning medical terminology in the process.

The cooperative efforts of all the AFSCs made this a very successful event. [147]

September. The 109th AES hosted the officers dining-in for the wing which was coordinated by Maj Barb Anderson and Capt Cathy Cisar. Elizabeth Strohfus, a pilot who shuttled aircraft to England during World War II was the guest speaker. An officer from another unit on base commented, "I can unequivocally state that I thoroughly enjoyed the event, and moreover, several officers I spoke to from various units within our wing expressed the same sentiment. The good-natured fun of the grog bowl and commensurate violations of the procedures, officer team building and camaraderie, excellent cuisine, delightful guest speaker, the bagpipes and drums all made for a well-rounded and memorable evening! My hat is off to all of you and my sympathy extends to the next committee who will indeed have to top this year's dining-in!" [148]

Photo courtesy of Col Karen Wolf
(L - R): Lt Col Karen Wolf, Maj Sue Schuldt, Capt Pat Howard, Maj JoEllen Evavold singing Karaoke at the wing's dining-in.

Lt Col Karen Wolf briefed the unit that 2001 would be a year in which the unit would concentrate on UTC training. Each person in the unit who was assigned to a mobility slot was assigned to a position in a UTC. Throughout the year, UTC managers would plan pertinent training for personnel assigned to that UTC.

October. SMSgt Timothy Evavold, Superintendent of Nursing Services, was promoted to Chief Master Sergeant.

November. Several unit personnel were recognized as national award winners. Maj Barb Anderson was selected as the ANG Flight Nurse of the Year, SSgt Tony Staut as the Outstanding Medical Services Airman of the Year, and Capt Dave Richter, ANG Young Healthcare Administrator of the Year.

December. The unit Christmas party for members and family was once again held on the December UTA. Post party reports indicated the event was a great success.

2001

January. The Commander commented that the most important activity of 2001 would be to accomplish the Operational Readiness Inspection. Training had already begun for this event, but there would be much more to come.

☆☆☆☆☆

The AE Commanders Council conducted a fly-in for all ANG AE units in San Antonio, Texas.

The agenda was to share information with other air evac units as well as to further camaraderie and fun. Breakout sessions represented the various sections such as Staff Development, Aircrew Training, Chief Nurse's Office and Stan/Eval.

☆☆☆☆☆

Lt Col Sharon Rosburg briefed the unit on the changing financial picture and its effect on the unit for the foreseeable future. Basically, things would be tighter due to overspending at the Guard Bureau level over the previous 12 months. Everyone was only allowed their annual fifteen days AT allotment. This meant that if someone attended a 30-day formal school, they were done for the year. A priority for all unit members was to maintain their flying currency as the unit continued to be tasked for worldwide deployments.

☆☆☆☆☆

The National Registry EMT-B Refresher course was conducted at the unit this month.

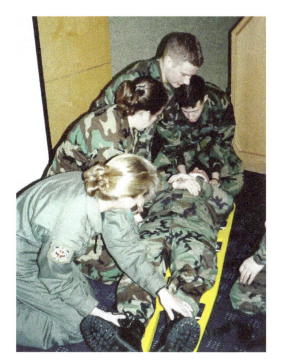

Photo courtesy of the 109th AES archives

(L - R): SSgt Emily Armon, SMSgt Cheryl Burton, SSgt Pat Clark, SSgt Sean Mitricska, TSgt Mike Granlund practicing longboard use during National Registry EMT-B Refresher.

Due to the extreme icy weather conditions, aeromeds no longer walked out to the aircraft for their training flights. For safety reasons, crewmembers and patients were being driven out to the flight line.

February. Seventy-one unit members were scheduled for block training this month. Many changes were made in the training to ensure the aeromeds were qualified for worldwide deployments.

March. This UTA was the first opportunity for the squadron to practice some of the skills needed for the Operational Readiness Inspection scheduled for July, with a strong emphasis on ATSO requirements. Unit members flew a mission as other UTCs (AELT, AEOT and MASF) participated in the training as well.

April. 1st Lt Kim Schmidt, TSgt Steve Burmeister and SMSgt Tom O'Keefe were selected to fly live C-141 missions to Puerto Rico. This was an opportunity to familiarize crewmembers with the C-141 aircraft and its mission.

☆☆☆☆☆

The American Heart Association recently made changes in CPR. Unit members underwent additional training incorporating the new standards. Aeromeds would be tested on these changes on flight evals beginning in July.

☆☆☆☆☆

The Total Force AE Commanders Conference hosted by the 109th AES was a tremendous success. One hundred sixty participants were squeezed into the CE classroom where many informative briefings were conducted. The success of the conference was due in part to the efforts of Lt Col Rosburg and MSgt Deb Flohr.

May. The UTA was used to build on the skills needed and the lessons learned in March as it was a dress rehearsal for the July ORI. Dubbed Early Bird '01, many members were required to spend Saturday night on base. The 24-hour plus exercise included mobility processing, UTC establishment, two flights, overnight shifts, ATSO, and the setup of radios. The 934th AES was also involved with their AEOT and crews. Personnel not participating in the ORI were tapped as patients. By all accounts, it was a long weekend. Although there were no major problems, some areas were noted that needed refinement.

☆☆☆☆☆

SMSgt Thomas O'Keefe was promoted to Chief Master Sergeant this month.

☆☆☆☆☆

It was determined that the current annual three-mile walk did not meet the DOD cardio-respiratory endurance/fitness and muscular strength requirements. A new fitness program was scheduled to begin in January 2002. The AF requirement until then was to practice push-ups and sit-ups (a better indicator of muscular strength). Each member would be scored on their performance of crunches and push-ups and advised on the requirements needed to successfully pass the fitness test next year. The overall goal was to promote good health and fitness.

June. On June 21st, the unit got an unexpected visit from the 187th AES in Wyoming. They were en route on a cross-country training mission when their aircraft experienced trouble with keeping the aircraft pressurized. The plane landed in Minneapolis to utilize Guard C-130 aircraft mechanics to fix the problem. They prepared to RON (remain overnight) after a brief check turned into nearly a five hour delay.

In a complimentary letter, the 187th Commander, wrote, "During this time period, the 109th AES offered their services and facilities to us. They did not hesitate to assist us with information, directions, and transportation. I would like to thank them for extending their services, along with a most heartfelt welcome to us. You have some super people in your unit!" [149]

☆☆☆☆☆

SSgt Drew Severt and TSgt Tony Staut designed and built equipment litter racks that saved time in getting ready for training flights.

☆☆☆☆☆

On the evening of June 16th, an ORI de-stressor was held at the dining facility between 1630 and 2100. Smoked pork chop sandwiches prepared by Maj Ed Howard and beverages were served. A slide show, "A Year in Review" with music was shown.

July. From July 21-24, the unit participated in an ORI at Camp McCoy dubbed Northern Eagle '01. It has been over a year since the first planning meetings took place for this activity. It grew from a small local joint exercise with an inspection thrown in for good measure to a two-unit inspection during a local joint exercise that was attached to a huge national exercise, Golden Medic, in which the 109th AES was the only AF participant.

Maj Jim Caldwell was recognized for his great planning efforts, especially as it related to interfacing with the Army and personnel at Camp McCoy. Due to his efforts, all of the unit's UTCs were inspected during the ORI with great success.

The IG gave honorable mention to SrA Cheryl Hackley (AEOT), 1st Lt Matt Peterson and 1st Lt Robert McDowell (AELT). The Commander also thanked the UTC managers, 1st Lt Matt Peterson (AELT), Maj Schuldt (MASF), Lt Col Rosburg (AEOT) and Capt Howard (AE crews) for a job well done in leading their UTC personnel to success. [150]

☆☆☆☆☆

The unit again provided medical coverage for Norman Conquest 2001 (formerly known as the Kaiser Roll). Lt Col Karen Wolf and Maj Jan Darling headed up this event.

August. The ninth annual Minnesota Stand Down for Veterans took place on 2-5 August in a tent city on the West Bank of the University of Minnesota. Over 1,000 veterans registered during searing hot, humid weather for this year's event. About 173 veterans visited the medical treatment tent where an array of medical, dental, and podiatry exams and services were offered.

Aeromeds who participated in the Stand Down had the opportunity to hone their skills at starting IVs, drawing blood, taking 12-lead EKGs and providing immunization and intradermal injections.

The hot weather added stress to these veterans in need and several suffered from chest pain, breathing difficulties, heat exhaustion and hypertension. Personnel in the medical treatment tent took vital signs, started IVs, provided cooling measures and offered soothing words of comfort.

109th AES celebrities, Maj J. Schacht and SSgt E. Nowlan were pictured in local newspapers as they provided patient care.

Many individuals (both patients and observers) who stopped by the medical tent commented about the professionalism, excellent nursing skills and "can do" attitude of the 109th. More than one health care practitioner stated, "Your unit (the 109th AES) has very, very good nurses. They are a knowledgeable and highly skilled group of professionals."

Capt John Janu and SSgt Shawn McMahon coordinated this activity. This was the sixth year that Maj Sue Schuldt served as the liaison for the Stand Down event. [151]

☆☆☆☆☆

This month, the aeromeds were also involved with the "Remember Pearl Harbor Days" at Fleming Field, South St. Paul, MN, as well as the Duluth airshow which featured the Blue Angels demonstration team. In addition, AEF rotations to Macedonia and Southwest Asia began and would continue through the first week in December.

☆☆☆☆☆

After taking a well-deserved breather, Lt Col Wolf wrote in her Vital Signs column that they needed to look to the next couple of years. The next big challenge would be the Initial Response Inspection scheduled for June 2002. This inspection would test the entire wing's preparedness in deploying personnel, cargo and equipment. Little did anyone realize that in less than a month the wing's ability to do just that would be put to the test, only this time for real.

CHAPTER 11
The Command of Lt Col Sharon Rosburg

(Sep 2001 - Feb 2003)

Photo courtesy of Lt Col Sharon Rosburg

Commander's Comments: Well, it seems this will be my final column. The last seventeen months, during which I was Commander, have gone extremely fast. Seems like just yesterday that we were responding to the disaster of September 11, 2001 and just minutes ago that I was visiting you as you served on state active duty. I just want to thank each of you for your support during my command. I also ask that you give your full support to the acting Commander, Major Espinosa and to whoever is named as the permanent Commander.

Looking back over my entire time with the 109th AES, since April 1999, we certainly have done a lot: JRTC, ORE, EORI (Expeditionary Operational Readiness Inspection), etc. I enjoyed working with you on each of our major taskings and involvements. I also want to assure you that although I will be retiring soon, you will remain in my thoughts and prayers.

See you at the Change of Command and as always: "When you want to point fingers, remember to shake hands."

That was my final column in the "Vital Signs" – a great resource that was part of the unit long before me. As most readers may not know, I was recommissioned from a line officer to a professional officer under the full-time officer reorganization under the 133rd Wing Commander, Col Heggemeier in 1999. I had enlisted time as well in Personnel and Finance. Those past assignments, especially as Wing Logistics Officer for 15 years, gave me detailed knowledge of the aeromedical mission, its deployments and Unit Type Codes. I was proud to serve with every aeromed, before, with me, and since me!

Lt Col Sharon Rosburg

September. Lt Col Sharon Rosburg became the new 109th AES Commander. Lt Col Karen Wolf transferred to State Headquarters where she pursued a variety of tasks including Chief Nurse initiatives, exercise evaluation team development and Employer Support of the Guard and Reserve.

Photo courtesy of MSgt Maloney
Lt Col Karen Wolf (left) presents "Change of Command" cake to new aeromed Commander, Lt Col Sharon Rosburg (right).

On Sep 11 (9-11), a series of four coordinated terrorist attacks were carried out by the Islamic terrorist group al-Qaeda on the United States. The attacks consisted of suicide attacks used to target symbolic U.S. landmarks.

Four passenger airliners—which all departed from airports on the U.S. East Coast bound for California—were hijacked by 19 al-Qaeda terrorists to be flown into buildings. Two of the planes, American Airlines Flight 11 and United Airlines Flight 175, crashed into the North and South Towers, respectively, of the World Trade Center complex in New York City. Within an hour and 42 minutes, both 110-story towers collapsed, with debris and the resulting fires causing partial or complete collapse of all other buildings in the World Trade Center complex, including the 47-story 7 World Trade Center building, as well as significant damage to ten other large surrounding structures. A third plane, American Airlines Flight 77, crashed into the Pentagon (the headquarters of the United States Department of Defense) in Arlington County, Virginia, leading to a partial collapse of the Pentagon's western wall. The fourth plane, United Airlines Flight 93, initially was steered toward Washington, D.C., but crashed into a field near Shanksville, Pennsylvania, after its passengers tried to overcome the hijackers. In total, the attacks claimed the lives of 2,996 people (including the 19 hijackers) and caused at least $10 billion in property and infrastructure damage. It was the deadliest incident for firefighters and law enforcement officers in the history of the United States, with 343 and 72 killed respectively.

It was officially announced that the U.S. was now engaged in a war against terrorism. What changes and challenges would this bring to the 109th in the future? Time would tell.

☆☆☆☆☆

Based on information that the 109th AS received at the recent ORI, the aeromeds were asked that whenever they were involved in real-world flying operations or local exercises that they were to be prepared to give information to the flight crew during the mission planning phase regarding the number of bodies (whether real or mannequins) and approximate weight of medical equipment that would be on board. This information was necessary for completing performance data prior to take off and landing. Weight and its distribution on the aircraft could be critical, especially on an actual short field dirt strip. Neglecting to share this information in advance could be especially costly on a hot landing zone and result in delays while the flight engineer performed the calculation.

☆☆☆☆☆

Sadly, a number of unit flight nurses left the unit for duties elsewhere. A great deal of experience and knowledge departed with them. Best wishes were given to Lt Col Darrell Rask, Lt Col Karen Wolf, Maj Lorraine Hennessy, Maj Linda Jensen, Maj Sue Schuldt and Capt Theo Williams.

November. Not one, but three aeromeds earned national recognition.

SMSgt Cheryl Burton was selected as the 2000 Outstanding Aeromedical Evacuation Crew Member of the Year. Cheryl stated, "I give all thanks and glory to God, for He has given me incredible mercy and grace. Through Him, I see things much differently in my life. Therefore, He can groom me to be the leader He sees fit. I also thank all the people in my unit, who contributed to my receiving this award and have warmly welcomed me back into the unit. God bless you all."

Capt Catherine Jacobson-Hanson was awarded the 2000 ANG Readiness Officer of the Year. "I would like to thank Lt Col Karen Wolf, Lt Col Sharon Rosburg, Capt Sharon Burt and MSgt Blair Sorvari for their confidence and guidance in assisting me to perform my job. Their leadership and mentoring allowed me to perform at the award level. I also would like to thank my husband and boys for their support and acceptance of the long hours away from home to deploy unit members in the AES," she said.

Maj Susan Schuldt was selected as the 2000 ANG Flight Nurse of the Year. She commented that "The MNANG has opened possibilities to expand my horizons both globally and locally. Not only have I had the opportunity to travel and work in challenging environments around the world, but through the state's tuition reimbursement program, I've expanded my understanding of cultural differences and gained a global perspective. Because of our unit's training incentives, I've achieved certification in several critical care areas important for providing optimal in-flight nursing care." [152]

☆☆☆☆☆

Lt Col Sharon Rosburg felt the end of the year was a good time to give the unit an idea of their service in the war on terrorism. She said, "Although we do not know what our future will hold, especially in the war against terrorism, I thought you would like a recap of participation during the current three operations. In support of the 11 September attack, we had 74 people on duty for a total of 311 days. In support of state active duty, we had 80 people on duty for a total of 811 days. In support of AEF, we had 21 people on duty for a total of 541 days. That is an average of over 10 days per member in only a couple of months. Just one more example of the commitment each of you makes to the unit!" [153]

December. All AEF rotations returned by the first week of December.

The unit collected over $500.00 in addition to many stuffed animals and art supplies for the King Family Salvation Army School. Capt Mark Kolar delivered the donations before Christmas which were greatly appreciated. This was a very underprivileged school with some very deserving children.

2002

January. The NAF (Numbered Air Force) visited in late January for a Staff Assistance Visit. They took a look at some of the programs and offered constructive feedback toward preparing for our ASEV.

☆☆☆☆☆

A U.S. Southern Command (SOUTHCOM) mission fell through due to a communication error at ANG level.

☆☆☆☆☆

The unit was asked to improve their supply discipline. It was noted that members left several pieces of equipment on board the aircraft following recent missions. These items were found by maintenance personnel and returned to the unit. They could have easily been discarded because maintenance didn't know where they came from. Instead, they used their supply discipline and tracked down the owning unit. Also, it was noted that some items were issued from the warehouse for deployers without hand receipts. In the future, it was asked that members sign out any items taken from the warehouse.

☆☆☆☆☆

The unit began to prepare for the ASEV Visit in September. The primary purpose of the ASEV was to assist in developing and maintaining the best possible Stan/Eval and training programs, which promoted safety and mission effectiveness. In addition, it ensured standardization of all training and Stan/Eval processes throughout the Air Force.

February. To date, over 100 wing members have deployed in support of Operation Enduring Freedom (OEF). Unit members are reminded that they must be ready to deploy at a moment's notice.

March. It was announced that the unit would not have the Metrics Oversight Visit scheduled for September. Instead, AE units would be getting a Health Services Inspection beginning in 2003.

☆☆☆☆☆

TSgt Potter, a radio operator, briefed the aeromeds that the communications setup that most of the "old timers" were familiar with would be changing in the near future. With the increasing use of satellite communications by the front-line units for the past several years, it was inevitable that the 109th AES would eventually become a beneficiary of those developments. Laptop computers and e-mail would be coming to the field with future unit exercises and deployments.

☆☆☆☆☆

The March UTA was focused on OJT training.

April. Lt Col Rosburg was notified that the unit would be receiving a new Designed Operational Capability (DOC) draft in May. This included several openings for flyers where they would not have to maintain currency, but must have prior flying experience. The aeromeds already had some of these positions in the MASF and AEOT. With the decreasing number of flying slots and the transfer of three non-flying AETs to other vacancies, the opportunity was opened up for the AETs. Although offered, the unit did not have sufficient nurses available at that time to take advantage of a similar situation.

☆☆☆☆☆

On a flight this month, Capt Howard recalled the following, "I had the privilege of flying one night this week with a crew that clicked really well. You've all had it, where the communication is uncanny and the coordination is as though we could anticipate the other's thoughts. Capt Behrens, TSgt Howk and SSgt Eubanks demonstrated not only experience and skill, but the pride in the 109th AES we all wish to emulate. The performance of SrA Zueli was impeccable. His preflight briefing was one of the finest I have attended and his participation with the rest of the crew made me forget he was in training. I also realized that night as a flight nurse, I rely on the technical skill of the AETs. Their ability and mastery of our equipment made our configuration and in-flight emergency run quickly and smoothly. I am proud of not only these AETs, but all of the AETs in our unit. Keep up the good work!" [154]

May. The Commander announced that Capt Matt Peterson was named ANG Outstanding MSC Officer of the Year. In addition, 1st Lt Julie Ritz was named ANG Outstanding Medical Readiness Officer of the Year.

☆☆☆☆☆

Twenty-four members of the 109th AES joined nearly 800 Boy Scouts, Girl Scouts, and Cub Scouts as part of the "Rocket's Red Glare" theme for the annual Kaposia District Camporee, held May 3-5 at Maltby's Nature Preserve, Cannon Falls, MN.

"This event gave aeromeds the opportunity to train and to interact with the community," said SMSgt Steve Campos, Human Resource Advisor (HRA), 133rd Airlift Wing, who coordinated ANG involvement in the weekend.

"It was not only a good PR (Public Relations) event," said TSgt Bryan Steven, "but served the dual role of training some of our new people on putting up tents, water purification and vehicle operations."

Members left at 0900 on 3 May with Humvees and M35 deuce and a half trucks pulling water buffalos and carrying equipment for four large tents, generators and other equipment for field setup and sustainment.

The majority of the training occurred on 3 May.

"What was really cool about that was we all had our AFSCs combined and working together," said Maj Georgeanne Johnson.

TSgt Steve Burmeister also felt it was a good training experience. He stated, "It's nice to go out and have some fun and get some training when you're not being evaluated."

Once set up, the unit shared its resources with the scouts. "The aeromeds provided our water, power and shelter for programs, as well as vehicles and equipment of interest for the scouts to see," said Carol Strom, Co-Coordinator of the Kaposia District Spring Camporee.

Some of the equipment the squadron members demonstrated to the scouts included the MNANG Museum's simulated F-4 Phantom cockpit, flak vests, Kevlar helmets, NVGs, face paint and a 20-person life raft.

The equipment was divided into different stations, which scouts took turns visiting throughout the day on 4 May. At one of the stations, scouts had to paddle a boat out to the middle of a pond and climb into the 20-person life raft. Once in the raft, Burmeister told them about its different survival features. "After explaining it so many times, I should get a perfect score on the next inspection," said Burmeister.

At the second station they set up, aeromeds painted the scouts' faces. "All the Girl Scouts in my troop got full face paint," said TSgt Mike Granlund.

Along with activity stations, troops took part in "adopt a hero for the day." This involved each troop taking one to two military members into their group, cooking for them, and including them in their day's activities. "It was a fantastic opportunity for the scouts to get to speak with and learn more about our military," said Strom. She added, "All in all, both scouts and military members enjoyed the experience. Parents and scouts have been overwhelmingly appreciative of the experience." [155]

Photo courtesy of SrA John Wiggins, Northstar Guardian (Jun '02)

SrA Tony Hallen demonstrates to the scouts on how to cook and eat an MRE.

Recently, 17 members of the 109th AES completed the first e-Mentoring program on base.

During the three-month program, each military member communicated once a week via e-mail with 9th grade science students at Roosevelt High School in Minneapolis.

"The students apply what they are learning in school to what you're doing," said Maj Georgeanne Johnson. "You get some real challenging questions about the environment and travel."

The 133rd Airlift Wing was one of four organizations that participated in this program designed by an organization called Youth Trust to build partnerships between schools, employers and community resources in order to help students achieve success in school and develop marketable job skills.

SMSgt Steve Campos, Human Resource Advisor, 133rd Airlift Wing, coordinated the program for the medical and aeromedical squadrons. "It provided the students with another part of the network, besides parents and teachers," said Campos.

The students had two opportunities to come out to the base to visit their mentors and to see where they work, once in March and again in May. "The aeromeds showed them where they work, who with and on what equipment," said Campos. "Then they went to lunch together."

Students and mentors alike enjoyed the program. "It was a good start to an excellent program," said Johnson. Students agreed. "The students enjoyed the program so much they were asking about next year," said Campos.

Next year, Campos said he would like to increase the number of students mentored to 50 and invite members of other units on base to participate. [156]

☆☆☆☆☆

At the Total Force Commander's Conference, held in Oklahoma from May 20-24, attendees were informed that there would be a new list of projected UTCs. Details would be announced in future months.

In addition, new changes were announced regarding JRTC. The Operations Plan was written by HQ AMC and units were required to sign-up UTC by UTC, not as a whole squadron. At this point in time, the unit had not determined which, if any, UTCs would participate next June. It would depend on the workload for the operations groups as a whole.

For the flyers, the unit would be rapidly converting to "universal" checklists rather than Mission Defense System specific, i.e. C-130, C-17, etc. Publications and regulations would be streamlined and the contents of the pubs (publications) kit would be reduced by about 75%.

(authors' note: See write-up and photos in the chapter entitled "Aeromedical Evacuation Training Flights (A Historical Perspective)".)

June. The unit conducted AEOT Training at Fort McCoy, WI. The training was focused on the configuration of the aircraft along with a review of the medical equipment. Since the original plan for the exercise was developed prior to 9-11, it had a different perspective than what was initially emphasized. Changes in theater requirements led the unit to try and gain some familiarity with new ways of doing business with troops in the field.

Photo courtesy of the 109th AES archives

109th AES personnel practice water survival skills in a 20-man life raft during Ft. McCoy FTX.

Photo courtesy of MSgt Rachel Maloney

Transfer of patients from MASF to C-130H during FTX training at Ft. McCoy.

<u>**July.**</u> The 109th AES and family members spent the day floating down the St. Croix River in life rafts (provided by the wing's C-130Hs) and canoes.

Photo courtesy of the 109th AES archives
Aeromeds and family members prepare the 20-man life rafts and canoes for a day of river floating.

August. The AF announced that stop-loss has been lifted for all AFSCs in the unit. However, squadron members were expected to fulfill whatever commitment they had before resigning.

☆☆☆☆☆

The 109th AES volunteered to help transport patients from the Minnesota Veterans Home to/from and around the Minnesota State Fair via wheelchairs.

☆☆☆☆☆

It was announced that the unit would have the much postponed ASEV in April 2003. Although eight months away, leadership felt that there was much preparation ahead. Along with getting ready for the ASEV, readiness for deployment (anytime, anywhere) was emphasized.

September. Construction continued at the front gate of the base which incorporated enhanced security measures.

October. ANG/SG mandated that all AETs be nationally registered EMTs as of 1 Oct. AETs without a national certification could not be deployed, promoted or upgraded.

It should be noted that the 109th began providing EMT training for their med techs back in July of 1971, once again putting the unit decades ahead of this Guard-wide requirement.

✰✰✰✰✰

Going into the fall, the 109th AES stepped up its preparation for the upcoming ASEV. Squadron members were given questions that would be asked of them during the evaluation and might be asked of them during the UTA.

November. Three unit members deployed to Ramstein AB, Germany as they began their turn in the "bucket" for their assigned AEF.

✰✰✰✰✰

After a two and a half year wait, the 109th AES received their new UTCs. One of the big changes was the addition of a Critical Care Team which included an assigned physician to the squadron.

2003

January. As the New Year began, the main focus of the unit remained on deployment readiness. With this goal in mind, the upcoming ASEV was still a priority. Two additional inspections were scheduled for the year; the Initial Response Inspection (IRI) and the Unit Compliance Inspection (UCI). Both would assist the squadron in preparing for the upcoming ASEV.

Deployed - Letters from the Field: Maj Georgeanne Johnson

Capt Jacobson-Hanson, TSgt Spangler and I are working in the Operation Enduring Freedom AEOT in Germany. Our job is to recover the crews, CCATTs and their equipment coming in from down range locations, taking care of logistical requirements here, locating returning flights and blocking them in, and launching them back to their locations. We coordinate with the owning element to keep them informed of the location of their crews and when to expect a return. In addition, I have been involved in some of the planning for the future AEOT, with the shift away from Operation Joint Guard (OJG).

It is a very interesting time to be here with much activity as the theater expands. We have talked with the crews from all the locations and are getting a pretty good feel for what their missions and living conditions are like. The locations vary from the well-developed, to the austere where there is bare minimum support. The weather is cold in some of the outlying "Stan" areas with an ice glazed landscape. Of course, these are the crews that most appreciate their warm billeting room with a private shower. Most areas do get quite cold at night. Like the living conditions, the missions vary. The missions between the bases in the theater (transporting patients from minimal support areas to the theater hospital) are done mostly with C-130s. The long-haul missions (i.e. Bagram, Afghanistan or Oman to Germany) are done with any available aircraft. We are seeing lots of C-17s, also C-141s, C-5s and KC

-135s. These are long killer flights, ranging from 8-17 hours, with refueling and diverts. In addition, the crews have to drag along their A and C bags and their weapons. They come in totally whipped and we send them out in less than 24 hours, sometimes even the same day. The reason we have such quick turnarounds is that the crews and CCATTs are needed back at their locations. If the base was left without their crews or CCATT, crews from other locations had to pack up their belongings and make a temporary move until a crew returned. Although we try to grant it when possible, crew rest is waived for OEF.

Even though I am not on the actual missions, a lot of info can be derived when crews come into the AEOT. We have seen some of the same trends that occur at home, including equipment operation/care issues and checklist discipline. Therefore, I emphasize that the training at home should attempt to emulate live missions and we all need to take maximum advantage of the opportunity to train realistically. I also repeat that ASEV preparation actually prepares us for live missions that we can and will be performing during our careers, some sooner than later.

Although we can't give details, we can tell you that if you hear about it on CNN (Cable News Network), the patients come here. If you have any questions that we can help you with regarding AEOT operations or what to expect as a crewmember in the theater, we would be glad to answer them … Have a good UTA.

February. The Vital Signs contained Lt Col Rosburg's final column as she was ending her term as 109th Commander and retiring. Maj Espinosa assumed the duties of acting Commander for the next two months.

☆☆☆☆☆

The unit coordinated efforts with the 934th to accomplish flying requirements as both units were dealing with deployment issues.

☆☆☆☆☆

The aeromeds hosted the ANG Assistants and Advisors Meeting while celebrating ANG AE day on 28 Feb. Attendees participated in a walk around on a static C-130H, observed offload of patients and equipment, and attended the crew debrief. The Distinguished Visitors (DV) were very excited to see unit aircrews at work.

March. The 109th AES was informed that Maj Augustine from HQ AMC was now attached to the unit and would be flying soon to maintain her currency.

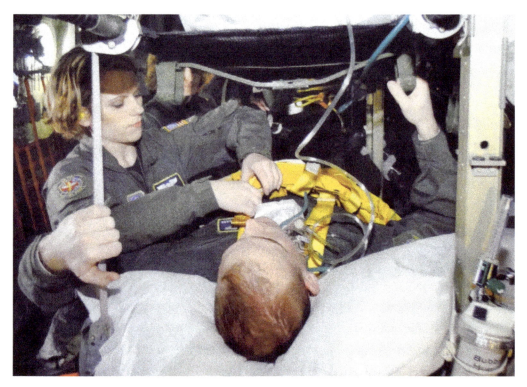

Photo courtesy of TSgt Devona Haher, Northstar Guardian (Mar '03)

TSgt Erika Miller secures SrA Dustin Sicard to a litter during a local training flight.

CHAPTER 12
The Command of Lt Col Georgeanne Johnson

(Apr 2003 - Jun 2009)

Photo courtesy of Lt Col Georgeanne Johnson

Commander's Comments: Recruited by Mike Germain, I joined the 109th Aeromedical Evacuation Flight in 1990 as a flight nurse; I had no idea of what was ahead. (Mike didn't tell me everything!) I was looking for an interesting and challenging role while serving the country. It certainly turned out to be all of that!

During my career I have been provided many opportunities to serve, learn, and grow. The training, deployments, exercises, teaching and humanitarian missions were amazing and took me to places I had never dreamed of. The best part was always the people who led me or were part of my team; I learned so much from and about them. They were not only fellow Airmen, but also people who offered their own special contributions. Whether it was their own special humor or innovative way of doing things, they taught me life lessons.

In March of 2003, I returned from a six-month deployment in Germany where we piloted the first ever Aeromedical Evacuation Stage Management Team. While deployed, I was part of the aeromedical war planning for a possible reinvasion of Iraq, so it was no surprise when President Bush launched Operation Iraqi Freedom about a week after my return. Immediately, members of the 109th AES were deployed to Scott AFB, IL for another first; ICMOP (Integrated CONUS Medical Operation Plan). In a matter of weeks, I took command of a unit that was being tasked all over the world.

The ops tempo during the following six years was one that we had never seen before. Rarely were all the members at home. Change became the norm. We received new equipment packages, new UTC packages, new regulations, and new inspections. Recruiting was a constant process and we were sending our newly qualified members on deployments as they returned from their schools and soon after the AECMs became qualified. AMC instituted the universally qualified crewmember concept, requiring our flight crewmembers to become qualified in multiple aircraft frames.

While members deployed globally to Iraq, Uzbekistan, Kuwait, Qatar, Scott AFB, IL, Andrews AFB, MD, Germany, and other locations, the unit continued its support for the Minnesota Stand Down for Veterans, exercise participation, annual hospital training tours, Border Patrol in the Southwest U.S. and operational missions from Ramstein to Andrews. Crews deployed for Hurricane Katrina, stood alert for others, and ground personnel deployed for flood support. The number and scope of support of demands increased, requiring more of Guard members around the country. Many members were facing challenges with their employers; missing opportunities for advancement or even having difficulty hanging onto their jobs. In 2004 with an AEF approaching, AE commanders struggled with the best way to help our people maintain good standing with their civilian employers. In partnership with our AEF partners, we petitioned the National Guard Bureau to task the deployments on partial mobilization rather than volunteer status. To this day, I believe this was the best thing we could do to protect our members.

A commander can only be as good as his/her people. I was blessed to have an amazing group of people. They worked hard and played hard! Their humor brought us through difficult times. The wing provided excellent people for vacant positions, starting with Lt Col Don Dahlquist, who not only was extremely knowledgeable; he provided great perspective and advice. When our First Sergeant and Chief positions were open, SMSgt Ray Kennedy and Chief Greg Close were sent to us. Although it was unusual at the time to have "outsiders" brought into the unit for those positions, they both were sound leaders and exceptional NCOs. Our Flight Instructor crew was made up of some very gifted instructors. The support of a dedicated full-time staff often made the seemingly impossible happen. There are too many more to mention. In the end, it is the outstanding people of the 109th AES that I admired and still miss.

Throughout the years I was always amazed at the patriotism and commitment of the unit. They continually stepped up the demands and surpassed expectations. The Airmen and women of the 109th AES, and their families, are true heroes! It was my privilege and honor to have been their Commander.

Lt Col Georgeanne Johnson

<u>April.</u> Maj Georgeanne Johnson was selected as the new Commander.

☆☆☆☆☆

Under the code name Operation Iraqi Freedom (OIF), U.S. forces invaded Iraq in the early morning hours of March 20, 2003. President George W. Bush's administration believed that the country's dictator, Saddam Hussein, held nuclear weapons as well as ties to al-Qaeda which allowed that organization to set up training camps in the Iraqi desert. Both were viewed as threats to the United States and her Allies. Approximately 148,000 U.S. men and women, 45,000 British, 2,000 Australian and 194 Polish special operations soldiers made up the initial invasion forces. U.S. Marine units attacked the airport on April 3rd and reached the outskirts of Baghdad. The airport was secured, cleared and the first U.S. aircraft, a C-130, landed on April 7th.

By the morning of April 9, 2003 U.S. tanks were patrolling the streets of the capital and the only Iraqis present were civilians who cheered them as they passed. Saddam had fled the city. His days as ruler of that country were over. Although the Pentagon declared on April 14th that all major combat had ended, the fighting in Iraq would continue for more than eight years.

The degree of commitment of unit members to the movement of casualties during this time frame would be substantial.

☆☆☆☆☆

The squadron received word from the 15th AF that the scheduled ASEV was placed on hold due to the large number of deployed or potentially deployed personnel. The 15th AF stated that the inspection would occur shortly after all of the crews had returned home.

☆☆☆☆☆

Members of the 109th AES and one member of the 133rd Medical Squadron deployed to Scott AFB, IL, in support of the first-ever expeditionary AE squadron in the continental United States. As part of the 775th EAES, 28 members of the 109th AES launched and recovered aircraft, and flew as crew on missions redistributing casualties from Operation Iraqi Freedom. Since early April, wing members had been working alongside personnel from active duty, Reserve and Guard bases. "There's been a tremendous amount of synergy between different units that has given us the capability to do missions as well as we have," said Maj DeDecker, Deputy Commander, 775th EAES.

The two biggest concerns on the missions were safety and patient care. "From pilots down to med techs, everyone has a goal of delivering them safely and as quickly as possible and taking the best care of them that we can," said TSgt Erika Miller.

An average mission day ran as long as 16 hours, flying out to Andrews AFB, MD, and then landing at up to seven different bases distributing patients. On the ground during launches and recoveries, personnel loaded, unloaded and replenished equipment and supplies, handled baggage, and assisted with patient handling.

One of the things members found especially valuable about this deployment was real-world experience. AlC Joe "Beeker" Tilseth, returned from Tech School only three days before deploying. "I was kind of nervous but also really excited," he said. "When I got here, it all came together and I used my Tech School experience."

TSgt Michelle Lambert, finished her clinicals for nursing school while at Scott AFB and found the real-world experience valuable as well. "I got some of the coolest firsthand experience for my clinicals," she said. "It was probably a lot more in depth than it would have been."

Beyond the work experience, personal experiences with the service members they are helping to bring home really make this deployment worthwhile. "To see it on the news is one thing, but to hear these stories and see their pictures firsthand truly makes it real to you," said Capt Patrick Howard. "That's why I'm satisfied that I could do something to support them doing their mission." [157]

Photo courtesy of SSgt Heather Gillette, Northstar Guardian, Jun '03
TSgt Michelle Lambert helps to transport a patient from the ambus (ambulance bus) to a waiting C-9.

Deployed - Letters from the Field: Maj Jim Caldwell

Greetings from the 775th EAES (Expeditionary Aeromedical Evacuation Squadron)! During the week of 4 April, twenty-eight members of the 109th AES joined personnel from nine other ANG and AFR units to form the 775th EAES, the first EAES ever activated in the continental United States.

The formation of the 775th marks the execution of the Integrated CONUS Medical Operation Plan in support of Operation Iraqi Freedom. Our mission is to provide patient movement to the unit of record for patients transiting the CONUS AE system. Members of the 775th are stationed at Scott AFB, IL and Andrews AFB, MD.

All 109th personnel are at Scott AFB where we make up the Squadron Command Cell, the AEOT, two aircrews and the B-MET (Biomedical Equipment Technician). When we arrived, this concept existed only on paper. Within less than a week we were flying live missions.

Lt Col Virginia (Ginny) Schneider of the 142nd AES Delaware ANG assumed command of the squadron on 24 April 2003.

Crewmembers are receiving C-9 certification and qualification as well as C-21 certification. In addition to the C-9 missions, we maintain C-130 and C-21 Bravo alerts at both locations. Three 109th crewmembers were quickly dispatched to Randolph AFB, TX to pull C-21 Bravo alert for several days. We've moved over 500 patients in a few short weeks. Needless to say we've been very busy.

Establishing a new squadron and implementing a new concept such as ICMOP is very challenging, but also very rewarding, knowing that we are having a positive impact on the lives of battle casualties and other patients we care for. Although we aren't all providing direct patient care, the missions would not have happened without the hard work of the entire team.

May. Maj Georgeanne Johnson pointed out that the balance of the year was going to be challenging for the unit. The Guard was still experiencing some steep financial restrictions. Money for active duty days and competency training was almost nonexistent. Unit members were reminded to watch their days carefully before planning active duty training days at the unit.

☆☆☆☆☆

Lt Col Don Dahlquist returned to the squadron after a five-year absence where he served as the Senior Health Administrator at the 137th AES in Oklahoma. He would perform these same duties upon his return to the 109th AES.

June. Lt Col Schneider sent the unit words of high praise regarding the caliber of the 109th personnel deployed to Scott AFB, IL in support of Operation Iraqi Freedom.

Deployed - Letters from the Field: Maj Jim Caldwell

If there is one thing we take away from this deployment it is the absolute necessity of flexibility. Over the many years we have all heard about and witnessed the need for AE to be flexible. However, flexibility has taken on a new meaning for those of us in the 775th EAES. SMSgt Gruel came upon an ancient AE proverb that says it best, "Blessed are the flexible, for they do not get bent out of shape." This is posted at the entrance to the Command Cell and reminds us all that things will change and change frequently. We either adapt and succeed or remain rigid and fail. Thus far we have maintained the flexibility we need to succeed.

As of 2 June, we have successfully moved 560 litter patients, 1101 ambulatory patients and 206 attendants on 151 missions encompassing 2814 total flying hours. Our missions have ranged from Guantanamo Bay to Hawaii and many points in between. We've moved patients on C-9s, KC-135s, C-130s, C-141s and C-21s. Our patients have ranged from critically injured combatants to a premature infant. The flexibility exhibited by quality personnel has been key to our success.

There continues to be an ebb and flow of the activity level of the 775th EAES. In mid-May, Andrews AFB, MD flight line was closed for five days during the Joint Service Open House. During this period, all AE missions from Europe were routed to Scott AFB, IL. Ten members of our detachment at Andrews deployed to Scott to help support this additional requirement. Maj Anderson and the AEOT did an extraordinary job ensuring that all missions were safely launched and recovered in a timely manner.

Our Flight Instructors and Flight Examiners trained and qualified two flight nurses and three AETs from the 375th AES and 932nd AES on the C-130. The C-9s have not been funded for fiscal 2004. The C-130 is slated to be utilized for CONUS missions in place of the C-9. The 375th and 932nd AES are very anxious to qualify as many AECMs as possible before 1 October.

The mission of the 775th EAES continues to evolve as the 375th AES and 932nd AES return from deployment. We have begun the process of integrating them into the ICMOP mission. This is quite an adjustment for them since they are accustomed to operating on a somewhat regular schedule. In the past, CONUS AE maintained an operating schedule and mission requirements had to work into the schedule. ICMOP is mission driven. Mission needs determine the number and frequency of missions on any given day. Final mission requirements are not known until 0300 to 0400. This makes for an interesting few hours for the Crew Management Cell.

A1C Tilseth was promoted to SrA effective 1 June. At his promotion ceremony, Lt Col Schneider noted that he was a prime example of "see one, do one, teach one." His OJT was self-directed and he has done an exceptional job as the AEOT "loggie." Be sure to ask SSgt Arndt about his meeting with the First Lady, Laura Bush, at Fort Campbell, KY when he returns.

Overall, this has been a very good deployment for members of the 775th EAES. We've learned a lot and have gained a great deal of satisfaction with our contribution to Operation Iraqi Freedom.

By the June UTA, over 25% of the unit was deployed. Even though some members returned to the unit during April, the squadron was already slotted for AEF 1 and 2, which was scheduled for September - November 2004.

While some wing members redeployed, many members and their families had the disappointment of their return delayed, including those in the 109th. Facing some of the longest deployments in our history caused stressful relationships for all involved.

Deployed - Letters from the Field: Maj Jacobson-Hanson

Guten Tag! TSgt Sally Spangler and I have been deployed in Germany since 29 Nov, 2002. Over this time period, we have gained valuable military experience.

During the first few months, TSgt Spangler and I fell under the command of Maj Georgeanne Johnson as part of the Aeromedical Evacuation Operations Team for AEF 7 and 8. The mission of the AEOT was to recover incoming AE missions from the Operation Enduring Freedom Area of Operation. After recovering the AE crews and CCATTs the AEOT would reserve billeting, secure narcotics and medical equipment, and transport the crews to billeting. While the crews were put into crew rest, the AEOT would utilize the Global Decisions Support System (GDSS) to find opportune airlift to return the crews to their geological locations. The AEOT would request the airlift through the Air Mobility Control Center (AMCC) and through the Air Terminal Operation Center (ATOC). Once airlift was confirmed, the AEOT would notify the MCD and launch missions to get the crews and their equipment back on the aircraft. The goal was to get the AE crews and CCATTs back intratheater ASAP so they would be available for future missions. On average most crews were back in the air within 24-48 hours and some less than 12 hours.

Under the direction of Maj Johnson, the AEOT piloted the first ever Aeromedical Evacuation Stage Management Team (AESMT) in AMC. I was part of the initial cadre of the AMC/CV (Vice Commander) vision for a seamless integration of AE stage management into command and control. After Maj Johnson deployed back to the unit, I became the acting Deputy Director for the AEOT and the ops tempo increased due to the war. On 27 March, everything took off and the AEOT was recovering/launching four to five missions a day going into both Operations Enduring Freedom and Operation Iraqi Freedom AORs. The eleven personnel that manned the AEOT worked around the clock to ensure all missions were covered. The first casualties from OIF including former POW (Prisoner Of War) Jessica Lynch were recovered at this location. In the first two weeks of the war, the AEOT recovered close to 200 patients alone - almost half of the amount during the last three months.

In the beginning weeks of April, the 491st Expeditionary Unit came to Ramstein. It contained a 32-person AEOT so the former AEOT was folded into the 491st AES. Since then the 491st has recovered/launched over 2000 patients. The tempo is starting to slow down although there is still a steady flow from the OIF AOR and missions to the States.

July. Most of the deployed unit members have returned to the unit. However, the last crew scheduled for deployment departed this UTA.

☆☆☆☆☆

The Unit Compliance Inspection was held during the UTA. The forty inspectors on base reviewed programs and asked questions of the program managers. Some of the areas of focus included OJT, Career Advisor, the Government Credit Card Program, Self-Inspection, Weight Management and Fitness Programs, Security, Medical Readiness, Deployment, and unit file plans. Some were disappointed that the inspectors did not check all of the unit's programs, especially with all of the work that went into preparing them.

☆☆☆☆☆

At the Minnesota Stand Down for Veterans, 26 members provided over 170 homeless vets with health care screenings for diabetes, high blood pressure, and tuberculosis. The goal was to positively impact and empower change in the lives of these former service members.

August. Maj JoEllen Evavold was selected as the OGV Flight Nurse, and now served as the Senior Flight Nurse Examiner.

☆☆☆☆☆

On 1 August, the 775th EAES and all of its assets moved from Scott AFB, IL to Andrews AFB, MD. There were still large numbers of injured Soldiers, Sailors, Airmen, and Marines arriving every day at Andrews AFB from the AOR, so an AE launch and recovery function at Andrews was maintained for several more months. In addition, the deactivation of the C-9 increased the use of C-130s for patient movement and crews were needed to fly that mission. Andrews continued to be a very busy location for some time.

During its existence, the 775th EAES at Scott AFB launched and recovered 389 missions with patient loads of 1,558 litter patients, 4,476 ambulatory patients and 715 attendants. They also flew a total of 117 missions with patient loads of 409 litter patients, 1,093 ambulatory patients and 257 attendants. What a truly impressive record!

Deployed - Letters from the Field: 1st Lt Mensen

After a twelve-hour layover at Baltimore/Washington International Airport and an agonizing rotator ride, we landed in Bishkek-Manas, Kyrgyzstan, and were then informed that our new home would be Uzbekistan. To our delight we made a quick hometown connection. Twenty-three of the 133rd Aerial Port members were running the ATOC. Although we did not personally know any of them, they quickly welcomed us fellow Minnesotans, gave us access to all their resources and took us under their wings!

There are two three-person crews and a CCATT team here. Our crews are kind of backwards, two nurses and one med tech. Our first week here we had three flights. SSgt Devine and her crew flew two combat missions to include a PUC (Prisoner Under Containment) run. TSgt Eubanks and I took the AOR tour flying to Pakistan, Kyrgyzstan, Germany, and Afghanistan and returning to Uzbekistan. That mission took us 27 hours of flying on three different aircraft - the C-130, C-141, and C-17. No flights since our first week here, so we sit in an eternal crew rest state.

We currently reside in tent city and had our door proudly painted with our very own 109th AES emblem! Brown and Root are here to feed us, but the food is comparable to an MRE anyway. We do have warm water for the showers, and no time limit on them!

Lessons learned so far are to stand your ground on what you know is right and rely on your training! Yes, you should wear your survival gear when the front-end crew put theirs on and you still preflight equipment before missions. Kudos to SSgt Devine on these issues! She made us all proud! Remember to use your checklists - it makes the preflight briefing a whole lot easier.

Deployed - Letters from the Field: 1st Lt Ehman

As of this writing, the crew of myself, 1st Lt Bartz, MSgt Burmeister, TSgt Gozel and SrA Maloney have just gone over one week in country (Camp Wolf at Kuwait City International Airport, Kuwait). Our trip and in processing went very smoothly and we all thank TSgt Sean Mitricska and SSgt Jason Arndt for their hard work getting us here!

There are several AE crews at this site and the five of us have been divided into three different crews. Within our first week here we have all flown missions already! There are several flights daily and we anticipate flying one to two times a week. Flexibility is definitely the key around here. Missions, tasking and assignments are constantly changing. As MSgt Burmeister and I found out, this sometimes can happen mid-flight.

If you need an idea for any upcoming ground training sessions, spend time configuring seats! A common mission here is the AE crew boarding a plane along with multiple pallets and 20+ PAX.

After landing you have very little time to reconfigure the aircraft for patients so a very good knowledge of how to take apart and install the center seats and sidewall seats is important. TSgt Gozel adds, "Fly, and if you think you're flying enough, fly some more." It is so critical in this environment to be completely comfortable with the aircraft and configuring.

We are flying with crews from Delaware, West Virginia, Tennessee, and California. Everyone here is C-130 qualified so it has been a smooth transition for all.

We are living in a tent city. The Minnesota crew plus MSgt Ringwald and SrA Vogt share a tent. SSgt Jeramy Hanzel and MSgt Pat Nowlan have also visited us for a short stay. We are offered four hot meals a day and they have excellent ice cream here! There are a few MWR (Morale, Welfare, Recreation) tents on the base. One has board games and ping pong tables, another shows movies continuously and a third was set up as a gym. Overall, it isn't too bad of an assignment.

Deployed - Letters from the Field: Capt Peterson

We arrived here (Al Udeid AB, Qatar), as a twelve-person AEOT on 11 July, but were quickly right sized into an eight-person AECMC (Aeromedical Evacuation Crew Management Cell). We dispatched our RDOs to Iraq (Fitzhenry) and Kuwait (Vogt) respectively and our two logisticians

(Howard and Wildes) were moved into positions that are responsible for AE logistics for the entire AOR. Our Support Cell (Hanzel and Nowlan) is busy traveling the theater in search of equipment repair needs.

Our primary function in the AECMC is to manage AE crews and CCATTs as well as to coordinate and execute AE missions. The ops tempo is high and we man the AECMC 24/7. We share our space with C-130 Tactics and Intel which helps to broaden our perspective and gives us other vital sources of information. The Aussies and Brits also share the AE mission. Working with our coalition brethren has been an outstanding experience and they truly are great people.

The living conditions are pretty decent. We live in tents with bunks. Each tent holds approximately 10-12 people. They have wooden floors and lockers to store your gear. As you can imagine, they are air-conditioned. The tents still get hot during the day but without the air-conditioning, they would be unlivable. The base has many amenities you would find back home such as a gym, media center, pub, rec center and a coffee shop just to name a few. You can actually get a drink here. In fact, there is a daily ration of three.

The lessons learned here are plenty. You always need to be prepared to relocate. If Fitzhenry or Voght wouldn't have brought the right gear, they would have been miserable. You also need to understand the new AE CONOPs (Concept of Operations). Everything in theater is done according to the new system. If you don't understand the parts and how it all fits together, you could be in for some pretty serious headaches. The good news is that nothing in AE is difficult. It just needs to be learned.

On a personal note, I am truly honored to be deployed with such a great group of people. Everyone jumped in, learned their job and displayed great attitudes. Obviously, if you enjoy one another and immerse yourself in your job, being deployed is a piece of cake.

P.S. It was 179.5 degrees on the ramp the other day. Who could live here?

September. During this month's UTA, Maj Judy Espinosa was named the OIC of Squadron Support, Maj Gary Prickett was selected as the new Chief Nurse, and Maj Barb Anderson became the new Assistant Chief Nurse.

☆☆☆☆☆

There was still pressure on unit members to meet the many deployment billets requested by the Guard Bureau. Maj Johnson stated, "There are still many slots available for many AFSCs in the 120-day Silver Rotations starting in November. Crews may sign up for 60 days of the tour. Crewmembers were also called a week ago with the opportunity to fill 35-day tours to Ramstein, providing patient movement from downrange locations, and also for 15-day tours for the ICMOP missions. These rotations will involve certifications in other airframes."

Deployed - Letters from the Field: 1st Lt Mensen

We are halfway through our deployment here in Uzbekistan. Overall things have gone well. As always there are logistical glitches here and there, but the missions always get off the ground and our patients get moved.

So far, between the two and three person crews here at K2, we have flown on the C-17 (a lot), the C-130 and the C-141. We've had a total of 11 missions and moved a total patient load of 9-7+2. We've seen everything from seizures and pregnancies to heart attacks and landmine encounters. Remember there is still a war going on here! SSgt Devine finally got to fly on a C-17 mission to Germany! It took nine weeks, but it was well worth the wait. I think most of her Christmas shopping is done!

We are a little lonely, due to the Minnesota Aerial Port members returning home from K2. I can say that they proudly represented us as the champions of the K2 Labor Day volleyball tournament!

As for our aeromed achievement, TSgt Eubanks, SSgt Devine, and I launched ourselves, configured the C-130 and loaded the patient within 20 minutes of being called for an urgent mission. Yes, the O2 and electrical were hooked up and preflighting done! Just remember to use your checklist, and our training does pay off. There have been numerous times when safety time-outs have been called here; don't be afraid of what you know is right! Fly safe and we are looking forward to coming home in November!

The C-9A Nightingale with its red cross was officially retired from the air evac mission at Scott AFB, IL this month. They received their first fleet of C-9A Nightingales for the aerovac mission in 1968. The C-130 was slated to be utilized for CONUS missions in its place.

October. MSgt Sue Malecha retired from the National Guard after twenty-one years of service. MSgt Pat Nowlan was selected as the 109th AES new First Sergeant. Due to the heavy demand on the unit for personnel deploying overseas, there were many unfilled positions within the squadron. The Executive Staff met in December and filled several open positions. Personnel who were temporarily assigned to sections were also reassigned.

☆☆☆☆☆

SSgt Shawn Fitzhenry, a ground radio specialist, has spent the last four months in Iraq with the 379th EAES Liaison Team. He moved throughout the country coordinating air evacuation for wounded Soldiers assigned to Army airborne divisions.

During this time, his team and the Army personnel have been living in tents without air conditioning. They do their laundry in tubs in front of their tents and attempt to dry the clothes on lines. While on the lines, clothes get full of dust. They used to get one shower a week, but now are allowed one three-minute shower a day.

For morale, they got one 15-minute e-mail session, for which they had to wait in line two to three hours, and one 10-minute phone call per week.

In e-mails written to his fiancée, Fitzhenry has been describing some of his daily activities. "I started off by going through town on a convoy with coalition security forces and some other Army folks," he said. "It is a little nerve racking not knowing who is good or bad out here. We drove around with our weapons pointed out the vehicle windows with a round in the chamber and the selective fire switch on semiautomatic. Our fingers were just barely on the trigger aiming at anyone that might be suspicious, but it is so hard to tell who is."

On another day, he wrote to inform her their unit had taken some losses. "We have had a rough day today," he said. "We lost three good guys and two more are getting worked on."

After writing to her about the difficulties of his deployment, Fitzhenry, who works as a Lakeville police officer at home, reassured his fiancée. "I will be okay out here," he wrote to her. "I am strong, and I have had a lot of training that has prepared me for what I need to do to complete my part of the mission out here."

Recently, Fitzhenry received a reminder of his purpose over there in the form of an interaction with local Iraqis. He had gone to the local tailor to get patches sewn on his uniforms. As he was leaving the shop, the 11-year-old boy whose parents owned the shop stopped him. "As I was getting ready to leave," wrote Fitzhenry, "it was funny because the boy extended his hand to shake mine and said, 'welcome, how can I do for you?' So I shook his hand and just smiled and said thank you. The boy's father then came over and shook my hand and said, 'thank you for helping us.'

"I guess the whole experience just brightened up my day. It was cool to actually get thanked by an Iraqi national family for being over here. It makes being over here worthwhile when you look at that little boy and know he will have a chance at freedom and to live a better life than what his parents did." [158]

November. It was announced that the long delayed ASEV would now be held next June.

Deployed - Letters from the Field: SrA Vogt

> Greetings from Ibn Sina Hospital in downtown Baghdad. It has been a very interesting two months with the 28th Combat Support Hospital out of Fort Bragg, NC. I am currently stationed in a fixed facility with other AF Airmen.
>
> We like to say that we are "embedded" with the Army because we support a large number of Army troops. Our area is heavily defended. This area of Baghdad is known as the Green

Zone and supports the Coalition Provisional Authority and Iraqi Governing Council. Our evacuation mission is very busy. Things have been really building in intensity around here in the last month. I'm grateful that Shawn, Pat, and Jeramy were able to come and see our location several weeks ago. It is hard to explain unless you've been here. This was one of Saddam's playgrounds that encompass the Ministry of Information, the Cultural Center, one of Saddam's many palaces, as well as houses used by his sons. Many of the buildings in the area have been bombed in the most recent war as well as in 1991.

Unfortunately, things have been getting much more dangerous around here lately. We always carry our weapons with us wherever we go, but attacks on soft targets in the area have made things more "exciting." Gunshots, mortar rounds exploding, rocket fire, tank fire and car bombs are daily occurrences in and around our area. Luckily, we have not been put into any life-threatening circumstances. However, we ate lunch at a hotel recently that was bombed the next day, so I guess one never knows.

We are currently supporting U.S. and coalition military personnel with life, limb, and eyesight issues. At any given time on the wards we have more Iraqi POWs and civilians than we do American personnel.

I have seen all types of people come through our doors, including some of the future leaders of the country as well as the current ones. It's an honor to know that we are responsible for the safekeeping of so many important people that have a stake in the future of this country. I look forward to seeing you all at December drill. Have a great month.

Deployed - Letters from the Field: 1st Lt Ehman

Hello from the desert plains of Southern Iraq! We have finally made the move rumored about for weeks. The end of October saw the five of us pack our bags and leave the comforts of Camp Wolf, Kuwait behind. A short flight later and we were relocated to Tallil AB in southern Iraq. Our mission here remains the same and since our arrival we have been very busy getting organized and setting up the AE shop here. We are the first AE crews assigned to this location so it has been a learning experience for us all.

Many of the luxuries of Kuwait are a distant memory now as we adjust to dining in tents, five minute "combat showers" and less than desirable toilet facilities. We asked about trips to the local Hilton but it doesn't appear that is an option for us! There is however an archeological site of interest nearby that we do hope to visit; the birthplace of the biblical figure Abraham is just a mile or so off camp.

We are all excited to be coming home this month and with any luck we'll be with our families on Thanksgiving Day. Look forward to seeing you all soon!

December. Just in time for the holidays, twenty-seven unit members returned home after a four month deployment in support of Operation Enduring Freedom. Members were based in Iraq, Kuwait, Qatar and Uzbekistan and flew missions throughout the area of responsibility.

☆☆☆☆☆

Nurse recruitment and retention was a high priority for the wing, with numbers well below the unit's needs for many years. A taxable $15,000 cash bonus spread out over three years with a continuing commitment was available for qualified flight nurses with more than four years but less than 17 years of time-in-service who had not previously received a medical bonus in any reserve component.

☆☆☆☆☆

Serving as part of the 379th AES in Southwest Asia, several 109th AES members waited for the call to collect and transport patients needing specialized care.

On any given day, they would be ready to transport patients from any airfield in the area of responsibility, either to collection points from which patients were airlifted to Europe or the U.S. according to their needs, or a number of specialized care facilities in Southwest Asia.

This meant long days. Some flying days would span up to 30 hours. However, the work was not without gratification.

"It was a long day, but rewarding," said MSgt Mike Granlund, med tech, of a four-city, round-trip mission through Iraq one day.

"It's very rewarding work," added fellow 109th AES crewmember Capt Matt Smith. As the MCD, his job was to oversee patient treatment and acted as a liaison between the medical team on board and the aircrew flying the plane.

Not only were the days long, but they could also be very stressful and dangerous as crews often carried critical patients in and out of combat zones.

For example, a Turkish national in Afghanistan needed transport to Baghdad to receive specialized care. Capt Smith and his crew jumped into action preparing a C-130H to airlift the patient to Baghdad. The crew loaded equipment and supplies and configured the litters on a co-located C-130H while waiting for what happened to be a 133rd Airlift Wing C-130H carrying the patient arriving from Afghanistan.

As the Minnesota cargo plane taxied into position on the tarmac, the captain's crew put the finishing touches on the C-130H about to receive the patient. Aircraft tail to aircraft tail, the patient transfer took place. The patient, who had a coma-producing concussion from a two-vehicle accident, was in guarded condition for his ride to Baghdad.

"From what I was told, I believe he was the only survivor in the vehicle he was riding in," said Capt Smith. The patient's prognosis was also unclear at the time of scheduled aerovac, according to Smith.

A CCATT kept watch over the patient until the touch down in Baghdad. Then, dressed in full battle gear, the team transferred the patient to a waiting Army helicopter, which immediately took off to a local hospital.

Of the danger and stress, 109th AES members say, "All in a day's work."

"I just have a job to do," said MSgt Granlund. "I don't consider myself to be courageous or a hero…We're all here together, and we support each other."

Other 109th AES members who served on this volunteer four-month deployment were: Capt Kim Schmidt, Maj John Mickelson, MSgt Bryan Steven, and TSgt Andrea Zondlo. [159]

Photo courtesy of NorthStar Guard, Spring/Summer 2004 - Courtesy Photo
MSgt Mike Granlund (front right litter bearer) helps to transport a critically injured patient from one C-130 to another.

Along these same lines, two 109th AES aeromeds partnered with active duty and reserve units to provide Squadron Medical Element (SME) and command support for the 379th Expeditionary Medical Support (EMEDS). Fifty plus combat sorties were flown with 100% readiness. Another 17 members provided comprehensive intratheater patient movement, in-flight patient care, and aeromedical communications systems management throughout the CENTCOM (Central Command) theater of operations.

2004

January. It was announced that due to the changes in the wing plans, the Executive Committee cancelled the 109th AES participation in the Fort McCoy exercise scheduled for July. In lieu of the July UTA, unit members were expected to attend the extended April and May UTA for scheduled exercises.

☆☆☆☆☆

It was noted that in post UTA walk arounds through different unit section areas that some sections were left in disarray and various food items were left in the working areas. The Commander has decided to create a monthly "award" that will go to the most "deserving" section called the "You Don't Want It" Award. It was hoped that it would garner the expected results.

☆☆☆☆☆

The priority training objective for this quarter was the use of the ventilator on the local missions. One patient on each flight was assigned as a ventilator dependent casualty. The expectation was for the crew to preflight and set up the ventilator and provide the expected care in-flight. This was a first for the unit as far as this piece of medical equipment went. The goal was for all aeromeds to become proficient with this critical device.

Deployed - Letters from the Field: Maj Mickelson

Hello from Baghdad International Airport. Hope y'all had a blessed Christmas or Happy Holiday. TSgt Zondlo and I got alerted at 2300 on Christmas Eve and we were in Germany on Christmas Day and got to see snow! We have two AE crews (½ compliments) and two CCATT teams. I would prefer to have all five of our crews, but that is how CENTAF (U.S. Air Forces, U.S. Central Command) utilizes AE assets in OIF. The other crew is from a C-141 unit out of March AFB, CA. It can be a challenging learning experience to fly with other crews. Flexibility and a constant focus on the mission is the key. Maintaining a sense of urgency at all times cannot be emphasized enough.

The 109th AES does an excellent job of preparing us to deploy. Baghdad International Airport is a target for the enemy. We have been attacked multiple times with mortars and rockets.

I assume you saw the news about the DHL (civilian) and the incident with the C-17. During a recent return "deadhead" flight, about 30 minutes out I heard the loadmaster say "the LZ is hot." The airfield was under a mortar attack. We circled awhile and landed safely. On my last mission, the crew "popped flares." Last night was New Year's Eve and again we were attacked. It is dangerous, but I put my continued safety in God's hands.

We are seeing a lot of seriously injured Soldiers. Today was the first time I have seen human remains loaded onto a plane. It was a moving, emotion-filled experience to watch the Army Soldiers carry their friend onto the plane. A chaplain said a few words and they stood in formation and saluted goodbye to their comrade in arms.

One thing I will warn of is that there are a bunch of rumors roaming about. There are changes occurring now; what the future needs of AE will be only God knows. Continue to train hard and be prepared to deploy if called. Take care.

February. Word came down from Guard Bureau detailing a change in direction regarding AEFs. Aeromeds would no longer be assigned to an AEF. Instead, all aeromeds would be identified as "Enablers." This meant that instead of having an assigned period of responsibility, everyone would be on volunteer status to fill AE requirements in much the same way that the unit had filled these vacancies since last fall. The squadron coordinated with the 156th AES from Charlotte (sister unit of 109th AES) to fill in the time frame that the unit was originally assigned - Sep to Nov '04.

☆☆☆☆☆

Maj Johnson let the unit know that there are services available to unit members returning from lengthy overseas deployments who may be having readjustment issues. The effect of deploying for this war has touched every person in some way. Some had more difficulties returning than others. "Just remember, you are not alone."

☆☆☆☆☆

The unit was notified that the equipment packages for our new UTCs had arrived and Logistics was busy doing inventories and storing them. As part of the packages, the squadron now owned a Humvee and a "new" deuce. Plans were developed by the vehicle instructors to train unit members on these vehicles.

☆☆☆☆☆

By the end of February, the majority of the squadron had returned home. Many of the job positions that had been vacant for a long time could now be filled and returning personnel needed to get up to speed with the preparations under way to prepare the squadron for the June ASEV.

March. Maj Johnson noted that the squadron has had close to 80 deployments over the past twelve months, with some members having deployed twice in support of the Global War on Terrorism.

Deployed - Letters from the Field: 1st Lt Matt Smith

MSgt Granlund and I were split up the first of the month. Since I last wrote, I spent a week in Tallil, Iraq, closing AE operations there in preparation for their move north. I have flown three times in seven days (the luck of the rotation).

One thing I learned is that there is usually a physician that comes to the plane with the patients. Always hit them up for extra pain medication. In the last week I have seen close to a dozen combat injuries; anything from fractures relating to explosions, shrapnel and gunshot wounds. I have seen colostomies secondary to shrapnel wounds to the belly. External fixators are a big thing for a lot of these fractures.

What I'm seeing is that the majority of these patients are being ordered Tylox or Percocet for pain control on the flight. The other day, a patient with a femur external fixator placed the day before was ordered Tylox for pain. He came on the plane crying from the pain. A physician was there and we were able to get a Morphine order from him - 2 mg IV. It was ineffective.

The physician was along for the trip and we were able to get 1mg extra after takeoff. We just happened to note that a flight surgeon was on the plane deadheading. We decided to try our luck with him. He looked at the patient (crying, squirming) and told us that as long as he was breathing, BP was above 100, and O2 saturations were above 90 to give him what he wants and needs. He received an additional 10 mg IV and we started getting his pain under control by the end of the hour and a half flight.

I know that we've been briefed on pain control, but there are some individuals who don't have the same vision as the rest of us.

April. The ASEV flight evaluations that began at the end of this month went very well with Maj JoEllen Evavold having received an "EQ" grade.

☆☆☆☆☆

Even though the unit's AEF cycle was still four months out, the increased tempo of activity in the Middle East increased requirements for AE support. The unit was already getting indications of the requirements it was expected to meet.

Just this month alone, the Radio Operations section traveled to Pope AFB, NC and several logistics personnel journeyed to Scott AFB, IL for additional training. One 109th AES aerovac crew traveled to Wright-Patterson AFB, OH for C-141 certification training by Jackson, MS instructors and then flew to Ramstein AB, Germany and back to Andrews AFB, MD.

From this, one can see that there was a lot of interaction with other units from around the world including Guard, Reserve, and active duty partners. In the history of the 109th AES there has never been a time with the operations tempo like the unit has experienced in the past 12 months. Although the 109th AES had the lowest number of deployed members than at any time during the past year, over the last month alone, some 20% of the squadron has traveled away from home station and interfaced with other units.

May. ASEV feedback from the evaluators continued to come in with very positive comments regarding the unit strengths in CRM, configuration, and realistic training scenarios. They also noted very positive interaction with the loadmasters and pilots.

Deployed - Letters from the Field: TSgt Miles

Missions are going well in Germany. So far I've had six flights. My crew knows many of you all back home. They are a very good team and we work well together. It seems to be that if something goes wrong it's going to happen to our crew. We've gotten to use our emergency skills very well. I want to share some of my flights with you all.

My first mission to Kuwait was with some cargo and passengers. We then picked up a couple of more patients and flew to Iraq. As we were loading patients in Iraq, one of them coded. They rushed her back to the MASF but she didn't make it. We finished loading, then they wanted to give us one more ambulatory patient. I made some room and said OK. This Marine came on with a broken arm. It was a smooth flight to Germany. During the unloading another patient coded. They got him off the plane and rushed him to the medical facility. We got the rest of the patients unloaded and finished with a 26-hour duty day (about 11 hours of flight time).

Nothing could have prepared me for the patients I saw and the codes I had.

This was my welcome into heavy AE. The next day I saw that last Marine we took on being interviewed on the Today Show talking with his family back in California via video. That made my day and the flight worth it.

My third flight was to Andrews AFB, MD. I was helping litter patients with different items. The way the Soldiers gave me a sincere, "Thanks Sergeant" gives me so much pride in my job and knowing the men and women we transport appreciate what we are doing for them as much as I appreciate what they are going through. During that flight we had to divert to Norfolk, VA to wait out the weather at Andrews. Patients don't like hearing that we are not there yet and will take off again in an hour or two - who can blame them?

Last week I had my first live mission as CMT (Charge Medical Technician). It started out with an aircraft emergency. As we were loading our equipment, smoke started coming from the front of the comfort pallet. We evacuated the plane and the fire department came. They couldn't find the cause of the smoke and we did a tail swap after it was safe to get our gear. When we got to Kuwait, we only had a load of nine litters, one ambulatory, and two attendants. On the down side it was the first mission I flew back with a casket; it was sad to see that. On the upside I got to pass out letters from 1st graders to the patients. They liked that!

I also saw the article from the Pioneer Press on 30 Apr '04 about the emergency landing of the C-130H back home. This reminds us all that we need to be ready anytime, anywhere.

For the newer members back home, I recommend that you deploy early in your careers.

I'll see you all in June!

(authors' note: The incident mentioned in the previous "Letters from the Field" referred to a recent crash landing at Minneapolis/St. Paul IAP with one of the wing's C-130s. The aircrew were unable to fully lower the starboard side landing gear. After touchdown the landing gear collapsed causing the aircraft to veer to the right causing damage to #3 and #4 engine as well as outer wing damage. All four crewmembers survived without injury. There were no aeromeds on board this flight. This was a stark reminder of the potential danger the aeromeds faced on a day to day basis during their training. One did not have to be deployed to be placed in harm's way.)

June. The last seven deployed members returned to the unit. The squadron continued to focus with increased intensity on preparation for the AEF scheduled for September.

☆☆☆☆☆

The ASEV team arrived to conduct their week-long inspection and spot flight evals.

☆☆☆☆☆

Col Terry Tripp retired as Wing Commander, and Col Cossalter took over command of the 133rd AW. The Change of Command ceremony and a reception at the dining facility took place on the Sunday UTA.

July. The unit did an excellent job during the ASEV visit. The final report revealed the combined scores with the airlift squadron for Aircrew Testing and In-Flight Performance were both graded "Excellent," while the Training and Equipment Programs were rated "Satisfactory." The overall grade for the wing was Mission Ready, with an "Excellent" grade for Aircrew Performance and "Satisfactory" for both Training and Stan/Eval.

☆☆☆☆☆

The next AEF for the unit was scheduled for the September to November time frame. In the past year, the 109th AES provided numerous volunteers for periods ranging from 30-120 days. Along with this notification, AMC sent out a partial mobilization order to all AE units to fill specific UTCs for the assigned AEFs. At the recent AE Commanders' Conference, ANG commanders discussed the subject of volunteerism versus PM (Partial Mobilization). The general consensus was that volunteerism was having many serious impacts on individual units and their members. After discussions with wing commanders and their solid support, the 109th and 156th AES sent a message to NGB that they intended to deploy for the AEF under the mobilization authority. This decision would allow the unit to perform their jobs as well as provide the necessary personnel needed to best fill the requirements stated by the mobilization order.

This was confusing to the unit and its members since the PM authority only covered specific UTCs and there was no plan conveyed to the unit as to how they would fill vacancies not covered under the order. This put unit members, their families and employers in a "wait and see" situation. The possibility existed that unit members who did not volunteer to deploy might be called upon to fill requirements of the AEF.

August. Word was received from the National Guard Bureau that a large number of unit members would be deployed in the next few weeks to meet the needs of the AEF. This increase was due to escalating activity in the Middle East.

☆☆☆☆☆

Family Day activities were scheduled for Sunday of the August UTA. Once again, it was an opportunity for the unit to recognize their families and show its appreciation to those who gave so much over the past year to support their military obligations. Military personnel were authorized to wear civilian clothes all day. It was a nice break in the midst of all the deployment activity.

☆☆☆☆☆

The AF celebrated the 50-year milestone of the legendary C-130 Hercules which was first flown on 23 Aug, 1954. Since that historic day (and up to 2004), more than 2,200 C-130s in 70 variants to five basic models have been produced, and 676 are in service with the Air Force. The Navy and Marine Corps fly C-130s, as do the armed forces of 66 other nations.

The first C-130A became operational in Dec 1956, replacing the far less capable Fairchild C-119 Flying Boxcar, revolutionizing aircraft performance and providing greater speed, range and takeoff ability. Continuous improvement was the norm for the C-130 system. Several new models included such enhancements as the new external fuel tanks allowing the aircraft to fight heavy winds in flights cross the ocean, more powerful engines with new propellers, beefed up landing gear, a modified model demonstrating short take offs and landings, and modified "Ski-130s" outfitted with ski landing gear to resupply Arctic expeditions.

The newest C-130 in the inventory, the "J" model, entered the AF inventory in Feb 1999. The basic design remains true to the original, but with 40-percent more range, 24-percent faster speed, shorter runway takeoff capability and greater cargo and passenger capacity. Its new avionics will also allow for better data capability and control, and requires a crew of three rather than five.

The C-130s combat record is an integral part of its distinguished history. The aircraft quickly earned its reputation as a tough aircraft for rough places. In the late 1950s, with Southeast Asia facing a communist takeover, the Herc quickly became the armed services' premier tactical airlifter.

In addition to flying in numerous contingency, peacekeeping, and humanitarian relief operations around the world, the C-130 continues to play a vital role in the United States. Equipped with Modular Airborne Firefighting Systems, these C-130s are deployed to help combat wildfires in the Western states, and WC-130s provide vital data as hurricane hunters over the Caribbean and Florida, collecting information for the National Hurricane Center.

These special duties, along with the daily tasks of deploying, supplying and redeploying joint service and Allied forces throughout the world will build upon the C-130s legacy of heroism as one of the premier, multirole aircraft in American history. [160]

☆☆☆☆☆

At the Minnesota Stand Down for Veterans, six 109th AES members provided over 175 homeless veterans with health care screenings for diabetes, high blood pressure, and tuberculosis.

September. Twenty-eight unit members deployed for the next four months. A large number of those were office supervisors which significantly affected all of the sections. "Temporary supervisors" were identified as necessary. For example, after her deployment, Lt Col Johnson returned to her duties as squadron commander full-time and covered the duties of Lt Col Dahlquist when he deployed.

Three members supported CENTCOM intratheater patient movement and in-flight patient care within the Afghanistan Area of Operations as part of Operation Iraqi Freedom.

Professionals from the Medical Group and the 109th AES provided outstanding medical care to many sick and wounded. They found themselves in places like Al Udied, Qatar, and Manas, Kyrgyzstan.

☆☆☆☆☆

As part of the Exercise Great Lakes Response, 35 members initiated, coordinated and planned a large-scale Homeland Defense/Weapons of Mass Destruction Exercise to improve coordination and response for emergency situations. The 109th AES was the first ANG unit (regionally) to deploy a 25+ member Expeditionary Medical Support package, combined with state and local civilian entities in support of over 5,000 personnel at a deployed or stateside location, to provide a full range of medical treatment in the event of a chemical or biological attack.

☆☆☆☆☆

Unit members participated in a live air evacuation mission to the Azores.

November. MSgt Gozel was selected as the Outstanding Enlisted Air National Guardsman of the Year at a local American Legion event. First Sergeant Nowlan accepted the award for MSgt Gozel who was recognized for his achievement after he returned from his deployment.

☆☆☆☆☆

Training was complete on the Zoll ECG monitor/defibrillator. All future checkrides would be using this new piece of medical equipment.

☆☆☆☆☆

The concept of Universal AECM was coming to fruition. This would entail all aerovac crewmembers to become qualified in the C-130, C-17, C-141, and KC-135. It was anticipated that all training and book tests would be completed by December 2005.

☆☆☆☆☆

Due to the demand for more nurses, associate degree nurses (meeting certain conditions) would be accepted into the unit as flight nurses.

December.

Deployed - Letters from the Field: Capt Mary Larson (excerpts)

FROM THE FRONT LINES... Actually, from the Ramstein library across from billeting. From all of us in Germany, we extend our Holiday Greetings to everyone back home and downrange. Last evening our crew had an early Christmas present; a 0-8+0 mission. We had time to bake cookies, roast hot dogs, and, well..."tap out"; a reprieve for all our crews from only a week ago.

While in Ali-Al-Salem waiting for a C-130 to bring us patients, our crew went to the chow hall to eat and watch game #4 NY/Boston. As I walked in I heard, "Mary Malek!" Capt Patty

Ehresmann, C-130 pilot, was sitting there with her front-end crew. I last saw her in '96 when she was in the 109th AES, and we deployed to Hungary together as AETs. Maj Kolar and his crew had brought us our patients we were so "patiently" waiting for.

On Nov 5th and with a 14-hour notice, my husband, Lee, and our three kids flew to Andrews, DC and stayed two nights at the Comfort Inn with the rest of our crew and CCATT.

As those in the 109th AES know, it is a humbling honor to be serving and caring for our country's wounded and injured warriors. It takes EVERYONE in so many different capacities, back at the unit and here, to launch a mission. SSgt Devine received the following note from one of our patients on 16 Sep '04 that says it all: "I hope this doesn't sound dumb but I just wanted to tell you all that I have so much respect for all you do. You are all so busy and there are so many of us to care for that I thought a note may be easier to say thanks. You are all doing a great job! Thank you and God bless you." (name withheld by book authors)

Continued Blessings to You All...

2005

March. By the UTA, all unit members had returned home from the latest set of deployments. The Wing Commander also directed that no one was to be deployed, unless mobilized, until after the ORI (scheduled later in the year) was accomplished.

☆☆☆☆☆

In the March Vital Signs, the Unit Career Advisor noted that the reenlistment bonus was set at $5,000.

April. From April 25-29, the 109th AES participated with the wing in the Combat Readiness Training Center Exercise at Volk Field, WI. The focus was strictly ATSO. Training was provided by an excellent cadre at Volk Field who specialized in preparing units for ORIs. After this event, the plan was to exercise squadron operations back at home with an ORE during the September UTA, and then accomplish the ORI in December. The 109th AES was scheduled to work with the Oklahoma aeromeds for this ORI.

☆☆☆☆☆

Select 109th AES personnel deployed to Baghdad and Balad, Iraq.

June. A four-day exercise over the UTA weekend was held by the wing to prepare for the upcoming Operational Readiness Inspection in Dec. The focus of the exercise was on two phases of deployment. The first phase, the Initial Response, consisted of personnel/cargo preparation, palletization, mobility processing and personnel/equipment deployment.

The second phase of the exercise was the employment phase. Squadron and wing UTCs actually set up to some degree and functioned according to their mission. This was a 12-hour day beginning at 0600 and continuing until 1800. UTCs "deployed" to various locations around base and performed the necessary activities to provide AE services as needed. The MASF and AELT facilitated the movement of the patients to the aircraft and our AE command squadron provided overall AE command and control responsibilities. This phase also strongly emphasized the Ability To Survive and Operate and the wear of CBWD (Chemical Biological Warfare Defense) ensembles, Self-Aid/Buddy Care (SA/BC), Post Attack Response (PAR) Teams, and squadron/wing level command and control functions. [161]

July. Wing members had the July UTA off with makeup days scheduled for the Sep ORE.

August. A two-day exercise was conducted which was the last opportunity to prepare for next month's ORE.

The 109th AES planned on operating with the 137th AES (Oklahoma City) for both the Sep ORE and the ORI in December.

September. Along with 300 medical crewmembers from across the nation, 10 Airmen from the 109th AES provided medical care to Hurricane Katrina survivors from Sep 2-15. One five-team crew returned Sep 5, with the second team returning Sep 15.

"When we are needed, we will sacrifice what we have to support those in need," said TSgt Robert Buresh, 109th AES. "We are always prepared to deploy when we get the call."

The aeromeds, based at Lackland AFB, TX, picked up and transported 12 patients from New Orleans International Airport, New Orleans Naval Air Station and Gulfport MS to Shreveport, LA., in addition to other locations in the southern region.

"Most patients had no shoes, no belongings," explained Lt Col Barbara Anderson, 109th AES MCD. "One patient, a little elderly lady who didn't speak English, was terrified as she had never flown before."

It was a mission unlike the aeromeds had ever seen. The medical team overcame language barriers, patient identification tribulations and operated in a chaotic environment to care for patients and save lives.

When the tasking was authorized, there was a very short notice to launch a base C-130H. Within a four-hour window, crewmembers were notified (some left their jobs to report), checked mobility folders, obtained medications and supplies from the VA, had orders printed, completed and loaded the in-flight kits, drew items from Base Supply, and finally launched the aircraft. This would not have been possible without overwhelming support from everyone involved, both at the unit and base level. [162]

Hurricane Katrina necessitated changes for the September ORE. The training site at Gulfport, MS was no longer operational and the 137th AES out of Oklahoma did not participate due to their commitments for Hurricane Katrina relief. Only a portion of the base deployed to Volk Field, WI - the aeromeds did not. The 109th AES was still a part of the Initial Response phase which included mobility and cargo processing as well as training flights that took place during the week.

Also in September, preparations were made for a possible 109th MASF tasking for personnel and equipment to provide patient evacuation for Hurricane Rita which ultimately made landfall in Louisiana. The mission was subsequently assigned to the active duty Air Force. At that point, all squadron volunteers were informed and released from all responsibility for the deployment. The tremendous response of unit members to the call for assistance (whether to deploy or assist in the preparation of people and equipment) was indicative of what an outstanding, committed group of people we have in the unit. [163]

November. The unit continued to train and prepare for the December ORI.

December. The wing as well as the 109th AES scored an "Excellent" rating for the ORI which was held this month. During both our individual debrief before leaving Volk Field and the formal wing debrief, the inspectors emphasized the outstanding attitudes that were especially evident during the harsh weather conditions. The senior inspector stated that participants displayed the best sense of urgency and attitude seen in the last two years.

☆☆☆☆☆

Also this month, CMSgt Cheryl Burton retired with over 22 years of military service. Two months ago she was asked to join a ministry full-time and she accepted the offer.

2006

February. SMSgt Kennedy began duties as the First Shirt for the unit, replacing MSgt Nowlan.

March. CMSgt Greg Close became the new Superintendent of Nursing Services. He previously served with the Medical Group.

April. The UTA focused on preparation for the rapidly approaching AEF. In addition, a cross-country mission was flown to Houston, TX. Six missions were scheduled, and in the process,

MSgt Gozel was upgraded to examiner while MSgt Burmeister, TSgt Schimek, and Maj Janu passed their instructor checkrides. To top it off, four spot evaluations were completed and a Ground Flying Training Period was accomplished.

May. By the UTA, most of the members were sent out on the AEF, deploying to Iraq and Qatar.

Photo courtesy of Vital Signs (Jun '06)
Capt Michael Cook (left) and Capt Dominic Ehman (right) deployed in Djibouti, Africa.

Deployed - Letters from the Field: Capt Ehman

Greetings one and all from hot and humid Djibouti, Africa! I know it is hot where the others are but only I can claim it being "Africa Hot!" which somehow makes it hotter than anywhere else!

By the time this makes print I will have completed over one month of this tour. Time has passed relatively quickly. I'm now just settling in for the middle two months which I remember seem to take a bit longer.

I am living on a relatively small base named Camp LeMonier - a former French base, and we are situated just a short distance from the Red Sea, adjacent to the Djiboutian International Airport. The food here is good, the workout facilities are top notch and I live in an air-conditioned room connected to my office. How convenient is that?

Probably the most interesting aspect of this job is the fact that I actively interact with all four branches of the military, as well as the civilian contractors. The medical facility on base is run by the Navy, they call themselves an EMU or Expeditionary Medical Unit, and they work in an EMF or Expeditionary Medical Facility, neat huh?! Honestly, the first thing I realized is that there are more acronyms than I could have imagined. The second thing I realized is that I have no idea how to identify Navy rank. I call them all sir and ma'am, seems to work OK. The flight line is run by civilian contractors and I have regular contact with them coordinating aircraft arrival/departure times, flight-line access and patient movement. Most of them are retired military and they have always been helpful.

My role is to assist the EMU in coordinating the transportation of patients from this location to higher levels of care. The base population is small and to this point I am averaging only one mission a week. Initially, there was a medical crew pre-positioned at this location, but they have recently been moved to another location to support other taskings. While this primary job is less than busy, I have been able to get involved in a few other areas. There is a group of pararescuemen here and the Liaison Nurse Officer (LNO) has historically provided ground medical support for them when they do their weekly parachute training jumps. I have been able to go out with them a couple of times including a night jump near the Ethiopian border. I have also been asked to work with them during their medical training, providing scenarios and evaluating/critiquing their performance.

In spite of these activities, there is plenty of down time. The Morale, Welfare, Recreation office offers many options to see the sights. In addition to shopping trips to the markets, there are tours to a cheetah refuge, a trip to a nearby island for snorkeling/scuba diving and evening trips into town to go bowling and go-cart racing. The chapel offers frequent trips to help out at the local orphanages and there are even classes on base to learn two of the local languages - Arabic and Swahili. Another opportunity I hope to take advantage of is an Embassy-sponsored English Discussion Group that travels to the local university to sit for an hour or so and talk with the students. This is an organized event with specific topics for discussion. The goal is to share cultures in an open and nonthreatening manner. The unfortunate part of this job is that I am the single LNO here so I am somewhat tied to the base. I will be able to do some of the shorter trips, but a trip to the island for snorkeling is a full day and not an option for me. One highlight of the tour so far was a USO (United Service Organization) visit and concert by Toby Keith on May 31st. In case anyone is wondering, there is a "Cantina" here with a three drink limit.

As I write this I currently have two patients waiting for transport from this location. I eagerly await the arrival of the aircraft and crew with the hopes of seeing a familiar face or two from the 109th. So far Capt Cook has been the only 109th visitor here.

Every day I am greeted by sunny blue skies and warm sand under my feet, I can't imagine a better way to spend my summer! Well...maybe I could come up with something.

Cheers to those of you keeping the unit functioning back home and to those enjoying the sandy landscape in areas not too far from me! I look forward to seeing you all in a few short months!

Photo courtesy of MSgt Rachel Maloney
Aeromeds in Iraq 2006.

(L - R): SrA Matt Monjes, Lt Col JoEllen Evavold, SSgt Amy Nordquist, SSgt Terry Dierkhising, Capt Kirsten Hoffoss

Deployed - Letters from the Field: MSgt Burmeister

Hello from Balad AB, Iraq. As we approach our halfway point of our deployment, I look back on the first two months here. Personally, I have deployed three times before, so nothing was too surprising to me. I learned not to expect anything, and I would do fine. However, several of our people have not deployed before, and I saw that their expectations did not meet reality. I guess there are a few points I would like to talk about.

The Learning Curve...
Everyone here hit a steep learning curve. Many of us had never been in these positions before, and were totally new to them. We only had a few days to learn from our outgoing

people what to do. We did not always like the way they did things, but we had to learn what they knew before it was too late. Even after they departed, we were still learning. As of now, halfway through, I am still learning different things.

Working Together...
I saw a lot of separation between people here. There were different shifts, different positions, and different crews. When everyone worked together and helped one another, things went fantastic. However, at times, people tended to just hang out with their own group, and not cross those barriers they erected. When that happened, people had problems, and the mission suffered. Don't get me wrong, we did the mission, no one got hurt, and everything that needed to get done, was done. I am proud of the job everyone has done. However, I think if we worked together more for the mission and not so much for ourselves, it would have been smoother.

Staying busy...
This time around, I have been busy myself working 12 hours a day (at least) six days a week. However, I know from past experience if you aren't busy, time drags, and the deployment goes slowly. In this instance, the time has flown by for me. I would suggest that you get involved in things. Here they have all kinds of events going on. I have seen dodgeball tournaments every other week, floor hockey, get-togethers, base tours, and many other functions. If that does not work, then get out and work at the hospital, help out at the AEOT or help out at the clinic. Many folks are keeping busy and from what I hear the tour has gone by quickly for them. The busier you are, the quicker the time goes.

I am proud of the job everyone has done, and look forward to the second half of the rotation going as quickly and as well as the first half. Take care.

Throughout the year there were many references to financial shortfalls and budgeting constraints for the wing. Even though the squadron continued in their attempts to be fiscally responsible, the 109th AES, like every other unit on base, was hit hard. Personal requests that would have been considered reasonable in the past were denied. However, resources to execute training and operational expenses for the year were available.

At the base level, the centralized clothing account experienced a heavy burden that affected some of the aeromeds. The requirements for deploying members took priority. Uniforms and fitness gear were in short supply at the base level. Members were able to place orders, but some items would not be available until the next fiscal year. Urgent needs were handled individually by the unit resource advisor.

July. The National Guard Youth Camp was held from July 29-August 4, while the National Guard Teen Camp was conducted from 5-13 Aug.

Unit members continued to deploy while others returned home from their AEF deployments. In addition, two unit members deployed to Operation Jump Start for the Southwest Border Patrol. Capt Collyard performed duty in New Mexico, while TSgt Devine served in Arizona. Both of them worked in medical clinics set up to support military personnel deployed to their locations.

September.

Deployed - Letters from the Field: 1st Lt Linn

I have been working as the Director of Operations of the Aeromedical Evacuation Operations Team. I work on the evening shift (1900-0700) here in Balad with Lt Col Evavold, SSgt Aranda (WV) and Capt Joseph (OK). The AEOT staff directly support the launch and recovery of air evac crews and CCATTs. We manage crew rest for our AE crews and coordinate any logistical issues that our personnel have here from weapons to travel arrangements. A majority of the missions actually launch during the evening shift, but we run a 24-hour operation here so missions may launch any hour of the day or night. We currently manage four CCATTs and three AE crews.

Our operations tempo varies widely from day-to-day. One night we might launch two CCATT missions and recover an AE crew plus an additional CCATT. The next night may be rather slow while we wait for another mission to develop. The next night we may be busy running again from the beginning of shift until the end. To quote the former DO of the AEOT, Capt Hoffoss, "We're like firefighters. We might sit around for hours and then suddenly it's time to GO." Launching a CCATT mission entails getting the team weapons from the armory, loading medical equipment on the trucks, transporting the team to Intel for their briefings and then getting the team to the hospital to "package" patients for AE. As the senior medical member of the AEOT, Lt Col Evavold will usually launch the CCATTs, but the other AEOT members must also be able to perform that task as well. When I'm assisting a CCATT at the hospital, I help with patient movement from beds to litters and help set up SMEEDs (Special Medical Emergency Evacuation Devices) and other medical equipment prior to transport. I will also periodically check with the flight clinical coordinator to ensure all patients are validated for movement prior to loading on the aircraft.

AEOT personnel currently work 12-hour days with two on-call days per week, so we spend a lot of time in the office. There are well-maintained fitness facilities on base and both an indoor and outdoor pool with late hours. I try to swim in the lap pool at least every other day and go to the fitness center on the other days. The base also has a nice theater, so I occasionally catch a movie with some of the crewmembers on one of my on-call nights.

I have enjoyed my experience here in Balad. It's personally satisfying for me to put some of my training to use, since this is my first deployment as an MSC officer. Most importantly, we're here to support the Soldiers and Marines who are literally on the front lines of combat, and it's an honor to serve them. Our AE crews, ground personnel and CCATTs are doing great work over here to ensure that mission gets accomplished.

Deployed - Letters from the Field: Capt Sellner

I don't think I fully understood what I was getting myself in for when I volunteered to be deployed for 120 days. I had heard the whisperings about past deployments and thought to myself—piece of cake. I took for granted the impact my being gone would have on my family and myself. Things have gotten better as time has progressed—having e-mail contact with family and friends helps the days go by faster. I've tried to establish a routine also. Every day I walk to the BX in hopes they have something new that I didn't see yesterday. Naps for me are like breathing now—that's a habit I'll have to curb once I get back home. The flights are long and hot. The worst is when we arrive out to the plane before the loadmasters have had a chance to open up the back. You're climbing up to hang straps or configure the aircraft and the sweat drips off of you like rainwater. But when you receive that first patient—everything else becomes secondary.

Since this was my first deployment as a member of the 109th AES, I can honestly say my learning curve had many sharp angles. Our training prepared me for the "hands-on" portion of our daily missions—that part is second nature now. The ability to multitask when engines are running and multiple people are vying for your attention at the same time is something I learned on the fly. I had no expectations with regard to how the schedule was set or which crews we were assigned to. Our CMC (Crew Management Cell) determined we would not fly with hard crews. As time progressed, I learned the strengths and weaknesses of both myself and the med techs with whom I had the opportunity to fly. I can honestly say I would have preferred to fly the first couple of missions with personnel from Minnesota—if only to give myself a buffer of familiarity.

There is a sense of family here. I believe I've gotten to know and become closer to the people I have deployed with. We watched out for one another both emotionally and physically. We listened to each other when things weren't going quite right and we needed to vent. I was lucky enough to stay in Balad for about a day and a half. The feeling of family was overwhelming - being able to see people from home, talking to them, laughing with them. It's amazing how much that lifts your spirits.

Now I'm looking forward to coming back home—in about 60 more days. It's bittersweet to send off people you've become close to and also be open to the new people coming in. The relationships we build in AE are transient—but you know eventually we will see each other again.

Photo courtesy of the Vital Signs (Sep '06)
Part of the MN crew available during a scheduled photo op.
(L - R): Capt Janu, Maj Jacobson-Hanson and Capt Sellner

All deployed unit members had returned from AEF 1 and 2. Three aeromeds were deploying this month in order to fill shortfalls for the next AEF.

2007

Regular missions to PACAF and EUCOM began.

January. Lt Col Dahlquist traveled to Scott AFB, IL in a "jump seat" to observe the 375th's HSI and bring back critical information to prepare the 109th AES for their upcoming HSI.

February. A Staff Assistance Visit was conducted this UTA weekend.

April. The Annual Hospital Tour was held at the San Diego Medical Center in California, and despite a lower census and level of patient acuity, it was deemed a success. POCs for the event included Capt Bougie, Capt Ehman, SMSgt Tracy and MSgt Peterson.

May. "Terminal Velocity," a five-hour Base Mass Casualty Exercise, was conducted on Saturday afternoon of the UTA. The primary players included the 133rd MDG (Medical Group) and the 109th AES. Primary emphasis concentrated on the completion of readiness requirements.

June. At the National Guard Association of Minnesota Convention, Lt Col Dahlquist was inaugurated as the President for a two-year term.

July. Two military medical aircrew members from Canada visited the unit and participated in several training events and interacted with squadron members.

August. Several months of preparation concluded this UTA in final planning for the HSI next month.

September. The 109th AES completed the HSI, scoring an "Excellent" rating. The wing also was awarded an "Excellent" grade on their UCI.

October. A local exercise simulated an earthquake in another state where the patients were evacuated to Minnesota on the C-130H aircraft and then transported to local hospitals. Organized through the Veterans Administration Medical Center and held at the MN ANG base at the airport, about 160 medical, logistics, security, administrative and other types of individuals participated. [164]

November. The Guard Recruiting Assistance Program (G-RAP) became a reality. This initiative incorporated Army and Air Guard personnel into the recruiting arena while providing a $2,000 incentive payment for each successful recruitment. Some members were already bringing new Airmen into the 109th AES and other units on base through this program.

☆☆☆☆☆

The AF ended the use of the base vehicle stickers to access their installations, including Guard and Reserve bases. The general guidance directed everyone to remove decals from all their vehicles immediately. The rationale was from an anti-terrorism perspective - why make military or family members stand out in public and potentially mark them as a target?

2008

February. An operational mission was flown on a C-17 that evacuated patients from Ramstein AB, Germany to Andrews AFB, MD. Included in the patient manifest was a military canine who was injured in the line of duty. The unit requested two additional operational missions for later in the spring/summer so that the squadron could make use of this unique training opportunity.

☆☆☆☆☆

Slots for the next AEF (Aug and Sep) for the 109th AES and 156th AES, (Charlotte, NC) were announced during the Feb UTA. Unit members were encouraged to sign up.

☆☆☆☆☆

Everyone in the squadron was directed to complete all required readiness training for the upcoming AEF cycle. They were given the option of attending the AECOT course at Volk Field, WI, the formal AECOT course at Sheppard AFB, TX, or attending the local readiness training at the unit. Those that chose training at Volk Field remained in place to participate in the Patriot '08 Exercise at the same location.

April. MSgt Potter became the First Sergeant, replacing SMSgt Kennedy who left for duties as the Wing HRA.

May. It was announced that the main body of the MASF, consisting of 13 people, was removed from the Unit Manning Document. This resulted in the loss of one MSC, one Medical Admin, four FNs, and seven AETs. It was anticipated that the UTC would be assigned to the 133rd Medical Group in the near future. Also, the MASF augmentation package was eliminated resulting in a loss of four FNs, six AETs, and a Medical Logistics person while two crews were soon added. The MASF changes resulted in a net loss of fourteen personnel. When the entire process was completed, the total squadron manning was reduced to 100 aeromeds.

Diaries of a Med Tech: SrA Noel Olson

You're sending me where for SERE (Survival, Evasion, Resistance, Escape)? Fairchild? This was a statement that kept going over and over in my head. With whom did I get on the wrong side of? I was getting nervous thinking about how many bruises and cuts I would have when I was done. Will I come back brainwashed? When it came for SERE training, I told myself that this is the only class I have left until I can start flying and nothing is coming between that.

So as of March 24th, I started my life-changing adventure. In the first two days I was taught that you can put 17+ AF personnel into a 20-man raft. If your LPU (Life Preserver Unit) doesn't inflate, you could at least hook yourself to the raft. Your exposure suit feet are filled with water and you need to lift these extra 100 pounds into the raft by yourself because the others don't believe you can do it. And to make the situation even more interesting, you are being sprayed with a fire hose at Minnesota garden hose temperature. After this class, all I could think about was going off for another adventure and 17 days to go.

After the water survival, I started the academics for outdoor survival. The class was full of information from using compasses, starting fires with cotton balls and Vaseline, tying knots, how 550 cord is used in survival situations and how important communication is to rescue. After these four days of indoor classes we went out to the glorious, spacious, outdoor classroom, the mountains of Washington. My element and I hiked with 60-pound packs up mountains that seemed to have no end, crossed creeks, slept outdoors in temperatures that froze our water and covered our tents in the morning with snow. We used compasses and maps to triangulate points, learned how to get around at night with only a compass and used only the most beautiful bathrooms. This phase of training was awesome even though I had to kill a rabbit and it took me four attempts to get rescued. I loved the outdoors and camping, as long as we didn't have to kill rabbits.

After the outdoor survival came the eight days that I would have to say everyone is afraid of. These last days of class were spent learning about resistance training for peacetime, wartime, and hostage situations. The only thing I can say about this training is that I feel everyone should go through this to realize who they are as individuals and how important they are to the military. This training also showed me how we as Americans are different from the rest of the world in our trust and faith.

If you have an opportunity to go to Fairchild, **GO!** Go with excitement, an open mind and a willingness to have faith and trust in others and yourself. My last advice to everyone is always exhibiting the 5 Fs;

1) Faith in family and friends
2) Faith in your country
3) Faith in your future
4) Faith in what you believe
5) Faith in yourself (you might really surprise yourself).

I want to say thank you for your support while I was gone and thank you all for being who you are. See you in the sky!

Also this month, Governor Tim Pawlenty announced the appointment of the Minnesota Chapter of the Military Officers Association of America's first Vice President, Col Julia Eszlinger Jensen (Ret) to a newly formed Veterans Health Care Advisory Council.

The nine-member Veterans Health Care Advisory Council was created by executive order as a result of a recommendation of the Governor's Veteran's Long Term Care Advisory Commission. The council provided the Department of Veterans Affairs with advice and recommendations on the current and anticipated future needs of veterans and also studied various issues and trends in the long-term care industry. [165]

June. The Trauma Nurse Core Course was conducted at the Hennepin County Medical Center. It was a required course for all FNs who completed their initial flight training or those whose course certification would expire within the next year.

August. Two of the deploying groups for the AEF departed just before the Aug UTA. The weekend itself was a four-day extended drill which focused on preparing other unit members deploying for the AEF. Family day activities commenced Saturday morning allowing some time for relaxation and socialization during the four-day stretch of training activities.

☆☆☆☆☆

Select members of the unit deployed to Qatar, Germany, and Iraq.

September. The last members to deploy for the AEF left the base for their respective assignments. Other unit members would be departing soon to begin the process of replacing those on 60-day rotations.

☆☆☆☆☆

Another channel mission to Germany with 109th AES aeromeds took place over the Labor Day weekend. While in Germany, the crew had the opportunity to see many of their squadron members who were deployed to that location. It was reported that they were in good spirits and all have flown missions downrange. One of the crews was even told by one of our nurses that he has a new appreciation for all the training we do at home and encouraged us to keep it up!

October.

Deployed - Letters from the Field: Lt Col Georgeanne Johnson

Greetings to everyone back home and to members at other deployed locations! Time is going quickly here and we are getting acclimated to the "warm" weather. I am personally looking forward to experiencing a "tropical" January. The base is an interesting collection of personnel, accommodations, and services. We certainly have everything we need here. The wing also has a variety of morale activities scheduled consistently. Today we are celebrating Halloween with some special events. The 379th EAES is put up a "Haunted Tent" as a team effort, with the inspiration from SSgt Roberts and organizational support from Chief Close.

Congratulations to our members who have been selected to represent the Group for Outstanding Airman of the Year (OAY) — SrA Serres and TSgt Hanson. Great job. We are all proud of you and know you will represent the Operations Group well!

In our absence, I can see that everyone at home has been dedicated to keeping the unit in tip-top shape and taking care of our people. Something tells me we all have some interesting "combat" stories of our own to share. Thanks to all of you in your dedicated efforts.

Photo courtesy of Lt Col Sue Behrens
109th AES contingent in Al Udeid AB, Qatar.

(L to R): MSgt Rob Potter, TSgt Chad Neihart, Maj Matt Peterson, Maj Sue Behrens, Lt Col Georgeanne Johnson, SSgt Aubree Roberts, CMSgt Greg Close, Lt Karl Bjellum

November. 109th AES members continued to rotate off and return from their AEF assignments. All seem to have enjoyed a positive experience and a few returning members would end up transferring to the Medical Group upon their return. By the end of the month, all deployers had left for their rotation assignments.

Deployed - Letters from the Field: MSgt Potter

Howdy squadron! I heard that the last drill was pretty quiet. Rest assured, "downrange" we haven't been too quiet. It's been a real eye opener to see how continuity changes from one AEF to another. The way one group will operate vs. the expectations we have coming in.

The ability to assume your position in a squadron on only a few days turnover and to be expected to fulfill those responsibilities in an unfamiliar role or environment can be a real eye opener. I never realized just how quickly a bunch of aeromeds could wreck multiple vehicles, lock their keys out, break gas caps, and experience maintenance problems. You guys are HIGH maintenance! Ha ha ha. If trends keep up, there may have to be an additional radio operator just to maintain the status quo! Seriously though, I have had a lot more experience dealing with vehicles than I ever thought possible.

No matter where, when or who you go with, you can always count on events happening that are unexpected, sometimes good, other times not so good. When things are going south, turn it to your advantage. There are always people on base who can help you. The biggest challenge is breaking the ice, talking to folks and shaping your discussions in the form of a question.

We had a haunted house for the unit on Halloween and yours truly was in the Psycho Ward. Go figure.

Already ¼ of the way down, time is flying. Happy Thanksgiving to everyone and if you happen to hunt deer in Wisconsin, good luck!

December. Some discussion took place around the UTA regarding the squadron coin. Based on inputs from unit members, it was decided that the aeromeds would keep the current coin, at least for the time being.

2009

January. The new 133rd Wing motto was released - "Citizens Serving America – Airmen Defending Freedom." The squadron coin issue again surfaced when the unit was asked if they wanted to adopt the new wing motto or if they had other ideas for the coin. It was again decided that no changes would be made at this time. (authors' note: A new coin would eventually be designed in 2013.)

☆☆☆☆☆

Unit members were encouraged to download the PureEdge Viewer to their home/off-base computers to enable them to view government documents remotely.

☆☆☆☆☆

1st Lt Gartner and the Awards and Decs personnel held a silent auction which raised $1,100. The unit entertained the possibility of scheduling this as an annual event.

Deployed - Letters from the Field: Lt Col Georgeanne Johnson

Hello squadron. Welcome back to the deployers. By the UTA, the crew with us will be back and settling in with their families and the command cell here will be only a few weeks from returning. Hopefully everyone has had a successful experience and learned lots. All of you should be proud of the job you have done during the past months—that includes the deployed members and the ones holding down the fort back home!

We have been quite busy over here and ironically the crewmembers that came in at the halfway point are catching up with the 120-day folks on the missions flown. There are certain people who always seem to attract those alert missions—this time it seems to be SMSgt Dan Cisar. Everyone here who stand alerts with him immediately pack their bags and are ready to go. Being deployed has not exempted us from inspections. We have had people standing in line here to do inspections or SAVs. There is even an AE/SG SAV being done by AMC and AFCENT (AF Central Command). The double whammy! It is spinning up to be much like an ASEV.

Speaking of ASEV ...I'm sure all the crewmembers have been studying, right? Time has come for us all to jump into that new game, now that deployments are almost done. After the past six months, I know this will be but a small obstacle. We are going to show the AMC Stan/Eval folks that the 109th is at the top of the game!

See you all next month!

Deployed - Letters from the Field: Lt Col Barb Anderson

I hope this finds you all well. It sounds like everyone has been very busy with the additional missions and the ASEV preparation, not to mention the everyday running of the unit.

Welcome to all the new members of the 109th! I'm so looking forward to coming home even though I have truly enjoyed my deployment. I work for a great boss and I'm learning an entirely different side of things, plus having TSgt Hanson around to harass has been a hoot. Not to mention that it has also been great having our other 109th members here; it really does help from being homesick. Just in case you might have heard through the grapevine that I was in the hospital, I was, but I'm fine now (no surgery was needed so that was great news). I'm almost 100%, but decided that I am a wimp and not into the pain thing at all.

See you sometime in February and hope you all had a wonderful holiday season!

February. By the UTA, the final deployed members of the 109th AES had returned to Minnesota.

☆☆☆☆☆

Several unit members transferred to the Medical Group with the MASF: Capt Kim Schmidt, Maj K. Dieter Bartz, Capt Tim Bougie, Capt Michael Cook, MSgt Ken Petersen, TSgt Jeff August and Maj Karen Gozel.

March. At the end of the month, several 109th AES radio operators were deployed as part of the North Dakota Flood Fight. 1st Lt Jeramy Browning, TSgt Shawn Fitzhenry, and TSgt John Flatten rounded out a seven-person team working with the JCP (Joint Communication Platform), manning a state-owned communication system trailer in Moorhead, MN. All of the radio operators received training on this platform during the March UTA. On Thursday, 26 March, SrA Jessica Serres and A1C Matthew Piringer got into the fight and swapped places with two of their team members.

The squadron aeromeds were also queried regarding their availability to respond if needed for emergencies created by the flooding on 27 March. This request was put out to all ANG AE units through their state JOCs (Joint Operations Center). They had a tremendous response with the capability to provide up to four full crews and augmentees. None of the crews were ever tasked.

April. During, and for a few days after the UTA, the unit underwent the scheduled ASEV. The ASEV was used as a tool to assess a unit's combat capability, readiness, and mission effectiveness while ensuring compliance with current directives. It also validated training, tactics, and standardization/evaluation programs. The ASEV provided unit commanders an opportunity to address operational issues with higher headquarters personnel.

The following areas were covered in the evaluation: Special Interest Items, Aircrew Examinations (100% Closed Book Testing), In-flight Performance (evaluations), Stan/Eval Administration, Training Programs and Administration, and Aeromedical Equipment.

"Mission Ready" was the overall assessment for the 133rd AW. A great deal of detailed preparation and hard work went into ensuring the unit's programs were in compliance, with the bulk of the responsibility laying on the Aircrew Training leadership. Kudos went to Maj Ehman and MSgt Howk and their team and to Capt Bochniak, who spent many hours putting the finesse on the medical equipment and medication processes. The ASEV inspectors awarded the Training Folders and Continuation Training Processes "Excellent" ratings. They also mentioned that they enjoyed flying with us and spoke highly of the unit training program and the crews. Two 109th AES members were cited as exceptional performers—Maj Ehman and MSgt Steven from OGV. [166]

☆☆☆☆☆

TSgt Flatten and TSgt Fitzhenry left the base to participate in a first of its kind overseas activity. TSgt Flatten writes:

> This past month TSgt Fitzhenry and I went to Poland to participate in ESKULAP '09. What a chance of a lifetime! We left on the 15th of April. We flew to Delaware and met up with the folks we would be working with while deployed to Poland for the exercise. The following day we met the C-130 from Illinois that would take us the rest of the way. It was wheels up and we were off to Poland. Our first stop was the New York ANG base as we had an equipment failure. After that we had stops in St. John's Canada and RAF Mendenhall, England. We arrived in Minsk at one of their Russian era air bases complete with blast proof hangers. On Sunday we were able to get a look at Warsaw. We spent the better part of the day exploring Old Town (and of course enjoying the local cuisine and beer). Monday was the kick off of the exercise. We then moved to the Wesola Army Base. We found ourselves driving back

and forth to Minsk a lot. Did I mention we had our own vehicle while there? We also did a slide presentation explaining how our AE system works. On Thursday, it was a dry run of the exercise. Fitz and I were able to watch the events from a berm that they have around their playing field. It was quite humorous as the wounded Polish soldiers complete with their moulage were doing a round of "ow's" that was just downright funny. They also brought in one of their helicopters to evac a patient. That was very cool! On Friday, it was the exercise complete with all the dignitaries and generals. The playing field was set up with the sound effects of a soccer game. Once the exercise began it was narrated by the Polish officers in charge. We then alerted the crew that things were kicking off and they were off to the aircraft. So we did an actual alert. During the week we had met one of their doctors who wanted to take us on a personal tour of downtown Warsaw. We met up with him on Saturday afternoon. He explained a lot of their history to us and how much they value their freedom. It was a very good time. We were able to see where the Ghetto walls stood that were constructed during World War II and we were able to see their Tomb of the Unknown Soldier. On Sunday it was time to leave. We loaded up the plane on Sunday and we were off to Scotland. Fitz and I got to play patients, so needless to say, we got to catch a little shut eye on the way. Once back stateside it was off to the airport and home again. It was a great two weeks. We would go back anytime.

Photo courtesy of the Vital Signs (May '09)
TSgt Flatten (left) and TSgt Fitzhenry (right) - ESKULAP 2009.

May. The theme for the UTA was Ability to Survive and Operate. The Readiness Safeguard exercise was held from May 12-18 at Volk Field, WI. On the first day, squadron and wing out-processing was accomplished. Upon arriving at the destination airfield on day two, everyone attended the in-processing brief, filled sandbags, unloaded baggage, checked in at billeting, and then attended several briefings from Volk Field personnel. Days three and four found everyone scheduled for training. Days five and six culminated in a two-day exercise which included two flying missions. This training exercise was the first step to prepare for the future ORI.

For those unit members who remained at home station, three days of training was conducted. Classes included Post Attack Recovery, Radio Communications, Litter Carrying, Expedient Bandaging, Facility Hardening, and Weapons Issue, Carrying and Clearing. [167]

CHAPTER 13
The Command of Col Penny Hodges-Goetz

(Jun 2009 - Jan 2013)

Photo courtesy of Minnesota ANG

Commander's Comments: A letter to myself on my time as the 109th AES Commander -

It was around Christmas time 2009 while deployed to Baghdad as the Chief Nurse of the EMEDS at Sather AB that I learned that I had been selected as the next Commander of the 109th AES. The e-mail came from then Col Dave Hamlar (Brig Gen Hamlar now). My reply back to Brig Gen Hamlar was, "Sir, I think you sent this e-mail to the wrong person." He replied, "No, it was intended for you." I replied, "Sir, you know that I'm not a flight nurse." Brig Gen Hamlar responded that he and wing leadership were aware, and that being a flight nurse was not required. After the e-mail from Brig Gen Hamlar confirming your selection, remember what you said, "What the hell!" Those aeromed folks are going to eat you for dinner. You were scared that you were going to be a big failure. During my time in the Medical Group, I had seen those cocky, self-assured flight suit wearing folks around the wing, and I didn't see myself fitting into that clique.

You returned home early 2010, and assumed command just in time to start prep for an ORE/ORI—no pressure! Additionally, the squadron was operationally active supporting the war effort in Iraq and Afghanistan. You had no idea what you were doing or what you were going to do. Shortly, after taking command you were at Volk Field, one of many weekends that you would lay under a table in MOPP gear trying to figure out how to sleep in a mask without getting caught. The outgoing Commander, Lt Col Georgeanne Johnson was showing you the ropes. We were in the dining facility, and Georgeanne introduced you to a table of AE folks, Maj Howard said to you, "Are you going to flight school?" I replied, "No, I hear that you all have enough exceptional flight nurses. I understand that what you all need is a commander." Score 1 for Penny! That moment defined my time at the 109th AES. I was the Commander, my role was not to be their peer, or an exceptional flight nurse. My role was to ensure that we had an exceptional organization that could execute the mission, and the squadron ROCKED the ORI!

You owe your success in the AES to the men and women of the 109th. You were no dummy; you knew that the members of the squadron were skeptical of having a non-flyer as a commander. But, you soon learned the true meaning of "integrity first, service before self, and excellence in all we do." Although the men and women of the 109th were skeptical, they never allowed their skepticism to get out in front of the mission.

You quickly learned that aeromed folks are attracted to shiny rock, and that you better keep them busy or they will keep you busy. And some of that mischief might just rub off on the commander. During the HSI, we scored a "Satisfactory." I fondly called the aeromed folks, my "flying monkeys," as there was never a dull moment. We all felt that our "Satisfactory" was unfair. So, before the inspectors had departed, I wrote, "Satisfactory My Ass" on a cake decorated with monkeys that we had purchased to celebrate the HSI. Well, we had the cake sitting out in the hallway for all to see, and Col Jim Johnson happened by, and it would be an understatement to say that he was very unhappy. Col Johnson talked to most of the leadership team -- Lt Col Ed Howard, SSgt Ryan Ketterling, the Chief Nurse Sue Behrens, the Chief Dan Cisar, the DO (Director of Operations) Lt Col Matt Peterson and the XO (Executive Officer) Capt Ann Feist—they all told Col Johnson that they were accountable for the cake. This was and remains the proudest moment of your military career. You were hooked, and knew without a doubt that aeromeds was the best mission in the Air Force.

The years flew by way too quickly, and although you were moved on to become the Commander of the Medical Group and promoted to colonel, you mourned your loss on leaving the best job in the Air Force. The organization had excelled, we were recognized as a "go to" unit in the AE community. Our motto was, "we can do that" followed shortly by, "how the heck are we gonna do that?" The combined effect of individual efforts and skills make the 109th an outstanding organization. None of us could do our jobs without the support of others. We counted on each other to do their part so we could do ours. We shared a common purpose and we knew that when we needed help, our wingman would be there to pitch in and make the mission a success.

As you think back on your time in the aeromeds, above all you have an overwhelming sense of gratitude. How lucky were you to have the opportunity to serve your country alongside such an elite group of individuals with the best mission in the Air Force. Forever, aeromeds!

Col Penny Hodges-Goetz

June. Lt Col Penny Hodges-Goetz took command of the 109th AES on 21 June, 2009. Lt Col Hodges-Goetz's position before that was Chief Nurse for the 133rd Medical Group. She had also served on active duty in the Army Reserve and Minnesota Army National Guard in jobs such as an operating room head nurse and officer in charge of statewide drug testing and physical exams. [168]

Lt Col Georgeanne Johnson, outgoing Commander, transitioned to MN Military Headquarters, St. Paul, MN.

CMSgt Close also left the unit to serve in his new position as the State Command Chief. His change of authority ceremony took place on 6 June on the State Capitol grounds.

☆☆☆☆☆

The 109th AES became "on-call" for hurricane response coverage. Responsibility included all UTCs, should they be needed. Recent history proved that this was a very real possibility. UTC WRM packages were moved back to the unit and narcotics were maintained in order to stage for a timely response. Members were asked to sign up for this assignment so the unit would have personnel to call on short notice.

July. The squadron picked up a 9-day PACAF flight manned by five of our aeromeds.

☆☆☆☆☆

At the end of the month, a unit furniture reorganization project was implemented, and consisted of a new layout for the squadron's office sections.

August. New training requirements enacted a change where all flight nurses and med techs were required to qualify on the M9 (Beretta 9mm handgun) every 24 months. All other personnel would fire just prior to deployment as dictated by the theater's reporting instructions.

☆☆☆☆☆

Unit training at Alpena's Combat Readiness Training Center in Michigan took place from 16-22 Aug '09. Squadron members flew via C-130H from Minneapolis to Alpena on 16 Aug and returned the following Saturday, 22 Aug. Aeromed training missions were conducted on both flights.

The opening training activity was quite a memorable event and provided a sense of realism with regard to work area security and checkpoint operations. The training surveys demonstrated a high regard for the Expeditionary Medical System orientation program, UTC setup and Readiness Skills Verifications (RSV) accomplishment.

The course instructors at Alpena were very excited to have AE personnel and UTCs as participants in both the training and the exercise at the end of the week. Many of the unit members benefited greatly by working with a user service that was not familiar with the aeromedical mission but would actually be the people supporting our mission. Numerous ground personnel were able to participate as patients during the training, gaining a better understanding of the mission from the patient's point of view. To round out the experience, additional team building drills were conducted for the aeromeds.

A review of the member feedback sheets demonstrated the participants met their defined training goals and it was by and large a very positive training experience. A special thanks went out to TSgt Fitzhenry and SMSgt Cisar for all their efforts and the outstanding training environment they created at Alpena. The relationships they established with the full-time staff were clearly visible and greatly enhanced the training experience. [169]

September. Seven of our crewmembers flew a 7-day USAFE live aerovac mission.

November. Many unit members participated in an ORE in Alpena, MI. There were some issues identified with the coordination between the aeromeds and the airlift squadron. Processes were refined for the one remaining ORE in January and ultimately for the ORI in March.

December. SMSgt Dan Cisar was promoted to CMSgt.

2010

January. From Jan 21-28, the unit participated in an ORE at Volk Field, WI. This was the last major "rehearsal" before the ORI scheduled for March.

☆☆☆☆☆

Col Julie Eszlinger Jensen (Ret) was named the Veteran of the Month by WCCO AM 830 radio.

March. The ORI was conducted from 21-28 March. The unit did very well, garnering an "Outstanding" rating.

April. During the April UTA, Maj Behrens assumed duties as the new Chief Nurse from Lt Col Barb Anderson. Lt Col Anderson looked forward to her last deployment, and then retired soon thereafter.

☆☆☆☆☆

The first deployers were already off and running before the April UTA in support of the unit's next AEF.

Photo courtesy of Maj Peter Mudge
Live aerovac mission in Kandahar, Afghanistan.

Deployed - Letters from the Field: MSgt Maloney

As I'm getting adjusted to my new settings, I wanted to pass along some tips on my experience so far. There are many seasoned deployers in the unit; however, there are a good number of folks who will be deploying for the first time.

–Be ready to stay in transient billeting before moving to long-term billeting. So you may want to pack items you'll need in one bag during the transient week, versus needing to dig through your entire luggage.

--Give yourself a break. Know it's going to take some time to adjust to the new schedule of working, sleeping, eating and working in time for PT (Physical Training). Also, your body will not instantly adjust to the extreme heat.

--Take care of your feet. If that means wearing orthotics or really good socks, it will be worth it. My feet feel like little ovens here in this heat.

--When the transfer of information occurs from the person you're replacing, be prepared that their teaching style may not be conducive with your learning style. You'll figure out the job as you go, but ask questions and learn as much as you can in the interim.

Deployed - Letters from the Field: Maj Pat Howard

You need a can-do attitude as you would in any military performance. Here, in Germany, that means knowing you are here to do the mission. Anyone who deviates from that expectation by wanting time off to tour, or thinking their crew is flying more or less than another, and being treated unfairly, will find themselves (and their unit) poorly thought of. Another issue to be aware of is that Bravo missions are often initiated only to be cancelled. Know this is because multiple options are started to give our wounded warriors the best care, and planned at higher levels. If cancelled, we should be proud of our leaders for investing in a better option. This leads me to...

Luck of the draw... I have four missions where all others that deployed with me have only two or three. I happened to have a Bravo that launched, and nearly a second which would have given me five. The flight schedule is written to accomplish the mission, not to be fair.

Additional thoughts:

- The new checklist came out and we're using it (although only in paper form).

- We use the wireless headsets, and they are fantastic for communication.

- Our two-hour training flights prepare us for performing to AF standards, but do not prepare us for the lengthy missions. I have not had less than a twenty-hour mission. Again, can-do is a must.

- You may have crewmembers that don't value the checklist in real-world missions. I challenged my crew twice now and found it improved our solidarity and morale.

Remember we are ambassadors for our wing and squadron. By having a can-do attitude and demonstrating flexibility, you will leave a lasting impression of yourself, your squadron and your wing.

July. No UTA was held this month due to previous extended weekends required for previous ORE and ORI.

☆☆☆☆☆

Twenty-seven aeromeds participated in the Patriot 2010 exercise at Volk Field, WI from 15-22 July. They sweated with their Dutch and Canadian aerovac counterparts in UTC operations and equipment, radio gear, a C-17 flight, static aircraft instruction, rotary aircraft exercises, EMEDS tours, as well as Dutch and NATO operations training.

The UTC training was beneficial, and the unit identified additional needs in the squadron. In the coming months, it was decided that the 109th AES would establish a process for standing up an AEOT on the UTAs that we are flying, with a goal of providing more consistent training for a wider scope of UTCs in the squadron.

☆☆☆☆☆

The AEF was still in full swing with the last scheduled group leaving at the end of July.

Deployed - Letters from the Field: CMSgt Dan Cisar

Hello from beautiful Camp Bastion, Afghanistan. I am on Day 14 at this location and am functioning as the Superintendent of the 451st EAES DET 1.

Both the AEOT and the CASF (Contingency Aeromedical Staging Facility) are aligned under the 451st EAES with the squadron located at Maj Peterson's location and DET 1 here with me. Showing up midway through the current group's rotation as the superintendent for a group of active duty people and for a CASF that I have never been part of has been both a challenge and an education.

Currently, we are working on establishing the first AF Enlisted Council here on Bastion/Leatherneck. Life on a Marine FOB (Forward Operating Base) could easily be enough reason to hate their situation but this is a really good group of Airmen and they are making the most of our situation.

MWR facilities are nonexistent here. The Marines must believe a shower and food is all people need. We do have Wi-Fi that works more than half the time, but it is very slow. There are a couple of gyms, a small AAFES (Army and Air Force Exchange Service) tent and a barber shop. My 12 roommates and I share a tent. We work in a tent, shower in a tent and eat in a tent. I don't think I have been in a building that wasn't a tent in over a week.

> I met a young Marine today who is on his second trip through the CASF in a month. It was a shrapnel wound last time, a bullet wound to the face (grazed) and shoulder this time. He will return to duty shortly. Another patient who recently came through had not had a shower in three months. I attended a ramp ceremony for another young Marine the other day. I think of these guys when I do not like my tent, or when we don't have bagels or ice cream because the convoy got attacked.

The unit had four personnel fill AEF shortfalls created by other AE units. These individuals had very little time to get ready, their training was up-to-date, and were able to meet the requirements to get to their location successfully. Not only was the 109th AES able to fill all of our slots, but stepped up to the plate once again when needed.

August. On August 31, 2010, President Obama announced that the American combat mission in Iraq had ended.

Photo courtesy of MSgt Chad Neihart

Airmen from 133rd Airlift Wing at Al Udeid, Qatar pause for a photo on August 10, 2010. The Command Chief for the 133rd AW, CMSgt David Speich (far left) was passing through on his way to a deployment in Iraq and caught up with many in the Minnesota ANG unit already deployed for the Air Expeditionary Force rotation.

(L - R): CMSgt Speich, TSgt Chad Neihart, SMSgt Bryan Steven, MSgt Rachel Maloney, Lt Col Dedra Tentis, Lt Col Barbara Anderson, 1st Lt Jeramy Browning, Lt Col Ed Howard, and SrA Sam Howard

September. The squadron was obligated to assist with hurricane support from September to November.

Deployed - Letters from the Field: CMSgt Dan Cisar

Hello all, not much has gone on at my location since my last article. Every day is the same, every night is the same and I don't pay attention to what day it is, except for Sunday: king crab legs day. I have been on two missions this last week. We fly Alpha alerts on an HC-130P. The only stanchions available for us to use are C and D. This makes it very interesting to load CCATT patients.

On one of the missions I flew to Kandahar to attend SMSgt Granlund and SrA Schaumann's promotion ceremony. It was an exciting and fun event that I am sure they will remember for years to come. Congratulations Mike and Meredith! All seem to be doing very well. While I was there, TSgt Applen was awarded performer of the week, Maj Bochniak was out flying, Lt Mudge was busy doing everything Maj Peterson had assigned him, and Maj Peterson was thinking of more things for Lt Mudge to do. A trip to Kandahar would not be complete without an opportunity to dive on the floor and head out to a bunker; very similar to the ORI except these bunkers are made of concrete instead of surveyors tape.

We are over 25% through our deployment. Most of it has gone by very fast. Hopefully that trend will continue.

Have a great UTA! I wish you were all here with me. I would love to be able to share this experience with all of you!

November. In this month's issue of the Vital Signs, Lt Col Hodges-Goetz, the 109th AES Commander, made a very interesting observation. She stated, "It is important that we are able to speak with facts about our mission. Approximately eighty-five percent of all the AE assets are in the Guard and Reserve. Our squadron completed twenty percent of all Guard operational missions in the last fiscal year. During the last AEF, we deployed forty-five members in eleven different movements to six different locations. Every squadron has good people in them, but facts help us to support what we know to be true. We are a world premier aeromedical evacuation squadron."

During the past year, the 109th AES had flown missions in Antarctica, EUCOM, AEF Qatar, Germany, Afghanistan, OCONUS and a Hospital Tour to Alpena, Michigan.

Photo courtesy of Lt Col Behrens
Mission Crew to Ramstein Germany.

(L to R): Lt Jim Mattson, TSgt Rob Buresh, TSgt Amy Lasserre, Maj Sue Behrens, SSgt Corey Stedje, SrA Lexi Holtz, Lt Keith Bryant

2011

<u>**January.**</u> Lt Col Hodges-Goetz and Lt Feist attended the Total Force AE Commanders Conference in St. Louis. Perhaps one of the most interesting aspects of the meeting dealt with math, and aerovac had a tremendous role in the outcome. It was stated that a military member injured in theater had a 90% chance of survival, and if they entered the AE system they had a 96-98% survival rate. Great numbers for aerovac! Other topics included patient safety, pain management, and the projection that the Electronic Medical Record was to be implemented in all squadrons by next year.

☆☆☆☆☆

This UTA marked the end of an era with CMSgt Small's retirement. Chief Small left behind a legacy of service before self and an unwavering commitment to all members of the squadron.

February. The USAF School of Aerospace Medicine at Brooks in San Antonio, TX was decommissioned. New school facilities were opened at Wright-Patterson AFB, OH later in the year.

April. Ten aeromeds deployed to the Democratic Republic of the Congo (DRC) from April 23 through May 4, to participate in MEDLITE 11, a medical exercise hosted at the DRC's Centre Superior Militaire Academy.

MEDLITE 11 offered a unique opportunity for Airmen from the 133rd AW to share medical knowledge and techniques with their African host nation's medical personnel.

"The Congolese military wasn't actually doing any in-flight care of their sick or their injured, and with the closest hospital 1,000 miles away, people were dying," said MSgt Robert Buresh. "We basically developed an air evacuation program for them, starting from square one."

"During the first week we instructed on altitude physiology, medical supplies and equipment, and in the second week we actually got them on a C-130 and configured the plane with litters to show them how to safely load and unload patients," said Buresh.

The exercise focused on improving the readiness of both countries' medical personnel by providing classroom instruction, an AE scenario and a mass casualty exercise to conclude the training.

The aeromeds worked alongside approximately 50 other U.S. Air Force active duty, National Guard and Reserve military personnel and 150 Congolese military personnel in the latest in a series of exercises that were initiated in 1987 as a now U.S./Africa Command-sponsored, bilateral medical exercise to facilitate an exchange of medical information and techniques with militaries in Africa.

"Everyone from the 109th who went there got a better global perspective," said Buresh. "We saw pretty much the opposite of what the American dream really is."

"The experience was worth any amount of inconvenience it caused us in our personal lives, being away from our families and our jobs and everything. It far outweighed it," he said.

Photo courtesy of Capt Chris Wolf
Capt Chris Wolf with three members of the Congolese military as part of MEDLITE 11.

Aeromeds from the 109th AES and medical professionals from the 133rd MDG participated in the annual Minnesota Stand Down for Veterans event at the Boy Scout Base Camp at Fort Snelling from Aug 2-3. The ultimate goal of the annual event was to provide as many services in one location in order to provide assistance to homeless veterans and those in need.

The collaboration between the 109th AES and 133rd MDG was executed by 20 medical professionals working shifts throughout the two-day event. Approximately 284 patients were seen for free medical screenings and follow up with doctors on site as needed. 1st Lt Amy Nordquist, a nurse from the 133rd MDG said that, "It's been great working together as a team with the 109th AES to put our education and practice to good use."

May. Twenty-two 109th AES aeromeds were part of a 32 member tasking which included personnel from the 133rd Medical Group, the 148th Fighter Wing and four other units from across the U.S. These servicemen participated in a MEDRETE in Catacamus, Olancho, Honduras, where they provided medical, dental, optometry and preventive medicine care to the partnering host nation.

These exercises, supported thousands of indigents in Central America and the Caribbean and provide U.S. military personnel training in the delivery of medical care in austere conditions.

On one busy day, 882 patients were treated!

"The most rewarding part of doing a MEDRETE is the ability to use your medical skills to help others with little or no access to medical care," said Lt Col Penny Hodges-Goetz, 109th AES Commander. "The personal satisfaction of giving back to the global community is immeasurable."

MEDRETEs also serve to promote diplomatic relations between the U.S. and host nations in Central America by providing humanitarian and civic assistance via a long-term proactive program.

"In addition to providing medical, optometry and dental care to an underserved population, we also had the opportunity to interact with our Honduran military colleagues," said Hodges-Goetz. "We had members of the Honduran military express to us that their opinion of people in the U.S. had changed because of their exchange with our group." [170]

June. A SAV was conducted from 10-16 June. This was a preparation audit of unit systems for compliance for the ASEV inspection scheduled in 2013.

☆☆☆☆☆

The squadron was notified that they would be flying with computers to trial using e-pubs (electronic publications) and electronic training tools in-flight. AMC was using the 109th as one of the test units for these trials.

July. Four aeromeds were honored during the July UTA for their extraordinary efforts over the years to ensure the success of the squadron. Lt Col Edward Howard, Lt Col Barbara Anderson, MSgt Shannon Culver and MSgt Michael Howk had a cumulative 100 years of service to our country.

September. The Readiness Plains exercise dominated the weekend activities.

October. Congratulations went out to the Squadron Outstanding Airman of the Year winners: SrA Corey Stedje, TSgt Travis Shore and MSgt Travis Miles.

November. As of 1 November, it became mandatory for all unit members to wear the ABU (Airman Battle Uniform).

Members from the 375th visited the unit during the UTA to conduct a SAV before the HSI next May. By all accounts, the visit went well with a report that there were no failing programs.

2012

January. All of the deployers had departed the unit to begin the next AEF rotation.

☆☆☆☆☆

The Battle Buddy concept was instituted for new deploying squadron members. Seasoned aeromeds were assigned to the "newbies", who were about to go on their first deployment, assisting them with the deployment process through their tour and eventual return to the unit.

February. Thirty-six of the remaining squadron members participated in Global Guardian 2012, which was held in Savannah, Georgia from 17-24 Feb. This was an ANG sponsored training exercise that emphasized full spectrum operations which provided personnel and units an opportunity to participate in a simulated deployed Joint Air Expeditionary Wing (AEW). The focus of the exercise was to provide a requirements-based training exercise, utilizing unit Mission Essential Task Lists (METLs). Global Guardian was designed to successfully prepare units for deployment to an AEW in theater, conducting direct and indirect combat operations, and redeploy safely to home base.

Lt Col Hodges-Goetz, 109th AES Commander, remarked that, "Global Guardian was a very successful exercise. The training on the various airframes and the collaboration and integration with the Dutch and Canadians was beneficial for all involved."

CMSgt Cisar remarked, "The crew integration between our squadron members and the Canadians had mixed results. Our crews with more experience were with the more experienced Canadian crews; the integration went well and this crew was able to function at a high level. Our less experienced crew with our students were with the less experienced Canadians; there were issues. The majority of the problems revolved around strong mission planning and Crew Resource Management. We could have predicted this outcome. If you don't have the experience to know your job really well, it will be difficult to successfully incorporate dissimilar crewmembers. With that being said, everyone was a very fast study and the lessons learned on day one resulted in very successful results on day two. These missions along with the capstone are not meant to evaluate performance, but are meant to challenge everyone and try to expose them to situations we don't normally see on local ARMs. I think everyone was challenged and everyone responded and performed very well." [171]

☆☆☆☆☆

It was announced that there were some projected changes being considered in regard to the local military structure in MN. The information received was promising for the ANG. The 934th was projected to lose all of their C-130s and Duluth was designated as an associate active duty base, which would increase their personnel footprint by 60-100 individuals.

Deployed - Letters from the Field: MSgt Miles

Hello from our nation's capital. Before deploying to Andrews, I was told that Ramstein AB was the busiest hub for patients and Andrews was the busiest hub for crews; I can now confirm that statement is true. We've seen just about everyone that is deployed to the 10th Expeditionary Aeromedical Evacuation Flight (EAEF) (Ramstein) and the 775th EAEF OL-B (Travis). One of the quickest things I learned is that over all my years of flying I should have looked at those boards, which I let the MCD worry about. I encourage everyone to look at the AEOT boards and read them and ask questions when passing through. From what I have seen, I believe you all. I would like to personally tip my hat to Capt Sellner down at the 775th OL-A Kelley Detachment. Sometimes we think we may have short supplies and resources, but Capt Sellner really does. She is instrumental in ensuring the KSAT (San Antonio International Airport)/KSSF (Stinson Municipal Airport, San Antonio, Texas) missions are successful and that the crews and equipment get where they need to be.

Remember to work hard and play hard. In fact, I discovered Fort Washington, which was used from the War of 1812 through WWII. I highly recommend it to anyone that comes this way. It's great for hiking.

Deployed - Letters from the Field: TSgt Lasserre

We are about one month into our four-month deployment and so far, everything is going great. We managed to stay mostly together as a crew. Capt McCarthy, SSgt Hemmingson, SrA White, and I are on a crew together along with an active duty nurse from Pope. We are all getting along well and learning quite a bit from each other. Lt Smith is on a crew with all active duty members including a Canadian nurse, so I'm sure he has had to teach them a few things, mostly about being (Minnesota) nice. We can't complain about our schedule. It seems that we have ample time to explore the area and there is so much to do. On our off days we are scheduled for ground duty where we launch and recover other crews but we still have plenty of free time to exercise, work on class work, PME, and also for volunteer opportunities. SrA White has been volunteering at David Grant, USAF Medical Center, Travis AFB, CA and is also working on finishing up his ALS (Advanced Life Support) course. SSgt Hemmingson is currently taking online courses. Capt McCarthy and I started volunteering at the local animal shelter. Hopefully neither of us comes home with anymore furry creatures.

One of the best parts of this deployment is that on every mission we get to see 109th members from all over the country. At Andrews, we always run into Miles, Wenaas, Rawling, and Hughes. On our last trip we even got to hang out with Asper and Brothers. We make it a point to have dinner and drinks with each other. It's just like old home week. When we stop in San Antonio, Capt Sellner is there to help us when the ramp opens up. Seeing her smiling face always brightens our day. We have the best mission in the AF and truly some of the most wonderful people.

Deployed - Letters from the Field: Lt Col Pat Howard

Our missions have been a consistent flow of patients from the one location we fly down to right now. We had a rash of missions that brought crews out of Al Udeid, but seem to have let up in the last week. It was fun to see our peeps come from down range. I'm told the crews in the "Deid" are flying a lot as a result of closing some of the bases in the AOR. They report so far to be happy with the activity.

A small group got to go spend a couple nights in Paris, some are going skiing and I got to see "Batman Live" in Frankfurt with friends. This is the beauty of what Ramstein has to offer for deployment: we get to practice the "work hard/play hard" philosophy! Illness has taken its toll; SrA Holtz was sent home, 1st Lt Arndt was down and out with a respiratory "wish for death" kind of illness which she was kind enough to share with me. These are things that we don't plan for, but occur nevertheless and must be managed. People here and back home are affected and have done a great job in supporting these issues. Capt Ringle had a death in the family and is waiting for approval to get leave to be with family. Please offer prayer in support for her and her family.

And...we are looking forward to receiving a SAV this month. That's Germany in a nutshell.

March. The unit continued to prepare for the upcoming HSI.

☆☆☆☆☆

Lt Col Pat Howard and his wife Kasia became the proud parents of a little girl. He was able to share in his daughter's birth via Skype from his deployed site.

Deployed - Letters from the Field: MSgt Buresh

Greetings from Helmand Province, Afghanistan. Camp Bastion is a wonderful place to visit this time of year. Temperatures are fairly mild, there's no snow, and the food is wonderful.

Actually, things are going very well. Living on a Marine Base (Camp Leatherneck, aptly named) is very different. The only places to go in your off time are the gym, the USO, or the

MWR tent. They've just recently started showing movies once a week, but they are older movies for some reason. We work on the British side of the world, which is also interesting. We've done training with the British ambulance drivers and the fire department for airfield familiarization. TSgt Nelson says that this is the ultimate camping trip. We have electricity (when the generators are working) and Internet (we can't download anything or watch Netflix or anything) and the girls go to the British coffee shop every morning. The baristas there know them by name.

It is the slow time of the year and there haven't been many casualties to get out of here, which is a good thing. Our CCATT teams are the busiest and our AE crews have just recently flown their first AE mission in over a month and a half. Some would think that it must be boring since there aren't any missions and there isn't any place to go. On the contrary, TSgt Nelson has reorganized the office and file plan in the AEOT. The amount of stuff that she cleaned out still baffles me. SrA Beers has completely cleaned and restructured the logistics area. She recently got congratulated on her efforts by the AFCENT/SG and the head of all AFCENT CCATT teams in the theater. I've been busy with aircrew schedules and balancing two different alert schedules and helping to prepare for a SAV. We haven't had a lot of idle time.

The most recent addition to our AE mission here is flying on fewer missions with the 76th Rescue Squadron. These are tactical missions flying out to the Forward Operating Bases and getting patients from there to bring them to larger hospitals. They fly patients of all nationalities and many times land on dirt airstrips. I sent the commander and Lt Feist articles last month that explain it a little better. These missions have been the sanity of our aircrews as it gives them missions to fly.

We hope everyone enjoyed being in Savannah and away from the cold and snow. We wish everyone well and have a great St Patrick's Day.

Deployed - Letters from the Field: TSgt Rawling

I was scrambling for a topic to write about, and then I helped a CCAT team drop off a Marine double amputee to his wife and parents.

What hits me every time, at my vulnerable 24 years of age, is how young these people are. I feel I have never experienced a loss like he or his family are feeling, and find myself trying to relate. The analogs come to me immediately: the Marine is my best friend, Tony, who enlisted right out of high school, and went mostly unseen to our social group for three years. Continuing the metaphor, the Marine's parents are my friend's; and the wife is Tony's high school girlfriend, and my close friend.

The Marine was on loose contact precautions. The family arriving was dressed in gowns and gloves before entering his room, and before I had time to realize they'd gone in, they were out again, wife in tears, parents helping her out of the gown. Both the Marine and his wife looked fresh out of high school; I insisted she was his little sister until I overheard otherwise. No one can prepare for that kind of loss in oneself or one's beloved, and it's unimaginable to be forced to do so with so much life ahead.

It's easy to be distracted and sated by the comforts aeromedical deployments offer us. One downrange base may be dry and made of tents; another may have beer and AC. Germany had the luxuries of Western shopping and touring only one shallow language-curve away. Being deployed to the States I can call home at will with no regard to Zulu time, I can shop without learning new words, and I can drive my car after signing its lease once, instead of signing its form 1800 daily. But one Marine pushes all that aside.

It's a coin toss as to what our lives will be like deploying in AE, but there's a trip segment by one of us from Dwyer to Bagram, Afghanistan to Germany, Middle East to America.

The 133rd AW Key Volunteer Program (KVP) was launched this month. The Key Volunteer Program is part of the Airmen & Family Programs for the 133rd AW and originated from the "Key Spouse Program" in the active duty Air Force. The wing chose to locally name it (as has the 148th FW in Duluth) the Key Volunteer Program, because they wanted to expand the potential volunteer base beyond spouses only. It is a squadron-based program designed to be a communication network between unit leadership and families of unit members. The KVP involved at least one non-military volunteer to represent each squadron, in addition to the involvement of other squadron members. The Key Volunteer could not be a paid member of the base populace. Unit members were asked to submit names of spouses/family members/friends who would be interested in representing the squadron as a KVP member. [172]

April.

Deployed - Letters from the Field: Capt Sellner

First a little background information regarding our operation in San Antonio. As of right now, the 775th EAEF does not currently have an official presence in San Antonio. MSgt Staut and I were sent TDY and basically operated as an AELT. Since we don't technically "exist", our office consists of a Dodge 2500 Diesel Turbo truck and two cell phones. Since there isn't an official order for our AEOT here, we are borrowing space from the 433rd ASTS (Aeromedical Staging Squadron) for storing equipment in their hangar right off the flight line. Kelly Base Ops also works with us in obtaining transportation for the crews and keeping us updated on inbound/outbound aircraft times. They also let the MCDs use their telephones and fax machines so the end of mission paperwork can be completed. The 59th CASF at Wilford Hall is also letting us utilize their liaison office when we are on site. This allows us computer, printer, fax capability so we can update our command cell at Scott AFB, IL.

Communication has been our key to success thus far. Since we aren't a full functioning AEOT, the majority of our time is spent on the telephone and utilizing computers where we can. MSgt Miles and SSgt Hughes have been great with updating us on wheels up times and anything out of the ordinary that heads our way. I've spoken many times to TSgt Monjes at ETAR (Ramstein AB, Germany) Stage to coordinate/communicate any equipment/crew returns we have; also working very closely with Maj Causey at Jackson, Mississippi when the AE crews/equipment transition through her location on their way back to Andrews or Germany. My prior experience in the AEOT has helped me tremendously with this unusual situation in San Antonio and being able to bounce ideas off of another experienced flyer is priceless. The week of Feb 14th, TACC (Tactical Airlift Control Center) and other entities headed to San Antonio to facilitate meetings in hopes of permanently moving the 775th OL-C from Scott AFB to San Antonio Texas. As of early March, we are still in a holding pattern.

Deployed - Letters from the Field: Lt Col Howard

Greetings to everyone. It surprises me that I encounter flyers that don't know or appreciate the history of "The Coin" and most notably "The Coin Check"! I won't take the time here to go into the history, but hope that one of the readers will take time to present the rich heritage at an upcoming Commander's Call.

Let me share with you a couple of personal examples of how "The Coin" can be utilized to give you an idea of its importance. SrA William Peralta, an admin assigned to my team has performed in an outstanding manner. To begin with, he volunteered to work with my team to cross-train and get more involved in the mission. This meant he took on additional duties right off the bat. Once assigned to me, he quickly demonstrated he could perform the work of three people. If that wasn't impressive enough, he has added a light-hearted spirit to the work environment with his positive, fun energy. After a particularly exhausting weekend the AEOT team went out for dinner. We recapped the events of the weekend and I offered special praise to SrA Peralta in the way of presenting him with a 109th AES unit coin via the customary handshake.

In a second similar experience, I presented the DO Maj Shawn Suber with a 109th AES unit coin in the same fashion. This was not only because of his work and attitude, but he also informed me at our outing that he didn't get the whole "Coin" thing and never carried one. Rather than educate him by causing him to buy me a beverage of my choice, I presented him the "Coin" filled handshake and warned him not to be in the presence of Airmen in a bar without it "ever again!"

I will finally add that I was presented with a coin by the Ambassador of Luxembourg. The Ambassador carries coins for the purpose of recognizing the efforts of those of us in uniform. In my case he felt I gave extraordinary attention to him, and his family, and orientation to our mission at the AEOT and the aircraft. We recipients would say we're just doing our job the way we feel it should be done. I was presented with the coin in the same customary handshake I had given others. The giver decides who gets "The Coin" and why. The receiver just enjoys the informal reward. I don't have a lot of coins, but I hold those I do have very special to me. I wish that all of us would have a drawer full of coins, but especially one on our person for the unpredictable "Coin Check" to avoid humiliation and undue expense.

Deployed - Letters from the Field: Sgt Hughes

Of course you all know this is my first deployment and I am in the ground position. It took me about two months to fully adjust to my deployment where I felt like I was ready to take on more. I find that four months does not seem long enough to accomplish everything I would like. The pros to this location include the ability to sightsee, learn more about American history, and I was able to vacation with my family here. The cons that I believed to be long hours actually turned out to be rotating shifts (from days to nights) for which I am fortunate.

Although I have odd work hours depending on the flow, I have adapted easily to this position. I picked up very quickly the position as a duty controller and have been recognized by my command in reference to doing a great job as a first time deployer in the ground position as a flyer. I have also taken the time to go to the ASF and learn about what they do for the patients, how they prep them and I have followed the LNO on a launch day. I would have liked to learn more of the AEOO role but understand that it requires experience and rank to fulfill that position. So with that, I've gone out to see a launch and still would like to accompany a CCATT mission.

I am thankful that I am having such a great deployment and fortunate to be where I am. I know that they all don't end up this way. I would also like to commend the ones I am deployed with. I don't know how I can express my gratitude to them except to say, "Thank you for your great leadership, positive attitudes and the motivation that you all have!" Not only do I work with great people from our unit, the North Carolina folks as well have made a positive impact. I have had the joy to be the North Carolina/Minnesotan linguist. One last con... I am happy to have put on rank but I am still the lowest ranking personnel in the AEOT. (sigh)

Deployed - Letters from the Field: Capt McCarthy

We send a big hello to the squadron, and hope all back home are surviving HSI awesomeness. Here are a few updates to report from our crew. Greg White was promoted to Staff Sergeant in March and was recognized at our Flyers Call. Sadly, no one forced him to recite the Airman's Creed. SSgt Mike Hemmingson, Capt Jason Carter (our active duty MCD from Pope) and SSgt White grew respectable mustaches for "Mustache March" which intimidated many PAX and patients. They clearly oozed with masculinity, so TSgt Amie Lasserre and I found them truly irresistible all month long. Lt Lee Smith enjoyed a visit from his wife and daughter, and is happy to announce they will be welcoming a baby boy in August!

We have been blessed with sunny weather for day trips to Squaw Valley near Lake Tahoe, San Francisco, and Yosemite National Park. Napa Valley is pretty lame (kidding) and we have become well versed in viticulture and the neighboring vineyards, especially the ones with free tasting! As the newest flyer of the crew, I have been taken under the wings of my experienced crew and have learned a thing or two, for which I am very thankful. Each flight brings different challenges and opportunities to improve as a flyer. I am continuously reminded that our mission is truly unbeatable. Despite being away from loved ones, it all seems worth it with each patient we care for and bring home.

I would like to share a quick story of a particularly memorable patient. His story is unique; a victim of friendly fire in the desert, with pictures and X-ray films to prove the accident could have been both tragic and catastrophic. With his injuries, he is most certainly on the road to rehab, another surgery, and a permanent career change for the Army. The patient shared with us the details of the accident and how being classified as a "non-battle injury" strangely affected his treatment by some. He was overlooked for a Purple Heart medal, and was rightfully disappointed. What surprised us most about this young Soldier was his positive, humble, and grateful attitude. While he was in obvious pain, both emotional and physical, his attitude never wavered as he explained the frustrating circumstances. While it may have been the Percocet talking, his attitude was truly inspiring... he consistently spoke highly of his commander, the Army, and especially those who cared for him along the way. As a crew, we were reminded to keep our attitudes positive in any circumstance for these 120 days, and count ourselves lucky to care for such courageous individuals. Happy Drilling... We will see you soon!

May. The HSI was conducted this month. The inspectors were extremely complimentary of the squadron, specifically the professionalism evident throughout the unit. They acknowledged the high operations tempo and training efforts experienced by the squadron in the past few months. The next HSI will occur five years down the road.

☆☆☆☆☆

About a dozen members of the 109th AES participated in the Tough Mudder on May 19th. The team was enthusiastic to represent the Minnesota ANG in the more than ten-mile obstacle course. It was laced with icy pools, high walls, electrified obstacles, and of course lots of mud. Most of all, they were happy to help out the Wounded Warrior Project, the main reason for the event.

The team explained how their military training helped, especially in the mental aspect of the course. They also said that it brought them together as a team. They were very motivated by the military emphasis before the start, as the host explained stories of wounded veterans completing the course. The National Anthem was played just before the 1000 start, as one last boost.

There were other members from the 133rd Airlift Wing scattered throughout the course also participating.

Tough Mudder events are hardcore 10- to 12-mile obstacle courses designed by British Special Forces to test your strength, stamina, mental grit and camaraderie. Tough Mudder has raised more than three million dollars to support the Wounded Warrior Project. [173]

☆☆☆☆☆

June. Jordan Garretson, writing at MLB.com, penned the following piece: MSgt Rob Buresh's homecoming from his recent deployment was quite a memorable one for his two daughters. Annie and Alex Buresh had no clue what awaited them as they ran the bases at Target Field on Sunday before the Twins' game against the Tigers.

As the sisters cruised past first base, their father, MSgt Robert Buresh, hid behind T.C. Bear (the mascot of the Minnesota Twins) near home plate. When they rounded third, he appeared, giving his daughters their first in-person glimpse of him since Jan 9th.

He went to a knee and dropped the three flower bouquets and two teddy bears from his arms, wrapping his two girls up and showering them with kisses as the 38,710 in attendance responded with a standing ovation.

Buresh returned stateside Saturday night after a near five-month deployment overseas. He completed his sixth career deployment at Camp Bastion, Afghanistan, as a member of the 109th AES, 133rd Airlift Wing, Minnesota Air National Guard. His wife, Julie, was aware of his return, but they kept it a secret to surprise Annie, 11, and Alex, 8.

Moments after the teary-eyed reunion, Robert struggled to compose himself and explain the rush of emotions. His hands shook, his feet wobbled, and perspiration glistened on his forehead.

"That was a lot more nerve-wracking than I thought it was going to be," he said. "It feels awesome. I can't put it into words."

Buresh originally planned on surprising his daughters at school. But when he learned his return was scheduled for Memorial Day weekend, he nixed that plan because he didn't want to wait until Tuesday to see them. Buresh learned from a squadron mate that the Twins were supplying free tickets to the unit and their families a day earlier. He contacted the team, which helped arrange the on-field surprise.

"The hardest part was not being able to come to the park," said Buresh, who lives in Kasson. "I was strongly encouraged to not be here any time before 12:20, so I was walking around downtown Minneapolis holding bears and flowers. Everybody looked at me like I looked funny."

But Buresh's patience was rewarded - and it went beyond the emotion of the initial surprise.

"When I found out I was coming to the game, I wanted my first meal here in the States to be a dog and a beer," he said. "And I get to have it with my family."

"I got to Baltimore last night at about 9:30 Eastern time. I ate on the plane before we landed. My butterflies were so bad I don't think it would have stayed down anyways."

He said he couldn't think of a better way to spend the day than watching baseball with his family.

"This is a moment they are going to remember for the rest of their lives," he said. "As a dad, I can't ask for any more. That's just fantastic. I can't tell you how grateful I am for doing this."

Annie and Alex thought their dad would be home at "the end of May or the beginning of June." They had no idea Sunday would be the day they reunited. The time apart had been "pretty hard," Annie said, but they couldn't wipe the ear-to-ear grins off their faces. Said Alex, "I thought that my mom kept a pretty good secret." [174]

Photo courtesy of SSgt Jonathan Young/U.S. Air Force/www.minnesotanationalguard.org
MSgt Robert Buresh was reunited with his two daughters at a Minnesota Twins baseball game.

<u>July.</u> In another Minnesota Twins event, the Twins held their annual Military Appreciation Day at Target Field on 1 July. The theme was women in the military and many of the activities were carried out by Minnesota women from all branches of the service.

Members of the 133rd AW were involved in the color guard and giant flag in center field. The most visible and audible representatives of the wing were sisters 2d Lt Darcy Reller, 109th AES and A1C Jessica Reller, 133rd AW, singing the National Anthem. They were particularly excited to be able to share the moment with their grandmother, who has been a lifelong Twins fan, the Rellers said. There were many tickets handed out to members of the wing who enjoyed a great day of baseball watching the Twins beat the Royals 10-8. [175]

Deployed - Letters from the Field: TSgt Nelson

Things are going well, but a little tired of seeing the dirt and rocks; grass and trees would be nice. We continue to learn things every day, which is amazing since we do the same thing every day, day after day after day.

SrA Beers went on a tour of the AF Osprey helicopters and got some neat pictures. Things are starting to get busier around here due to the time of the year, which is great because time is going by fast now. SrA Beers and I go to the Green Bean a few times during the week instead of the British coffee shop; we needed to change things up a little bit. They also have a better selection of coffees and offer some good smoothies.

We have been talking to our replacement, which is very exciting because now it feels like the end is near. Communicating with people from 12 different bases (2-3 people from each base) - it makes a person's head spin a little. It is definitely a big learning experience and I'm glad to be doing it because it has been keeping me busy.

We haven't had the best vehicles; it seems something goes wrong then they go for repair and don't come back for days or weeks (depending on the vehicle) so then we are short. The Internet goes down a lot or is really slow. The generators for our tents have broken several times so the air conditioners freeze up. The generator for our living areas seemed to quit working at least on a weekly basis. But at least we have each other! Secretary of Defense Leon Panetta visited the base but not our compound, while Gen Green and quite a few other VIPs (Very Important Persons) did come to visit our AEOT. It seems like every few weeks some VIPs came by to see us.

August. Gen Raymond E. Johns Jr., Air Mobility Command Commander, paid a formal visit to the 133rd AW on 23 Aug. Johns, Col Greg Haase, 133rd AW Commander and staff members spent time touring the base and discussing the facilities, the aircraft and the people of the Minnesota ANG. While visiting the 109th AES, the four-star general presented coins to SrA Sara Beers and TSgt Erika Nelson.

October. Capt Chris Wolf deployed to Antarctica in support of Operation Deep Freeze. His role was to provide medical care at the walk-in clinic/hospital at McMurdo Station, Antarctica. During his 7-week deployment, they ended up evacuating five patients for a variety of conditions (such as an appendectomy) that were too big to handle at their facilities. Patients were flown to Christchurch, New Zealand when an aerovac mission was necessary.

Photo courtesy of Capt Chris Wolf
Capt Chris Wolf deployed in support of Operation Deep Freeze at McMurdo Station, Antarctica.

November. MSgt Flohr retired from the unit, while MSgt Trelstad became the new First Sergeant, replacing MSgt Flatten who was acting as the interim First Shirt.

CHAPTER 14
The Command of Col Matt Peterson

(Jan 2013 - Nov 2014)

Photo courtesy of Col Matt Peterson

Commander's Comments: I began my career in 1990 by enlisting in the North Dakota ANG as a member of the "Happy Hooligans." I was attending the University of North Dakota and my job was in Operational Resource Management (today known as a SARM - Squadron Aviation Resource Manager). After graduation, I moved to the Twin Cities and eventually transferred to the 109th AS of the MN ANG in the same role. In 1997, I applied for a commission in the 109th AES as an MSC officer and the rest is history.

As I think back on my 17 years in the unit, I think of the unit in three distinct phases. Early on, we focused entirely on training and were inwardly focused. The unit was very tight and laser focused on the flying mission. We participated in numerous exercises including JRTC, Golden

Medic, Northern Eagle and of course an ORI. We were a well-trained unit with great leadership under Col Carlson and Col Wolf. Then, September 11th happened and the next phase began.

Phase two was all about contingency deployments. In 2002, we deployed half the 109th AES to Scott AFB, IL to do the In Conus Patient Redistribution mission otherwise known as ICMOP. The rest of the aeromedical evacuation squadron was assigned to UTC taskings that were waiting to be validated to support an invasion of Iraq via Turkey. Those were some crazy times! I can remember getting calls every day from the command post as we would constantly receive new taskings. It was an exciting time, but stressful as well. Eventually, Turkey would not allow the U.S. to invade Iraq via its territory and then the buildup in Kuwait began. Over the next 5-6 years, the unit deployed on a continuous cycle to support OIF and OEF in numerous locations throughout the globe.

The third phase was when we began to become more outwardly focused and more balanced between flight and ground operations. In 2009, under the leadership of Col Hodges-Goetz and eventually as I became Commander, the unit began to spread its wings on the national and international scenes. The 109th AES became the lead planning unit for Global Patriot and eventually Global Guardian. Both of these were international exercises that included didactic training and exercises and the unit was the driving force behind their success. In addition, the squadron took on a key role as the lead planner for JRTC, the graduate school of AE. Finally, the unit became immersed in global health engagement that led to numerous missions in Africa, Europe and Latin America.

I really enjoyed my time as Commander. The unit was well oiled by the time I took the stick and the squadron continued its successful execution of deployments, exercises and global health engagement missions. We also successfully passed an ASEV, completed a hospital tour and pulled off the wonderful Founders Day/Reunion event. By the end of my time, the pace and scope of deployments began to decrease and the unit began to turn over with a lot of new blood. Although we received authorization to begin recruiting to three extra crews and received an additional AELT equipment package, the unit was definitely entering a new phase of inward focus on training, recruiting and reconstitution. Although I was sad to leave the state for a new role in the state of Washington, I was happy to see Lt Col Behrens take the helm and lead the unit into this new phase.

Col Matt Peterson

2013

Jan. Lt Col Matt Peterson replaced Col Penny Hodges-Goetz as Commander, who moved to the MDG as their new commander.

April. A continuing resolution to the defense budget was passed last month which restored the flying hours for the unit. This gave the squadron the ability to train new aircrew members, complete upgrades, maintain currency and prepare for the upcoming deployment. The 934th

AFR was very helpful in sharing some of their flights with our unit. In the future, the 109th would look to them for more opportunities to train with their organization.

☆☆☆☆☆

Lt Col Matt Peterson, 109th AES Commander, created a team to look into overhauling the Vital Signs, so the publication would be more relevant to each unit member and less about writing articles for the sake of writing articles. The goal was to leverage the unit's Facebook page to communicate outside of the unit and focus the Vital Signs more toward internal needs.

☆☆☆☆☆

This UTA started the kickoff towards the ASEV prep for next year. Capt Arndt was named the lead project officer and briefed the unit on the project plan.

☆☆☆☆☆

The Military Ball was also held on Saturday evening of the UTA weekend.

Deployed - Letters from the Field: SSgt Rawling

This round in Germany has certainly had its ups and downs. We have one more crew and four fewer missions than we had in 2010-2011, and the patient loads have decreased as well. On the upside? Fewer broken Soldiers. The drawback is finding enough to do to fill the downtime.

Many of us have alternated between touring and volunteering through our local Red Cross representative. I managed to see Paris for cheap and use that language I studied for seven years for the second time in my life! My crew was also able to see Belgium and Italy by way of a weather divert. We certainly put the brews in Bruges and the icy in Sicily.

A highlight of my trip was meeting the NGB Senior Enlisted Advisor, Chief Jelinski-Hall. We spoke briefly about a few things to expect in the near future. Like we've been hearing from our own senior enlisted, EPRs (Enlisted Performance Report) and CCAF (Community College of the Air Force) requirements are incoming, so take the opportunity and be ready. I know I'm certainly going to need a review when EPRs start.

Deployment, or any time on an active duty base is perfect for piling on credits to your CCAF degree. There are a few members in our flight who completed their CCAF last month; I will join them soon. Many others have taken advantage of the various college courses offered on base to complete applications to other undergrad and graduate programs.

Well, that's my trip thus far. Here's looking forward to seeing y'all again this summer!

May. It was anticipated that with the decreased funding projected in the coming months, the off-base training opportunities might be decreased. The unit would probably be looking at on-base or local FTXs for training practice to make the best use of available funds.

June. Plans were underway for a Founders Day/Reunion celebration. As part of the preparation activities, the unit coin was redesigned. (authors' note: Please see the "Squadron Coin" section at the back of the book for further details.)

It was also at this time that the authors of this book were asked to write a history of the 109th AES for the event. Given the time constraints, we decided to concentrate on the first seven years of unit history, with an emphasis on the efforts and accomplishments of our founders. A fifteen page "early" unit history was drafted and distributed at the event, with the promise that we would build on this document and write a complete and comprehensive history of the 109th AES, which culminated in the writing of this book.

August. A 109th AES Founders Day/Reunion celebration was held from 16-17 August.

The genesis for these two events began when Lt Col Henry Capiz (Ret), former Commander of the 109th AMEF, called Col Julie Eszlinger Jensen (Ret), also a former Commander of the 109th AES to suggest that a red cross be placed on the C-131 Samaritan aircraft parked at the Minnesota ANG Museum. The Samaritan was flown by 109th AMEF crews in the early 1960s during domestic aerovac missions. At his request, Eszlinger Jensen began the process. It was through many years and many hurdles and with the help of her husband, Lt Col Russ Jensen (Ret) and the Hunt family assistance that it was finally accomplished. The Hunt family donated all memorials from the passing of Maureen to the Air Guard Museum C-131 project.

In addition, the desire to bring the founders back to the 109th AES was a goal of Col Eszlinger Jensen for many years. It seemed natural to do so during the dedication of the red cross on the C-131 aircraft in honor of their colleague and founder, Col Maureen A. Hunt. Together with founder Dorthea Tenney and Col Penny Hodges-Goetz, the current 109th AES Commander, planning enthusiastically began. Other key players for this event included Lt Col Darcy Anderson, Col Sandy Carlson, Col Alice Graner, Lt Col Ed Howard, CMSgt Mark Latourelle, and Col Karen Wolf. What began as a Founders Day only reunion developed into an all 109th AES reunion - past and current membership.

Photo courtesy of Minnesota ANG Museum
Col Maureen A. Hunt

On Friday evening, a buffet and program were held in honor of the founders at the 934th United States Air Force Reserve Services Club.

Photo courtesy of Stacie Wescott
The Founders.

Back Row (L - R): Terrance Ripley, Brig Gen Leo Goodrich (former MN Adjutant General's Staff), Maj Gen John Dolny (former 133rd ATW Wing Commander)
Middle Row (L - R): Robert Hecht, Carol Osteboe, Richard Vosika, David Lund
Front Row (L - R): Dorothea Tenney, Betty Cook, Lt Col Jerry Nelson (former Commander), Jean Cool, Geraldine Hendrickson, James Mulroy

The following day, the official ceremony and dedication of the red cross was held at the Minnesota ANG Museum.

Photo courtesy of Stacie Wescott

Unveiling of the red cross on the C-131 aircraft parked at the Air Guard Museum was in honor of Col Maureen A. Hunt, who was one of the founders of the 109th AMEF, went on active duty, was a rising star, had an outstanding USAF career, invented and patented two aeromedical equipment items and unfortunately was medically retired. The C-131 is recognized and especially significant to the 109th AMEF as it was the aeromedical aircraft for domestic aerovac flown in by Col Hunt and many of the early 109th AMEF flight nurses and med techs.

After the event, Col Eszlinger Jensen received many phone calls, e-mails, and the following two letters:

"Julie--Greetings from both of us with much gratitude for our wonderful two days!! We were awed, thrilled and humbled by 'our' aeromedical evacuation squadron of today. We were treated like royalty (it will take a while for our heads to return to normal size), impressed with the unit of today and forever grateful for the honors and thank-yous and presentations we experienced. After returning home, and taking the time to read the histories in the booklet, we realized more fully the number of people involved and the hard work put into this endeavor. We wish to thank each and every one of them. It was an A-1 effort, truly successful for us!! It brought back so many memories which are still coming forth - many thanks to all. Dorothea assures us you will be able to forward these kudos to all those involved. We felt pride wherever we went!"

Gratefully--Capt Betty Cook and Capt Jean Cool

"Julie--We can't imagine how much work the reunion weekend was; we know you had a lot to do with all of the stages! It was wonderful. We had such a nice time the whole weekend and really appreciate all the work it involved. According to everyone we talked to, it was a huge success." Love--Carol and Terry Ripley

September. By the UTA weekend, the first two groups of the current AEF cycle were deployed. The remaining groups left a few weeks after the drill weekend.

Photo courtesy of MSgt Rachel Maloney
Deployed in Germany.

(L - R): SMSgt Bryan Steven, Capt Lee Smith, MSgt Travis Miles, Maj Jason Arndt, TSgt James Kreiman, TSgt Sam Dennis, CMSgt Dan Cisar, TSgt Matt Monjes, Capt Meg Grout, MSgt Rachel Maloney

The Boreas Reach exercise was held on the UTA weekend as well. Many unit members found themselves in UTCs and leadership roles to which they were not accustomed. The exercise was a pilot to determine if it could be substituted for the next ORI.

October. Nearly half of the squadron was deployed for the AEF rotation. The remaining squadron members prepared in earnest for the ASEV scheduled for next May/June.

Photo courtesy of Capt Andrea Payne

October 2013 flight from Germany back to the States in a C-17. Capt Andrea Payne recalls a patient load of 15 litter, 13 ambulatory, and 8 attendants. Several were blast victims from an IED (Improvised Explosive Device).

Deployed - Letters from the Field: Capt Wolf

Greetings from Travis deployers!

We hope everyone is doing well and that those that deployed to other locations have made it there safely. From what we are hearing through various outlets, it sounds as though people are adjusting to their missions and duties. The Travis crew (Wolf, Reller, Goodman, Mitricska, and Shore) all made the long drive to our location and have spent the past few weeks getting into a routine. We have mixed crews and everyone quickly adjusted into their roles; we seem to have pretty high performing teams. The majority of our mixed crews are from the New England area - so we are learning a creative blend of lingo somewhere between Minnesooota (dontcha know, eh) and Boston (I have to go pawk the caw and get a cup of cawfee).

We've spent a lot of our time doing training. Physical fitness is generally 5-6 days per week and skills training also; we are only averaging about five patients on our flights, so we are accomplishing quite a bit of training on our required medical skills.

This has been far different from other missions and deployments that I have been a part of. I have to say one of my most gratifying moments has been seeing an injured Soldier stepping off of the aircraft at Miramar and having his wife and kids there to greet him after nearly ten months away. Those are the moments that I feel privileged to be a part of…and part of why we do what we do. From all of us at Travis…be safe.

November.

Deployed - Letters from the Field: CMSgt Dan Cisar

Hallo aus Deutschland Geschwader! I have to keep reminding myself that this is indeed a deployment, a wonderful deployment. Funny how in the desert time seems to drag on at a snail's pace but here time is flying.

A very rewarding aspect of the superintendent job here at the 10th is being able to spotlight our mission and Airmen on almost a weekly basis to the constant stream of Distinguished Visitors that tour this place. Our most recent and to date our favorite visitor is Command Chief Master Sergeant James Hotaling of the ANG. Chief Hotaling spent a couple of hours with some of the guardsmen deployed here. MSgt Applen and MSgt Miles gave the Command Chief a tour of the building and an overview of our mission, then Chief Hotaling was able to sit down for an hour-long question and answer session with a group of us.

A definite highlight was when the Command Chief coined MSgt Eric Applen for his hard work and dedication to the AE mission. Have a wonderful Thanksgiving! I know we will!

Photo courtesy of the Vital Signs (Nov '13)
Command Chief Master Sergeant James Hotaling of the ANG and MSgt Eric Applen.

December. It was noted in the Vital Signs last month that many unit members did not pass their PT test, with several having a history of multiple PT test failures.

Lt Col Hesser (acting Commander) and Capt Truscinski rolled out some voluntary squadron fitness challenges to help build some accountability and competition within the squadron. The goal was not to look for the "fastest" or the "most," but who has the greatest improvement. The fitness challenge was posted to a Facebook page and unit members were asked to join. The first challenge was a "Biggest Loser" contest along with push-ups and sit-ups. The greatest percentage of improvement was tracked through the February UTA. Prizes for the winners were yet to be determined. The ultimate goal was to get 100% of the squadron to 80 or better on the fitness assessments.

2014

February. Germany and Afghanistan deployers returned this month. Epic snowstorms in the Southeast, cancelled flights, breakdowns and missing crewmembers made the return trip from Bagram quite the experience.

★★★★★

Much of the activities this UTA centered around preparation for the upcoming ASEV - the number one objective for 2014. Capt Laura Mitricska was coordinating this activity.

March. A new inspection system was introduced this month - the Commander's Inspection Program (CCIP) which replaced the familiar Self-Inspection Program. CCIP was designed to change the existing mindset from "passing an inspection" to "ensuring capability." The goal was to improve mission readiness by taking a sustained, proactive approach throughout the year to achieve compliance rather than a reactive approach that typically equated to a flurry of activity 2-3 months prior to a unit inspection. In addition, Unit Effectiveness Inspections (UEIs) replaced the Health Services Inspections with the UEIs scheduled on a 48 to 60-month cycle.

April. The Chief Nurse, Lt Col Pat Howard, asked everyone to actively pursue recruiting nurses for the squadron. He anticipated a need for a minimum of eight new nurses to meet the anticipated attrition in the next several months.

May. The ASEV team administered a closed book and Boldface examination to all available personnel. ASEV tests are derived from a minimum of 85% Master Question File (MQF) questions, with the balance coming from Flight Publications, Safety/Operational Supplements, Flight Crew Information Files (FCIFs), and local directives. The minimum passing grade for an ASEV closed book exam is 85%, while Boldface exams are graded "Q" or "U" (Qualified or Unqualified).

After the 90-day ASEV notification, all AECMs were fair game to receive a flight evaluation from HQ AMC Flight Examiners. Normally, 5%-25% of each crew position would be administered ASEV flight evaluations. AMC Flight Examiners administered flight evaluations to Flight Instructors and/or Flight Examiners. Flight evaluations looked at a cross section of the unit's operational mission. Instructors were asked to demonstrate maneuvers to help assess their abilities. All crewmembers were asked to accomplish specific tasks or maneuvers for their crew qualification to assess proficiency.

A unit-level overall ASEV grade would then be awarded. At the conclusion of the visit, the ASEV team chief provided feedback (oral and written) to the unit commander and staff. Individual programs are awarded a grade using the following scale:

> **Outstanding**: Program exceeds all requirements and is noted as a "best practice" by program evaluators.
>
> **Excellent**: Program exceeds requirements with only minor deviations noted.

Satisfactory: Program meets requirements with some deviations noted. This is the "standard" ASEV program grade – equivalent to a Q1 flight evaluation.

Marginal: Program meets most requirements with significant discrepancies noted.

Unsatisfactory: Major discrepancies noted that degrade program effectiveness. [176]

After conducting the inspection this month, the ASEV team awarded the following grades:

Overall grade: **Mission Ready** (possible grades are either Non-Mission Ready or Mission Ready).

Aircrew Performance: **Excellent**

Stan/Eval: **Satisfactory**

Training: **Satisfactory**

Tactics: **Excellent**

Capt Katherine Gartner was also recognized as a "Top Performer." Her role was critical to the success of the ASEV "and she absolutely knocked it out of the park" according to Lt Col Peterson, 109th AES Commander. Other individuals credited with the success of this inspection included Capt Laura Mitricska, Maj Arndt, MSgt Buresh and MSgt Brothers. [177]

November. This UTA marked the Change of Command of the 109th AES. Lt Col Matt Peterson relinquished command to become the Commander of the 194th Medical Group at Camp Murray, Washington. Lt Col Sue Behrens became the new 109th AES Commander.

After leaving the 109 AES, Col Peterson completed a two-year assignment as the 194th MDG Commander. He then transferred back to the Minnesota Air National Guard and entered the Air National Guard Assistants and Advisors Program (NGAP). Col Peterson's first assignment in the NGAP program was as the ANG Assistant to SG3X for Global Health Engagement at Headquarters Air Force. As of the writing of this book, Col Peterson is currently engaged in a second NGAP assignment as the Assistant Director, Office of the Joint Surgeon at National Guard Bureau.

CHAPTER 15
The Command of Lt Col Sue Behrens

(Nov 2014 - Mar 2019)

Photo courtesy of Lt Col Sue Behrens

Commander's Comments: As I sit on one of our C-130Hs, waiting to take off for a training mission to Travis AFB, CA, I thought what better time to write about the current 109th AES. I have been Commander for three years now and it has never been dull. This dynamic, fast paced squadron continues to set the bar high and I have never seen a group of forward-thinking individuals that have a synergy which goes beyond compare as in this one. Our predecessors can rest assured that our squadron's legacy is in excellent hands.

I have been in the unit since 1999 and have seen numerous changes. We have gone from carrying a bag full of regulations (small suitcase) to where now the flyers carry an iPad Mini with all the regulations on that device. The training requirements have tripled for all AF

Specialty Codes and Unit Type Codes. We have simulator mannequins that we use for training and one of them is certified for training flights. This is in addition to members portraying and being moulaged up as patients.

We have continued to deploy and at this time do not see it changing. Our deployments have taken us to Afghanistan, Kuwait, Iraq, Qatar, Djibouti, Travis AFB, CA, Andrews AFB, MD, Germany, and Kelly AFB, TX. We do exercises with all U.S. military branches - active duty, reserves, and guard units across the United States - as well as international exercises with Poland, Croatia and an exercise in Columbia, South America with 11 other nations. In addition to participating, we have some very dynamic planners who also did the planning of many exercises both CONUS and OCONUS. One of our primary missions as a major player in the Department of Homeland Security (DHS), requires us to take our turn "in the bucket" for terrorist attacks, hurricanes and other natural disasters. It seems there are always at least two directions we are going.

I am not sure how long I will continue as Commander as there are so many rising stars within the unit. In my opinion, that is how we will continue to get better and better, sustaining the legacy that was started in June of 1961, by continuing to pass the torch. However long I am in this chair, it has been one of the greatest honors I could have been a part of.

The drill weekends are nonstop for me. They start on Thursdays and go until about 1800 on Sundays. My two-hour drive home is made without the radio on so I have some silence and time to reflect. I am truly mentally exhausted but it is a good exhaustion. But as most commanders know, this job is not just a drill weekend position - now known as RSDs (Regularly Scheduled Drills, previously known as UTAs). It is a 24/7 job, and with modern technological capabilities I can work from home as well as at the base. While for the most part this is a plus, it also gives one little time for yourself. We are so well connected this day and age that commanders have not only laptops but iPads or iPhones. As a matter of fact, this is being written on my iPad with a Bluetooth keyboard.

We have our motto that we have carried since Col Penny Hodges-Goetz was Commander. "We are the 109th, we can do it!" And there is no doubt in my mind that this squadron does and will do anything that is thrown in their path and will excel at it. Minnesota should be proud of these quiet warriors!

Lt Col Sue Behrens

November. Lt Col Sue Behrens returned to the 109th AES and replaced Lt Col Matt Peterson as Commander.

December. In the December Vital Signs, Lt Col Behrens outlined her expectations as the new Commander - integrity, hard work, and assurance that unit members take care of each other.

☆☆☆☆☆

On December 28, 2014, after 13 years of combat operations, President Obama and Secretary of Defense Chuck Hagel announced the end of OEF, a conflict that claimed the lives of more than 2,200 American troops.

Photo courtesy of TSgt Richard Childs and Col Michael Germain

"DEDICATED TO THE MEN AND WOMEN OF THE 109TH AES WHO SERVED DURING OPERATION IRAQI FREEDOM, OPERATION ENDURING FREEDOM, AND THE GLOBAL WAR ON TERRORISM"

Photo courtesy of TSgt Richard Childs and Col Michael Germain
Detailed close-up of previous picture.

2015

February. This was the final UTA for CMSgt Dan Cisar who retired this month after 28 dedicated years of service with the 109th AES - an icon who would surely be missed in the years ahead. On one of his last deployments, ANG Command Chief Hotaling labeled Chief Cisar a "Field Chief" and summed it up by saying "a Field Chief is the Chief who is in the business of taking care of his people with his people, and usually without the knowledge of his people."

March. The Chief's Board was held on the UTA weekend to select the new Chief for the 109th AES. Chief Lance Burg was selected for this position.

May. Several unit members had been deployed and were already flying missions. It was suggested that members of the 109th AES stay connected with them via Facebook, e-mail, and Internet-based texting.

June. SrA William Peterson graduated from the in-residence Airman Leadership School. Out of the 180 Airmen in the class, he was chosen as the recipient for the Commander's Leadership Award for outstanding leadership and performance. [178]

Photo courtesy of the Vital Signs (Jun/Jul 2015)
SrA William Peterson with the Commander's Leadership Award Trophy.

July. TSgt Taylor Juvland Nielsen had an interesting experience during a Patriot exercise this month. She recalls, "I had an opportunity to go on a training exercise with a team of USAF pararescuemen (PJs for para-jumpers). I was working as ground personnel when I was approached by the OIC. He asked if I would like to accompany the PJs on one of their drills. I readily agreed to help! They required additional medical assistance at a site where they would rescue the "patients" and I would help provide medical care while they worked on those who had more complex medical needs. It was very different from any simulated mission I had ever done! I followed one of the PJs through buildings, and helped them rescue several mannequins that served as patients. I provided care to them based on the injuries presented and they worked on the other patients. We 'saved' all of them and I have a memory that I will never forget!"

August. The capabilities of the 109th AES was a natural fit for Vigilant Guard, a statewide exercise testing the ability of military and civilian organizations to work together.

"Our role in the exercise is to stabilize and transport patients from the field to higher echelons of care," said 109th AES Director of Operations Maj Jeramy Browning. "We strive to provide the best care in the air. Our highly trained flight medics care for sick and wounded patients, maintain their health and well-being aboard the plane - getting them to the definitive care they need. Being able to participate in this exercise helps us refresh protocol and procedures of working with civil authorities, sister services as well as state and local entities."

During the exercise, the aircrew and medical team of the 109th AES transported role-playing patients from the 133rd Airlift Wing in St Paul to Camp Ripley. On arrival, the team worked with other National Guard medical personnel to transport additional mock patients from UH-60 Black Hawk helicopters to the unit's C-130H Hercules aircraft to simulate the continuation of care during a state emergency.

"This exercise gives us a great opportunity to practice improving our interoperability with the Army Guard, civilian healthcare providers and emergency response personnel," said SSgt Britt Monio. "In the event of a future, real-world scenario like this, we know that we will be prepared and the incident command system should run effectively, helping patients get the medical care they need in the fastest and safest way possible."

Litter carries across the flight line, checking patient's vital signs and maintaining the overall care of patients in-flight are just a few of the things the team trained on. The 109th AES spent nearly an entire day practicing in-flight processes and procedures in a scenario that could happen if they were activated by the governor during a state emergency.

"Every single person in our squadron loves what they do," said Browning. "I'm so proud of my unit and the great work they do - whether it's on base during a drill weekend or flying around the state or world helping people with an outstanding level of care."

Vigilant Guard is a United States Northern Command and National Guard Bureau sponsored exercise designed to improve emergency coordination, response and recovery management with federal, regional, local, civilian and military partners. [179]

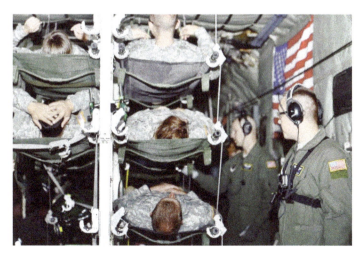

Photo courtesy of TSgt Lynette Olivares/TSgt Paul Santikko, Northstar Guard Online (Aug '15)
Aeromeds check their "patients" on board a C-130H for the Vigilant Guard exercise.

November. The unit held a silent auction which raised $922 for the unit fund. This fund is supported only by donations and used to fund retirements, BBQs, comradery, etc.

December. The holiday was celebrated with a chili cook-off on Sunday of the UTA.

2016

January. Donations of various items (computer accessories, food items, etc.) were requested from unit members for the Minnesota Veterans Home. Members of the 109th AES collected the items and delivered them to the Veterans Home as they volunteered for other duties for the veterans.

☆☆☆☆☆

SSgt Taylor Juvland Nielsen comments on her first live aerovac mission. She recalls, "I was in college at the time, and I received a call from the squadron asking if I would be interested in participating in the first (and only) live mission out of Minneapolis that we knew of. I was told that an Airman had been injured by an IED blast in Afghanistan, and had been brought back to the U.S. but still required some extensive care that a hospital in Minnesota could provide. Due to the nature of his injuries, he was not able to take a civilian aircraft back to his home station. As soon as I heard there was someone who needed help, I immediately responded 'absolutely' and got my gear ready to go. This was exactly why I had joined aerovac - to take care of the wounded and get them home. I drove to the squadron the next day and was a mix of nervousness and excitement. I had only been on simulated missions before and it was thrilling to imagine having a real patient on the plane. We followed our checklists and waited anxiously for the patient to arrive at the aircraft. Finally, we saw an ambulance approach and I prepared to do the job I was trained for. We got the patient safely transported within a few hours and he received a hero's welcome the minute we landed. It was like nothing I had ever seen. There were camera crews, friends, family in addition to many posters/banners awaiting our arrival. To this day, I feel absolutely privileged to have been part of getting that Airman home."

March. MSgt Rachel Maloney was one of five members of the Minnesota ANG selected by the Adjutant General to represent the Minnesota National Guard as the 2015 Civil Servant of the Year. Winners were honored at the 39th Federal Civil Servant of the Year Recognition Awards Program held in Bloomington, MN.

May. Through the eyes of an orientee:

When you enlist you are told you have to go to "drill" once a month even though you haven't gone to basic yet. On your first drill weekend you show up not knowing what to wear or where to go. As an orientee, you feel like you are wearing a sign on your forehead that says, "I'm new," simply because of the fact that everyone else is in some kind of uniform; some in camo and others in pajama pickle suits.

Everyone else is walking around, laughing really loud, and talking as if they have known each other forever. Sitting in the orientation room is very awkward when you're new, because when people walk by and make eye contact over the cubicle wall you don't know what to do, so you glance at the wall to make yourself look busy. People who were in charge of orientation walk in the cubicle and say it's time for Commander's Call. Whatever that means. You follow the herd of people into a classroom, and cut straight to the back. Why do you go to the back? Because it somehow makes you feel like your civilian clothes blend in with all the camouflage. Just when you think, "perfect, I'm safe in my chair" someone who looks like they have been in the Marines for years asks, "Are there any new people here?" At this point everyone in the room is turned around in their chair staring at you. As you stand up trying to remember what your name is, you realize you really don't know what you are doing here. Once you rattle off your name and where you're from, you quickly sit down and pray no one looks at you again. As the gathering continues, multiple really important people talk to the group about things that sound like singing the alphabet in random order... MPF (Military Personnel Flight), ADLS (Advanced Distributed Learning Service), AROWS (Air Reserve Orders Writing System), DTS (Defense Travel System), IMR (Individual Medical Readiness), MYPAY (website for all issues dealing with military pay), CCAF (Community College of the Air Force) and DOD (Department of Defense). Suddenly the Marine man by the door yells, "Room, tench-hut!" You look around and quickly realize you're the only one sitting and jump up trying to make it seem like no one saw you mess up.

After that meeting is done you walk back to the cubicle and get a sheet that has a bunch of titles of people that you are told to go and find. You nod your head as if you know what any of it means. Walking around the maze of cubicles, you start remembering people's faces and start asking anyone that will make eye contact with you, "Who is this?" while pointing to the checklist. Walking around, you run into a grumpy man in the corner, and a bunch of people who keep trying to make jokes that you don't understand. At this point, you don't know what to say, so you awkwardly laugh and walk away. After walking around for what seems like hours, you head back to the cubicle having made no progress on your checklist and hope for better luck tomorrow.

Fast forward two years and you're finally done with all required training to be a part of the 109th AES. You have been through two months of basic training, four months of Tech School, one month of phase two, two months phase three, three weeks of SERE, two days of water survival, one month of FN-AET, one month of FTU (Formal Training Unit), and two months of seasoning. After you have completed all of that training you will still be trying to figure out what's going on. It is sure worth the ride to be a part of this AE family. [180]

August. On August 12th and 13th, a team from the 109th AES completed the Great River Ragnar. The adventure began in Winona and ended in Minneapolis with plenty of miles through the back roads of Wisconsin. After 200-ish miles and nearly 31 hours of minimal sleep, some rain, plenty of sunshine, and night running, all participants made it safely home. The adventure should have been with 12 runners but they did it with only 11. This was a great team building opportunity and Maj Jason Arndt said that he was fairly certain it will not be the last Ragnar our members complete. A special thanks went out to volunteer Emily Applen who was given the power to stop traffic and enjoyed every minute of it! [181]

Photo courtesy of the Vital Signs (Jul/Aug '16)
Great River Ragnar Team #43 109th AES.

Back Row (L - R): Mark Hesser, Rory Connolly, Jason Arndt, Rob Buresh
Front Row (L - R): Stu Rawling, Alex Hofschulte, Sarah Schutta, Kristin Dudas, Meghan Grout, Shawn Fitzhenry, Tina Ruyle

December. Lt Col Pat Howard retired this month after 24 years of service. This brings an end to an era of the three "Howard" siblings. Since 1970, there has been at least one "Howard" in the 109th AES, and between the three of them, they have proudly served continuously for the past 47 years!

Photo courtesy of Lt Col Ed Howard
(L - R): SMSgt Liz Howard, Lt Col Pat Howard, Lt Col Ed Howard at Pat's retirement.

Photo courtesy of the 109th AES archives
(L - R): 1st Lt Ed Howard, 2d Lt Pat Howard, and MSgt Liz Howard 24 years earlier at Pat's swearing-in!

The authors asked Lt Col Pat Howard for his thoughts on this incredible family history within the 109th AES. He writes:

Thank you for asking me to write about the Howard sibling members of the unit. The authors of this book thought it would be a unique item to note as collectively we served the military as members of the 109th AES for over 90 years.

Ed Howard was the first of the three of us enlisting in 1970 and serving as an AET and an MSC for more than 20 years each, retiring as a Lt Col. Elizabeth Pierson (Howard) served for 24 years as an AET, retiring as a SMSgt, and I, Patrick Howard served 24 years as a FN, retiring as a Lt Col.

Ed, the oldest of 10 siblings, joined during the Vietnam conflict and provided inspiration in our youth by allowing us to wear his uniforms and wig for Halloween costumes. Yes, that's no mistake. The wig was commonly worn by men in that era to tuck their hair under and be "in regulation" for inspection, allowing them to have the fashionable long hair of the period. There are other not-so-inspirational lessons of Ed teaching us how to make our beds tight enough to bounce a quarter, properly hanging our clothes to avoid wrinkles or the ever popular, inspection of the drawers and closets after everything was put away. But…, Liz enlisted anyway and learned intimately how Ed's lessons were acquired, and Pat was commissioned (so I got the light version).

Liz offered two valuable lessons to me when I first joined. First was the tradition of the first salute rendered by an enlisted to an officer. She proudly attended my commissioning, walked me outside, saluted me and told me I owed her a silver dollar. Lesson, take care of your enlisted! Second lesson, experience trumps rank. That was when the butter bar after getting out of flight school and having just passed his checkride, thought he was going to suggest to the 11-year experienced MSgt the correct way to enplane a patient. Lesson: respect your senior enlisted.

All three of us worked hard and played hard. Often on Sunday after the drill we would recap drill and talk politics, unit and family. Work was reflected by all of us having been instructors, examiners and eventually leaders. We played together at the base, exercises and even on deployments whether it be in games or positions we were assigned. Liz and I braided hair for all the ladies at JRTC for ease of chemical warfare play, swam in the ocean in Hawaii and played countless sets of volleyball. Ed and I danced with a performer in Ecuador, bunked together and toured the base in Balad. While I shared these same experiences with many members, the three of us will be able to revisit these experiences far more often.

Everyone who joins the ANG will likely make friendships that will last the rest of their lives. The Howards were already family so the long-term relationship was a lock. Like working in the family store, or sharing in the family chores - this was just another way for us to work together, but more lasting. We didn't share the household or store duties together except for a few years, but all three of us were together for 13 years as aeromeds offering us a bond that few in life will be able to enjoy.

I would like to note that while family members serving in the same unit is not common, family serving in the ANG has been the model since the first militia. In fact, the first militias commonly served in the same organization. Three sons, a brother and nephew have or are still serving the wing in other career fields adding to the time-honored heritage of the Minuteman. We were very proud and happy to have served and shared this bond over the years we were together as aeromeds and while we have the same last name, we are just part of the entire Guard Family.

2017

February. The 109th AES sent one of their own out to do a bigger job. Chief Lance Burg was recently selected as the next Command Chief of the 133rd Airlift Wing! His parting words to the unit follow.

"I am deeply honored and humbled to be selected for the Command Chief position and look forward to working with the entire wing's enlisted personnel to continue the upward growth that I have seen in the last few years. With that said, a significant part of me is genuinely sad about not being able to continue in my role as the Chief of the 109th AES.

"In a little less than two years (wow, that was fast), I have grown to love and appreciate the passion and work ethic that the Airmen of the 109th AES bring to the mission. I'm so excited for this squadron's direction for the future and the desire to grow as displayed by our mid-level personnel, both officers and enlisted. You have an excellent group of leaders in your Senior NCO and FGO (Field Grade Officer) core that will enable a strong forward projection to ever greater things both in the field and home station. That's what makes this even harder. The 109th AES is ripe for even greater things with the folks here and I wanted to be a part of that and was hoping to be able to say I contributed to the 109th AES's legacy of excellence.

"I've gained so much in such a short period of time to include understanding the mission, understanding some of the trials you go through, and getting to know some of your talents and skills that will benefit the wing as a whole as well as the squadron. I am a better Chief and will be a better CCM (Squadron Chief Master Sergeant) because of the 109th AES and both I and the wing have AE to thank for that. I've spent 27 years learning and developing my leadership/followership skills, but the last two have been the finishing school that prepared me to move to an even higher position of responsibility. As scary as that is for me to move to the Command Chief position, I'm excited and feel ready and I have you to thank for giving me the confidence and skills to do so. Don't forget to come see me up at the 'big house' (not prison) when you get a minute; you'll always be a crucial part of my career and hold a special spot in my heart. I will be with you Saturday morning to wrap up the staff sergeant EPRs and a few other things, but after that I will sit up at 631 if you need anything. Thanks again for the willingness to accept me into the fold, I'll never forget it." [182]

☆☆☆☆☆

In addition to being an aeromed with a primary mission of caring for patients in-flight, most aircrew members also have "additional duties" within the unit. Some serve in areas of Aircrew

Training, Staff Development, etc. If this wasn't enough to do, a few of the aeromeds volunteer for duty as honor guard members who represent the military branches of service at veterans funeral services to show the nation's deep gratitude to those who have faithfully served the country.

Photo courtesy of MSgt Rachel Maloney
TSgt Vaughn Hanson - aeromed and honor guard.

Deployed - Letters from the Field: MSgt Travis Miles

Greetings from Germany! Once we got to the 10th EAEF they split us up into different crews. SrA Ewert and Lt LaBlanc are on a crew together. SSgt Bo Peterson is on a crew by himself. Maj Ruyle and I are on a crew together. Currently the loads are pretty light. My smallest load has been four patients and my largest load has been 19.

The experience level at the 10th this rotation is limited. Knowing the regs (regulations) has been very critical and I think you can easily tell the difference between how the 109th trains compared to some units. My crew has members with experience ranging from 1-3 years, so I'm the old guy that puts us over 10 years of experience for our ORM (Operational Risk Management). However, my crew acts and performs like they have all been flying for over five years. They are quick to adapt and overcome any obstacle. We were alerted for a Bravo mission with only two pallet positions to use. Without stressing, the crew got our gear loaded and prepared for the patient. When we got to the location, the patients came out but they didn't have any meals and one patient (our priority) was missing. The Soldiers that brought out the patients had no idea who the other patient was. Maj Ruyle got on the phone with TACC and then was connected to TPMRC so they could help find this patient, that no one seemed to know about. He was finally located in the wrong line at the Kuwait International Airport. He was supposed to have been driven straight to the aircraft.

We've been exploring history since we arrived. During our Bravo days we have been watching Band of Brothers. On our down time we went to Bastogne and Foy and saw the woods where the 101st were dug in during the Battle of the Bulge. We also stopped at the American and German Cemeteries in Luxembourg. A member of the crew set up PT in the morning. One day we went to Cologne and climbed to the top of the Cologne Dom which turned out to be 533 stairs! So we counted that for leg day.

I do have to tip my hat to SrA Ewert. He has been setting up some great BBQs with chicken, ribs, candy bacon, bacon explosion, and a brownie cooked in an orange peel. Once again showing the lead, all five of us Minnesotans took on additional duties as well serving at the 10th EAEF.

Photo courtesy of MSgt Travis Miles

Repositioning flight to Ramstein AB, Germany. MSgt Miles and his crew picked up Lt Jessica LaBlanc and SrA Joshua Ewert at Andrews AFB, MD after their aircraft "broke" en route to Ramstein. MSgt Miles is kneeling on the left side of the photo securing the Neonatal Transport System (NTS). SrA Ewert is hunched over in the center of the picture securing the oxygen cylinder while Maj Tina Ruyle is second from the right. The rest of the crew are from the reserves and active duty that made up the crews.

March. MSgt Eric Applen became the new First Sergeant in the 109th AES. He comes with 10 years in the ANG and 17 total in the Air Force.

April.

Deployed - Letters from the Field: MSgt Travis Miles

The downhill slope of the deployment is here. The five of us at Ramstein have been doing well. Thank you to all of you that have reached out to us to see how the deployment is going. This is the point of the 90-day itch aka "Short Timer Disease." It's when people want to get home because they know it's almost the end. Some people may become complacent and start taking short cuts. Many of us have checkrides shortly after we get back so we are keeping each other in focus on the mission and preparing for checkrides. Always be ready and Semper Gumby (always flexible) is very important, especially as regulations change.

On one recent flight I had a patient with a hernia complaining of a headache and his neck was bothering him. He said his pain was 5/10. I knew there used to be a reg that allowed us to give Tylenol, but now there is the 48-307 with its three volumes. It took a little time, but I found that I could give Tylenol based on the OTC (Over The Counter) AE protocol. Within the protocol it also directed that we had to complete a 2852 (Near Miss Event) for giving him Tylenol from the AE stock. Remember to dig into the new regs and the recent MQF update. Many things have changed since the days of flying with a Life Pack 10 and a few backpacks of medical supplies!

As I mentioned, always be ready. On one flight we stopped at McGuire to pick up cargo before deadheading back to Germany. I had just started to sleep when I was awakened by Maj Ruyle. She had noticed a diesel fume smell in the aircraft. She notified the front-end crew to see if there was a chance cargo was leaking fuel. They said there shouldn't be as nothing was declared as hazardous cargo. The loads went to the back and found the smell of fumes and a wooden crate leaking. The crate was marked as "General Cargo." We had to turn around to land at McGuire and put on EPOS (Emergency Passenger Oxygen System). Fire Rescue was asked to check it out. Since it was marked as "General Cargo" they had to call out the HAZMAT (Hazardous Material) team. It took a good amount of time before they could establish that it was safe to open the cargo door, since the cargo had leaked a large amount of fluid. Prior to the flight, some individuals didn't bring their jackets along since it was "nice outside". As we waited for them to check out the problem, an evening chill set in and they began to feel the cold. At any temperature, remember your flight jacket. You may never know when you may need it. Later it was determined that it was a ship pump with diesel fuel still in it. Thankfully Maj Ruyle recognized the odor and questioned the load masters. Her actions prevented a larger mishap and protected us from illness and injury.

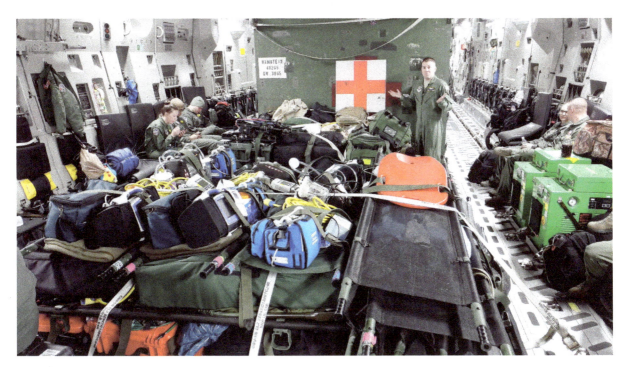

Photo courtesy of MSgt Travis Miles

SSgt William "Bo" Peterson poses with equipment for three AE Crews and one CCATT all trying to return to Ramstein from Andrews AFB, MD. It was crowded, but the crews were able to secure all of the equipment.

<u>August.</u> The squadron clarified the wear of leather flight jackets. According to the 36-2903, leather flight jackets could be worn when an Airman is permanently awarded an aeronautical badge. Aeronautical badges were permanently awarded after three years of aeronautical orders or after ten combat missions IAW 11-402.

<u>September.</u> SSgt Emily Stanzyk and SSgt Byrnes attended the Advanced Trauma Training Program (ATTP) at Rush University in Chicago. She writes:

"'The more tools you have in your toolbox, the more prepared you'll be.' ——Dr. Louis Hondros. At first, this statement might seem a little redundant, a little obvious. Yes. Of course, we've heard it a thousand times: the importance of these 'tools' people speak of, and this imaginary 'toolbox' - the immeasurable value of education and preparation. Dr. Hondros made this comment on the first day of our training. That day, this almost cliché metaphor struck a different chord in me; and throughout the week, the summation of our training rested on these simple, but vital words. The more tools you have, the more prepared you will be.

"It was week-long training that included didactic, hands-on, and observational learning. We studied all kinds of traumatic injuries including: thoracoabdominal trauma, TBIs (traumatic brain injuries), blast injuries, burns and others. We also got to spend an evening with the Chicago Fire

Department, and an evening in the ER - it's Chicago, which means…GSWs (gunshot wounds)! The program also included BDLS (Basic Disaster Life Support) and ITLS (International Trauma Life Support) training/certification with mass casualty simulation. The major highlights of the program are the Live Tissue Lab and Cadaver Lab. The Live Tissue Lab was by far the coolest thing I've ever seen or done medically. I was partnered with a nurse and we each sutured a laceration of a live, BEATING pig's heart! And the great news: we saved the pig! Twice! My first life was saved! In the Live Tissue Lab, we also got to perform a chest tube insertion, needle decompression and we practiced applying pressure to a severed femoral artery. This was also my first time getting to do a human cadaver lab, which was really cool! We practiced intubating with the laryngoscope and performed a cricothyrotomy. In BDLS and ITLS we learned about disasters with an emphasis on mass casualty situations. The program concluded with linking all of our skills and learning together in a simulated MASCAL (Mass Casualty) exercise.

"In light of the recent mass shooting in Las Vegas, this training is incredibly relevant. The reality is we don't know where or when it's going to happen next. But we can be certain it will, whether it's an active shooter, a natural disaster, or some other catastrophe. That's why tools and training like this are so important. I'm deeply grateful to have had this opportunity. Mr. Rogers once said, 'When I was a boy and I would see scary things in the news, my mother would say to me, "Look for the helpers. You will always find people who are helping."' How cool that we've been given the knowledge, skills, and compassion to be a helper." [183]

☆☆☆☆☆

Also this month, a portion of the unit deployed in support of Hurricane Irma. Capt Emily Applen recalls: "The 109th AES knew that we were 'in the bucket' for disaster relief for the quarter. Lt Col Susan Behrens, Commander, watched the news closely and several days before Hurricane Irma was set to hit, she was already asking for members' availability to provide assistance. We were finally tasked late morning on September 6, 2017 to report to the unit. Both of our augmented crews arrived and were put into crew rest the same day by 1500. The crews waited with anticipation while the hurricane took out power and completely devastated Puerto Rico. Our ground crew continued to watch the news and get updates from the CAT (Crisis Action Team) Cell to determine when we would be needed for potential AE missions. On September 9, our two crews were forward deployed to Scott AFB, IL for prepositioning. Prior to leaving the unit, we were fed a grilled steak and salad dinner cooked by our ground crew. The evening we departed was also the same night of the Air Force's 70th Anniversary Gala, which was held in the hangar at the 133rd AW. Senator Amy Klobuchar was in attendance, and she came out to the flight line just prior to us departing to thank us for our service and to bid us safe travels.

"Support for moving crews and equipment for this storm relief was great because it involved a Total Force effort. With help from an active duty front-end crew out of Dyess AFB, TX our two ANG crews were transported by C-130H to Scott AFB. This same front-end crew and plane were also transporting an AE crew from the 934th Reserve who were completing a separate mission first before picking us up to go to Scott on their way back to Texas.

"Once our crews got to Scott AFB, we continued being postured and ready to support. We were given a waiver to sit in Bravo alert for the week, which allowed us to launch within three hours at any time. Unfortunately, we never got any closer to the impacted area than Illinois and did not have an opportunity to transport any patients. We were flown home on a C-17 the afternoon of September 14. While it was difficult to be sent only to Illinois, this activation demonstrated that our unit is mission ready and able to provide support at a moment's notice."

Photo courtesy of Capt Emily Applen

The two augmented air evac crews who were activated and deployed to Scott AFB, IL for prepositioning in support of Hurricane Irma in Florida.

Back Row (L - R): Aric Sonnenschein and Annie Oberg
Front Row Standing (L - R): Tina Ruyle, Robert Buresh, Rory Connolly, Matt Monjes, Kathryn Kjellesvig, Susan Behrens (109th AES Commander), Kayla Goorhouse, Amber Hull, Brandon Reshetar, Lee Smith, Emily Applen, Brian Brothers, Elizabeth Lapolice

October. Exercise Southern Strike was held at Gulfport, Mississippi. SSgt "Jeff" Schmitt had this to say about unit members' participation: "Aeromedical evacuation crewmembers had a small part in this bigger joint multiple branch exercise. They operated out of a smaller base that housed some cockroaches. For this exercise, two of three primary aircraft utilized were the C-17 and C-130. Mixed crews deployed from Delaware, New York, Mississippi and North Carolina.

It was great to work with and share knowledge from other AE units that train in similar, but variably different ways. The 109th AES stood out as elite flyers."

Deployed - Letters from the Field: SSgt Taylor Juvland Nielsen

I remember one mission in particular when I was deployed. Throughout flight school and on simulated missions, we were taught to always prepare for a psychiatric emergency. It was typical on these missions to practice as if this was a real scenario. This is to prepare you so when/if it occurs, your muscle memory kicks in. Although we always prepared for this emergency, and you hear from your flight instructors stories that they experienced, you never think it will happen to you.

One day we were tasked with a routine mission, and everything had gone off without a hitch. We got our patients on the plane, sat down and prepared to taxi. I was sitting by one of the flight nurses, and in between us was a psychiatric patient. The patient had been very relaxed and calm all through the briefing. The plane began to taxi and as soon as it did, the patient began crying profusely. I asked the patient if he was okay and tried to reassure him that we would get him safely transported. I tried every manner of distraction and to get the flight nurse's attention. All of a sudden, the patient tore off his seatbelt and started to make a run toward the flight deck as we began taking off. At this point, it all became muscle memory and I remember getting up and grabbing the patient before he could make it any further. We were able to eventually calm down the patient and the rest of the mission went smoothly. This incident taught me a valuable lesson - you have to prepare for every situation. You just never know when something like this could happen to you.

Another mission that I participated in was an unexpected one. I and three other members of my crew had run a 10K race that night and had just finished huge plates of spaghetti. After returning to the dorm, we received a call that we were needed. One member of my crew got the call while she was still in the shower and ran out into the hallway with shampoo still in her hair. Another, had just started a load of laundry. A third member of my crew had just taken a laxative. Needless to say, we put our uniforms on as quickly as possible and ran out the door. We flew to where our patient was and brought him aboard. At this point, it struck us just how serious the situation was. The patient had gotten a hand caught in machinery and needed emergency surgery to save it. We needed to get this patient transported immediately or he would lose his hand. We alerted the pilots and prepared for takeoff.

I went to check on the patient after we were airborne, and noticed the oxygen level appeared to be dipping. I quickly put the patient on one of our machines and started monitoring vitals. The flight nurse and I figured out that the opioids the patient had been given for pain, was causing him to not breathe properly. We followed protocol and got the patient to an appropriate oxygen level. As we continued on, the patient's respirations continued to get worse. We did everything we could, and he was finally able to maintain an acceptable oxygen saturation. I ended up strapping myself in and sitting with the patient for the remainder of the mission. We got him to the hospital and later found out that they did save the hand and he was doing fine. To this day, I still think about that mission. I wonder what happened after his discharge from medical care? But I know that whatever happened afterwards, my crew and I provided the absolute best care we could.

Photo courtesy of SSgt Taylor Juvland Nielsen

SSgt Taylor Juvland Nielsen - our "military" editor for this book.

SMSgt Mark Grieme retired on 1 Oct. Mark spent 38 total years of service (6 years as an Army medic, 17 years as an aeromed, and 15 years as an airfield manager). Although thirty of these years were served in technician status in various positions with the Minnesota Air National Guard, his heart remained with the aeromeds!

Photo courtesy of Lt Col Darcy Anderson
SMSgt Mark Grieme configuring a C-130 for a flight.

At some point in time, the authors found it necessary to cease writing the history of the unit and move on to the editing and publishing phases required to complete this project. Near the end of 2017, we decided this was the appropriate point in time to do so.

As we continued to work on this book through 2018 and into 2019, the unit gained a new Commander and we felt compelled, in the interest of a complete history of past and present commanders, to include one final chapter. Even though we have not added any written history following Lt Col Mathsen's comments, his stated goals for the future of the 109th indicate that the unit will continue to have a powerful presence in aerovac. The torch is now passed to a future generation in hopes that the next chapter of this exceptional squadron will continue to be recorded for posterity.

CHAPTER 16
The Command of Lt Col Curtis Mathsen

(Mar 2019 -   )

Photo courtesy of Lt Col Curtis Mathsen

Commander's Comments: I am writing this five months into my command.

Several things are clear:

1. *The 109th AES is a national leader in AE. It is comprised of dedicated, hard charging Airmen who love the mission.*
2. *The operational tempo with training and mission is extensive.*

My road to Commander was rather circuitous. I spent the first 11 years of my military career on active duty. I joined the Air Force out of nursing school and had assignments at Lackland AFB in Texas, Andrews AFB in D.C., Wright Patterson in Ohio and Mountain Home AFB in Idaho.

At Wilford Hall, I started as a clinical nurse on a cardiothoracic unit and then transitioned to the cardiothoracic ICU. While in the ICU, I developed an interest in anesthesia and was selected for Certified Registered Nurse Anesthetist (CRNA) school at Uniformed Services University for Health Sciences in Bethesda, MD with clinical training at Wright Patterson AFB. I returned to Wilford Hall for my first CRNA position. In 2003, there was a need for a CRNA at Mountain Home AFB. I enjoyed the chance to move from Wilford Hall, the "mothership" of the Air Force to a much smaller medical group with unique opportunities and challenges.

My 11 years of active duty can be summed up in one term - clinical focus. It was all about patient care. I enjoyed the readiness exercises, but never looked for or pursued leadership opportunities. In those 11 years I had minimal contact with the Air National Guard or Air Force Reserve. This is particularly odd, since Boise, ID has an ANG base, but we never trained together.

After 11 years of active duty, my wife and I decided it was time to return to the Midwest, plant some roots and look for a nice town to raise our two girls. I took a CRNA job in Wausau, WI.

Once you hit 10 years on active duty, halfway to retirement, the prevailing culture was to commit to staying for 20 or get out and finish up your career in the Guard or Reserve. The Mountain Home recruiter searched and found a potential opening for a nurse in the Medical Group at the 133rd Airlift Wing.

My sole clinical focus could not transition to Air National Guard nursing. This was the beginning of gaining a broader perspective of everything it takes for a medical group to run, an air wing to run, and how we fit into the big picture with DOD, reserve forces, other guard units, and local and state civilian entities. I found I enjoyed the challenge of working with teams and running programs.

I did stints as OIC of Awards and Decorations, Medical Readiness Officer, OIC of the Self-Aid/Buddy Care program and OIC of Education and Training. I was also a founding member of the Minnesota Chemical Biological Radiologic Nuclear (CBRN) high yield explosive Enhanced Response Force Package (CERFP). This is a Joint Air Guard, Army Guard team tasked to respond to disasters within our FEMA region. It provides search and rescue, decontamination, and emergency medical care and transport. I served as an Assistant Chief in the Medical Group and was then selected as the Chief Nurse of the CERFP team. Next, I applied for and was selected as Chief Nurse of the Medical Group.

I have been fortunate to have great mentors who helped me hone leadership skills, seek career developing opportunities, and network. I had seen the procession of the last two 109th AES Commanders, Lt Col Penny Hodges-Goetz and Lt Col Sue Behrens come over from the MDG

Chief Nurse position. I distinctly remember having lunch with Col Hodges-Goetz (after AES, she was selected as MDG Commander) at Highland Grill one drill weekend. She looked at me and said, "You should look to become the next AES Commander." Fast forward a few years, and my present MDG Commander, Col David Nelson, came over to the billeting lodge to "have a beer." His real reason was to inform me that I could expect to be named AES Commander in the next few months and offer some words of wisdom on assuming command.

Due to the nature of drill weekends with trying to pack as much as possible into the two days, I was not familiar with many of the 109th AES personnel even though they were only a building away.

Military people like to use the term "drinking from a firehose." When getting oriented to the position by Lt Col Behrens, I realized just how appropriate the term is.

My initial goals and thoughts:

1. *Get to know the people.*
2. *Get to know the mission.*
3. *Maintain the tradition of excellence that the 109th AES has established. It is definitely a leader in deployment excellence and training center for EMT Refresher courses, and the new TCCC (Tactical Combat Casualty Care) requirement.*
4. *I am blessed with a core of dedicated and knowledgeable full-time staff that keep me informed.*
5. *Transition from the focus on taking care of the wing members and domestic operations to focus on taking care of our ill and wounded warriors throughout the world.*
6. *The Airmen of the 109th AES have extensive training requirements of both ground and flight training.*

I am looking forward to getting all the aspects of my flight physical finalized so I can schedule flight school. The ability to train and deploy as a flight nurse will enhance my knowledge of the mission and allow me to care for our wounded warriors.

Projects I'm walking into:

1. *State-of-the-art C-130 fuselage trainer going into our warehouse. Combined training for Guard and Reserve flight teams.*
2. *Addition of three new flight crews and two AELT teams. Where are we going to fit these new Airmen in?*
3. *Upcoming deployment in the spring.*

I have had the opportunity to fly on some training missions and be able to observe the process from start to finish. I was impressed by the detailed orientation of the medics and nurses in ensuring safe setup, knowledge of incoming patients and being prepared for in-flight emergencies - either patient or aircraft related.

In future conflicts, AE may be tasked with caring for unregulated patients. We may encounter near peer adversaries and increased presence of Anti-Access/Area Denial (A2/AD) areas. The possibility of having a plane maximized with casualties and requiring triage and emergency care becomes a possibility. These scenarios and needed skills will be incorporated into exercise training plans.

Remember - your focus can change, always be open to opportunities, seek out and listen to strong mentors, and actively network. Always work hard.

Lt Col Curtis Mathsen

Photo courtesy of Tech. Sgt. Amy Lovgren, 133rd Airlift Wing's Public Affairs

Maj Meghan Grout directs the onload of patients up the ramp on a local training mission... the doorway to "The Best Care in the Air!"

Squadron Patch History

An effort was made to capture all the 109th AEF's/AES's patches, both official and unofficial.

Since the authors were members for only a portion of the 109th's history, our knowledge of all possible patches that existed was quite limited. Even though other patches may exist, we made every effort to get the word out to past and present aeromeds to help us out by letting us know what patches were associated with the 109th AEF/AES.

The results are what follows.

In 1964, the unit received its first "official" shoulder patch. The design evolved primarily from the unit's activation and deployment during the Berlin Crisis in 1961. The patch was a deep blue globe on a shield of light blue representing day and night (24-hour capability) as well as the world mission of the squadron. The arrow encircling the globe denoted speed and directness. The winged staff of Asclepius (the god of healing) symbolized the medical mission and the airborne nature of the unit's medical operation. [184]

(Photo courtesy of TSgt Richard Childs / Col Michael Germain)

In 1967 our parent command, the 133rd, was deactivated and the 109th AMEF became an autonomous unit. At that time, flights were not authorized a unit patch. Our original patch was retired and members began to wear the first of two unofficial patches, or "gopher patches."

These patches consisted of a caricature of the University of Minnesota Golden Gopher, holding a large syringe. The significance of the large white star behind the gopher is unknown. In 1969 or 1970 this patch was retired because of the concern about the image it portrayed, especially with the hippie and drug counterculture becoming a facet of the American scene.

(Photo courtesy of TSgt Richard Childs / Col Michael Germain)

It was replaced with a patch depicting a gopher holding a small medical bag. Some people, not knowing we were a medical unit, thought it represented a lunch box or tool kit. Period photos document that early members of the unit wore this patch into the mid-1980s. How long after, is not known.

(Photo courtesy of TSgt Richard Childs / Col Michael Germain)

In the course of our research into the history of the unit's initial shoulder patches displaying the Minnesota Gopher, the authors have documented just two such patches as displayed on the previous page. Dates of issue and length of service are still under investigation. However, we have been told by a number of former members they believe a "third" gopher patch was created sometime after 1975.

They described this patch as very similar to the second patch - the one with the gopher holding a small medical bag embossed with a minute red cross. This "third" patch was a duplication of the previous Golden Gopher only this time not holding the small medical bag.

As of this date, the authors have uncovered no evidence to support this belief. No definitive photo, sketch, or any written reference, "official or unofficial", has surfaced to date describing this "third" patch.

It is the conviction of the authors that only two "Gopher" patches were created and worn by unit members. The belief of a "third" patch might be explained by the following. Because of the white color and the minuscule size of the bag held against a white background (the gopher's stomach), the medical bag is virtually invisible. Thus when viewed, even from a short distance, the medical bag is extremely difficult if not impossible to visualize. Therefore, we believe that the many members who viewed this second patch and did not distinguish the small medical bag came to believe a "third" patch had been created.

If in fact a "third" patch was indeed created with just the gopher as describe above, the authors would be extremely grateful for hard evidence documenting its existence.

The Gopher patches were produced in limited numbers and by the mid-1980s had all but disappeared.

However, in 2018, the original Gopher patch (the one with the syringe) was reproduced and authorized for wear by the squadron as a "morale patch" as a tribute to the heritage of the unit.

In 1986, we were again authorized an "official" unit patch, similar in some respects to the original patch. The heritage was continued with the retention of the globe and winged staff. A significant change was the large red cross which dominated the globe and the addition of "TAC Evac" across the top.

(Photo courtesy of TSgt Richard Childs / Col Michael Germain)

Later, "TAC Evac" would be replaced with "Air Evac." "AEF" would become "AES" when we became a squadron in 1992.

(Photo courtesy of TSgt Richard Childs / Col Michael Germain)

SQUADRON PATCH HISTORY ★ 367

Instructors within the 109th AES wore this patch. Notice the AMC designation.

(Photo courtesy of TSgt Richard Childs / Col Michael Germain)

Examiners within the unit (who were also instructors) were issued this patch.

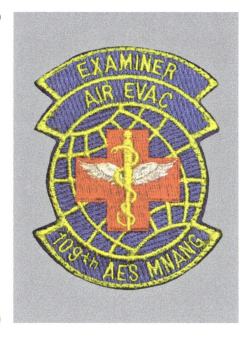

(Photo courtesy of TSgt Richard Childs / Col Michael Germain)

Examiners within the Stan/Eval shop were entitled to wear this patch.

(Photo courtesy of TSgt Richard Childs / Col Michael Germain)

The "Grim Reaper" patch was designed by Maj Kirsten Boehm when she was a radio operator for the 109th AES. This moral patch was created because it was determined that radio operators could not wear the unit medical patch as they were considered non-medical combatants. Feeling shut out, this new patch was developed and they were allowed to wear it on the shirts under the uniform or on PT gear. These patches quickly gained popularity and exchanged with other radio operators in the aerovac community. The symbol of the grim reaper over the regular squadron patch signified combatants in a medical unit.

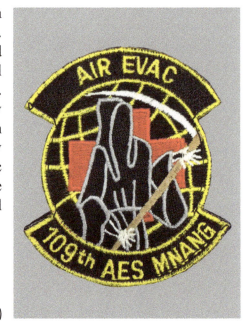

(Photo courtesy of MSgt Rob Buresh)

SQUADRON PATCH HISTORY ★ 369

This Provisional (P) patch was created for Operation Desert Shield/Storm and worn by all deployed air evac units in theater. The "1611" was developed by adding up all the participating air evac unit numbers (i.e. 109 for the 109th and so on).

(Photo courtesy of TSgt Richard Childs / Col Michael Germain)

Maj Gary Horton recognized that after Desert Shield/Desert Storm only generic contingency patches were available. He came up with the idea of designing a 109th AES patch to commemorate the service of our aeromeds during the war effort. Horton gave the patch sketch to his 17-year-old son who finished the computer design and sent it off to have 100 patches made - the minimum order. They were sold at cost and with only 100 available, are hard to come by today.

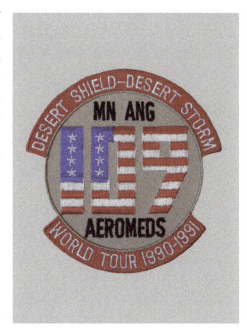

(Photo courtesy of TSgt Richard Childs / Col Michael Germain)

Squadron Coin, Flight Scarf, Hat History

Photo courtesy of TSgt Richard Childs / Col Michael Germain

Photo courtesy of TSgt Richard Childs / Col Michael Germain

While serving in Hungary for Operation Joint Endeavor in 1996, SSgt Michael Granlund, SSgt Steve Burmeister and SSgt Bryan Steven made the dream of a 109th AES coin come true, making the squadron the wing's first to produce an official coin.

The process actually began before the aeromeds deployed. After SSgt Burmeister came up with the idea, he and SSgt Steven came up with some preliminary sketches. The final design for the face of the coin would be a C-130 imposed over the state of Minnesota. SSgt Steven found the state outline on a phone book and SSgt Granlund got the C-130 image from a postcard.

Costs for producing a coin would be high, but in Germany, a lot of money could be saved, even on an exceptionally high-quality coin made of solid pewter. The coins were also numbered, with two framed for display: #109 for the Aeromed building and #133 for the Wing Headquarters. Only 800 were originally minted.

As for the cash backing, SSgt Burmeister and SSgt Granlund came up with the $250 down payment, and then SSgt Granlund came up with the $1,800 to cover the remainder when the coins were delivered.

The new coins went on sale for $10 each, beginning with the December holiday party on 14 Dec, 1996. As a limited edition coin, the mold was scheduled to be broken after 1000 coins were produced. [185]

Photo courtesy of TSgt Richard Childs / Col Michael Germain

Photo courtesy of TSgt Richard Childs / Col Michael Germain

In 2013, the unit coin was redesigned.

Capt Ryan Ketterling remembered, "In 2013, the squadron was preparing for the 109th AES Founders Day/Reunion. It was decided that it might be a good time to redesign the unit coin, and do so in a way that would honor the history of the organization. Col Matt Peterson, CMSgt Dan Cisar and I discussed the concept of creating a Heritage Coin, with unique attributes that would focus on the organizational changes throughout the last 50 years.

"The front side of the coin focused on three key areas: the global impact on AE, the C-130 aircraft, and the state of Minnesota. One of the most notable changes that would signify the transition of the organization throughout the years were the different unit patches. We decided to use three patches as a foundation for the back of the coin."

Col Matt Peterson recalled, "During the run-up to the Founders Day/Reunion, many members of the squadron were curious about the heritage of the unit. Of course, they had heard the many stories that had been shared by senior members, but there were few artifacts that tied the rich history together. That was the inspiration of the coin...to create an artifact that represented all of us that have served and continue to serve in the 109th AES."

✫✫✫✫✫

All C-130 units transferred to Air Combat Command in Oct of 1993. At this time flyers were issued flight scarves which were to be worn at all times with the flight suit except when flying. The scarf was worn until the unit returned to Air Mobility Command in April of 1997.

Photo courtesy of TSgt Richard Childs / Col Michael Germain

It should be noted that the following unit hats were not an issued item. They had to be purchased by individual aeromeds.

Photo courtesy of Lt Col Robert Hecht
First known aeromed hat from the late 1960s.

Photo courtesy of Col Glen Ramsborg
Aeromed hat, circa 1977.

Photo courtesy of SMSgt Mark Grieme
Trio of aeromed caps from the late 1980s.

Photo courtesy of SMSgt Mark Grieme
Latest aeromed hat, circa 2002.

Credits

Prologue	[1]	Video interview with Brig Gen Goodrich, Aug 2013
	[2]	Phone interview with Maj Gen Dolny, Aug 2017

Chapter 1   The Command of Maj Edward Doyle
- [3] Northstar Guardian, May 1961
- [4] Interview with Capt Dorothea Tenney, Dec 2016
- [5] Interview with Capt Jean Cool, Dec 2016
- [6] Video interview with Capt Dorothea Tenney, Aug 2013
- [7] Letter from A1C David Lund, Sep 2017
- [8] Interview with Capt Dorothea Tenney, Dec 2016
- [9] Interview with Capt Dorothea Tenney, Dec 2016
- [10] Interview with Capt Jean Cool, Dec 2016
- [11] Video interview with Lt Col Robert Hecht, Aug 2013
- [12] Letter from A1C David Lund, Sep 2017
- [13] Interview with Capt Dorothea Tenney, Dec 2016
- [14] Video interview with Lt Col Robert Hecht, Aug 2013
- [15] Interview with Capt Dorothea Tenney, Dec 2016
- [16] St. Paul Pioneer Press, 24 Jun 1962
- [17] Interview with Capt Betty Cook, Dec 2016
- [18] Northstar Guardian, Nov 1962
- [19] Interview with Capt Dorothea Tenney, Dec 2016
- [20] Interview with Capt Dorothea Tenney, Dec 2016

Chapter 2   The Command of Col Harry Nelson
- [21] Video interview with Col Harry Nelson, Aug 2013
- [22] Interview with Capt Dorothea Tenney, Dec 2016
- [23] Jackie Germann, Staff Writer, St. Paul Pioneer Press, 30 Jun 1963
- [24] E-mail exchange with Lt Col Russ Jensen, Jul 2017
- [25] Lt Col Georgeanne Johnson, Vital Signs Supplement, Mar 2008
- [26] Interview with Capt Dorothea Tenney, Dec 2016
- [27] Northstar Guardian, Mar 1964
- [28] Lt Col Georgeanne Johnson, Vital Signs Supplement, Jun 2008
- [29] "A Fit, Fighting Force," The AF Nursing Services Chronology, 2005
- [30] Northstar Guardian, Jun 1964
- [31] Video interview with Col Eszlinger Jensen, Aug 2013

	[32]	Northstar Guardian, Mar 1966
	[33]	Fred Bereswill (pilot) as written in "Once a Jock…" by Roy Mantz
	[34]	Northstar Guardian, Dec 1966
	[35]	Interview with Col Julie Eszlinger Jensen, Dec 2016
Chapter 3		The Command of Lt Col Henry Capiz
	[36]	"A Fit, Fighting Force," The AF Nursing Services Chronology, 2005
	[37]	Northstar Guardian, Feb 1986
	[38]	Northstar Guardian, Mar 1971
	[39]	Northstar Guardian, Nov 1971
	[40]	Northstar Guardian, Mar 1971
	[41]	"A Fit, Fighting Force," The AF Nursing Services Chronology, 2005
	[42]	Northstar Guardian, Jun 1972
Chapter 4		The Command of Col Harry Nelson
Chapter 5		(known command vacancy)
	[43]	A Commemorative History of the 133rd Airlift Wing (1996)
Chapter 6		The Command of Lt Col David Molin
	[44]	Northstar Guardian, Jun 1978
	[45]	TSgt Jo Ann Anders, Northstar Guardian, May 1979
	[46]	A Commemorative History of the 133rd Airlift Wing (1996)
	[47]	Northstar Guardian, Jun/Jul 1980
Chapter 7		The Command of Col Julie Eszlinger Jensen
	[48]	Interview conducted with Col Julie Eszlinger Jensen, Dec 2016
	[49]	Northstar Guardian, Feb 1981
	[50]	Northstar Guardian, Oct 1981
	[51]	Northstar Guardian, Oct 1981
	[52]	Northstar Guardian, Jan 1983
	[53]	Northstar Guardian, Nov 1981
	[54]	Northstar Guardian, May 1982
	[55]	Northstar Guardian, Aug 1982
	[56]	"A Fit, Fighting Force," The AF Nursing Services Chronology, 2005
	[57]	Northstar Guardian, Nov 1982
	[58]	"A Fit, Fighting Force," The AF Nursing Services Chronology, 2005
	[59]	Northstar Guardian, May 1984
	[60]	Maj Darcy Anderson, 109th AEF, Northstar Guardian, Feb 1985
	[61]	Northstar Guardian, Feb 1985
	[62]	Northstar Guardian, May 1986
	[63]	Northstar Guardian, Jun 1986

[64] Lt Col Neal Gendler, Northstar Guardian, Jul 1986
[65] Northstar Guardian, May 1987
[66] Northstar Guardian, Jul 1988
[67] Northstar Guardian, Jun 1987
[68] Sgt Kirsty McNee, Northstar Guardian, Jan 1988
[69] News Release from the Dept. of Military Affairs, Office of the Adjutant General, St. Paul, MN, 29 Feb 1988
[70] Sgt Kirsty McNee, Northstar Guardian, Fall 1988
[71] Northstar Guardian, Oct 1989

Chapter 8   The Command of Lt Col Darcy Anderson
[72] Northstar Guardian, May 1989
[73] Northstar Guardian, Jun 1989
[74] SSgt Dale Eckroth, AF Recruiting Service, Northstar Guardian, Aug 1989
[75] MSgt Robert Janssen, 109th AEF, Northstar Guardian, Jan 1990
[76] Northstar Guardian, Apr 1990
[77] Capt Kathleen Zappia, 133rd TAW/PA, Northstar Guardian, Jul 1990
[78] Capt Kathleen Zappia, 133rd TAW/PA, Northstar Guardian, Sep 1990
[79] Northstar Guardian, Sep 1990
[80] militarybases.com
[81] "A Fit, Fighting Force," The AF Nursing Services Chronology, 2005
[82] Vital Signs, Sep 1990
[83] St. Paul Pioneer Press, 4 Oct 1990
[84] TSgt Joseph Shafer/Capt Kathleen Zappia, Northstar Guardian, Nov-Dec 1990
[85] Northstar Guardian, Oct 1990
[86] A Commemorative History of the 133rd Airlift Wing (1996)
[87] Philip Shenon, The New York Times, 26 Dec 1990
[88] Northstar Guardian, Jan 1991
[89] Lt Col Donna Alt, 109th AEF Chief Nurse, Northstar Guardian, Apr 1991
[90] Northstar Guardian, Mar 1991
[91] MSgt Robert Janssen, 109th AEF, Northstar Guardian, Feb 1991
[92] Northstar Guardian, Apr 1991
[93] Northstar Guardian, May 1991
[94] A Commemorative History of the 133rd Airlift Wing (1996)
[95] SSgt Richard Childs, 109th AEF, Northstar Guardian, Aug 1991
[96] Maj Kathleen Zappia, 133rd TAW/PA, Northstar Guardian, Sep 1991
[97] "A Fit, Fighting Force," The AF Nursing Services Chronology, 2005
[98] Northstar Guardian, Jan 1992
[99] 1st Lt Gail Fellman, Vital Signs, May 1992
[100] SrA Kim Graupe, Vital Signs, Aug 1992
[101] Lt Sue Schuldt, Vital Signs, Aug 1992

[102] Patty Johnson, Vital Signs, Nov 1992
[103] Northstar Guardian, Jan 1993
[104] Vital Signs, Nov 1992
[105] A Commemorative History of the 133rd Airlift Wing (1996)
[106] Maj Cherie Huntington, 133rd AW/PA, Northstar Guardian, Aug/Sep 1993
[107] Capt Bill Horvath, Vital Signs, Apr 1993

Chapter 9   The Command of Col Sandy Carlson

[108] Northstar Guardian, Aug - Sep 1993
[109] Northstar Guardian, Oct 1993
[110] TSgt Kelly Lovely, 133rd AW/PA, Northstar Guardian, Oct 1993
[111] Northstar Guardian, Oct 1993
[112] Joe Winter, The Hudson Star-Observer, Hudson, WI, Northstar Guardian, Jan 1994
[113] Capt Kevin Gutknecht, HQ PA, Northstar Guardian, Nov/Dec 1993
[114] Maj Cherie Huntington, 133rd AW/PA, Northstar Guardian, May 1994
[115] TSgt Kelly Lovely, 133rd AW/PA, Northstar Guardian, Apr 1994
[116] "A Fit, Fighting Force," The AF Nursing Services Chronology, 2005
[117] Maj Cherie Huntington, 133rd AW/PA, Northstar Guardian, Jun 1994
[118] A Commemorative History of the 133rd Airlift Wing (1996)
[119] Vital Signs, Aug 1994
[120] Maj Sandy Darula, Vital Signs, Oct 1994
[121] Maj Cherie Huntington, Public Affairs, Northstar Guardian, Oct 1994
[122] TSgt Kelly Lovely, 133rd AW/PA, Northstar Guardian, Jan 1995
[123] TSgt Kelly Lovely, 133rd AW/PA, Northstar Guardian, May 1995
[124] Capt Susan Schuldt, Vital Signs, Aug 1995
[125] Vital Signs, Sep 1995
[126] Vital Signs, Mar 1996
[127] Lt Col Sandy Carlson, Vital Signs, Apr 1996
[128] "A Fit, Fighting Force," The AF Nursing Services Chronology, 2005
[129] Vital Signs, Sep 1996
[130] Capt Jim Caldwell, Vital Signs, Aug 1996
[131] Vital Signs, Sep 1996
[132] Northstar Guardian, Dec 1996
[133] Maj Cherie Huntington, Public Affairs, Northstar Guardian, Nov 1996
[134] Vital Signs, Jan 1997
[135] Vital Signs, Aug 1997
[136] Capt Hennessy, Vital Signs, Sep 1997
[137] Northstar Guardian, Dec 1997
[138] Capt Lorraine Hennessy, Vital Signs, Mar 1998
[139] "A Fit, Fighting Force," The AF Nursing Services Chronology, 2005

CREDITS ☆ 379

[140] TSgt Doug Oswald, Northstar Guardian, Jun 1998
[141] Minnesota Militia, Dec 1998
[142] Northstar Guardian, Aug 1998
[143] Vital Signs, Nov 1998
[144] Northstar Guardian, Dec 1998

Chapter 10   The Command of Col Karen Wolf
[145] Northstar Guardian, Sep 1999
[146] Vital Signs, Oct 1999
[147] Vital Signs, Aug 2000
[148] Vital Signs, Oct 2000
[149] Lt Col Karen Wolf, Vital Signs, Jul 2001
[150] Lt Col Karen Wolf, Vital Signs, Aug 2001
[151] Vital Signs, Aug 2001

Chapter 11   The Command of Lt Col Sharon Rosburg
[152] Northstar Guardian, Jun 2001
[153] Lt Col Sharon Rosburg, Vital Signs, Nov 2001
[154] Capt Pat Howard, Vital Signs, Apr 2002
[155] SSgt Heather Gillette, Public Affairs, Northstar Guardian, Jun 2002
[156] SSgt Heather Gillette, Public Affairs, Northstar Guardian, Jun 2002

Chapter 12   The Command of Lt Col Georgeanne Johnson
[157] SSgt Heather Gillette, Public Affairs, Northstar Guardian, Jun 2003
[158] SSgt Heather Gillette, Public Affairs, Northstar Guardian, Oct 2003
[159] SSgt Heather Gillette, Public Affairs, Northstar Guardian / AF Print News, Feb 2004
[160] Betty Kennedy, AMC History Office, Northstar Guardian, Sep/Oct 2004
[161] Lt Col Donald Dahlquist, Vital Signs, Jun 2005
[162] 2d Lt Sheree Savage, Wing Public Affairs, Northstar Guardian, Dec 2005
[163] Lt Col Johnson, Vital Signs, Oct 2005
[164] MSgt Mark Moss, Wing Public Affairs, Northstar Guardian, Dec 2007
[165] The MN Chapter of the Military Officers Association of America, May 2008
[166] Lt Col Johnson, Vital Signs, May 2009
[167] Lt Col Johnson, Vital Signs, May 2009

Chapter 13   The Command of Col Penny Hodges-Goetz
[168] Northstar Guardian, Fall 2009
[169] Lt Col Howard, Vital Signs, Sep 2009
[170] TSgt Amber Monio, Wing PA, Northstar Guardian, Summer 2011
[171] Vital Signs, Mar 2012

[172] Vital Signs, Mar 2012
[173] SSgt Jonathan Young, 133rd AW, Northstar Guardian, Summer 2012
[174] Jordan Garretson, MLB.com, 27 May 2012
[175] SSgt Jonathan Young, Northstar Guardian, Fall 2012

Chapter 14   The Command of Col Matt Peterson
[176] Capt Laura Mitricska, Vital Signs, Oct 2013
[177] Vital Signs, Jun 2014

Chapter 15   The Command of Lt Col Sue Behrens
[178] Vital Signs, Jun/Jul 2015
[179] TSgt Lynette Olivares/TSgt Paul Santikko, Northstar Guard Online, Aug 2015
[180] SrA Hope Tucker and SrA Jordan Paige, Vital Signs, May 2016
[181] Maj Jason Arndt, Vital Signs, Jul/Aug 2016
[182] Vital Signs, Feb 2017
[183] SSgt Emily Stanzyk, Vital Signs, Oct 2017

Chapter 16   The Command of Lt Col Curt Mathsen

Patch History   [184] Northstar Guardian, Dec 1964

Coin History   [185] Northstar Guardian, Dec 1996

Past and Present Flight and Squadron Commanders

AES Lt Col John Drayna   (June 1961 - Sep 1961)
     Maj Wayne Janzig   (Sep 1961 - May 1966)
     Maj Franklin Snapp   (May 1966 - Aug 1967)

(squadron deactivated and units under its command became autonomous units)

AEF Maj Edward Doyle   (Jun 1961 - Apr 1963)
     Col Harry Nelson   (Apr 1963 - Jul 1967)
     Lt Col Henry Capiz   (Jul 1967 - Aug 1973)
     Col Harry Nelson   (Aug 1973 - Feb 1977)
     known vacancy   (Feb 1977 - Oct 1977)
     Lt Col David Molin   (Oct 1977 - Nov 1980)
     Col Julie Eszlinger Jensen   (Nov 1980 - Mar 1989)
     Lt Col Darcy Anderson   (Mar 1989 - Jul 1993)
     Col Sandy Carlson   (Jul 1993 - Apr 1999)
     Col Karen Wolf   (Apr 1999 - Sep 2001)
     Lt Col Sharon Rosburg   (Sep 2001 - Feb 2003)
     Lt Col Georgeanne Johnson   (Apr 2003 - Jun 2009)
     Col Penny Hodges-Goetz   (Jun 2009 - Jan 2013)
     Col Matt Peterson   (Jan 2013 - Nov 2014)
     Lt Col Sue Behrens   (Nov 2014 - Mar 2019)
     Lt Col Curt Mathsen   (Mar 2019 -   )

Aeromedical Evacuation Training Flights (A Historical Perspective)

What made the strongest impression upon the authors over the course of the research for this book was how aeromedical evacuation training had evolved over the years for the 109th AES. Having begun our flying careers 35 years ago, we found this change to be profound. We envisioned that the aeromeds from the past would be interested in how current AECMs train for real-world contingencies, and along those same lines, we felt that current crewmembers would enjoy a historical perspective on how training had evolved over the years.

In addition, since the inception of the unit, the medical equipment utilized and available to our aeromedical evacuation aircrews has gone through numerous permutations and upgrades. We will highlight several of the more important pieces of equipment that illustrate these changes.

What better way to accomplish this task than to fly with the unit on a local training mission. Arranging such a flight, however, proved to be a daunting task. We thought that it would be a slam dunk for two retired aeromeds with over 2,000 hours of flight time in the C-130 - including multiple deployments during Operation Desert Shield/Storm - to get permission to ride along on a local training mission to gain an insight on the evolution of training over the years. Even though the wing was frequently granting flights for a variety of youth groups, we were officially turned down after nearly three years of requests beginning at the unit level and ending up with an official denial from a brigadier general at State Headquarters in Minnesota. Two options remained. One was to fly on a cross-country training flight in the Space-A (Space Available) status as retired military. Since these flights were very infrequent, difficult to arrange with our civilian work schedule and nearly impossible to arrange with the wing's aircraft availability during numerous ongoing contingency operations, this option was ruled out. The remaining possibility was to "fly" with the aeromeds on a ground mission in a static aircraft - otherwise known as a Ground FTP. This goal was finally accomplished when the authors were granted the opportunity to observe a Ground FTP training mission in October of 2019.

Hopefully we are able to convey many of the differences in training over the years for our readers in the following pages. Please keep in mind that the time frame by which we are comparing training activities range from the 1980s and 1990s to the present.

As for the mission itself, we met with the crewmembers at 1700 in the Mission Briefing Room at the 109th AES. Several things stood out once we entered this setting. World maps covered the walls to orient everyone to the existing scenario. High tech audiovisual equipment and a telephone speaker system were also apparent. Perhaps one of the most striking discoveries was the new two-piece camouflage flight suit that most crewmembers were wearing - much different than the one-piece green Nomex flight suit that had been worn in previous decades.

Once introductions were made, the crewmembers were told to get out their checklists to begin the mission brief. To our amazement and surprise, they all pulled out their own issued iPad Mini! Of everything that we were able to see on this training mission, this, in our opinion has to have been the biggest advancement in the aeromedical evacuation toolkit in the past 30-40 years. The iPad incorporated two items that had been used in the system for decades - the traditional crew checklist and current publications/regulations used in aerovac. The old crew checklist consisted of paper pages enclosed in individual plastic sleeves, bound with circular ring clips and was usually carried in the lower leg pocket of the flight suit for easy retrieval during the flight. As aerovac progressed throughout the years, crews became tri-qualified on three different airframes - the C-130, KC-135, and the C-17. Needless to say, the traditional checklists increased in size as well.

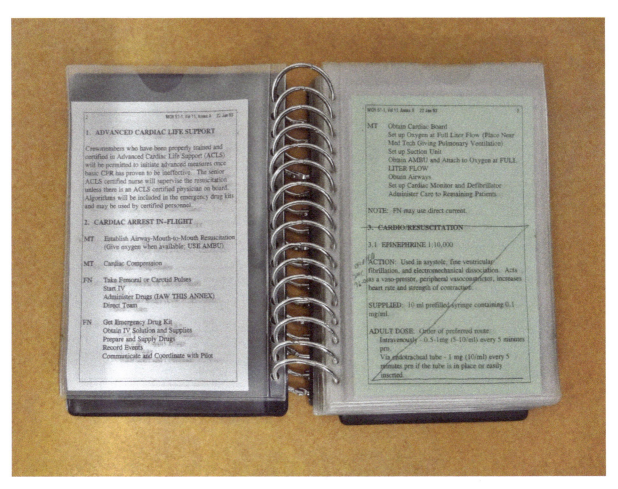

Photo courtesy of TSgt Richard Childs and Col Michael Germain
Old crew checklist.

In the past, crewmembers also carried copies of their pubs and regs in a large, bulky, heavy, brown briefcase on every flight.

Photo courtesy of TSgt Richard Childs and Col Michael Germain
Old pubs and regs briefcase.

The iPad replaced both of these items with a tremendous savings in weight and a much improved ease of accessibility. In addition, back in the day, individual "pen and ink changes" had to be painstakingly made to each crewmember's paper pubs and regs, sometimes taking hours to accomplish this menial task. Today, changes are automatically "pushed" or updated from the Internet weekly so the information is always up-to-date with no effort required by the crewmember to do the updating. It should be noted that the crews still fly with one paper copy of the pubs and regs as a backup. More on the iPad later.

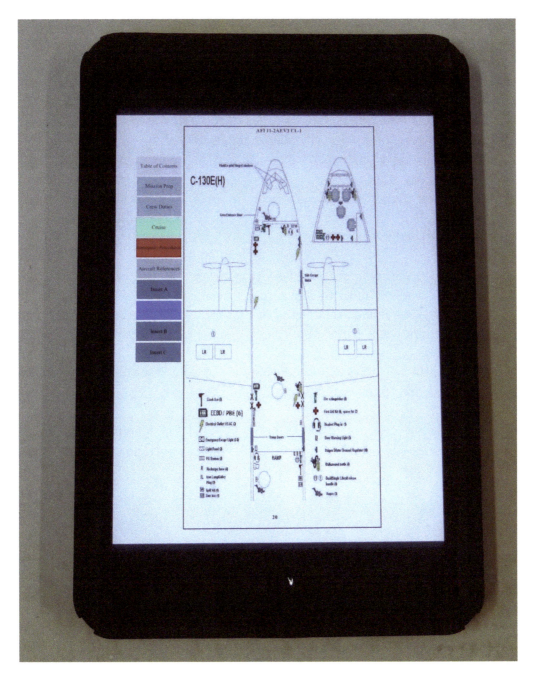

Photo courtesy of TSgt Richard Childs and Col Michael Germain
iPad.

We also noticed that safety (as in the past) was a high priority item. A new AECM Risk Management Worksheet was utilized to assess factors that might negatively affect the flight, such as a crewmember's health status and stress level, sleep, flight time, number and severity of anticipated patients, etc. Approval for a high risk flight was required and additional crewmembers might be assigned to the mission to deal with this increased risk.

Unlike flights earlier in the unit's history, numerous calculations are now required to satisfy current regs. The CMT was responsible for calculating the amperage required of all of the electrical medical equipment for the flight. They also totaled the weight of the equipment that they would bring on board to satisfy weight and balance requirements for the aircraft. This was a requirement that has been observed since about 2004. When deployed, this might amount to 1,800 pounds of gear. In comparison, early aeromed flights carried only a couple hundred pounds or less. Total oxygen requirements were also calculated for the duration of the flight to ensure the aeromeds had enough oxygen for patient needs.

Communications channel assignments were made (more on this later), infection control station setup was discussed, BLS and ACLS crewmembers were identified and duties assigned, and egress and ditching procedures were reviewed.

We were impressed with the comprehensive review that was conducted of all of the patients which included an in-depth assessment of their diagnoses, medication requirements, past treatments at the medical facility, anticipated treatments in-flight, etc. This was accomplished patient by patient with an opportunity to ask questions that any of the crewmembers might have had.

Training goals were also discussed so all of the crew was aware of what was to be accomplished, ensuring that all these objectives would be met.

Our simulated mission was an urgent aerovac on a C-130H which consisted of five adults and one child who were injured in a mortar attack. Three attendants would accompany the crew and patients.

We noticed that the briefing took longer than earlier aeromed briefings, but included much more critical information which was presented in greater detail. Time was used efficiently and everyone (including the patients) knew exactly what was to be accomplished on the training mission.

The medical equipment had already been loaded in an enclosed truck instead of being loaded in the back of a pickup, exposed to the elements as on early aeromed flights. Today, aeromedical gear is housed in a warehouse with most of it already secured on litters, ready to load right onto the aircraft. Back in the day, we utilized a very small room and all of the equipment was stored on shelves which had to be individually pulled and secured to litters for each flight. Current practices also utilize computer scanning of the equipment litters as they were removed and returned to the warehouse. All in all, it was a very efficient way to handle and account for all of their gear.

Photo courtesy of TSgt Richard Childs and Col Michael Germain

Medical equipment in the warehouse, preloaded and secured to litters in an "always ready to go" status.

The configuration of the aircraft was much more involved than in the past. In the early years, we had no oxygen or electrical lines to string, no walkaround oxygen bottles to charge, and very little medical equipment to secure. In contrast, oxygen lines and electrical cables were strategically weaved in and amongst the aircraft superstructure so it was available for all contingencies. In addition, much of the medical equipment that was secured to litters was strategically placed for emergency use.

The MCC, as in the past, functioned as the medical facility representative and gave a very thorough and detailed accounting of each patient which included recent medications and changes in medical status, along with the handing off all the paperwork and the anti-hijacking form. This event was covered in much more detail than we remember from earlier aeromed flights. Today MCCs are also qualified as flight instructors. Graduation from a two-week course is required for this certification. This allows the MCC to coordinate with the instructor, thus greatly improving the quality of training given the student med tech/nurse on each flight.

The onload of patients appeared to have remained the same over the years except for one added detail. We had the same "prepare to lift - lift" command where, in one movement, we would lift the litter and place it into the stanchion brackets. Today, they lift the litter vertically on that command and then use a second statement "prepare to rack - rack" to move the litter laterally into the brackets.

Once airborne, the first duty of the crew was to check their patients. Almost immediately, the psych patient became agitated and uncooperative. The crew quickly responded to the simulated crisis and when unable to "deescalate" the situation, resorted to medication to get the patient rapidly under control.

Crewmembers informed us that on deployed missions they are able to accomplish their patient charting on laptops, an option that earlier aeromed crews did not have. At the end of the flight, they simply burned the patient's charting information to a disk and with the other records turned it over to the receiving medical facility. This was a major time-saving advantage allowing for a detailed and accurate record of treatment administered during the flight.

Back to the iPad. This device was introduced to the general public in 2010 and issued to unit members in 2013. In addition to containing the information and resources mentioned above, crewmembers are able to access the Aeromedical Evacuation Clinical Protocols (AECPs) on their iPad which gives detailed data concerning different medical conditions and diagnoses that they may encounter on various missions. Background information, signs and symptoms, medications and treatment protocols were available at the click of a button. This is a tremendous and timely resource available to each and every crewmember on their iPad. We noticed all of the crew referencing this material during the two patient emergencies encountered on this flight. We were also told that simulated patients can reference this publication before being prompted to act out during a medical emergency to enhance the realism of the signs and symptoms that an actual patient might exhibit in a real-world situation.

In the past, most simulated medical emergencies were treated in accordance with the medical expertise that each flight nurse and med tech had experience-wise. For the most part, this was not a comprehensive and standard way to treat patients. We carried the Lippincott Manual of Nursing Practice as a reference and it is still carried on all missions today. Neither of us can remember ever opening that book on a mission. In stark contrast, the Aeromedical Evacuation Clinical Protocols is a great reference that current aeromeds have at their fingertips and use quite often.

After each of the medical emergencies we observed, a thorough debrief of the emergency took place discussing in great detail the diagnosis, treatment and medication administered (which included contraindications, duration of action and alternative drugs that could be used). We saw this as a mini-learning opportunity and thought it was a great way to wind up each emergency. In addition, real-world experience was discussed as many of these crewmembers had numerous deployments under their belt.

The aircraft emergency for our flight was a rapid decompression. Current crewmembers carry the latest personal oxygen equipment for this emergency and for a smoke/fire situation on the aircraft. When we started flying, there was no aeromedical crew oxygen. Later, walkaround oxygen bottles were added which incorporated an oxygen mask and a yellow rubber strap that went around the head to secure the mask. This was followed by a quick don mask that consisted of a spring-loaded bracket that one could quickly place around the head to secure the mask. There was still no way to protect one's eyes from smoke and other noxious agents until they came out with a separate set of goggles to use with the oxygen mask. Now, the aeromeds have a whole facemask/goggle system for these emergencies.

Photo courtesy of TSgt Richard Childs and Col Michael Germain
Walkaround oxygen bottle and facemask.

One last piece of equipment needs to be mentioned that has undergone numerous and innovative changes over the years - communications gear for the aeromedical crew. The C-130 is a loud environment to work in and combining hearing protection with communications capability was a real challenge to overcome.

Early aeromed crews simply shouted commands during the flight. In the event of a medical emergency, a "runner" often had to be employed to get additional help or supplies. It was a challenging way to operate and train.

In the late 1970s, the 109th AEF developed a solution - at least for training. Per their request, the 133rd Maintenance Squadron developed two aluminum "Comm (Communication) Boxes." Each one was about the size of a large tackle box and contained six 25-foot cables which could be connected to aeromed headsets. Powered by the aircraft electrical system, six aeromeds could now communicate with each other with relative ease.

These "Comm Boxes" quickly became the staple for training missions and offered many options for use. With two of them, personnel could run two missions at once on a cross-country flight, or leave one at home base for local training missions and use the other on a cross-country mission. Connecting both "Comm Boxes" together enabled twelve aeromeds to be in constant communication during the flight.

However, this newest innovation was not without fault. On some training missions with examiners, instructors, students and crewmembers, they often approached the maximum of twelve crewmembers all trying to talk over one another on the only "channel" available. Throw into this mix the twelve 25-foot cords that snaked all over the aircraft and it made for one interesting situation. Having a headset jerked from one's head was not an uncommon occurrence when the comm cord got caught on some aircraft structure or another aeromed tripped over the cord. Needless to say, this was both annoying and dangerous.

Many crewmembers found that while the headsets did not provide "adequate" hearing protection, hearing conversations in the headset with both earplugs in made it difficult to use it effectively. As a result, some aeromeds would resort to using only one earplug while using the headset.

In addition, the "Comm Boxes," although used for regular training, were left home during field exercises where we trained in a more realistic environment. Since they were built specifically for the 109th AEF, they were not available Air Force-wide and therefore not used during Operation Just Cause in Panama nor were they deployed with crews in the Middle East during Operation Desert Shield/Desert Storm.

Photo courtesy of Joe Jensen
**Aeromeds using headsets and "Comm Box" communication cables, circa 1980.
(actual "Comm Box" not shown)**

Enter the cordless headset. Sometime around the mid-1990s, the aeromeds tried out a dozen cordless, battery powered headsets. Since the communications channel was voice activated and was not always "hot" or "on" like the old "Comm Box" system, we soon discovered that the first few syllables of one's communication was needed to activate the device. Therefore, sentences were often clipped short, communications were hampered and for the most part the headsets were useless. If a crewmember yelled a single syllable word such as "Fire!", it wouldn't even be broadcasted over the communication system!

Today, a much advanced version is used with multiple channels available so instructors and examiners could go "offline" on another channel and privately talk to a crewmember without disruption of other mission communications. These Bose headsets also featured active noise cancelling features that enhanced the communication capabilities to a level never experienced before and provided more intrinsic hearing protection than the first headsets that were used with the older "Comm Boxes." This latest version of in-flight aeromed communications has greatly enhanced training, patient care and safety for all involved.

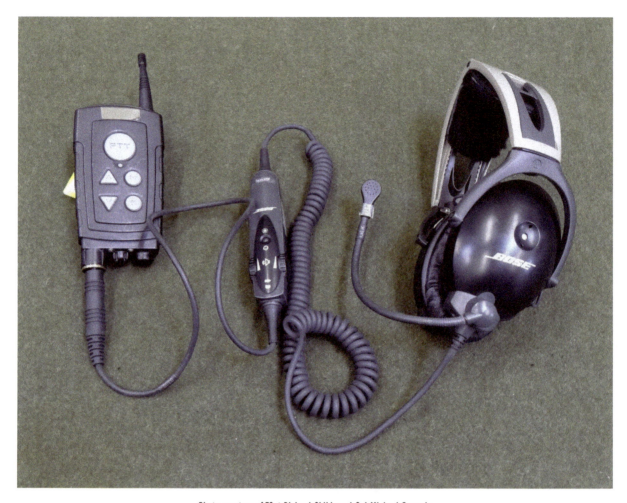

Photo courtesy of TSgt Richard Childs and Col Michael Germain
Aeromed wireless communication headsets.

As a side note, in the early 1990s an aeromed came up with a homemade "comm box" the size of a deck of cards that could be placed in the upper left chest pocket of the flight suit. This was powered by a 9 Volt battery and up to three individuals could connect to this personal "comm box." Unfortunately, when a non-aeromed crewmember discovered that we were using these unauthorized devices, they were banned from all future flights.

What training that was practiced in the past is no longer taught? Current aeromeds no longer train on the Stryker frame as it is in the process of being deleted from the system. In addition, due to safety concerns, aeromeds no longer practice actually exiting the three overhead escape hatches as we did in the past.

Photo courtesy of the 109th AES archives
Stryker frame.

Looking back over the years, it might appear that we have slighted or even disparaged the training of our early aeromeds. That is definitely not the case nor our intention. Like everything else over time, training has become more intensive, equipment has improved, and new procedures have been developed and refined. We want to acknowledge that the early aeromeds did a great job with what they had, as evidenced by the numerous awards and successful early deployments that are documented throughout this book.

What we did come away with was the incredible training and skill sets that current aeromeds possess today. It is quite easy to see that the med techs are functioning at the level that nurses did years ago and flight nurse competency and patient care rival what physicians were doing a few decades in the past. They also displayed the same high level of enthusiasm for the mission that unit members have demonstrated since the unit's inception. We can see that this was built upon the early training and experiences from all former aeromeds. The GFTP we observed was very detailed, comprehensive, and the aeromeds were very professional medical caregivers.

The authors wish to thank the following aircrew for their help and assistance during this Ground FTP as they observed how training had changed over the years:

Photo courtesy of TSgt Richard Childs and Col Michael Germain
Ground FTP (historical flight comparison) crew.

Back Row (L - R): Maj Lee Smith, A1C Nathan Wallgren, SrA Matthew Bauske, SrA Jeremy Teneyck, MSgt Rob Buresh
Front Row (L - R): Maj Kristin Dudas, Maj Jennifer Rosetta, SSgt Elizabeth Kolquist

Dates of Conflicts

(where and when 109th aeromeds served)

Conflict	Country	Dates
Vietnam War	Vietnam	1955 – 1975
Operation Deep Freeze	Antarctica	1955 - Present
Berlin Crisis	Germany	1961 - 1962
Operation Just Cause	Panama	1989 - 1990
Operation Desert Shield	S.W. Asia	1990 - 1991
Operation Desert Storm	S.W. Asia	1991 - 1991
Operation Restore Hope	Somalia	1992 - 1993
Operation Provide Hope	Somalia	1992 - 1994
Operation Southern Watch	S.W. Asia	1992 - 2003
Operation Sea Signal	Cuba	1994 - 1996
Operation Nomad Vigil	Albania	1994 - 1996
Operation Joint Endeavor	Bosnia	1995 - 1996
Operation Joint Guard	Bosnia	1996 - 1998
Operation Enduring Freedom	Afghanistan	2001 - 2014
Operation Iraqi Freedom	Kuwait	2003 - 2010
Operation Jump Start	SW U.S. border	2006 - 2008

Mission Aircraft of the 109th AES

109th AES Aircraft

(mission aircraft flown by the Minnesota ANG)

1961

Boeing C-97A Stratofreighter

cargo capacity: 96 troops or 69 litters
cruise speed: 300 mph
maximum altitude: 35,000 feet
maximum range: 4,300 miles

Photo courtesy of USAF

1963

Boeing C-97G Stratofreighter

cargo capacity: 96 troops or 69 litters
cruise speed: 300 mph
maximum altitude: 35,000 feet
maximum range: 4,900 miles

Photo courtesy of USAF

1971

Lockheed C-130A Hercules

cargo capacity: 92 troops or 74 litters
cruise speed: 336 mph
maximum altitude: 33,000 feet
maximum range: 2,050 miles

Photo courtesy of USAF

MISSION AIRCRAFT OF THE 109TH AES ★ 397

1981

Lockheed C-130E Hercules

cargo capacity: 92 troops or 74 litters
cruise speed: 336 mph
maximum altitude: 33,000 feet
maximum range: 2,360 miles

Photo courtesy of USAF

1996

Lockheed C-130H Hercules

cargo capacity: 92 troops or 74 litters
cruise speed: 336 mph
maximum altitude: 33,000 feet
maximum range: 2,360 miles

Photo courtesy of Osakabe Yasuo, USAF

Other Units' Aircraft

(mission aircraft from other units)

1961

Boeing C-135A Stratolifter
(KC-135A [refueler] depicted in picture)

cargo capacity: 126 troops or 44 litters
cruise speed: 530 mph
maximum altitude: 50,000 feet
maximum range: 3,500 miles

Photo courtesy of USAF

1962

Convair C-131A Samaritan
(C-131B depicted in picture)

cargo capacity: 27 litters or 32 ambulatory
cruise speed: 296 mph
maximum altitude: 23,000 feet
maximum range: 1,500 miles

Photo courtesy of USAF

1962

Douglas C-54 Skymaster

cargo capacity: 18 litters and 24 ambulatory
cruise speed: 190 mph
maximum altitude: 22,300 feet
maximum range: 4,000 miles

Photo courtesy of USAF

1962

Fairchild C-119G Flying Boxcar
(C-119B depicted in picture)

cargo capacity: 62 troops or 35 litters
cruise speed: 250 mph
maximum altitude: 23,900 feet
maximum range: 2,280 miles

Photo courtesy of USAF

1962

Boeing C-97C Stratofreighter

cargo capacity: 96 troops or 69 litters
cruise speed: 300 mph
maximum altitude: 35,000 feet
maximum range: 4,949 miles

Photo courtesy of USAF

1964

Lockheed C-121 Constellation

cargo capacity: 44 troops or 20 litters
cruise speed: 327 mph
maximum altitude: 25,000 feet
maximum range: 4,000 miles

Photo courtesy of USAF

1966

Lockheed C-141 Starlifter

cargo capacity: 154 troops or 80 litters
cruise speed: 550 mph
maximum altitude: 41,000 feet
maximum range: 4,000 miles

Photo courtesy of USAF

1976

McDonnell Douglas C-9 Nightingale

cargo capacity: 40 ambulatory with 4 litter patients or 40 litter patients
cruise speed: 504 mph
maximum altitude: 37,000 feet
maximum range: 2,000 miles

Photo courtesy of USAF

1992

Learjet C-21

cargo capacity: 5 ambulatory/1 litter patient
cruise speed: 530 mph
maximum altitude: 45,000 feet
maximum range: 2,306 miles

Photo courtesy of USAF

2006

Boeing C-17 Globemaster

cargo capacity: 134 troops, 36 litters, 54 ambulatory patients
cruise speed: 515 mph
maximum altitude: 45,000 feet
maximum range: 2,420 miles

Photo courtesy of USAF

From "Breakfast with Zak" to 109th Get-Togethers, No Stronger Bond!

Tom Stangl came up with the idea of frequent get-togethers for some of the "old-timers." We asked Tom about the genesis of his idea and how it has evolved over time. Tom writes:

"Sometime around February of 2016, I ran into Dan Tracy. We decided we needed to go have breakfast with Zak (SMSgt Al Zakariasen). So on Feb. 8th, 2016, Joe Jensen, Dan Tracy and I met Zak over at the Perkins in Hopkins for breakfast. Somewhere in the conversation we agreed we should do this more often."

Photo courtesy of Tom Stangl
***"Breakfast with Zak," 8 Feb, 2016.
(L - R): Tom Stangl, Dan Tracy, Al Zakariasen, Joe Jensen***

"More often turned out to be 16 months. But on June 29th, 2017, we did it again, at the same Perkins in Hopkins. This time there were eight of us."

Photo courtesy of Tom Stangl
"Breakfast with Zak," 29 June, 2017.

(L - R): Tom Stangl, Tim Evavold, Al Zakariasen, Chip Childs, Darrell Rask, Norm Hendrickson, Dan Johnson, Larry Bild

"During that get-together, we got a little more in depth about how often to meet, maybe rotating to different places in the Twin Cities, and alternating weekdays with weekends. When I posted the picture on Facebook, a certain Tracy Soderholm commented, 'Why is it all Guys?' I tried to defuse the situation by saying something like, 'Because it was during the week, the women had jobs, or a life, or something like that.'

"Her comment actually made me realize I needed to find an easy way to notify people when we would be having these 'little' get-togethers. Somewhere along the way, I saw a Facebook page for Guard members. I think this was started by Mike Cunniff. I started adding everyone I was friends with on Facebook to this Guard page. I also realized that not everyone is on Facebook, so I started my own e-mail list for people that may not be on Facebook. It's not perfect, but the lists are getting longer and with everyone's help, I'm hoping we can reach as many people as possible for future get-togethers.

"On May 15th, 2018 we met again at the same Perkins, 13 people this time. It was fun to see the breakfast group growing. It's obvious this guy named Zak had, and still has a major impact on everyone's life. I know he has on mine."

Photo courtesy of Tom Stangl
"Breakfast with Zak," 15 May, 2018.

(L - R): Joe Jensen, Chip Childs, Norm Hendrickson, Paul Walker, Tim Evavold, Al Zakariasen, Tom Stangl (standing), Barb Anderson, JoAnn Schauer, Nancy Dimunation, Mark Grieme, Dan Bougoeis, Eric Lee (not shown)

"That brings us up to the breakfast on September 8th, 2018. Norm and Barb Hendrickson graciously opened up their home for breakfast that morning, and it's a good thing they did, because I think the head count was around 35! It was a bright sunny Saturday morning. We all said the Pledge of Allegiance and sang the National Anthem, (something that we started at Zak's 80th birthday party a couple of years ago). Good food and lots of smiles, laughs and hugs."

Photo courtesy of Barb Hendrickson
"Breakfast with Zak," 8 Sep, 2018.

"It's obvious that not everyone can make it to these breakfasts every time. I'm just trying to set up opportunities for people to reconnect with Zak and each other and reminisce about old times if their schedule permits it.

"Let's fast forward to 14 Sep, 2019. This time Micki (King) and husband Wayne opened up their home to this motley crew. And what a beautiful home it was. This, however, was a bittersweet get-together."

Photo courtesy of TSgt Richard Childs
Get-together at Micki's, 14 Sep, 2019.

"You may have noticed that Zak is not in the picture. As it turned out, he called JoEllen Evavold that afternoon to tell her he would not be going to the party that night. Whatever reason he gave JoEllen, she wasn't buying it, and proceeded to escort Zak to the hospital. This was the moment when they told him the cancer had metastasized into his liver and lungs. They admitted him that day, but Zak was home that night saying, 'Why stay in the hospital if there is nothing else to do?'

"Albert E. Zakariasen fought the good fight, but on 19 Oct, 2019 he succumbed to cancer.

"In the memorial bulletin was the following statement: Albert Elsworth Zakariasen, age 83 of Hopkins, MN, transitioned October 18th, 2019. Albert, with integrity and compassion, touched thousands of hearts and will be loved forever. Served 31.5 years in the Armed Forces of the United States of America. Received Certificate of Appreciation for honorable service from Bill Clinton, Commander in Chief. Retired from the 109th AES as a SMSgt. Albert gifted his body for research to the Mayo Clinic.

"Please note that last sentence. Zak wanted to continue to help people even after his passing. That's the kind of person he was.

"So where do these gatherings go from here? We will continue to come together, hopefully twice a year. People have already stepped up and volunteered to host future gatherings. We will continue to reminisce about the good old days and honor the friends we've lost while we continue to cement the relationships that we have made with each other. We will also share in our joys, our sorrows and certainly have a good laugh or two - just like Zak would have wanted.

"I have now been retired for over 20 years now, but I feel like the bonds and the friendships I have from all those years ago are just as strong as when I left. When I saw everyone at the most recent breakfast, I felt like I had just seen them yesterday. Lots of love and respect. That's why we get together."

Respectfully submitted,

Tom Stangl

Abbreviations

1st Lt	First Lieutenant
2d Lt	Second Lieutenant
A1C	Airman First Class
A2/AD	Anti-Access/Area Denial
A2C	Airman Second Class
A3C	Airman Third Class
AAFES	Army and Air Force Exchange Service
AB	Airman Basic (rank)
AB	Air Base (location)
ABLS	Advanced Burn Life Support
ABU	Airman Battle Uniform
ACC	Air Combat Command
ACLS	Advanced Cardiac Life Support
ACSC	Air Command and Staff College
ADLS	Advanced Distributed Learning Service
AE	Aeromedical Evacuation
AECC	Aeromedical Evacuation Control Center
AECM	Aeromedical Evacuation Crew Member
AECMC	Aeromedical Evacuation Crew Management Cell
AECOT	Aeromedical Evacuation Contingency Operations Training
AEF	Aeromedical Evacuation Flight (after 1992, Air Expeditionary Force)
AELT	Aeromedical Evacuation Liaison Team
AEOO	Aeromedical Evacuation Operations Officer
AEOT	Aeromedical Evacuation Operations Team
AES	Aeromedical Evacuation Squadron
AESMT	Aeromedical Evacuation Stage Management Team
AET	Aeromedical Evacuation Technician
AEW	Air Expeditionary Wing
AF	Air Force
AFB	Air Force Base
AFCENT	Air Force Central Command
AFIA	Air Force Inspection Agency
AFORMS	Air Force Operations Resource Management System
AFR	Air Force Reserve

AFRES	Air Force Reserve
AFROTC	Air Force Reserve Officer Training Corps
AFSC	Air Force Specialty Code
AFTP	Additional Flying Training Period
AGE	Aerospace Ground Equipment
ALS	Advanced Life Support
AMC	Air Mobility Command
AMCC	Air Mobility Control Center
AME	Aeromedical Evacuation
AMEF	Aeromedical Evacuation Flight
AMEG	Aeromedical Evacuation Group
AMES	Aeromedical Evacuation Squadron
Amn	Airman
AMSUS	Association of Military Surgeons of the United States
ANG	Air National Guard
ANGRC	Air National Guard Readiness Center
AOIC	Assistant Officer In Charge
AOR	Area Of Responsibility
APC	Armored Personnel Carrier
ARM	Aeromedical Readiness Mission
ARNG	Army National Guard
AROWS	Air Reserve Orders Writing System
ARTEP	Army Training and Evaluation Program
AS	Airlift Squadron
ASEV	Aircrew Stan/Eval Visit
ASF	Area Staging Facility
ASTS	Aeromedical Staging Squadron
ATLS	Advanced Trauma Life Support
ATOC	Air Terminal Operation Center
ATSO	Ability To Survive and Operate
ATTP	Advanced Trauma Training Program
ATW	Air Transport Wing
AW	Airlift Wing
BAQ	Bachelor Airman's Quarters
BDLS	Basic Disaster Life Support
BDU	Battle Dress Uniform
BG	Brigade
BLS	Basic Life Support
B-MET	Biomedical Equipment Technician
Brig Gen	Brigadier General

BTLS	Basic Trauma Life Support
BX	Base Exchange

C4	Combat Casualty Care Course
Capt	Captain
CASF	Contingency Aeromedical Staging Facility
CAT	Crisis Action Team
CBPO	Consolidated Base Personnel Office
CBRN	Chemical Biological Radiological Nuclear
CBWD	Chemical Biological Warfare Defense
CC	Commander
CCAF	Community College of the Air Force
CCATT	Critical Care Air Transport Team
CCEP	Comprehensive Clinical Evaluation Program
CCIP	Commander's Inspection Program
CCM	Squadron Chief Master Sergeant
CENTAF	U.S. Air Forces, U.S. Central Command
CENTCOM	Central Command
CERFP	CBRN Enhanced Response Force Package
CMC	Crew Management Cell
CMSgt	Chief Master Sergeant
CMT	Charge Medical Technician
CNN	Cable News Network
Col	Colonel
Comm	Communication
COMSEC	Communications Security
CONOP	Concept of Operations
CONUS	Continental United States
COT	Commissioned Officer Training
CPR	Cardiopulmonary Resuscitation
CRM	Crew Resource Management
CRNA	Certified Registered Nurse Anesthetist
CRTC	Combat Readiness Training Center
CV	Vice Commander

DET	Detachment
DFAC	Dining Facility
DHS	Department of Homeland Security
DO	Director of Operations
DOC	Designed Operational Capability

DOD	Department of Defense
DRC	Democratic Republic of the Congo
DTS	Defense Travel System
DV	Distinguished Visitor
EAEF	Expeditionary Aeromedical Evacuation Flight
EAES	Expeditionary Aeromedical Evacuation Squadron
EASTAF	Eastern Tactical Air Force
EMEDS	Expeditionary Medical Support
EMF	Expeditionary Medical Facility (Navy)
EMT	Emergency Medical Technician
EMU	Expeditionary Medical Unit (Navy)
EORI	Expeditionary Operational Readiness Inspection
EPOS	Emergency Passenger Oxygen System
EPR	Enlisted Performance Report
EQ	Exceptionally Qualified
ER	Emergency Room
ERO	Engine Running Onload
ESGR	Employer Support of the Guard and Reserve
ETAR	Ramstein AB, Germany (four letter airport code)
EUCOM	European Command
FCC	Flight Clinical Coordinator
FCIF	Flight Crew Information File
FE	Flight Examiner
FEMA	Federal Emergency Management Agency
FGO	Field Grade Officer
FI	Flight Instructor
FN	Flight Nurse
FOB	Forward Operating Base
FTP	Flying Training Period
FTU	Formal Training Unit
FTX	Field Training Exercise
FW	Fighter Wing
GDSS	Global Decisions Support System
Gen	General
GFTP	Ground Flying Training Period
GPMRC	Global Patient Movement Regulating Center

G-RAP	Guard Recruiting Assistance Program
GS	General Schedule
GSW	Gun Shot Wound
HAZMAT	Hazardous Material
H/H Co	Headquarters and Headquarters Company
HIV	Human Immunodeficiency Virus
HQ	Headquarters
HRA	Human Resource Advisor
HSI	Health Services Inspection
HSRI	Health Services Readiness Inspection
HUMVEE	High Mobility Multipurpose Wheeled Vehicle (HMMWV, colloquial: Humvee)
IAP	International Airport
ICMOP	Integrated CONUS Medical Operations Plan
ICU	Intensive Care Unit
IED	Improvised Explosive Device
IG	Inspector General
IMA	Individual Mobilization Augmentee
IMR	Individual Medical Readiness
IRI	Initial Response Inspection
ISBN	International Standard Book Number
ITLS	International Trauma Life Support
JCCP	Joint Casualty Collection Point
JCP	Joint Communication Platform
JOC	Joint Operations Center
JRTC	Joint Readiness Training Center
KSAT	San Antonio International Airport (four letter airport code)
KSSF	Stinson Municipal Airport, San Antonio, Texas (four letter airport code)
KVP	Key Volunteer Program
LNO	Liaison Nurse Officer
LPU	Life Preserver Unit
Lt	Lieutenant

Lt Col	Lieutenant Colonel
Lt Gen	Lieutenant General
MAC	Military Airlift Command
Maj	Major
Maj Gen	Major General
MASCAL	Mass Casualty
MASF	Mobile Aeromedical Staging Facility
MASH	Mobile Army Surgical Hospital
MATS	Military Air Transport Service
MAW	Military Airlift Wing
MCD	Medical Crew Director
MDG	Medical Group
MDS	Medical Squadron
Med	Medical
MEDRETE	Medical Readiness Training Exercises
Med Tech	Medical Technician
MEI	Management Effectiveness Inspection
METL	Mission Essential Task List
MILES	Multiple Integrated Laser Engagement System
MIMSO	Military Indoctrination for Medical Service Officers
MNANG	Minnesota Air National Guard
MOPP	Mission Oriented Protective Posture
MOVSM	Military Outstanding Volunteer Service Medal
MPF	Military Personnel Flight
MQF	Master Question File
MRE	Meal Ready to Eat
MSC	Medical Service Corps
MSgt	Master Sergeant
MWR	Morale, Welfare, Recreation
NAF	Numbered Air Force
NAS	Naval Air Station
NATO	North Atlantic Treaty Organization
NC	Nurse Corps
NCO	Non-Commissioned Officer
NCOIC	Non-Commissioned Officer In Charge
NDMS	National Disaster Medical System
NGAP	Air National Guard Assistants and Advisors Program
NGB	National Guard Bureau

NHANG	New Hampshire Air National Guard
NTS	Neonatal Transport System
NVG	Night Vision Goggles
NWA	Northwest Airlines
NYANG	New York Air National Guard
OAY	Outstanding Airman of the Year
OCONUS	Outside Continental United States
OEF	Operation Enduring Freedom
OGV	Operations Group Standardizations/Evaluations
OIC	Officer In Charge
OIF	Operation Iraqi Freedom
OJG	Operation Joint Guard
OJT	On-the-Job Training
Ops	Operations
OPTEMPO	Operating Tempo, Operations Tempo, Ops Tempo
ORE	Operational Readiness Exercise
ORI	Operational Readiness Inspection
ORM	Operational Risk Management
OTC	Over The Counter
PA	Public Affairs
PACAF	Pacific Air Forces
PAR	Post Attack Response
PAX	Passengers
PBI	Performance Based Inspections
PHTLS	Pre-Hospital Trauma Life Support
PJs	Pararescuemen (PJs for para-jumpers)
PM	Partial Mobilization
PME	Professional Military Education
POC	Point Of Contact
POW	Prisoner Of War
PPD	Purified Protein Derivative (Tuberculin)
PR	Public Relations
PT	Physical Training
PTSD	Post-Traumatic Stress Disorder
Pubs	Publications
PUC	Prisoner Under Containment

Q	Qualified
QA	Quality Assurance
QAFA	Quality Air Force Assessments

RAF	Royal Air Force
RDO	Radio Operator
REFORGER	Return of Forces to Germany
Regs	Regulations
Ret	Retired
RN	Registered Nurse
RON	Remain Over Night
ROTC	Reserve Officer Training Corps
RPG	Rocket Propelled Grenade
RPM	Revolutions Per Minute
RSD	Regularly Scheduled Drill
RSV	Readiness Skills Verifications

SA/BC	Self-Aid/Buddy Care
SAC	Strategic Air Command
SARM	Squadron Aviation Resource Manager
SAV	Staff Assistance Visit
SCPS-M	Survivable Collective Protection System-Medical
SERE	Survival, Evasion, Resistance, Escape
SG	Surgeon General
SICU	Surgical Intensive Care Unit
SII	Special Interest Item
SME	Squadron Medical Element
SMEED	Special Medical Emergency Evacuation Device
SMSgt	Senior Master Sergeant
SORTS	Status Of Resources and Training System
SOUTHCOM	Southern Command
Space-A	Space Available
SrA	Senior Airman
SSgt	Staff Sergeant
Stan/Eval	Standards and Evaluation

TAC	Tactical Air Command
TAC	Tactical
TACC	Tactical Airlift Control Center

TAES	Tactical Aeromedical Evacuation System
TAG	Tactical Airlift Group
TAS	Tactical Airlift Squadron
TAW	Tactical Airlift Wing
TB	Tuberculosis
TBI	Traumatic Brain Injury
TCA	Traditional Commander in Chief Activities
TCCC	Tactical Combat Casualty Care
TDY	Temporary Duty
THREATCON	Terrorist Threat Condition
TNCC	Trauma Nursing Core Course
TOPSTAR	Sustainment Training to Advance Readiness
TPMRC	Theater Patient Movement Requirement Center
TRANSCOM	Transportation Command
TSgt	Technical Sergeant

U	Unqualified
UAE	United Arab Emirates
UCI	Unit Compliance Inspection
UEI	Unit Effectiveness Inspection
US	United States
USAF	United States Air Force
USAFE	United States Air Forces in Europe
USNR	United States Navy Reserve
USO	United Service Organization
UTA	Unit Training Assembly
UTC	Unit Type Code

VA	Veterans Administration
VADEX	Veterans Affairs Department of Defense Exercise
VAQ	Visiting Airman's Quarters
VIP	Very Important Person

WRM	War Readiness Materials
WWII	World War II

XO	Executive Officer

Validating Our Early Research

The authors met with several of the original unit flight nurses in Alexandria, MN in December 2016. The first several years of written unit history for the book were carefully examined and scrutinized for accuracy. The authors also interviewed these nurses on an individual basis to review and authenticate their personal memories and photographic contributions.

Photo courtesy of Col Michael Germain

Authors meet with early 109th AES flight nurses and former Commander.

(L - R): Julie Eszlinger Jensen, Jean Cool, Betty Cook, Dorothea Tenney, Chip Childs, (not shown, Michael Germain - photographer)

The authors also met with founding med techs at a local Twin Cities library to verify the accuracy and completeness of the early portions of the manuscript. Personal photos they submitted were reviewed for relevance before placement in the book.

Photo courtesy of Col Michael Germain
Authors meet with early 109th AES med techs and former Commander.

(L - R): David Lund, Richard Vosika, Julie Eszlinger Jensen, Chip Childs, Terry Ripley, Dick Oehlenschlager (not shown, Michael Germain - photographer)

For over the past 60 years, the 109th AES has responded to the medical and humanitarian needs of both the federal government and the state of Minnesota. During the course of meeting the many demands placed upon it over the decades, it has undergone numerous changes with equipment, personnel and its mission. One thing that has not changed, is the spirit of squadron unity, pride, and the willingness to persevere until the challenge is met. This attitude was manifested at its inception, constantly demonstrated through its many challenges and will remain the cornerstone of its commitment in the future. Through its actions, the 109th AES truly embodies the title of this book, "The Best Care in the Air."

Photo courtesy of Sue Carmody

Index

Page numbers in **bold** indicate pages with illustrations.

Numbers

1st Aeromedical Evacuation Group (AMEG), 56, 59, 60
1st Aeromedical Evacuation Squadron (AES), 64, 68, 69, 76, 83, 89, 98, 121
10th Expeditionary Aeromedical Evacuation Flight (EAEF), 315, 334, 350–351
11th Aeromedical Evacuation Squadron (AMES), 14
12th Air Force, 59
12th Military Air Transport Service (MATS), 15
15th Air Force, 225, 259
23rd Aeromedical Evacuation Squadron (AES), 202
24th Medical Group, 183, 202
47th Aeromedical Evacuation Flight (AEF), 97
47th Aeromedical Evacuation Squadron (AES), 36
47th Aeromedical Evacuation Squadron (AMES), 33
56th Aeromedical Evacuation Squadron (AES), 75
57th Aeromedical Evacuation Squadron (AES), 53, 63
68th Aeromedical Evacuation Squadron (AES), 154, 155
75th anniversary of Ray Miller flight, 198
76th Rescue Squadron, 317
109th Aeromedical Evacuation Flight (AEF) attitudes toward, 113–117, 124, 129
109th Aeromedical Evacuation Flight (AMEF), vii, 2, 3, 5, 11, 12, 14, 16, 18, 21, 24, 25–26, 33, 37, 41, 46, 47, 57, 58, 59, 60, 62, 64, 66, 160, 329
  change to designation to a squadron, 160
  charter members, 2–3. *See also* individual names
109th Aeromedical Evacuation Squadron (AES), ix, 2, 47, 113, 160, 162, 164, **164**, **165**, 171–172, 182, 185, 203, 220, **220**, 247, 258, 276, 278, 303, 418, **418**
  Ecuador, 222–224, **223**, **224**
  Founders Day/Reunion, 329–332, **330**, **331**
  historical perspective, training flight, 382–394
  Howard legacy, 346–349, **347**
  MEDLITE 11, 311, **312**
  Peru and Ecuador, 215–219, **216**, **217**, **218**, **219**
109th Aero Squadron, 198
109th Air Expeditionary Force (AEF), 160, 228, 233, 234, 294, 295
109th Airlift Squadron (AS), 176, 190, 225
109th Air Transport Group, 25
109th Tactical Airlift Squadron (TAS), 126
133rd Aeromedical Evacuation Flight (AMEF), 2, 12, 15, 31, 43
133rd Aeromedical Evacuation Squadron (AMES), vii, 2, 5, 6, 17, 18, 25–26, 31, 36, 43, 46
133rd Air Defense Wing, vii

★ 419

133rd Airlift Wing (AW), 53–55, 188, 203, 204, 219, 221, 250, 277, 318, 349
   50th anniversary, 53
   75th anniversary, 205
   75th anniversary of Ray Miller flight, 198
   Military Appreciation Day, 323–324
   motto, 296
133rd Air Transport Wing (ATW), vii–ix, 2–3, 15, 24, 25
133rd Civil Engineering Squadron, 170–171
133rd Dispensary, 6, 46, 211
133rd Medical Squadron (MDS), 129, 185, 202, 222, 230, 234, 259–260, 303
133rd Operations Group Standardizations/Evaluations (OGV), 225
133rd Tactical Airlift Wing (TAW), 55, 58, 62, 81, 86, 94, 127, 129
   Air Force Outstanding Unit Award, 105
133rd Tactical (TAC) Hospital, 88, 90
137th Aeromedical Evacuation Flight (AEF), 153
137th Aeromedical Evacuation Squadron (AES), 262, 282, 283
139th Aeromedical Evacuation Flight (AMEF), 2, 14, 15, 25
142nd Aeromedical Evacuation Flight (AEF), 69, 261
148th Fighter Wing (FW), 202, 312, 318
150th Aeromedical Evacuation Flight (AEF), 25, 43
156th Aeromedical Evacuation Flight (AEF), 69
156th Aeromedical Evacuation Squadron (AES), 274, 278, 292
167th Aeromedical Evacuation Flight (AEF), 69
170th Air Transport Group, 25
183rd Aeromedical Evacuation Squadron (AES), 215
187th Aeromedical Evacuation Flight (AMEF), 52, 240
189th Airlift Wing (AW), 202–203
204th Medical Battalion, 89–90, 126
210th Rescue Squadron, 91
374th Tactical Airlift Wing (TAW), 54
375th Aeromedical Evacuation Squadron (AES), 263, 290, 314
379th Expeditionary Aeromedical Evacuation Squadron (EAES), 268, 271, 294
379th Expeditionary Medical Support (EMEDS), 273
491st Expeditionary Unit, 264
775th Expeditionary Aeromedical Evacuation Flight (EAEF), 315, 318–319
775th Expeditionary Aeromedical Evacuation Squadron (EAES), 259–262, 262–263, 265
903rd Aeromedical Evacuation Squadron (AES), 42
911th Aeromedical Evacuation Squadron (AES), 202
934th Aeromedical Evacuation Flight (AEF), 97
934th Aeromedical Evacuation Squadron (AES), 204, 214, 240, 255
934th Air Force Reserve (AFR), 327–328, 354
934th Tactical Airlift Group (TAG), 85, 97, 315
1453rd Aeromedical Evacuation Squadron (AES), 25
1502nd Air Transport Wing (ATW), 25
4410th Aeromedical Evacuation Flight (AEF), 191
4410th Aeromedical Evacuation Squadron (AES), 190

A

Ackerman, Douglas, 160, 233
Active Federal Service, 11, 17, 41
Adams, Timothy, 90–91
Additional Flying Training Period (AFTP), **67**
Administration section, 98, 221, 226, **227**
Advanced Trauma Life Support (ATLS), 159
AECC. *See* Aeromedical Evacuation Control Center

AECOT. *See* Aeromedical Evacuation Contingency Operations Training
AELT. *See* Aeromedical Evacuation Liaison Team
Aeromedical Evacuation Contingency Operations Training (AECOT), 168, 233, 293
Aeromedical Evacuation Control Center (AECC), 6, 162, 186, 191
Aeromedical Evacuation Liaison Team (AELT), 141, 148–149, 196, 231, 282
Aeromedical Evacuation Museum, 164
aeromedical evacuation technician (AET), 66, 222, 225, 234, 248, 253, 292
Aeromedical Staging Facility, 142–143, **143**
Aerovac Schoolhouse, 156
AET. *See* aeromedical evacuation technician
Afghanistan, 254, 265, 271, 279, **305**, 309, 322, 344
Africa, 185, 284–285, **284**, 311, **312**
AFSC. *See* Air Force Specialty Code
AFTP. *See* Additional Flying Training Period
Air Combat Command (ACC), 160, 180, 203, 372, **372**
Aircrew Stan/Eval Visit (ASEV), 166, 185, 225–226, 247, 259, 275, 276, 277, 298, 336
Air Expeditionary Force (AEF), 160, 274, 309, 332
Air Force, U.S., viii, 4, 17, 73, 120, 166
  8th Air Force, 202–203, 283, 311, 318
  12th Air Force, 59
  15th Air Force, 225, 259
  Chief Nurse of the United States Air Force, 77, 78, 79, 80, 85, **86**, 110
Air Force Reserve (AFR), 42, 73, 85, 110, 142, 149–150, 327–328
Air Force Specialty Code (AFSC), 36, 201, 253, 267
Air Mobility Command (AMC), 156, 160, 174, 191, 210, 258, 278, 313, 367, 372
Air Mobility Control Center (AMCC), 264
Airmen, 6–8, 11, 15, 17, 46, 58, 62, 146, 282, 291, 342. *See also* individual names

Air National Guard (ANG), vii–ix, 1, 2, 4, 6, 9, 10, 12, 15, 16, 17, 21, 27, 32, 36, 38–40, 42, 43, 46, 47, 48, 52, 54, 57, 58, 62, 63, 72–73, 76–80, 82, 85, 86, 90, 91, 94, 95, 97, 100–104, 105, 107, 110, 113, 116, 118, 120, 121, 126, 129, 130, 135, 136, 142, 149–150, 153, 171, 175, 178, 182, 184, 200, 202, 203, 204, 207, 210, 214, 220, 225, 228–229, 233, 238, 247, 248, 253, 255, 261, 278, 280, 291, 298, 314, 315, 321, 322, 324, 326, 337, 344, 348, 352, 354, 357, 360
Air War College, 80, 100
Alaska, 91–92, 107–108, **108**
Albania, 191
al-Qaeda, 245, 259
Al Saud, Fahd bin Abdulaziz, 128
Alsip, Judith, 44
Alt, Donna, **68**, 121, 124, 142, 166
AMC. *See* Air Mobility Command
American Nurses Association Convention, 85, **86**
American Red Cross, 7, 97, 135, 185, 215
AMSUS. *See* Association of Military Surgeons of the United States
Anderson, Barbara, 151, 217–218, **218**, 224, 232, 237, 238, 263, 267, 282, 297, 305, **308**, 313, **403**
Anderson, Darcy, **68**, 69, 71, 80, **87**, 96, 97–98, **99**, 105, 106, **112**, 113, 115–116, 122–125, 128, 137, 138, **138**, 140, 141, 145, 151, 153, 158, **163,** 329. *See also* Simmons, Darcy
  biography, 112–113
  command, 112–172
  command notes, 113–117, 122–125, 129, 133, 137–138, 140, 144, 170–172
  "Final Formation", 178–179, **179**
  plaque, wing presentation, 156, **156**, 157
  WCCO-TV, **147**
Anderson, Linnea, 128, **130**, **137**
Anderson-Ray, Kelly, 166. *See also* Tracy, Kelly
Anderson, Robert, 9, 48

Andreotti, Eugene, 106, 124, 176, 178, 200
Andrews Air Force Base, 42, 75, 260, 261, 263, 265, **351**
Antarctica, 309, 324, **325**
Antonini, Edmund, 22
Applen, Emily, 346, 354, **355**
Applen, Eric, 309, 334, **335**, 352
April Touchdown '88, 105–106, **106**
Arlien, Cortland, **87**
Armed Forces Radio/Television, 118
Armon, Emily, **239**
Army National Guard (ARNG), 89–90, **90**, 125–127, 129, 153, 178, 303, 343, 360
Army, U.S., ix, 18, 69, 89, 91, 92, 95, 107, 126, 141, 153, 176–177, 231, 232
Arndt, Jason, **235**, 263, 266, 316, 328, **332**, 337, 346, **346**
ASEV. *See* Aircrew Stan/Eval Visit
Ash, George, 3
Association of Air National Guard Nurses, 62, 77–78
Association of Military Surgeons of the United States (AMSUS), 77–80, 90, 96, 101, 105, 120–121, 156, 199, 206, 220
attitudes toward unit, 4, 7, 18, 73, 79–80, 113–116, 129, 170, 171
August, Jeff, 297
Augustine, Major, 255
Ausen, Ardyce Marlene, 47, 85, 94, 100, 110
Azores, 232, 280

B

"Baghdad Bertha", 135
Bahrain, 139
Ballenger, Ray, 49
Balow, John, 62
Barbi, Susan, 120
Bartz, Dieter, 266, 297
Battle Buddy concept, 314
Battlefield Nursing, 57, 87–88
Bauske, Matthew, **394**
Beers, Sara, 317, 324

Behrens, Susan, 248, **295**, 302, 305, **310**, 327, 337, **338**, 339, 354, **355**, 361
  command, 338–358
  Commander's comments, 338–339
Belanger, Raphael, 3, 9
Belgium, 328
Belize, 224
Benson, Patricia, **68**
Berg, Steve, 165
Bergland, Jarl, 66, **68**
Bergren, Terrance, **68**
Berlin Crisis, 7, 14, 17, 33, 46, 363
Bild, Lawrence, 66, **68**, **70**, 76, 88–89, 91, 92, **96**, **106**, 178, **182**, 191, 200, **402**
Bild, Sharon, 155, 183
Bjellum, Karl, **295**
Black Hawk helicopters, 181, 343
Blilie, Gerald, **68**, **70**, 76, **96**, 110, 128, 134–135, **135**, 136, 152, 166, 183, 185, 207, **207**
Blue Angels, 242
Boab, Patrick, 80, **104**
Bochniak, Captain, 298, 309
Boehm, Kirsten, 368, **368**. *See also* Hoffoss, Kirsten
Boeing. *See* individual aircraft
Boisclair, Robert, 3, 9
"Boneyard", 55
Booen, Sherm, **35**, 57
Boreas Reach exercise, 332
Bornhofen, Colette, 151, 165
Borrego, Earnest, 237
Bosnia, 191, 202, 206
Boswell, Billy, 53
Bougie, Tim, 290, 297
Bougoeis, Dan, **67**, **68**, **403**
Bouthilet, James, **96**
Boy Scouts, 104, 248–249, **250**
Brady, Arlene, 143
Bramsford, Dan, **68**
Brannon, Robert, 127
Brazil, 233
Brcka, Rich, 196

Brede, Shawn, **68**, **70**
Breth, Rolland, 30
Brewer, Barron, 2, 8, 17, 49
Brim Frost exercise, 91–92, 107–108, **108**
Brock, Don, **177**, 190, 203, 235
Broman, John, 141, 150–151, 176
Brooke Army Medical Center, 121
Brooks Air Force Base, 11–12, 29, 48, 49, 50, 58, 73, 87, 112, 150, 164, 311
Brothers, Brian, 316, 337, **355**
Browning, Jeramy, 297, **308**, 342–343
Bruesewitz, Kim, 183
Bryant, Keith, **310**
Building 641, 174, 176, 198, 202, 204, 205, 210, **212**, 213
Building 644, 105, **132**, 174, 211, **211**, 212
"Bullpen" concept, 201
Buresh, Robert, **182**, 282, **310**, 311, 316–317, 337, **346**, **355**, **394**
 homecoming, 322–323, **323**
Burg, Lance, 341, 349
Burmeister, Steve, 202, 207–208, **209**, 220, 239, 249, 266, 284, 286–287, 370
Burton, Cheryl, 225, 229, **239**, 246, 283
Bush, George H.W., 128, 150
Bush, George W., 258, 259
Bush, Laura, 263
Bushey, Sandra, 151
Byrnes, Staff Sergeant, 353

C

C-5 Galaxy, 134, 150, 254
C-7 Caribou, 42
C-9A Nightingale, 50–52, **51**, 63, 88, 206, 261–262, **261**, 262, 265, 268, **399**
C-17 Globemaster, 121, 251, 254, 265, 268, 274, 280, 291, 307, **333**, 355, 383, **400**
C-21 Learjet, 262, **399**
C-47 Chinook helicopter, 89, **90**
C-54 Skymaster, 28, **398**
C-97A Stratofreighter, vii, 3, **4**, 22, 24, 29, **396**
 compared to C-130A Hercules, 54, 76
C-97C Stratofreighter, **398**
C-97G Stratofreighter, 24, **24**, 54, 55, 57, **396**
C-119G Flying Boxcar, 28, 278, **398**
C-121 Constellation, 31, 52, **399**
C-130 Hercules, 42, 63, 66, 81, 95, 107–108, 121, 129, 130, 134, 143, 149, 150, 160, 174, 180, 187, 200, 204, 210, 225, 240, 251, 254, 259, 262–263, 265, 266, 268, 278–279, 280–281, 298, 311, 315, 355, **358**, 361, 370–371, 372, 382, 383, 389, **418**
C-130A Hercules, 54–55, **55**, 57, 58, **59**, 76, 109, **396**
 comparison of C-130A/E, 81–82
C-130E Hercules, 81–83, **82**, 88, 89, 91, 93, **106**, 117, **127**, 135–136, 146, **146**, 154, 164, 166, 170, 176, 178, 186, 188, 198, 199, 204, **397**
 comparison of C-130A/E, 81–82
C-130H Hercules, 91, 121, 204, 205, **205**, 206, 209, 210, 215, 216, 222, 226, 231, 232, 252, 255, **262**, 271–272, **272**, 277, 282, 291, 304, 309, 338, 343, **343**, 354, 386, **397**
C-130J Hercules, 279
C-131A Samaritan, 28, **31**, 73, 75, 329, 331, **331**, **398**
C-135A Stratolifter, 14, 16, **16**, 18, 28, 49, 52, **397**
C-141 Starlifter, 42, **43**, 52, 75, 108, 121, 143, **144**, 149–150, 154, 155, 166, 232, 239, 254, 262, 265, 268, 273, 276, 280, **399**
Caldwell, Jim, 176, 241, 261–262, 262–263
Camp Able Sentry, 206, **206**
Camp Bastion, 307, 316, 322
Campbell, Lou, 74
Camp Bullis, 159
Camp LeMonier, 284
Campos, Steve, 190, 203, 217, 223–224, 248, 250–251
Camp Posey, 159
Camp Ripley. *See* Ripley, Camp/Fort
Camp Superkids, 88

Canada, 22, 107–108, 160, 291, 298, 307, 314, 315
Capiz, Henry, 33, 36, **45**, 46, 47, **53**, **54**, 56, **59**, 60, 62, 329
    biography, 45–46
    command, 45–60
Carew, Rod, 155
Caribbean, 201, 279, 313
Carlberg, George, **54**
Carlson, Dayton, 66, **67**, **87**, 91, 118, 169, 180
Carlson, Sandy, **173**, 203, 229, 230, **230**, 327, 329. *See also* Darula, Sandy
    command, 173–227
    Commander's comments, 173–175
Carlton, Paul K., 111, 236
Carmody, Susan, 151
Carr, Donald, 11
Carroll, Tony, **68**, **70**, 84
Carswell Air Force Base, 146
Carter, Jason, 320
Causey, Major, 319
challenges, 35–36, 149, 233, 258
Cheney, Dick, 149–150
Chesney, Murphey, 94
Childs, Margaret, **195**
Childs, Monica, 195, **195**
Childs, Richard H., 117–118, 119, 132, 133–134, **137**, **138**, 165, **402**, **403**, **405**, **416**, **417**
    50th anniversary of flight nursing poster, 164, **164, 165**
    plaque, wing presentation, 156, **156, 157**
Christmas party, 183, **183**, 233, 238
Cisar, Cathy, 225, 237. *See also* Milsten, Cathy
Cisar, Dan, 165, 170, 199, 202, 235, 297, 302, 304, 307, 309, 314, **332**, 334, 341, 371
Civil Air Patrol, 104, 118, 135, 231
Clark Air Force Base, 17, 42, 46, 50, 75
Clark, Pat, **239**
Clark, Susan, 105, **145**
Clobes, Senior Airman, 201
Close, Greg, 258, 283, 294, **295**, 303

Coast Guard, U.S., 91, 107, 149
coins, squadron, 202, 220, 296, 329, 370–372, **370**, **371**
    coin check, 319–320, 324
Colombia, 224, 339
Colomy, John, **54**
Combat Readiness Training Center (CRTC), 184, 281, 304
Commander's Inspection Program (CCIP), 336
"Comm Box", 390–392, **391**
Como, Perry, 74
Comprehensive Clinical Evaluation Program (CCEP), 198–199
Conaway, John B., 80, 94, **102**
Confederate Air Force, 57
Congress, U.S., 41, 58, 150, 176, 200
Connolly, Rory, **346**, **355**
Conrad, Eugene, 91, 128, **135**, 165
Contact Club, 66, 158
Convair. *See* individual aircraft
Cook, Betty, 8, **9**, 17–18, 48, 73–74, **330**, 331–332, **416**
Cook, Michael, **284**, 285, 297
Cool, Jean, 7–8, **9**, 12,18, **19**, **25**, 30, 48, 73, 74, **330**, 331–332, **416**
Cordova, Joseph, 84, 92, **96**, 106
Coronet Gopher, 194
Corrigan, Debra, **148**
Courage Center, 86
crew checklist. *See* equipment, flying
Cronemiller, Lawrence, 188–189, **189**, **190**, **216**
Cub Scouts, 248–249
Cuba, 193–194, 194–195, 198, 201
Culver, Shannon, 225, 313
Cunniff, Michael, Jr., 66, **67**, **68**, **70**, **96**, 402
Curtiss Oriole, vii, 198

D

Dahlquist, Don, 128, 129, 132, 136, 176, 183, 194, 258, 262, 279, 290, 291
Dahlquist, Doug, 66, **68**, **70**

Damiani, Darren, 136, 146, **177**, 184
Darling, Jan, 241
Darula, Sandy, 129, 132, **138**, 160, **163**, 175, 194. *See also* Carlson, Sandy
Daudt, Larry, 9, 27, 38–40, 47–49
David Grant Medical Center, 221–222, 315
Davidson, Christine, **148**, 165, 222
Davis Monthan Air Force Base, 55, 57
Dawson, Joan, **87**
DeDecker, Major, 260
dedication, collage, **340**, **341**
Dehen, Robert, **54**
Deming, Colonel, 200
Democratic Republic of the Congo (DRC), 311, **312**
Dennis, Sam, **332**
Department of Defense (DOD), 67, 77, 210, 240, 245, 345, 360
Department of Veterans Affairs, 145, 219, 293
deployment bags, **132**
de Rosier, John, **54**
DeSanto, Rose, 162, 177
Desert Shield, 114, 121, 127, 128–141, 148–150, 153, 156, 169, 171, 369, **369**. *See also* Gulf War, Persian
Desert Storm, 121, 127, 131, 140–146, 148–150, 153, 154, 156, 158, 169, 171, 179, 198–199, 210, 219. *See also* Gulf War, Persian
    Comprehensive Clinical Evaluation Program (CCEP), 198–199
    homecoming, **146**
    patients, **144**
    plaque, wing presentation, 156, **156**, **157**
    traveling tribute, **151**
Deutsch, Julianne, 184
DeVaan, Catherine, **68**, **70**
Devine, Erika, 265–266, 268, 281, 288
Dhahran, Saudi Arabia, 130
Diem, Ngo, 41
Dierkhising, Terry, **286**
Dimunation, Nancy, **403**
Djibouti, 284–285, **284**, 339

Dodd, Lloyd, 203
Dolny, John R., viii–ix, **viii**, 22, 24, 72, 77–78, **330**
domestic air evac system, 3, 6, 11, 14, 17, 28, 52, 71, 74, 121, 329, 331, 361
Douglas. *See* individual aircraft
Doven, Eugene, **148**, 165
Dover Air Force Base, 42, 75, 130, 133, 134
Doyle, Edward, **1**, 3, 5
    biography, 1
    command, 1–19
Drayna, John, 2, 4, **5**, 6, **6**, 10
Dudas, Kristin, **346**, **394**
Duncan, Stephen M., 150
Durand, Michael, 181
Dvorak, Linda, 124
Dwyer, Patricia, 77

E

Eastern Tactical Air Force (EASTAF), 2, 31
Eckelberg, Carol, **9**, 10, 15, 21
Ecuador, 215, **216**, 222–225, 348
    San Lorenzo Clinic, **224**
    San Lorenzo Hospital, **223**
Edwards, Staff Sergeant, 148
Eglin Air Force Base, 15
Egypt, 166, 181
Ehman, Dominic, 266, 270, 284–285, **284**, 290, 298
Ehresmann, Patty, 184, 280–281
Eielson Air Force Base, 107, **108**
Eisenhower, Dwight D., 41, 71, 76
Elmendorf Air Force Base, 75, 91–92, 107
El Salvador, 224
Emahiser, Lorraine, 151
Emergency Medical System, 75–76
Emergency Medical Technician (EMT), 57, 233, **239**, 253
Emergency Medical Technician Refresher, 233, 238, **239**, 361
employers flight, 115, 155, 163, 220
EMT. *See* Emergency Medical Technician

Enduring Freedom, Operation, 247, 254–255, 264, 271, **340**, **341**
England, 18, **19**, 71, 142–143, **143**, **144**, 146, **146**, 237, 298, 333
equipment, flying
    Comm Box, 391–392, **391**
    crew checklist, 383, **383**
    headset, wireless, 391–392, **392**
    iPad, 383–385, **385**
    pubs and regs briefcase, 251, 313, 384, **384**, 386
equipment, medical
    oxygen equipment, 386, 387, 389, **389**
    preloaded litters, 386, **387**
    Stryker frame, 392, **393**
Erdman, Diane, 49
Erhsmann, Patty, 280–281
Erickson, Connie, 183
Eriksen, Robert, 75
Eskan Village, 130–131, **131**
ESKULAP 2009, 298–299, **299**
Espinosa, Judy, 225, 243, 255, 267. *See also* Hill, Judy
Eszlinger Jensen, Julie, 32, 34, 35, 36, 42, 43, **43**, 48, 52, **53**, 64, 69, **72**, 80, 83, 85, **86**, **87**, 91, 96, 101, **104**, 111, 113, 118, 121, 229, **416**, **417**
    Air National Guard Medical Advisory Council, 62, 78
    Air War College, 80
    Association of Air National Guard Nurses, 62, 78
    command, 72–111
    Commander's comments, 72–80, 109–111
    Founders Day/Reunion, 329–332, **330**, **331**
    Fraternity of Air National Guard Nurses, 78
    Minnesota State Medal for Merit, 71
    People-to-People Goodwill Tour, 71
    Veteran of the Month, 304
    Veterans Health Care Advisory Council, 293
Eubanks, Staff/Technical Sergeant, 248, 265, 268
European Command (EUCOM), 151
Evavold, JoEllen, 170, 185, 199, 203, **206**, 225, 231, 235, **237**, 265, 275, **286**, 288, 405
Evavold, Timothy, 83, 88–90, **96**, 183, 238, **402**, **403**
Ewert, Joshua, 350–351, **351**

F

F-89 Scorpion, vii
F-94C Starfire, vii
Fabio, J.D., 50
Fagula, Nicole, 180–181, **182**
Fairchild. *See* individual aircraft
Farrell, James, 3, 10
Farris, Diane, 199
Federal Emergency Management Agency (FEMA), 117, 360
federal recognition, ix, 2, 125
Fee, Gary, 84, **85**
Feist, Ann, 302, 310, 317
Fellman, Gail, 159, 183
Ferretti, Dennis, **68**, **99**
field training exercise (FTX), 38, 76, 77, 78, 89–90, **90**, 92, **92**, 101, 107, 113, 115, 121, 123, 126, 129, 160, **163**, 172, 186, 196, 229, **252**, 329
Finn, Julie T., 151, 164, 188, 193–194
    Juanita Redmond Award, 201, 206–207
Fitzhenry, Shawn, 266–267, 268–269, 297–299, **299**, 304, **346**
Fitzsimmons, Dennis, 9, 48, 50
Flatten, John, 297–299, **299**, 325
Fleming Field, 242
flight nurses, 3, 4, 6, 7, 8, **9**, 12, 13, 14, 15, 16, 18, 21–23, 28, 29, 30, 31, **31**, 36, 38, 47, 48, 49, 50, **53**, 57, 58, 60, 63, 66, 70, 71, 73–74, 75, 77, 78, **87**, 89, 94, 95, 97–98, 100, 116, 118, 122–123, 125, 126, 129, 130, 141, 155, 156, 161, 168, 177, 185, 199, 202, 225, 235, 242, 245, 248, 263, 265, 302, 303, 315, 356, 387, 388, 393, 416, **416**. *See also* individual names

recruitment, 11, 17, 18, 27, 36, 44, 46, 60, 67, 75, 90–91, 94, 113, 120, 122–123, 124, 132, 165, 271, 280, 291, 336
requirements, 7–8, 120
shortage, 67, 120
uniforms, 7, 12, 21, 74, 76
flight nurse school, 36, 49, 50, 58, 133
flight nurse training syllabus, **13**
flight surgeons, 73, 77–78, 91, 191, 275. *See also* individual names
Floden, Jerry, **54**
Flohr, Deb, **227**, 240, 325
flying schedule, **52**
Fogleman, Ronald, 209
Ford, Gerald, 102
Forsythe, Thomas, Jr., 2
Fort McCoy. *See* McCoy, Camp/Fort
Fort Polk, 200, 227, 231
Fort Wainwright, 91–92, 108
Fort Washington, 315
Foster, Walter, Jr., 33–34, **34**, **54**, 62, 63, **68**, 69, 76, 81, 96, **104**, 109–110
Founders Day/Reunion, 329–332, **330**, **331**
Fox, Richard, 18, 33
Fraternity of Air National Guard Nurses, 77–78, 110
Fredericks, John, 9
Freund, Mark, 96, **169**, 217–219
    Surgeon General of the Peruvian AF, **219**
FTX. *See* field training exercise
Funk, Paula, **68**

G

Gapstur, Julie, 125, 136, 199, 217
Garracht, Claire, 78
Garretson, Jordan, 322
Gartner, Katherine, 296, 337
George Schafer Award, 80, 101–103, **103**, **104**, 110, 170, 171–172, 175, 182, 220, **220**
Georgia Air National Guard, 82
Germain, Cindy, **93**
Germain, Michael, **96**, 106, 128, 131, **135**, 139, 176, 180, 182, 183, 199, 207, **416**, **417**
"Baghdad Bertha", 135
television commercial, 94
Germany, 14, 16, **16**, 17, 18, 21, 27–30, 50, 83, 105, 118–119, **119**, **120**, 134, 140, 160, 165, 166, 191, 192, 206, 208, 254, 263–264, 265–266, 268, 273, 276, 280–281, 291, 294, 306, 309, **310**, 316, 318–319, 328, **332, 333**, 334, 350–351, **351**, 352, **353**
Gibbons, Captain, **25**
Gilbert, Lloyd, 9, 16, **16**
Girl Scouts, 248–249
Glaeser, Nancy, 66, **68**, **70**
Global Guardian, 314, 327
Global Patient Movement Requirements Center (GPMRC), 190, 203
Golden Medic, 241
"Good Company", 94
Goodrich, Leo, viii–ix, **viii**, **330**
Goorhouse, Kayla, **355**
Gozel, Karen, 297
Gozel, Stan, 266, 280, 284
Grand Forks Air Force Base, 166
Graner, Alice, 52, **53**, 63, **67**, 68–69, **68**, 76, 80, **87**, 90, 110, 121, 329
Granlund, Michael, 202, 207–208, **209**, 210, 220, **220**, 221, 223, 231, **239**, 249, 271–272, **272**, 275, 309, 370
Great Lakes Response exercise, 280
Great River Ragnar Team, 345–346, **346**
Green, John, 184, **216**
Grieme, Mark A., 107, 128, 166, 357, **358**, **403**
Grout, Meghan, **332, 346, 362**
Gruel, Scott, 225, 262
Grundberg, Helen, 3, 8, **9**, 17, 48
Guam, 50
Guantanamo Bay, 193, 194, 198, 201, 262
Guard Recruiting Assistance Program (G-RAP), 291
Gulf War, Persian, 134, 141, 145, 149, 171, 191, 198–199, 210, 219. *See also* Desert Shield, Desert Storm

Gunelius, Judith, 58, 66, **68**, **70**, 84
Gunter Air Force Base, 11, 17–18, 48

H

Haase, Greg, 324
Hackley, Cheryl, 241
Hagel, Chuck, 340
Hahn Air Base, Germany, 118–119, **119**, **120**
Haiti, 193–194, 194–195, 198, 201
Hall, Wilford F., 67–68
Hallen, Tony, **250**
Hamlar, Dave, 301–302
Hanoi Hannah, 135
Hanson, Clyde, 17
Hanson, Vaughn, 294, 297, **350**
Hanzel, Jeramy, 266
Hanzel, Kelly, **235**
Hart, Grace, 77
hats, flight and squadron, 187, 373, **373**, **374**
Haun, James H., 2, 3
Hawaii, 25, 26, 27, 29, 49, 50, 56, 155, 176–177, **177**, 210, 262, 348
Hayes, Tammy, 121, 128, **130**, 156, 176, 199
Health Services Management Inspection, 66–67
Health Services Readiness Inspection (HSRI), 125, 128, 131, 153
Hecht, Robert, 3, 9, 12, 14, 27, 49, 50, **53**, **330**
Hedin, Thomas, 9, 48
helicopters, 38–40, 89, 95, 98, 126, 150, 178, 181, 200, 206, 219, 231, 232, 272, 299, 324, 343. *See also* individual types
Hemmingson, Mike, 315, 320
Hendrickson, Barbara, 404
Hendrickson, Geraldine, **9**, 10, **330**
Hendrickson Get-Together, **404**
Hendrickson, Norman, 32, **68**, 76, 80, 87, **87**, 119, 121, 133, 160, 166, **169**, 194, 204, 207, **402**, **403**, 404
Hengemuehle, Tad, 99
Hennessy, Lorraine, **216**, 217, 245
Hernandez, Claudia, 128, **130**, 134, **135**, 161
Hesser, Mark, 335, **346**
Hickam Air Force Base, 25, 56, 176, 177
Hickey, Thomas, 100–101
Highstrom, Todd, 121
Hill, Judy, 107–108, 176, 190. *See also* Espinosa, Judy
Hill, Robert, Captain **53**
Hill, Robert, Airman First Class, **54**
Hilliker, Dan, 32
"Hilton Crew", **96**
Hodges-Goetz, Penny, **301**, 303, 309, 310, 313, 314, 327, 329, 339, 360–361
    command, 301–325
    Commander's comments, 301–303
Hodnett, Debra, 95
Hoffoss, Kirsten, 231, **286**, 288. *See also* Boehm, Kirsten
Hofschulte, Alex, **346**
Hoim, D.L., 50
Holmen Field, 46
Holtz, Lexi, **310**, 316
Honduras, 224, 312–313
Honor Guard, 350, **350**
Hope, Bob, 139, **139**
Hope, Delores, 139
Horton, Gary, 369
Horvath, Bill, 160, 168–169
Hotaling, James, 334, **335**, 341
Howard Air Force Base, 81, 88, 121
Howard, Edward, **54**, **67**, 69, 76, 109, 132, 140, 145, 223–224, 232, 241, 302, **308**, 313, 329, 346–349, **347**
Howard, Elizabeth, 117–118, 132, 136, 152, 160, 161, 183, 225, 346–349, **347**. *See also* Pierson, Elizabeth
Howard, Pat, 183, 186, 194, 226, **237**, 241, 248, 260, 306, 316, 319–320, 336, 346–349, **347**
Howard, Sam, **308**
Howk, Mike, **206**, **216**, 248, 298, 313
HSRI. *See* Health Services Readiness Inspection
Huber, Mary, **53**
Huddleston, Lieutenant General, 160

Hudson, Bill, **147**
Huey helicopter, 89
Hughes, James, 33, **54**, 57, **67**, **68**, **70**, 76, **96**, 109, 132, 136, 175, 185, 196, **197**
Hughes, Nicole, 316, 319, 320
Hull, Amber, **355**
Hungary, 71, 202, 208, **209**, 281, 370
Hunt, Maureen A., **9**, 10, 14, 17, 48, 50, 74, 77, 84, 329–332, **330**
Hurricane Irma, 354, **355**
Hurricane Katrina, 258, 282, 283
hurricane response, 279, 303, 309, 339
Hurricane Rita, 283
Hussein, Saddam, 128, 139, 259

I

Iceland, **138**, 232
ICMOP. *See* Integrated Conus Medical Operational Plan
Idaho Air National Guard, 360
Integrated Conus Medical Operational Plan (ICMOP), 258, 261, 262, 263, 267, 327
Iraq, vii, 128, 135, 139, 141, 190, 210, 266, 268, 269, 270, 271, **272**, 275, 276, 281, 284–285, 286, **286**, 294, 302, 308, 327, 339
Iraqi Freedom, Operation, 258, 259, 261, 262, 263, 264, 279, **340**, **341**
Italy, 328

J

Jacobson-Hanson, Catherine, 192, 217, 220, **220**, 229, 231, 246, 254, 263–264, **290**
Janke, Otto, 47
Janssen, Robert, 170, 214, **214**
Janu, John, 232, 236–237, 242, 284, **290**
Janu, Shirley, 232
Janzig, Wayne, 10, **10**, 19, 22, 36
Japan, 42, **43**, 45, 50, 52, 54, 75, 160
Jensen, Joe, 76, 84, 85, **87**, 92, **96**, **145**, 401, **401**, **403**
Jensen, Linda, 165, 183, 245

Jensen, Russell, 24, 329
Jillian, Ann, 139
"Joe-Bag-O-Donuts". *See also* Rodke, Charles
Johannsen, Janet, **53**
Johns, Raymond E., Jr., 324
Johnson, Alan, 66
Johnson, Daniel, 119, **148**, **402**
Johnson, Georgeanne, 151, 166–167, **168**, 184, 185, 199, 206, **206**, 226, 229, 249, 250–251, 254–255, **257**, 259, 262, 264, 267, 274, 275, 279, 294, **295**, 296–297, 302, 303
  command, 257–300
  Commander's comments, 257–259
Johnson, H.T., 121
Johnson, Jim, 302
Johnson, Lyndon B., 41–42
Johnson, Marlene, 126
Johnson, Patty, 163
Joint Endeavor, Operation, 202, 206, 207, **206**
Joint Readiness Training Center (JRTC), 174, 200, 227, 229, 230, 231, 243, 251, 326, 327, 348
Joseph, Stephen, 198–199
JRTC. *See* Joint Readiness Training Center
Just Cause, Operation, 121, 127, 390
Juvland Nielsen, Taylor, 342, 344, 356–357, **357**

K

Kaiser Roll, 86, 88, 104, 151–152, 161, **161**, 182, 185, **186**, 197, 225, 241
Kane, Elizabeth, 49, 50
Kapfer, Brent, 146, 183
Kaposia District Camporee, 248–249, **250**
Kazek, General, 150
KC-135, 150, 254–255, 262, 383, **397**
Keesler Air Force Base, 123, 232
Keith, Ron, **230**
Keith, Toby, 285
Kelly Air Force Base, 37, 164, 318, 339
Kelly, Linda, 58
Kennedy, John F., 41
Kennedy, Ray, 258, 283, 292

Kenya, 184
Ketterling, Ryan, 302, 371
Key Volunteer Program, 318
Killey, General, 122–124
King get-together, 405, **405**
King, Micki, 99, 128, 200, 405, **405**
King, Wayne, 405, **405**
Kisser, Airman First Class, 165
Kjellander, Michael, 148, **169**, 184, 200
Kjellesvig, Kathryn, **355**
Klosowski, Colonel, 200
Kolar, Mark, 246, 281
Kolbo, Robert, 32, **33**, **68**, 76, 84, 109
Kolquist, Elizabeth, **394**
Koontz, Daniel, 3
Korea, 50
Korean War (Conflict), vii, 4, 46, 65
Kreiman, James, **332**
Krinke, Leslie, 2
Kunze, Lorraine, **53**
Kuwait, 128, 133, 134, 141, 190, 234, **235**, 258, 266, 270, 271, 276–277, 327, 339, 351
Kyrgyzstan, 265–266, 279

L

LaBlanc, Jessica, 350, **351**
Lackland Air Force Base, 10, 11, 18, 49, 67, 125, 146, 222, 282, 359–360
Lahman, Marianne, 62
Lambert, Michelle, 260, **261**
Langemo, Helen, **9**, 10, 16, **16**, 17
Langley Air Force Base, 77, 84, **85**
Lapolice, Elizabeth, **355**
Larson, Mary, **206**, 222, 280–281
Larson, Steve, 200
Lasserre, Amy, **310**, 315–316, 320
Latourelle, Mark, 76, 92, **96**, 121, 133, 152, 161, 180, 329
Learjet. *See* individual aircraft
leather flight jackets, 100, 353
Lee, Deborah, 201
Lee, Eric, 227, **403**
Lee, Richard, **68**
Leonard, David, **54**
Lincoln Del Races, 75–76
Linn, Duane, 288–289
Lockheed. *See* individual aircraft
Lockridge, Judine, 151
Lord, Edward, 118, 135
Ludwig, Dorothy, **9**, 10, 15, 37, **37**, 47, 50
Lumpkin, Gary, 94
Lund, David, 3, 9–10, 12, 49, **330**, **417**
Luxembourg, 319, 351
Lynch, Jessica, 264
Lynch, Margaret, 23, **23**, **25**, **26**, 35–36

M

MAC. *See* Military Airlift Command
Macedonia, 206, **206**, 242
Mae West life preserver, 25, **26**, 27, 38–39
Malecha, Susan, 187, 221, **221**, **230**, 268
Maloney, Rachel, **227**, 266, 305–306, **308**, **332**, 344
Mangin, Howard E., 85
Marabella, Raymond, 9, 17, 49
March Air Force Base, 146, 273
Marines, U.S., 39, 46, 48, 135, 141, 149, 259, 265, 276, 278, 289, 307–308, 316, 317–318, 345
Martin, George, 188
MASF. *See* Mobile Aeromedical Staging Facility
Mathsen, Curtis, 358, **359**
  command, 359–362
  Commander's comments, 359–362
MATS. *See* Military Air Transport Service
Mattson, Dave, 210
Mattson, Jim, **310**
Matula, Wayne, **54**
Matus, Theresa, 151
Maxwell Air Force Base, 100, 229
May, Patricia, 129
McCann, Kim, 201, 203
McCarthy, Captain, 315, 320–321

McChord Air Force Base, 225
McCormack, Don, 17, 49
McCormick, Alan, 75
McCoy, Camp/Fort, 45, 89–90, **90**, 95–96, **95**, **96**, **99**, 103, 241, 251, **252**, 273
McDill Air Force Base, 101, 111
McDonnell Douglas. *See* individual aircraft
McDowell, Robert, 241
McElvain Scholarship, 27, 49
McGuire Air Force Base, 15–16, 18, 21, 28, 43, 74, 77, 352
McGuire, Chaplain, 162
McGuire, Major, 123
McLean, Cheryl, 94
McMahon, Shawn, **206**, 236, 242
Medical Service Corps (MSC), 17, 46, 77, 79, 91, 116, 130, 138, 141, 168, 174, 175, 191, 192, 221, 232, 235, 236, 248, 288, 292, 326, 348
medical technician, 6, 8, 11, 12, 16, 17, 18, 21, 22, 23, 27, 29, 30, 31, 32, 38, 47, 48, **54**, 55, 57, 58, 60, 63, 66, 67, 70, 71, 73, 75, 78, 89, 91, 94, 95, 97, 98, 99, 108, 109, 110, 118, 129, 130, 132, 141, 152, 155, 156, 161, 177, 180, 184, 185, 192, 197, 200, 202, 207, 222, 224, 225, 228, 253, 260, 265, 271, 277, 289, 292, 303, 387, 388, 393, 417, **417**. *See also* Aeromedical Evacuation Technician
MEDLITE 11, 311, **312**
MEDRETE, 223, 312–313
Mensen, Karen, 265–266, 268
Mickelson, John, 272, 273–274
Miles, Travis, 276–277, 313, 315, 316, 319, **332**, 334, 350–351, **351**, 352
Military Airlift Command (MAC), 35, 42, 50, 56, 58, 62, 76, 78, 88, 90, 109, 111, 121, 128, 156, 160
Military Air Transport Service (MATS), 15–16, 18, 25, 31, 35, 42
Military Appreciation Day, 323–324
Military Indoctrination of Military Service Officers (MIMSO), 123–124, 205

Miller, Erika, **256**, 260
Miller, Ray, vii, 198
Miller, Robert, 9, 48
Milsten, Cathy, 160. *See also* Cisar, Cathy
MIMSO. *See* Military Indoctrination of Military Service Officers
Minh, Ho Chi, 41
Minneapolis-St. Paul International Airport (MSP), 2, 21, 196, 232
Minnesota Air National Guard (MNANG), vii–ix, 2–4, 6, 73, 86, 150, 153, 178, 204, 206, 357
Minnesota Twins, 229, 322–324, **323**
Mitricska, Laura, 333, 336, 337
Mitricska, Sean, 266, **239**
Mobile Aeromedical Staging Facility (MASF), 63, 64, 68, 69, 89, **90**, **92**, **95**, 98, 107, 113, 118, 121, 122–123, 126, 148, 168, 174, 176, 178, 181, 185, 186, 196, **196**, 203, 208, 215, 216, **217**, 222, 231, 232, 239, 241, 258, **252**, 276, 282, 283, 292, 297
Mobile Army Surgical Hospital (MASH), 107, 181
Moehring, Minna, 47
Moen, Major, 124
Mogadishu, 166–167, **168**, 178, 180–181, 184
Mohr, Eileen, **53**
Molin, David, **65**, 66, **68**
    command, 65–71
    Commander's comments, 65
Monio, Britt, 343
Monjes, Matt, **286**, 319, **332**, **355**
morale, 138, 158, 269, 294, 365
Moran, Helena, 15
Morrow, Ken, 49
Mortindale, Major, 170
Moss, Robert, 9, 48
MSC. *See* Medical Service Corps
Mulroy, James, 3, 9, 49, **330**
Munsterman, Lynette, 151
Murray, Kathleen, 77

Museum, Minnesota Air National Guard, 198, 249, 329, 331, **331**

N

Napurski, Laura, **206**
National Disaster Medical System (NDMS), 97–98, 103, 105–106, **106**, 117–118, 135–136, 231
National Guard, 115, 138, 148–150, 178, 195, 311, 343, 344
National Guard Bureau (NGB), vii, viii–ix, 25, 57, 62, 63, 73, 77, 79, 80, 90, 109–110, 113, 121, 122–125, 127, 128, 130, 133, 136, 137, 149, 151, 166, 183, 185, 229, 238, 258, 267, 274, 278, 328, 337, 343
Navy, U.S., 28, 38–40, 41, 48–49, 74, 84, 113, 120, 121, 135, 141, 197, 202, 204, 215, 232, 278, 284–285
Neihart, Chad, **295**, **308**
Nelson, David, 361
Nelson, Erika, 317, 324
Nelson, Harry, 2, 5, **6**, 11–12, **20**, 32, 46, **61**, 62, 64, 73, **330**
    command, 20–44, 61–63
    Commander's comments, 20, 61
New Guinea, 45
New Hampshire Aeromedical Evacuation Flight (AEF), 2, 12, 15, 31, 43
New Zealand, 324
Nomad Vigil, Operation, 191–192
Non-Commissioned Officer Academy, 62
Nordquist, Amy, **286**, 312
Noriega, Manuel, 121
Norman Conquest, 241
Norman, Mark, 184
Northern Eagle, Operation, 229, 232, 241, 327
Northstar Guardian, 57, 144, 219
Northwest Airlines (NWA), 48
Norton Air Force Base, 154
Nosbisch, Donald, 146
Nowlan, Emily, 242
Nowlan, Pat, 266, 267, 268, 280, 283

Nurse Corps, 17, 72, 88, 94, 182
nurses, 10, 47, 58, 62, 73, 75, 77, 78, 79, 80, 84, 87, 88, 90–91, 95, 110, 113, 131, 154, 184, 191, 201, 215–218, 222, 229, 285, 303, 312, 354, 360
Nygaard, Mark, 136

O

O-38 aircraft, vii
O-47A/B aircraft, vii
Obama, Barack, 308, 340
Oberg, Annie, **355**
Oehlenschlager, Richard, 75, **417**
officers dining-in, 229, 233, 237, **237**
O'Keefe, Tom, 132, **138**, **216**, 239, 240
"Old Spice" policy, 201
Olson, Brenda, 49
Olson, Bruce, 52, 55–56, **70**
Olson, Leslie, 3, 10
Olson, Noel, 292–293
Oman, **142**, 254
Operational Readiness Exercise (ORE), 194, 201, 202, 281–282, 283, 304
Operational Readiness Inspection (ORI), 31, 57, 58, 162, 174, 202–203, 205, 241, 283, 302, 305
Operations/Aeromed building, 174, 176, 198, 202, 204, 205, 210, 211, **212**, **213**
ORE. *See* Operational Readiness Exercise
ORI. *See* Operational Readiness Inspection
Osmond, Marie, 139
Osteboe, Carol, 48, **330**
Otis Air Force Base, 79

P

P-51B/D Mustang, vii
Pacific Air Forces (PACAF), 6, 42, 74, 75, 76, 290, 303
Pakistan, 265–266
Panama, 81, 83, 88, 121, 127, 183, 202, 224, 390
Pandicio, Captain, 17

Panetta, Leon, 324
Panzella, Emmett, 16, **16**
patches, flight and squadron, 33, 187, 363–369, **363**, **364**, **366**, **367**, **368**, **369**, 371
Pate, George, 77
patients, 4, 14, 17, 21–23, 28, 31, **31**, 42, **43**, 51, **51**, 63, 66, 67, **67**, 69, 71, 74, 75, 82, 84, **85**, 86, 88, 89–90, **90**, 91–92, **92**, 94–96, **95**, 97–98, 99–100, 105–106, **106**, 117–118, 121, 125–127, **127**, 135–136, 142–143, **144**, 148–150, 155, 161, **161**, 162, 166–167, 180–181, 188–189, **189**, **190**, 190–192, 193–194, 196, **196**, 197, 198–199, 200, 206, 208, 215–218, **217**, **218**, 221, 222–224, **223**, **224**, 226, 231, 232, 235, 239, 242, **252**, 253, 254–255, **256**, 260, 261–262, **261**, 262–263, 263–264, 265, 268, 271–272, **272**, 273, 275, 276–277, 280–281, 282–283, 284–285, 288–289, 291, 299, 308, 309, 311, 312–313, 315, 316, 317, 320, 321, 324, 328, **333**, 334, 342–343, **343**, 344, 350–351, 352, 355, 356–357, **362**, 386, 387, 388, 391, 393
Patriot 2010 exercise, 307
Pawlenty, Tim, 293
Payne, Andrea, **333**
Pease Air Force Base, 43, 77
Pentagon, 94, 245, 259
Peralta, William, 319
Performance Based Inspections (PBIs), 153
Perkins, Larry, 85, **96**
Perpich, Rudy, 106
Perry, William, 198
Peru, 215–219, **217**, **218**, 224
    Surgeon General of the Peruvian AF, 218–219, **219**
Peterson, John, 17
Peterson, Kenneth, 165, 184, 200, 225, 235, 290, 297
Peterson, Matt, 241, 248, 266–267, **295**, 302, 309, **326**, 327, 328, 337, 339, 371
    command, 326–337
        Commander's comments, 326–327

Peterson, Robert, **37**
Peterson, William (Bo), 342, **342**, 350, **353**
Philippines, 17, 42, 45–46, 50, 52, 75, 108
Pierson, Elizabeth, 235, 348. *See also* Howard, Elizabeth
Pitha, Robert, 3, 9
Plombon, Lisa, 99
Pointer Sisters, 139
Poland, 71, 298–299, **299**, 339
Pope Air Force Base, 56, 64, 66, 68–69, 70, 76, 83, 89, 98, 160, 190, 202, 204, 235, 275, 315, 320
Potter, Rob, 247, 292, 295–296, **295**
Powell, Colin, 150
Prickett, Gary, 161, 166–167, **168**, 191–192, 199–200, 267
Provide Hope, Operation, 166–167
Puerto Rico, 83, 224, 232, 239, 354
Purple Penny exercise, 160
Pursley, Debra, 136

Q

Qatar, 258, 266–267, 271, 279, 284, 294, **295**, **308**, 309, 339
Quality Air Force Assessments (QAFA), 188

R

Ramsborg, Glen, 66
Ramstein Air Base, 105, 254, 258, 264, 267, 276, 280, 291, **310**, 315, 316, 319, 351, 352, **353**
Rangers, 181
Rask, Darrell, 190, 194–195, 245, **402**
Rawling, Stu, 316, 318–319, 328, **346**
Readiness Safeguard exercise, 300
Redalen, Sue, 95
Redmond, Robert, Jr., 66
Reed, Elinor, 78
REFORGER. *See* Return of Forces to Germany
Reinhardt, Andy, 237
Reller, Darcy, 323–324, 333

Reller, Jessica, 324
Rempfer, Paul, 50
Reshetar, Brandon, **355**
Response '89, 117–118
Restore Hope, Operation, **168**, 172, 184
Return of Forces to Germany (REFORGER), 165, 172
Rhein Main Air Base, 14, **16**, 18, 21, 28–30, 50, **116**, 140, 160, 191
Richards-Gebaur Air Force Base, 97
Richter, Dave, **216**, 229, 238
Riley, Captain, 162
Ringle, Crystal, 316
Ringwald, Bob, 266
Ripley, Camp/Fort, 92, **92**, 98–99, 103, 115, 125–126, **127**, 129, 153, 176, 178, 186, **187**, 194, 196, **196**, 232, 343
Ripley, Terrance, 3, 9, 49, **330**, 332, **417**
Ritz, Julie, 236, 248
Roadman, Charles, II, 210
Roberts, Aubree, 294, **295**
Robinson, Harry, 200, **216**
rodeo, 169, 225, 235
Rodke, Charles, 125–127, 132, 133–134, 158, 165, 176, 183, 227, **227**. *See also* "Joe-Bag-O-Donuts"
Roiger, Dale, 99–100, 200
Rosburg, Sharon, 129, 227, 229–230, 233, 234, 238, 240, 241, **243**, 244, **244**, 246, 247–248, 255
    command, 243–256
    Commander's comments, 243–244
Rosetta, Jennifer, **394**
Rotell, Henry, **54**
Routhier, Anita M., 12
Royal Air Force (RAF), 18, 142–143, **143**, **144**, 146, 298
Ruff, Violet, 83
Ruyle, Tina, **346**, 350–351, **351**, 352, **355**
Rwanda, 185, 192

S

Sabo, Martin, 176, 198
SAC. *See* Strategic Air Command
Samaritan, 64, 78, 172
Samaritan II, 66
Samaritan III, 68–69, **70**, 76
Samaritan V, 92, **92**
Samaritan VIII, 98–100, **99**, 103
Samaritan IX, 125–127, **127**
Sand Eagle, Operation, 162
Sarah P. Wells Award, 200, 210
Saudi Arabia, 128, 130–131, **130**, **131**, 133–134, 139, 141, 142, 150, 152–153, 167
scarf, squadron flight, **179**, 180, 372, **372**
Schacht, J., 242
Schauer, JoAnn, 202, **403**
Schaumann, Meredith, 309
Schaumann, Robert, 79–80, 86
Schenk, Tim, **96**
Schimek, Jennifer, 284
Schmenti, Carmalleta, 80
Schmidt, Diane, 66, **68**
Schmidt, Kim, 239, 272, 297
Schneider, Scott, 86
Schneider, Virginia, 261–263
School of Aerospace Medicine, 11, 14, 29, 50, 73, 87, 311
Schuessler, Bill, **230**
Schuknecht, Colonel, 78
Schuldt, Susan, 229, 232, 233, **237**, 241, 242, 245, 246
Schulz, Carol, 84, **87**
Schutta, Sarah, **346**
Schweigert, James, **54**
Scott Air Force Base, 14, 28, 42, 50, **51**, 63, 75, 111, 117, 121, 156, 170, 183, 190, 258–263, **261**, 265, 268, 275–276, 290, 318–319, 327, 354–355
SCPS-M. *See* Survivable Collective Protection System-Medical
Sea Signal, Operation, 193, 194–195, 201
Seeley, Owen, 136, **137**, 158, **159**

Self, Robert, 80
Sellner, Jacqueline, 289, **290**, 315, 316, 318–319
Sentry Independence, 94–96, **95**, **96**, 98–100, **99**
September 11, 2001, 243, 245, 246, 327
Serres, Jessica, 294, 298
Severt, Drew, 241
SH-34J helicopter, 39–40, **40**
Shegstad, Stephanie, **227**
Sheldon, Carolyn, 164
Shelly, Pamela, **68**
Sheppard Air Force Base, 50, 52, 146, 204, 233, 292
Shields, Gregory, **54**, 56
Shore, Travis, 313, 333
Shults, Jennifer, **216**, 231
Sicard, Dustin, **256**
Sicily, 328
Sieben, James, 81, 104
Silliman, John, Jr., 129
Simmons, Darcy, **53**. *See also* Anderson, Darcy
Simpson, Katherine, 15, 17, 18, 23
Sister Kenny Institute, 86, 88
Sitta, Steven, 136, 152, 185
Skaro, Thomas, **54**
Small, Colleen, 310
Small, James, **68**
Smith, Bruce, 3
Smith, Dennis, 66
Smith, Lee, 315, 320, **332**, **355**, **394**
Smith, Matt, 271–272, 275
Snapp, Franklin, 36
Soderholm, Tracy, 101, 192, 402
Somalia, 166–167, **168**, 178, 180–182, **182**, 184
Sonnenschein, Aric, **355**
SORTS. *See* Status of Resources and Training System
Southern Watch, Operation, 190
Spaatz, Carl S., vii
Spain, 33
Spangler, Sally, 254, 263–264
Speich, David, **308**
spouse flight, 92–93, **93**, 163

Staff Assistance Visit (SAV), 60, 123, 246, 290, 297, 313, 314, 316, 317
Stand Down for Veterans, 115, 176, 187–188, 197, 204, 214–215, 225, 229, 231–232, 236–237, 241–242, 258, 265, 279, 312
Stangl, Thomas, 108, 137, 155, 156, 165, 180, **183**, 192, 227, 401, **401**, **402**, **403**, 401–406
Stanzyk, Emily, 353–354
Status of Resources and Training System (SORTS), 122–125
Staut, Tony, 203, 204, 235, 238, 241, 318
Stedje, Corey, **310**, 313
Steven, Bryan, 201, 202, 207–208, **209**, 214, 220, 226, 248, 272, 298, **308**, **332**, 370
Stibitz, Karel, 136, 152, 161
stop-loss program, 131, 154, 253
St. Patrick's Day Parade, 147, **148**
St. Paul Ramsey Hospital Training Program, 47, 57, 60, 71, 104, 154, 182, 185
Strategic Air Command (SAC), 121, 160
strategic air evac system, 3, 11, 14, 15, 17, 18, 28, 29, 71, 143, 148–150
Strohfus, Elizabeth, 237
Strom, Carol, 249
Stucky, William, 2, 8, 17, 49, **54**
Suber, Shawn, 319
successes, flight and squadron, 14, 15, 47, 78, 90, 110–111, 116–117, 162, 171–172, 188, 202–203, 225, 291
Sullivan, Mary, 151
Surgeon General, 36, 62, 77–80, 94, 102, 110, 120, 236
Survivable Collective Protection System-Medical (SCPS-M), 105
Sustainment Training to Advance Readiness (TOPSTAR), 57, 222, 233
Sweden, 71

T

T-33A Shooting Star, vii
TAC. *See* Tactical Airlift Command
Tachikawa Air Base, 42, 75

Tactical Aeromedical Evacuation Conference, 56
Tactical Aeromedical Evacuation System (TAES), 89, 160
Tactical Airlift Command (TAC), 17, 56, 58, 59, 60, 78, 109, 160
TAES. *See* Tactical Aeromedical Evacuation System
Taylor, Marie, 84, **87**
Technical Training School (Tech School), 146, 185, 260, 345
Technician Program, 18
Tech School. *See* Technical Training School
Teneyck, Jeremy, **394**
Tenney, Dorothea, 7, **9**, 10, 12, 14, 18, **19**, 21–23, 26, 27, 35, **35**, 36, 48, 74, 329, **330**, **416**
Tentis, Dedra, **308**
Theater Patient Movement Requirement Center (TPMRC), 203, 351
Theodore C. Marrs Award, 101–104, **102**, **104**, 170–172, 182, 220, **220**
Theriot, Olivia, 50
Thompson, Christina, 44
Thunnel, Thomas, 3, 9, 49
Tilseth, Joe, 260, 263
Tokyo Rose, 135
Tomerlin, Betty, 227, **227**
TOPSTAR. *See* Sustainment Training to Advance Readiness
Torkelson, Michelle, 136
Tough Mudder, 321–322
Tourville, George, **54**
Tracy, Dan, 166–167, 290, **168**, 401, **401**
Tracy, Kelly, **168**, 206. *See also* Anderson-Ray, Kelly
Tracy, Michael, 160, 165
training 7–8, 11–18, 22–23, 27–30, 32, 47, 57, 60, 64, 66, **67**, 68–69, **70**, 71, 77, 84, 89–90, **90**, 110, 125, 142–143, 154–155, 156, **163**, 169, 176–177, **177**, 185, 202, 206, **207**, 210, 232, 235, **252**, 258, 273, 280, 290, 303, 307, 313, 314, 339, 353–354, 362, 382–393
SERE (Survival, Evasion, Resistance, Escape), 292–293
water survival training, 25–26, **26**, **27**, 38–40, **40**, 59, 83, **83**, **252**, **253**, 292
winter survival training, 234
TRANSCOM. *See* U.S. Transportation Command
Trauma Nurse Core Course, 57, 202, 233, 293
Travis Air Force Base, 36, 42, 56, 74–75, 221–222, 315, 333–334, 338–339
Trelstad, Brad, 325
Tripp, Terry, 277
Truman, Harry S., 41
Truscinski, David, 335
Turkey, 17–18, 151, 327

U

Unit Compliance Inspection, (UCI), 254, 264, 291
United Arab Emirates, **137**, 139
United Nations, 166, 180
Unit Effectiveness Inspection (UEI), 336
Unit Manning Document, 6, 15, 62, 73, 113, 122–123, 236, 292
Unit Type Codes (UTC), 6, 148–149, 174, 186, 199, 201, 204, 231, 236, 237–238, 239, 240, 241, 244, 251, 254, 258, 274, 278, 282, 292, 303, 304, 307, 327, 332, 339
University of Minnesota, 1, 30, 46, 48, 81, 112, 136, 231, 241, 364
USAFE. *See* U.S. Air Forces in Europe
U.S. Air Forces in Europe (USAFE), 6, 17, 74, 76, 160, 234, 304
U.S. Transportation Command (TRANSCOM), 121, 203
UTC. *See* Unit Type Codes
Uzbekistan, 258, 265–266, 268, 271

V

VADEX. *See* Veterans Affairs Department of Defense Exercise

Vandevoort, John, Jr., 146
Van Sambeck, Judy, 58, 63
Veteran's Administration, 120, 187, 198
Veteran's Administration, hospitals, 85, 97, 106, 135, 136, 154, 169, 182, 185, 201, 204, 214, 232, 234, 237, 283, 291
Veterans Affairs Department of Defense Exercise (VADEX), 190
Veterans Home, Minnesota, 253, 344
Vietnam Veterans of America, 146, 180
Vietnam War, 41–42, 46, 50, 53–54, 73, 75
Vigilant Guard, 342–343, **343**
Villagran, Sharon, 183
Vinland National Center, 86, 88
Vital Signs (publication), 91, 114, 132, 152, 242, 244, 255, 281, 309, 328, 335, 339
Vogt, Brent, 266, 269–270
Volk Field, 60, 62, 63, 94–96, **95**, **96**, 98, 184, 201, 203, 281, 283, 292, 300, 302, 304, 307
Vosika, Richard, 9, 27–30, 49, **330**, **417**

W

Walker, Paul, 76, 91, 227, **403**
Wallace, Mary, 78
Wallgren, Nathan, **394**
War Readiness Materials (WRM), 118–119, **119**, **120**, 175
WCCO-AM 830 radio, 304
WCCO-TV, **35**, 57, 147, **147**
Weaver, James, 77–80, 110
Webster, Dennis, **54**
Weinzetl, Carolyn, 3, 8
Wellner, Terrance, **68**, **87**, 88–89, 91–92
Wells, Sarah P., 79, 85, **86**
Wenaas, Dave, 316
White, Greg, 315, 320
Wilford Hall Hospital/Medical Center, 67–68, 77, 105, 121, 125, 146, 318, 360
Williams, Theo, **216**, 245
Wold-Chamberlain Field, 15
Wold-Chamberlain Naval Air Station, 46
Wolf, Chris, **312**, 324, **325**, 333–334
Wolf, Karen, 76, 80, 81, 94, 95–96, 100, 153, 176–177, 185, **187**, 194, **195**, 196, 201, **216**, 220, **220**, 225, **228**, **230**, 232, 237, **237**, 241, 242, 244, **244**, 245, 246, 327, 329
  command, 228–242
  Commander's comments, 228–230
Wolf, Lewis, 81, 100
women, 3, 53, 58, 62, 76, 79–80, 121, 175, 221, 323, *See also* individual names
  Air War College, 80, 100
  attitudes toward, 7, 18, 79–80, 116, 134, 139
  Ausen, Ardyce Marlene, 94, 100
  "Role of Women in the Military", 106
Women's Wellness Day, 106
"World of Aviation" TV program, **35**, 57
World War II, vii, 41, 65, 100, 135, 174, 211, 237, 299, 315
Wright-Patterson Air Force Base, 105, 276, 311, 360
WRM. *See* War Readiness Materials
Wyland, John, **145**, **169**
Wyoming Air National Guard, 52, 110, 240

Y

Yantz, Valerie, **68**, 76, 84, **87**
yellow ribbons, 145
Yokota Air Base, 42, **43**, 75, 160
Young Field, 94, 98
Youth Camp, 153, **154**, 178, 182, 186, **187**, 195, **195**, 287
Youth Trust, 250–251

Z

Zakariasen, Al, 162, 165, **183**, 192, **192**, 401, **401**, **402**, **403**, **404**, 405–406
Zappia, Ben, 237
Zilka, Richard, 153
Zondlo, Andrea, 272, 273
Zueli, John, 248

The Authors

Richard H. Childs Jr., nicknamed "Chip," was born in New England where he spent his early years. In 1956 his family moved to Lincoln, Nebraska where he attended high school and the University of Nebraska. In 1966 while attending the University, he joined the U.S. Navy Reserve, enrolling in their 2 by 4 Program, which required two years of active duty plus four years of service in the active reserve. In December of 1968, Childs began his active duty tour and was assigned to an amphibious vessel which deployed to Southeast Asia in support of the United States efforts in Vietnam. Honorably discharged in 1970, he returned to Lincoln and the University, graduating in 1972 with a Bachelor of Arts Degree in History with a minor in English and Journalism. In July of 1973, he returned to active Naval service

Photo courtesy of TSgt Richard Childs

graduating from Naval Officer Candidate School in November. Over the course of his four years as a Line Officer, he served on commands in Japan, the Philippine Islands and Virginia. Leaving the Navy in 1977, he moved to Minnesota and joined the 109th Aeromedical Evacuation Flight, Minnesota ANG, a decade later in November 1987. He graduated from the U.S. Air Force School of Aerospace Medicine in September 1988 and earned his wings later that fall. In 1990, he made two deployments to "the Desert" in support of Operation Desert Shield/Desert Storm, operating from Oman and the UAE flying live aeromedical evacuation missions. Childs retired from the National Guard in 1999, completing 21 years and 11 months of active duty and active reserve service. Always involved in historical organizations, he was a frequent contributor to the Old West Society of Minnesota's monthly Gazette, as well as having articles published in the Minnesota Weapons Collectors Association Quarterly, the Leather Crafters and Saddlers Journal and The Shootist, the official publication of the National Congress of Old West Shootist. Chip currently resides in Minneapolis, MN with his wife and two grown children.

The Authors

Col Germain was born and raised in Osceola, WI. After graduating from high school he attended the University of Minnesota, and St. Paul Ramsey Hospital and Medical Center's School of Nurse Anesthesia. Upon completion of his anesthesia training in 1982, he was commissioned as a 2d Lt in the Minnesota Army National Guard as an anesthetist. One year later, he joined the Minnesota ANG's 109th Aeromedical Evacuation Flight. Over the next 14 years he held various positions including OIC of Aircrew Training, Chief of Stan/Eval, and Chief Flight Nurse. Col Germain volunteered for three deployments during Operation Desert Shield/Storm and served six months in Saudi Arabia, the United Arab Emirates, and England, flying live aeromedical evacuation missions.

Photo courtesy of Col Michael Germain

Due to conflicts with his civilian job and flying duty requirements, he transitioned to the Air Force Reserve and became an Admissions Liaison Officer, recruiting for the Air Force Academy and AFROTC (Air Force Reserve Officer Training Corps). Here, he became the Liaison Officer Director for both Minnesota and North Dakota, retiring as a colonel in 2012 with over 30 years of service.

During this time period, he was also a full partner and owner of an independent anesthesia practice north of the Twin Cities. He and his wife Cindy, are retired and live in East Tennessee.

Col Germain's most memorable experience during his time in service was the commissioning of all three of his sons in the Air Force - a fighter pilot and two dentists.

CPSIA information can be obtained
at www.ICGtesting.com
Printed in the USA
LVHW070541291221
707426LV00004B/191